U0453253

深圳经济特区建立 40 周年改革创新研究特辑

陈金海 主编

深圳故事：
经济、社会、环境转型

The Story of Shenzhen:
Its Economic, Social and
Environmental Transformation

中国社会科学出版社

图书在版编目（CIP）数据

深圳故事：经济、社会、环境转型 / 陈金海主编 . —北京：中国社会科学出版社，2020.10（2021.1 重印）
（深圳经济特区建立 40 周年改革创新研究特辑）
ISBN 978 – 7 – 5203 – 7223 – 7

Ⅰ . ①深… Ⅱ . ①陈… Ⅲ . ①区域经济发展—研究—深圳②社会发展—研究—深圳 Ⅳ . ①F127.653②D676.53

中国版本图书馆 CIP 数据核字（2020）第 175336 号

出 版 人	赵剑英
项目统筹	王 茵
责任编辑	马 明　李 沫
责任校对	胡新芳
责任印制	王 超
出　　版	中国社会科学出版社
社　　址	北京鼓楼西大街甲 158 号
邮　　编	100720
网　　址	http://www.csspw.cn
发 行 部	010 – 84083685
门 市 部	010 – 84029450
经　　销	新华书店及其他书店
印刷装订	北京君升印刷有限公司
版　　次	2020 年 10 月第 1 版
印　　次	2021 年 1 月第 2 次印刷
开　　本	710×1000　1/16
印　　张	24.25
字　　数	361 千字
定　　价	156.00 元

凡购买中国社会科学出版社图书，如有质量问题请与本社营销中心联系调换
电话：010 – 84083683
版权所有　侵权必究

陈金海

现任中共深圳市委宣传部常务副部长，在推动深圳国际化和城市文艺创新发展等领域，作出了大量卓有成效的探索，推动联合国教科文组织授予深圳"全球全民阅读典范城市"称号，作为"深圳故事"项目总负责人，推动深圳与联合国人居署开展研究合作，项目成果在"联合国人居署第一届人居大会"和"联合国第 74 届大会"上成功发布，并在联合国人居署 2020 年世界城市论坛"城市图书馆"中精彩展出。近年来，在《人民日报》《光明日报》《南方日报》等刊物发表研究深圳经济社会文化发展的系列理论文章二十余篇。

深圳经济特区建立40周年改革创新研究特辑
编 委 会

顾　　　　问：王京生　李小甘
主　　　　任：王　强　吴以环
执 行 主 任：陈金海　吴定海
主　　　　编：吴定海
编委会成员：（以姓氏笔画为序）

　　　　　　王为理　王世巍　刘婉华　李凤亮
　　　　　　杨　建　肖中舟　何国勇　张玉领
　　　　　　陈少兵　罗　思　赵剑英　南　岭
　　　　　　袁易明　袁晓江　莫大喜　黄发玉
　　　　　　黄　玲　曹天禄　谢志岿　谭　刚
　　　　　　魏达志

总　　序

先进的文化，来自对先进的生产方式和生活方式的能动反映；先进的生产力，来自对生产前沿审时度势的探索。40多年来，深圳一直站在生产力和生产关系新模式探索的最前沿，从生产实践，到制度建立，再到观念更新，取得了系统的、多层次的成果，为改革开放全面成功推广，提供一整套系统的观念与经验。当然，深圳的改革历程，是一个步步为营的过程。如果说，改革开放之初所取得的成功，主要在于以一系列惊心动魄的实践，按照市场经济发展规律，循序渐进地突破制度的坚冰，在摸索中逐步确立社会主义市场经济的新制度、新机制、新关系，形成新的发展模式；那么，在完成试验田式的探索之后，深圳取得的新突破，则是在国内经济转型和国际新经济背景之下，结合自身优势而完成的产业升级和观念升级。在升级换代过程中，深圳已经取得开阔的国际视野，在国际上也形成自身的影响力，在国内则拥有党中央强有力的支持和更成熟的制度后盾。

在这个过程中，深圳作为探索者、排头兵所探索出来的一系列成功经验，已经成为社会主义市场经济体制的基本构成部分；在这个过程中，深圳人为社会主义市场经济模式的建立与繁荣，做出系列有利于国、有益于民的大胆探索，其间所形成的开拓进取精神，已经凝聚成为一种可以叫作"深圳精神"的东西。正如习近平总书记在深圳考察时说的："如果说，深圳是中国改革开放的一本样板书，那这本书上，给人留下印象最深刻的两个字，就是'敢闯'！"同时，深圳的系列探索实践，也是对党的老一辈革命家改革开放、发展生产力理想的具体实践。从全国来看，改革开放40余年，在我国沿海、沿江、沿线甚至内陆地区建立起国家级或省市级高新区、开发区、自贸区、保税区等，形成了类型众多、层次多样的多元化改革发展新格局。

党的十八大以来，中央对深圳提出的新要求，正体现着这种一贯思路的延续和战略高度的提升。深圳的拓荒意义不但没有过时，而且产生了新的内涵。深圳被赋予了中国特色社会主义先行示范区的新角色，从改革开放试验田，到社会主义先行示范区，这种身份的转变，是新时代进一步深化改革开放的新成果，也是深圳作为中国这个世界第二大经济体经济发展的重要驱动力在国际经济新格局中扮演的新角色。在习近平新时代中国特色社会主义思想指导下继续解放思想、真抓实干，改革开放再出发，在新时代走在前列，在新征程勇当尖兵，是新时代赋予深圳的新任务。在深化改革的过程中，不论是国家，还是以北京、上海、广州、深圳为代表的大城市所面对的国际政治形势和经济形势，比以往都要复杂很多，需要我们做出更睿智和更高瞻远瞩的决策，以应对更复杂的产业形势和政治形势。从这个角度看，新时代深圳改革开放、开拓进取的任务不是轻了，而是更重了；需要的勇气和毅力不是少了，而是更多了。

习近平新时代中国特色社会主义思想，是我们继续深化改革的指导思想和行动指南。在以习近平同志为核心的党中央的坚强领导下，因世界大势，应国内态势，以满足人民不断增长的物质文化生活需求为动力，在经济特区已有的经验基础上，围绕新时代经济特区发展进行深入理论思考和实践探索，完成城市发展与国家发展的统一，完成继承与创新的统一，为习近平新时代中国特色社会主义思想增添新的生动范例，为践行中国特色社会主义理论提供新的经验，推进新时代经济特区在经济、政治、文化、社会和城市生态等方面实现更高层次的发展，是新时代赋予深圳的新使命。

新时代推动新实践，新实践催生新思想，新思想呼唤新理论。讲好深圳故事既是时代所需，也是中国学者的责任。为了总结深圳经济特区建立40年来改革探索的经验，为深圳改革探索提供学者的观察和视角，深圳市社科院组织市内外的专家学者对深圳经济特区40年经济社会发展的路径进行了深入研究，形成了十部著作，作为《深圳改革创新丛书》的特辑出版。《深圳改革创新丛书》作为深圳推进哲学社会科学发展的重要成果,此前已经出版了六个专辑,在国内引起了一定的关注。这套《深圳经济特区建立40周年改革创新研究特辑》,既有对改革开放40多年来深圳发展历程的回顾,也有结合新使命而做的新探索。希望这些成果,为未来更深入和更高层面的研究,提供新的理论资源。这套丛书也是学界和中国社会科学出版社对深圳经济特区建立40周年的一份献礼。

编写组

2020年6月

序　　一

中国东南部的沿海港口和贸易历史，与我的家乡东南亚紧密相关。几个世纪以来，中国人冒险远下南洋，即现在的东南亚或南大洋，发展密切的贸易伙伴关系，甚至定居。这种开拓精神为两地人民创造了大量的机遇。深圳——这个中国东南部现代化的龙头城市，再一次被证明是一个令人振奋的地方。

本书分享了深圳实施的有关经济、城市规划和环境的政策和战略，在短短的40年内，深圳已经成为中国的硅谷。基于高科技、制造业和服务业，深圳取得了举世瞩目的经济社会发展。如今，知识型产业已成为深圳发展的驱动力，根据2017年全球金融中心指数，深圳的经济产出在659个中国城市中排名第三，深圳在全球最具竞争力的金融中心中排名第22位。2016年，深圳对中国GDP的贡献为3030亿美元，仅次于上海和北京。

然而，城市不仅仅是人们居住的地方，也不仅仅是生产商品和服务的场所。依靠内部动力，城市是经济增长和发展的关键驱动力。作为创新和变革的中心，城市创造了财富和繁荣，促进了资产和机会的再分配，提高了生产力，并为实现领土均衡发展做出了贡献。

要让这40年的奇迹延续下去，我们需要践行中国传统的高瞻远瞩的思维模式，追求可持续发展，以应对当前全球面临的日益加剧的贫穷、社会不平等、环境退化和气候变化等挑战。当前全球城市化进程加快，一半以上的人口在城市生活，城市可持续发展的议题日益凸显。我们必须深刻反思，如何才能提高城市居民的生活质量，同时确保城市保持经济生产力，创造一个对今世后代良好的社会和生态环境。

深圳的确是一个非凡的成功案例。许多成长中的城市、经济特区和新城可以从中吸取很多经验。我很荣幸向你们介绍这本书，书中涵盖了各个领域和机构的专家的专业知识，将有助于我们理解深圳经验的许多故事。

联合国副秘书长、联合国人居署执行主任

Preface Ⅰ

Southeast China, its coastal ports and history of trade, is particularly close and related to Southeast Asia, my home region. For centuries, the Chinese have ventured into the Nanyang, which is modern day Southeast Asia or the Southern Ocean, developed close trading partnerships and even established settlements. This pioneering spirit has created a wealth of opportunities for the people of both regions. It is not surprising that Shenzhen, the modern day leading city of Southeast China, once again proves to be an inspiring place.

This book shares economic, planning and environmental policies and strategies implemented by Shenzhen, which in a just four decades has emerged as the Silicon Valley of China. This remarkable economic and social development has been built on high-tech, manufacturing and service industries. Today, it is knowledge-based industries that drive Shenzhen's development. Its economic output is ranked third highest among 659 Chinese cities and according to the 2017 Global Financial Centres Index, Shenzhen is the twenty-second most competitive financial center in the world. In 2016, Shenzhen's contribution to China's GDP was USD 303 billion, surpassed only by Shanghai and Beijing.

Yet, cities are not merely places where people reside or sites where the production of goods and services takes place. Through their own internal dynamics, cities are key drivers for growth and development. They generate wealth and prosperity, serve as hubs of innovation and transformation, create multipliers, facilitate redistribution of assets and opportunities, increase productivity and contribute to balanced territorial development.

For this four decade-old miracle to continue, the old Chinese practice of long-term thinking needs to be practiced. Sustainable development must be pursued in order to address current global challenges of rising poverty, social inequity, environmental degradation and climate change. In our rapidly urbanizing world, with more than half of the population now living in cities, the question of sustainable urban development comes to the fore. We must ask ourselves how we can improve the quality of life of urban citizens, while ensuring that urban areas remain economically productive, socially inclusive and environmentally sound for both present and future generations.

Shenzhen is truly a remarkable success story. Many growing cities, special economic zones and new cities can learn a lot from its experience. I am pleased to present to you this book, which draws upon the expertise of specialists representing various fields and institutions. It will help us understand many stories that make up the Shenzhen experience.

United Nations Under-Secretary-General and Executive Director
United Nations Human Settlements Programme (UN-Habitat)

序 二

我很荣幸能为这本书《深圳故事：经济、社会、环境的转型》写下序言。

自1980年深圳经济特区成立40年以来，深圳经济社会取得了巨大的发展。本书从经济、社会和环境的角度记录了深圳多年来的进步。2018年，中国庆祝了改革开放40周年。2019年是深圳市建城40周年，2020年是深圳经济特区成立40周年。联合国人居署能够在这个对于深圳来说意义非凡的时刻出版这本书，我十分高兴。

联合国人居署致力于促进经济、社会和环境上可永续性人居发展，以达到所有人都有合适居所的目标。其他国家的许多城镇和经济特区都可以借鉴深圳的城市发展经验。我希望这本书能够为城市发展提供经验，城市领导人、城市规划者、学者和经济学家也能够从中受益。

深圳市对外文化交流协会会长

Preface II

It is with great pleasure that I write this brief message for this book *The Story of Shenzhen: Its Economic, Social and Environmental Transformation*.

Shenzhen has achieved tremendous economic and social development within the last four decades since the establishment of Shenzhen Special Economic Zone in 1980. This book documents Shenzhen's progress over the years from economic, social and environmental perspectives. In 2018, China celebrated the 40th anniversary of its reform and opening up. In 2019, we celebrated the 40th anniversary of the establishment of the city of Shenzhen, and in 2020 we will welcome the 40 th anniversary of the inauguration of Shenzhen Special Economic Zone. I am pleased that UN-Habitat is publishing this book at this important time for Shenzhen.

UN-Habitat is committed to promote economically, socially and environmentally sustainable human settlements development and the achievement of adequate shelter for all. Many cities, towns and special economic zones in other countries can be inspired by Shenzhen's experience in its urban development. I would hope that this book will contribute to the body of knowledge on urban development, and benefit city leaders, urban planners, academics and economists.

President of Shenzhen Association for International Cultural Exchanges

目 录

导 言 ………………………………………………………… (1)

上 篇

第一章 深圳和珠三角地区的全球价值链 …………………… (15)
第二章 城市融资、企业融资和创业融资 …………………… (38)
第三章 现代经济增长、经济特区与工业化 ………………… (67)
第四章 城市增长与城市规划：面对人口
　　　 增长的挑战 …………………………………………… (86)
第五章 基本服务和当地基础设施 …………………………… (107)
第六章 环境与生态城市 ……………………………………… (135)

下 篇

Chapter 1　The Global Value Chain in Shenzhen and the
　　　　　 Pearl Delta Region ………………………………… (165)
Chapter 2　Financing the City, Financing the Firms and Financing
　　　　　 Entrepreneurship …………………………………… (196)
Chapter 3　Modern Economic Growth, Special Economic Zone and
　　　　　 Industrialization ……………………………………… (232)
Chapter 4　City Growth and Urban Planning: Encountering
　　　　　 the Challenges of Population Growth ……………… (258)

Chapter 5　Basic Services and Local Infrastructure ……………（277）
Chapter 6　Environment and Eco-City ………………………（310）

参考文献 ………………………………………………………（353）

后　记 …………………………………………………………（367）

导　　言

一　故事的缘起

"深圳故事"这个项目，缘于一次偶然的拜访。2017年联合国人居署城市经济局局长马可·卡米亚先生（Mr. Marco Kamiya）和中国社会科学院城市与竞争力研究中心主任倪鹏飞教授一起到访深圳。交流过程中，深圳改革开放创造出的经济社会发展奇迹，令见多识广的马可先生也大为惊叹，深受启发。他说，一直以来，联合国积极推动南南合作，促进全球国家和地区，特别是发展中国家及欠发达国家和地区开展合作，深圳改革开放的成功经验是一个难得的案例，值得对外讲好"深圳故事"，分享深圳发展经验。

在这一倡议下，我们觉得，讲好"深圳故事"，不仅是深圳城市外宣的需要，也是联合国组织寄予这个城市的一份责任和期待。这个倡议，得到市委市政府主要领导的大力赞同。很快，深圳与联合国人居署开展合作，启动"深圳故事：经济、社会和环境的转型"课题研究，借此为世界城市发展提供中国经验和中国智慧。（2017年11月，深圳与人居署达成合作意向。2018年5月，深圳对外文化交流协会与人居署签署项目合作协议，项目正式启动。2019年4月，项目完成，形成"深圳故事：经济、社会和环境的转型"课题报告）

2019年5月，应联合国人居署邀请，我率深圳市文化代表团到人居署阿拉伯地区总部进行"深圳故事：经济、社会和环境的转型"项目成果推介，并在肯尼亚内罗毕人居署总部，出席"联合国人居署第一届人居大会"，以及大会专门设置的边会议程："深圳故事"项目成果发布会。

代表团到达开罗正值盛夏，庞杂的开罗大城喧嚣地铺洒在尼罗河下游的冲积扇面上。代表团在惊叹辉煌的古埃及历史和尼罗河壮丽的地理景观的同时，对开罗今天的现代化现状却也倍感诧异。当我们穿过年久失修、到处开肠破肚的城市中心和城郊一眼望不到边的烂尾楼和"城中村"，开罗的这幅现代化面孔，着实超越了大多数人的想象。

我们在走访街区的途中，不时有社区的孩子们围上前来，我们把预先准备的清凉油送给了他们，没想到孩子们想要的却是我们包里的签字笔。

夕阳的余晖炽烈地烘烤着这个古老的大埠，到处是临街破墙开店的小商铺，地下管网在精致的高档社区与平民区的交接处裸露，孩子们在淹没脚面的尘灰中奔跑嬉闹……这个氛围不禁使人想起20世纪70—80年代许许多多的中国城市，勤劳的人民渴求发展的眼神，这一切也使得我们一行对开罗的亲切感油然而生。

开罗之行，意义非凡。在人居署阿拉伯地区总部，原本只是一场简单的分享交流，没想到的是，"深圳故事"的精彩，一下点燃了大家的兴趣点。人居署阿拉伯地区总部主任海娜女士（Mrs. Rania Hedeya）觉得"深圳故事"非常新鲜，对深圳发展十分惊讶。一个边陲小镇，在40年的时间里发展成为一个现代化国际化大都市，像阿拉伯神话一样，简直是"天方夜谭"，令人不可思议。这是一次"拖堂"的交流，大家沉浸在一种欢愉的情绪中。他们对深圳经济发展、社会管理、移民文化、社区交流、医疗教育等方面层出不穷地提问，原定半小时的会谈，后来拖成了近三个小时，大家依然意犹未尽。

在交流中我们也了解到，人居署阿拉伯总部在过去的二十年间曾指导当地政府沿尼罗河两岸星罗棋布地规划建造了十几个中小城市，试图消化开罗的人口压力并更好地解决当地人民的城市化和就业问题，遗憾的是并未成功。这十几个建设成的城市至今依然荒置在静水深流的尼罗河两岸。人们由于就业、生活成本和发展机遇及城市公共品匮乏等原因，宁愿挤在污水横流的贫民社区，也不想迁到清洁宽敞的小镇,于是开罗大城继续这么摊大饼似地延展着。这或许正是海娜女士她们对深圳40年变迁感兴趣的原因所在吧。

"深圳故事"在阿拉伯地区引发热议之后,代表团来到肯尼亚内罗毕出席"联合国人居署首届人居大会"。这场大会是联合国人居署成立近20年来,首次举办的世界性峰会,全球100多个国家和地区的代表、30多个国家的首脑与会,参会人数超过3000人。这届大会的主题是"创新让城市和社区生活更美好","深圳故事"项目高度符合会议主题,联合国副秘书长、人居署执行主任迈穆娜·穆赫德·谢里夫女士(Mrs. Maimunah Mohd Sharif),为项目成果作序,指出"深圳无疑是一个引人注目的成功故事,其发展经验值得全球其他新兴城市和经济特区借鉴"。谢里夫女士,在百忙之中亲自为项目成果签名题词,特意委托项目司司长拉夫先生(Mr. Rafael Tuts)会见深圳市文化代表团。发布会现场,各国城市主官、专家学者、科研人员对于"深圳故事"给予极大关注,供会议交流的项目资料瞬间"秒光",94家海内外媒体进行了热潮式报道,全网阅读点击量超过5700万次,"深圳故事"一时间洛阳纸贵。

"深圳故事"这个项目无疑成为人居署近年来主导的旨在推进全球城市发展经验相互借鉴、相互促动的一个精彩案例。项目整合全球学术资源,采取国际研究视角,跨界组建不同学术领域、不同理论背景的国际学人多维度解析深圳。项目团队的13名专家来自联合国人居署、德国慕尼黑大学、意大利恩纳科雷大学、博茨瓦纳大学、中国社科院、南京大学、哈尔滨工业大学等。"深圳故事"项目共分为六个章节,力图从深圳在全球城市价值链中的位置、财政政策、经济增长、城市规划、基础服务、环境保护等方面深度挖掘,从内外结合的多面视角剖析深圳、解读深圳,试图为世界勾画出隐匿在深圳40年改革发展巨大实践中的工业化、城市化和国际化的深层逻辑。

二 一样的城市化,不一样的历史语境

纵观全球,当今世界城市演化的历程始终未能脱离从大航海和

殖民时代所开启的贸易化和全球化的主导历史语境，尽管深圳40年的城市发展同样必须承受来自全球化先发城市和地区在经济、文化、分工和规则等诸多方面的巨大压力，但深圳的工业化、城市化和国际化的故事却为全球发展中国家的城市，创造了一个在夹缝中生存，从配角到主角、从边缘到中心的一个发展传奇，同时也为那些渴望摆脱传统困境、闯出生路的城市和地区创造了一种全新的发展语境。

传统语境中的城市化，是在欧洲文艺复兴、地理大发现之后产生的，开创了人类有史以来声势最为浩大、历程最为复杂的全球化新航道。在这一航道里，西方先发国家的城市化，一直伴随着贸易、航海、工业革命以及技术进步，与殖民和战争同步伐，呈现出脉络分明的兴衰迭代。

13世纪末14世纪初，资本主义最早在意大利萌芽，佛罗伦萨、热那亚、威尼斯等城市，成为意大利乃至整个欧洲文艺复兴发源地和商贸中心。威尼斯海运发达，用商船从东方运回羊毛，从欧洲其他国家运来白银，在与热那亚的战争中赢得胜利后，威尼斯成为欧洲的经济中心，在贸易、航运、金融、奢侈性消费、艺术、建筑等方面达到高峰，一度成为风向标。

由于航海业的发达，特别是新大陆的发现，使得葡萄牙和西班牙相继脱颖而出。15世纪上半叶，葡萄牙突破海岸线的限制向外扩张，开启了地理大发现时代。此后，前赴后继的航海家到达好望角、印度西海岸港口城市科泽科德。特别是哥伦布和麦哲伦，相继刷新航海纪录，西方贸易的版图持续快速地扩张。葡萄牙、西班牙源源不断地从亚洲、非洲、美洲等地掠回大量的黄金、资源、物产，甚至人口，成就了这一历史阶段欧洲国家与城市的繁荣，西班牙首都巴塞罗那盛极一时。

欧洲各国对海运、资源、土地以及奴隶等控制权的争夺，导致经济霸权中心不断交替。荷兰从1585年开始崛起，大批由于战争破坏而逃到荷兰的商人、银行家、产业工人，在荷兰特别是阿姆斯特丹定居，使得荷兰在商业、航运、渔业、贸易、工业、金融以及教育等方面突飞猛进，到17世纪中后期在世界贸易中处于经济霸权地位。

此后，荷兰衰弱，英国后来居上。1688年的光荣革命确立了英国君主立宪政体，18世纪60年代至19世纪30年代英国成为世界上第一个完成工业革命的国家。通过一系列的贸易与战争，英国在18世纪至20世纪初统治的领土跨越全球七大洲，成为当时世界上最强大的国家和第一大殖民帝国。伦敦在政治、经济、文化、科技等领域影响力巨大，是当时世界上最大的城市。即便是今天，伦敦依然享有着这一历史遗产的余荫庇护，仍然是世界上最大的经济中心之一，也是欧洲最大的城市，与纽约并列为全球顶级国际大都会。

二战结束后，美国凭借世界大战获胜国的特权优势，并借助其地缘优势以及先进的武器工业，跃居资本主义国家首位，通过在全球贸易、金融、科技、军工等领域一系列的制度设计和全球治理体系的设置，美国最终登顶全球新霸主地位，纽约更是一跃而成为全球的金融中心、科技中心，纽约都市圈进一步塑形成为世界上最大的城市圈。纽约湾区的GDP总量，相当于北上广深4座城市之和。

由今察史，史以鉴今。从西方发达国家城市群大约500年间的兴替可以看到，几乎每一个国家或城市跃升为世界经济霸主的过程，都伴随着掠夺、殖民和战争，伴随着把自身的政治、经济制度以及价值观，强加给其他国家和地区。时至今日，在一些亚非拉国家和城市依然存在"殖民后遗症"。这种带有殖民语境下的城市化路径，决定了第三世界的城市化和全球化只能是被动的、被抑制的、处在垂直分工底层的城市化路径。现在看来，当初"人类文明的新航道"有着天然的"劣根性"，人类城市发展方需要开辟另一个全新的航道。

东方风来满眼春。1978年12月，中国共产党第十一届三中全会，让世界再次进入"中国时间"。从那一刻起，一个冲破西方全球化模式的全新航道悄然开启。改革开放成为社会主义现代化建设的总方针、总政策，中国由此走上了一条中国特色社会主义道路，经济社会实现全面发展。

城市是人类文明最为集中也最为精彩的现实表达。芒福德说：

"一代新文明必然有其自己的城市"。有外媒惊叹道:"中国大变革的指针正轰然鸣响。"1980年8月26日,《广东省经济特区暂行条例》在第五届全国人大常务委员会第十五次会议顺利通过,标志着经济特区在中国正式诞生。英国《经济学人》评价说:"改革开放以来,中国最引人注目的实践是经济特区;全世界超过4000个经济特区,最为成功的莫过于'深圳奇迹'。"尽管深圳从西方全球化、城市化中得到了产能外溢带来的巨大机遇,但这是一个完全不同于欧美模式的崭新城市化模式,是一个在打压中抗争、在被动中学习、在创新中奋进、在合作中共赢的新模式,它拥有完全不同的新逻辑,是一种内生发展动力所驱动的城市化。这也正是"深圳故事"的魅力所在。

> 深圳故事的关键在于,坚持改革开放,融入世界潮流,突破僵化的经济体制,释放出巨大的市场活力。

深圳率先冲破思想束缚,积极发挥市场在资源配置中的决定性作用,破除行政指令分配资源模式,实行以市场为取向的经济体制改革,在全国率先建立起社会主义市场经济体制基本框架。正是因为深圳尊重近代西方市场经济价值规律,主动在既有的"国际游戏规则"下参与竞争合作,深圳才能顺利抓住20世纪80年代,西方发达国家低端产业海外转移的重大机遇,凭借着艰辛的努力,赚来了来之不易的"第一桶金"。

马可先生指出,制度创新、剩余劳动力的聚集、全球分工、城市治理等是中国城市崛起中相互作用的四个引擎。他特别提到,建立市场经济的改革为其他三个引擎创造了条件和驱动力,深圳充分发挥改革开放"试验场"的有利条件,在实践探索中建立社会主义市场经济,为本土发展提供了强大的动力和吸引力。同时,政府在应对外部压力方面发挥了"微妙作用",引导市场发挥了决定性的作用,使这座城市得以攀登到全球产业链的上游。

1979年7月8日,蛇口工业区"开山第一炮"如同一声春雷炸响神州,开启了中国改革开放40年的华彩乐章。深圳率先打破

"大锅饭",迸发出"时间就是金钱,效率就是生命"的呐喊,以思想大解放,催生生产力大解放。作为中国大陆第一个出口加工工业区,蛇口工业区从当初占地 1.24 平方公里的荒凉之地,不断引进加工贸易企业进驻,后来催生了招商银行、平安集团、华为等世界 500 强企业。倪鹏飞教授和马可先生认为,这里的一系列改革可以称之为"蛇口模式",对深圳及中国改革开放产生了重大而深远的影响。

敢为天下先,深圳不断创出新纪录。"中国土地第一拍"在深圳落槌,盘活了特区土地,换回了建设亟须的资金,促成了宪法的修改;得益于学习国际招投标制度,深圳创造了"三天一层楼"的深圳速度;深圳向新加坡取经,全国首创养老保险个人账户;深圳证券交易所破茧而出,成为改革开放后第一家按国际惯例进行集中交易的证交所;在全国率先进行物价体制改革试验,率先取消一切票证,率先成立外汇调剂中心,率先统一内外资企业所得税税率,率先试行工资制度改革,率先试行商店承包经营……改革开放"试验田"从经济领域改革到全面深化经济、政治、文化、社会、生态文明体制和党的建设制度改革,闯出千余项"国内第一",深圳 GDP 从 1979 年的 1.96 亿元增长到 2019 年的 2.69 万亿元。创造了世界工业化、现代化、城市化发展史上的奇迹。

近年来,深圳继续全面深化改革,扩大对外开放,不断激发市场活力。在全国首创多主体供给、多渠道保障、租购并举的"4+2+2+2"住房供应和保障体系,被誉为"深圳二次房改";深圳发挥前海蛇口自贸片区重要开放平台作用,在更广领域扩大外资市场准入、全面实施准入前国民待遇加负面清单管理制度,推动现代服务业、制造业、金融业等领域全方位对外开放。

> 深圳故事的精彩在于,这是一座拥有全球视野,尊重国际规则,把创新植入 DNA 的城市。

深圳的全球化过程异常艰辛,西方国家在转移产能的同时,牢牢占据着产业链顶端,拥有绝对的话语权和定价权,深圳企业和工人只能靠自己的劳动与汗水承接由西方外包的低附加值的产品，商品要贴西方厂商的标签，才能销售到全球市场，赚取很少的加工费。比如，早期生产一部电话12美元，西方人挣了11美元，深圳企业只能赚取不到1美元的微薄利润。一件售价几千元的电器产品，常常也只能挣到几十元甚至更低的利润。

即便是在这样恶劣的环境下，深圳遵循国际规则，忍辱负重、不畏艰难，在劣势中与对手同台竞技。直到现在，"深圳制造""深圳创造"依然在国际竞争中遭遇各种技术壁垒，受到贸易保护主义的打压。但是，深圳硬是在这风风雨雨中艰难地挺下来了，靠始终如一的坚守、不顾艰辛的付出，靠做脏活、苦活、累活一点一滴地发展起来，像一粒种子在悬崖峭壁间顽强地发芽生长起来，以其成熟的耐心、持续的创新，源源不断地向国际市场供给物美价廉的优质产品。最终，在以西方为主导的制度化、法治化和主权化的全球化强势语境之中，创造出属于深圳的一片天地，赢得全球市场的普遍认可和尊重。

深圳拥有一颗不甘平庸的雄心。如何突破西方强势语境，主动打破路径依赖，深圳交出了自己的"答卷"，那就是：坚持把创新驱动作为城市发展主导战略，把创新融入深圳的血脉，成为经济社会发展的"核心密码"。在每一次社会发展的重要关头，深圳启动的全方位创新，都为经济社会发展注入了强劲动力、澎湃活力。在"三来一补"产业还很吃香时，深圳探索发展高新技术产业，从简单的加工制造，到设计加工，再到自主品牌；从最初的"山寨"，到完全自主知识产权，深圳始终鼓励科技创新，加大研发投入，布局创新载体，培育创新人才，有效激发了企业、高校、科研院所等各类创新主体的激情与活力。

唐杰教授指出，深圳具有许多引人入胜的品质，其中最突出的就是企业家精神在城市的每个角落都在"震动"。深圳"6个90%"，即深圳90%以上的研发机构设立在企业、90%以上的研发人员集中在企业、90%以上的研发资金来源于企业、90%以上的创新型企业是本土企业、90%以上的职务发明专利出自于企业、90%以上的重大科技项目发明专利来源于龙头企业，早已成为企业创新活跃的代名词,世界级企业不断涌现,平安、招商、华为、腾讯、万科、正威、恒大等7家企业跻身世界500强,大疆、优必选、奥比中光等创新型企业活力十足,创新成果从深圳走向全球。经过不断的转型升级,深圳成功实现创新驱动发展,成为国家创新型城市、全球知名创新之都,成为是全球产业价值链的中坚力量。深圳R&D投入强度远超国际创新型国家标准,超过以色列、韩国、瑞士、日本、美国等世界公认的创新领导型国家水平。截至2019年底,深圳创新载体2260家,国家级高新技术企业超过1.7万家,PCT国际专利申请量连续17年居全国城市首位,技术创新由"跟跑"向"并跑""领跑"转变,5G、超材料等领域成为国际标准引领发展的佼佼者。

作为中国的"硅谷",深圳高新技术产业发展成为全国的一面旗帜。全球创新资源加速向深圳聚集,国际研发机构和知名企业加快"抢滩"深圳,在深投资或开设分支机构的世界500强企业超过100家,格拉布斯研究院等多家诺贝尔奖实验室相继落地,苹果、高通、甲骨文、空中客车、埃森哲等"大鳄"选择深圳,投资设立以高端研发为主的创新中心。空客公司首席执行官托马斯·恩德斯说,深圳高新技术产业优势、创新创业氛围和良好的营商环境,是吸引跨国公司前来投资的重要原因。

深圳故事的另一个特质在于,它是一座志存高远、不断革新、全面可持续发展的城市。

深圳对标国际一流,在建设现代化国际化城市时,坚持"绿水青山就是金山银山"理念,推动形成人与自然和谐发展新格局。曾经一度,深圳的生态环境受到了破坏,江河受到了污染,但这并没有拖慢城市化的进度。曾经污染了的山河,深圳反过来正在以超常规的手段和气力进行全面治理。

深圳对发展道路的探索,始于经济,而最终致力于全面。从一骑绝尘的"深圳速度",到以高产出、低消耗、低污染为特征的"深圳效益",再到结构优化、创新驱动、绿色低碳的"深圳质量",

再到对标国际一流、打造更具时代引领性的"深圳设计""深圳品牌",深圳高质量发展的坐标系从来不是单向的、平面的、固定的,而是多维的、立体的、延展的。

在资源紧约束、环境强负荷的基础上,深圳始终秉承低碳发展、绿色发展、可持续发展,真正实现了"天蓝、地绿、水清",为国家探索出了一条超大型城市的可持续发展路径。深圳成为"国际花园城市""国家森林城市""首批国家可持续发展议程创新示范区",在全国率先实现公交车、出租车电动化,PM2.5平均浓度为每立方米24微克,接近欧盟标准。深圳能源消费增速低于GDP增速,单位GDP能耗逐年降低,为全国平均水平的一半左右,已与发达国家水平相当。

当然,深圳故事的特别之处,还在于它在国际化现代化进程中,形成的敢为天下先的移民精神和海纳百川、开放包容的城市特质。

"深圳故事"是几代人共同创造的全球化故事,"来了,就是深圳人",这是深圳多元包容移民文化的精神内核。作为一座移民城市,从最初全国各地支援干部、几十万建筑工程兵、数百万农民工,到众多高校毕业生、海归人员,深圳移民呈现出不同的时代特色,一茬又一茬的移民,从当初的深一代,到现在的深二代甚至深三代,在这里默默奉献青春。

这样的移民故事曾经发生在威尼斯、巴塞罗那、阿姆斯特丹、巴黎、伦敦、纽约、东京、香港等国际化大都市。现在,相同的故事依然在深圳继续,来自五湖四海的优秀人才不断会聚、创新创业、艰苦奋斗,成就了年轻的深圳。这座城市常住人口1300万,平均年龄33岁,他们来自170多个国家,涵盖中国56个民族,这是深圳的宝贵财富和重要竞争力。

奇妙的是,人们并未被深圳本土"官话"的广东话和客家话同化,来自五湖四海的居民自觉选择用普通话进行交流。研究团队学者戴维斯教授认为,仅此一点,就足以证明深圳是一个伟大的中国里程碑式的城市，克服强烈的地方性和特殊性倾向，建设更广的世界性语言环境。而且，深圳是一个如此特殊的城市，越来越多的人将自己标识为深圳，而不是原籍地。

文化是一个国家、一个民族的灵魂。放眼世界，但凡经济繁盛之地，往往文化交流碰撞也十分活跃。40年来，深圳成功撕掉"文化沙漠"的标签，培育出自身特有的文化内核。敢为天下先；大胆地试，大胆地闯；空谈误国，实干兴邦……这些，都是深圳文化的精神内核。

鼓励创新，包容失败，是深圳文化的重要气度。正是这种精神理念，让深圳成为全球创新的乐土。大疆创新科技有限公司创始人汪滔说，当年他怀揣技术谋求创业的时候，首先就想到了深圳，因为这里宽容失败，鼓励创新。他常常想，这一群初出茅庐的年轻人，不用去阿谀奉承、投机取巧，就可以在埋头苦干当中达到创业之巅，这样的故事恐怕只有深圳才可以实现。

三　关于深圳故事的未来想象

每个时代都有每个时代的使命，每座城市都有每座城市的机遇。面对当今世界发展百年不遇之大变局，人类文明的发展进入新时代，引领人类发展的"接力棒"已经传递到了世界的东方。深圳，必将也终将成为新一轮发展中的领跑者。

回顾历史，深圳充满自豪，展望未来，深圳满怀自信。在新的航道上，深圳放眼美好未来，对标国际一流。2019年2月公布的《粤港澳大湾区发展规划纲要》，赋予深圳粤港澳大湾区四大中心城市和区域发展四大核心引擎之一的重大使命；2019年8月印发的《中共中央、国务院关于支持深圳建设中国特色社会主义先行示范区的意见》，明确赋予深圳高质量发展高地、法治城市示范、城市文明典范、民生幸福标杆、可持续发展先锋的五大战略定位，擘画了深圳未来的发展蓝图：到2025年，深圳将建成现代化国际化创新型城市；到2035年，建成具有全球影响力的创新创业创意之都，成为中国建设社会主义现代化强国的城市范例。深圳正在抢抓"双区驱动"重大历史机遇，阔步走向世界舞台的中央。

相比中华民族伟大复兴的中国梦，深圳是中国这条大河当中的一道涓涓溪流，并汇聚到新的全球化浪潮之中。我们能在500年西方为主导全球化语境下，走出一种独有的全球化之路，靠的是勤劳与汗水，靠的是创新和资源的密集付出，靠的是低附加值的交换。在新的全球化的征途上，深圳将在道路、理论、制度、文化全面自信的新时代，全力构建人类命运共同体。

正是看到了"深圳故事"的成功与精彩，人居署调集了全球资源对"深圳故事"进行研究与推广。深圳的昨天，是很多城市和地区的今天；深圳的明天，也必将是这些城市和地区美好的明天。深圳需要向世界讲述自己的故事，世界也期待聆听深圳的故事。

潮平两岸阔，风正一帆悬。"深圳故事"正在继续，相信后续的故事会越发精彩。西方500多年城市化进程，威尼斯、巴塞罗那、阿姆斯特丹、巴黎、伦敦、纽约等，它们是西方城市化模式下的产物，是大航海时代殖民语境或者说前现代语境下的延续，而今，世界需要新的叙述，人类需要新的更加平等、持续的繁盛。从以西方为主的传统全球化缝隙当中生长出来的深圳故事和文化，是忍辱合作的文化、包容感恩的文化、创新共赢的文化，我们愿意分享自己的故事，激励更多的城市，以自身的勤劳和智慧，创造出属于自己的全球化和城市化发展的全新"故事会"。

上 篇

第一章 深圳和珠三角地区的全球价值链

一 介绍

深圳被誉为中国的硅谷。分析人士称,深圳的地位在不久的将来会更加重要,因为深圳的软件行业不仅与美国平分秋色,其硬件行业也发展飞速。诸多中国大型企业在深圳落户,如全球电子巨头华为、微信和QQ的运营商——互联网领军者腾讯,电子和汽车制造商比亚迪,从事生命科学和基因组研究的前沿机构华大基因(BGI),从事无人机及航空技术研发的大疆创新科技有限公司(DJI),以及致力于人工智能的商汤科技(SenseTime)等。

一个小村庄是如何从1979年起跃居成为全球技术中心的?本章将从改革开放、金融、治理、政策等方面揭示深圳的崛起。更重要的是,在城市规划和扩张的监测之下,深圳用全新的方式推动了城市扩张与生产能力齐头并进,取得了突飞猛进的发展。

二 典型化事实

根据中国社会科学院和联合国人类住区规划署(联合国人居署)联合发布的《2018—2019年全球城市竞争力报告》,深圳在经济竞争力方面排名世界第五,中国在国家排名中高居榜首。世界知识产权组织(WIPO)等多家机构发布的2017年全球创新指数显示,深圳是全球第二大创新集群,仅次于东京,已赶超硅谷。从

1978年到2018年的40年间,深圳从一个贫穷的边远渔镇崛起成为全球创新大都市,从世界产业链的底层跃居成为领头羊。深圳以其迅猛的发展创造了世界历史,这座城市的演变表现在以下几个方面。

(一) 从一个基础设施薄弱的农业城镇成为一座现代化大都市

从城市建设面积和环境发展来看,深圳在1978年曾是一个3平方公里的小城镇,1979年和2010年分别扩大到390平方公里和1997平方公里。改革开放以前,深圳几乎为一片荒地,经过40年的发展,这里已被绿地覆盖,城市化程度很高。在深圳成立之前和早期,几乎没有任何基础设施。现在,深圳为全球城市中心,拥有世界先进的基础设施。截至2017年,深圳共有8条地铁线路,总长285公里,成为全球地铁里程排名前十的城市之一。深圳通过航空连接了超过36个海外城市。深圳港的吞吐量已增至每年2520万个20英尺标准箱(TEU),连续五年成为世界第二大港口。

(二) 从一个拥有2万居民的小镇到一个拥有千万人口的大都市

在城市人口和社会发展方面,改革开放之前,广东省及宝安县有成千上万的居民逃往香港。1978年,宝安县深圳镇的人口约为25000人。1979年,宝安县改建为深圳市,常住人口为31.4万。在接下来的40年中,数百万年轻人和大学毕业生移居深圳。2018年,常住人口为1522.83万,地方政府实际服务人口超过2000万,城市化率为100%。2017年,各类人才超过510万,占常住人口总数的40.7%;常住人口的平均年龄为32.5岁,年龄在15—44岁之间的主要劳动力占76%。同时,城镇居民人均可支配收入从1985年的1915元增加到2017年的52938元,是32年前的27.6倍,年均增长率10.9%(图1-1)。

(三) 从一个小渔镇成为全球技术中心

在城市工业和经济发展方面,国内生产总值由1979年的1.96亿元猛增到2.2万亿元以上,38年中增长11223倍,年均增长率

27.8%。同期，人均国内生产总值由 606 元增长到 183100 元，增长 301 倍，年均增长 16.2%。2019 年，深圳 GDP 总值达到 2.69 亿，首次超过香港（图 1-2 和图 1-3）。

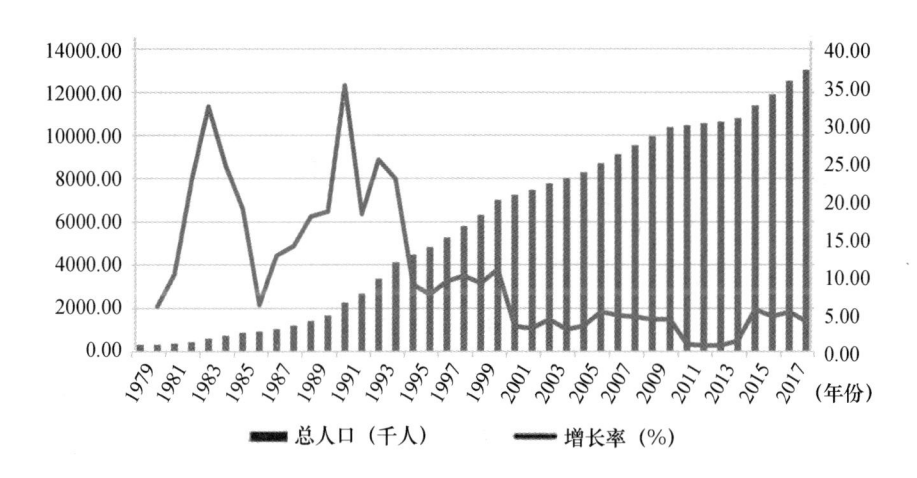

图 1-1 过去 40 年深圳人口及其增长情况

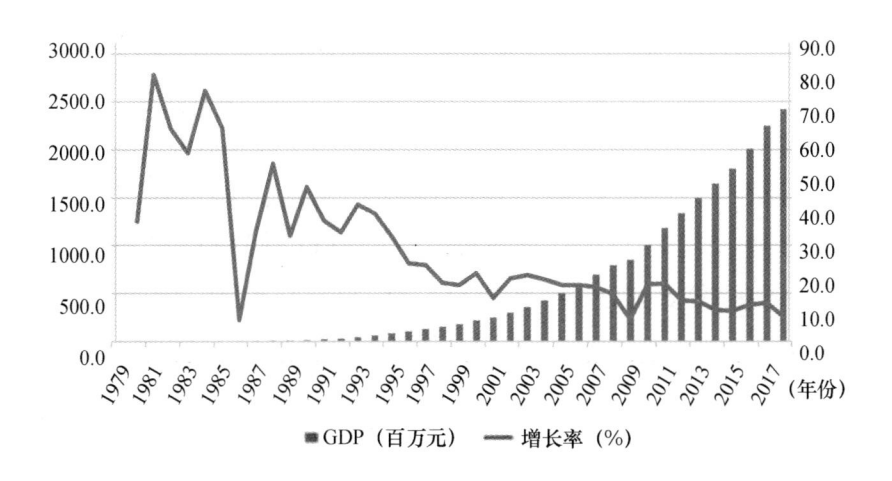

图 1-2 深圳过去 40 年的国内生产总值及增长率

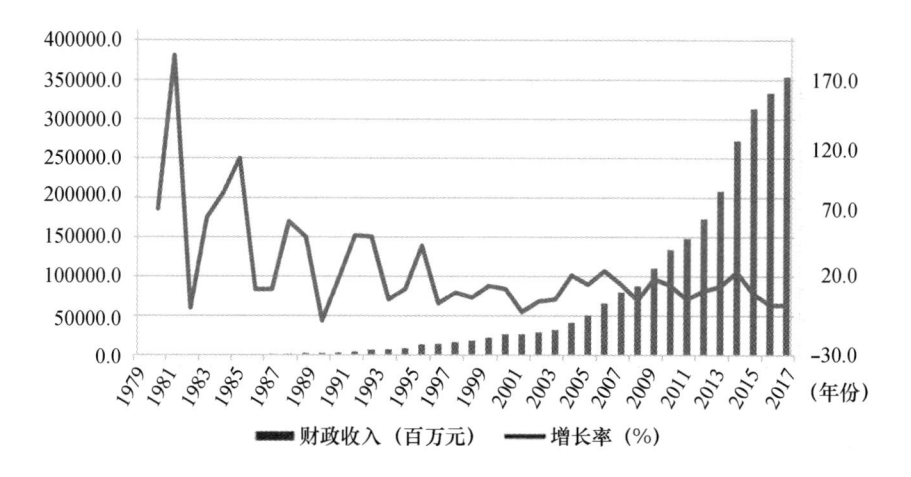

图 1-3　深圳近 40 年财政收入及增长速度

从 1979 年到 2017 年，深圳出口总额从 930 万美元增长到 2442.21 亿美元，增长 26259 倍，38 年来年均增长率 27.3%（图 1-4）。

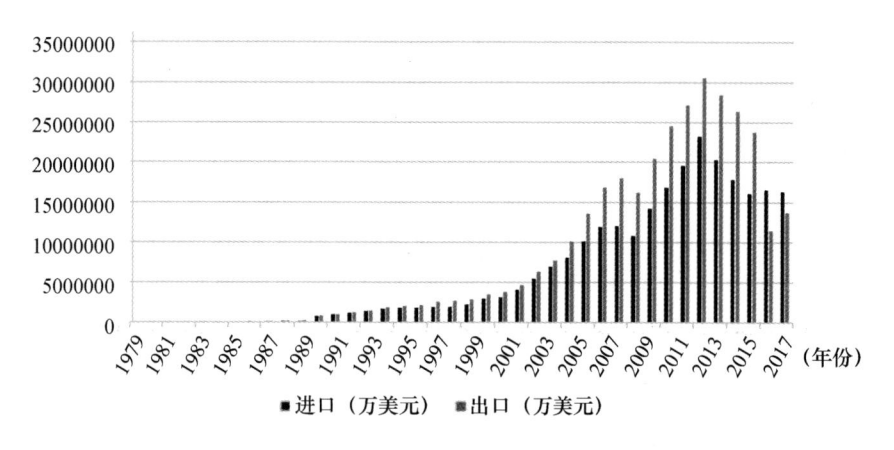

图 1-4　深圳近 40 年进出口情况

1978 年，深圳是一个传统的农业和渔业小镇。1979 年，开始从事加工和小生产行业，即加工材料或给定样品和组装部件。2018 年，深圳成为区域金融中心、中国经济中心和全球技术创新中心。

深圳从少数小型棉纺厂和农机维修车间起步，迅速发展到拥有320万个新兴经营主体，其中企业188万个，国家级高新技术企业1.2万个。2017年，全市微机设备产量是1983年的381230倍，集成电路产量是1983年的4260倍，所生产的产品技术价值高。深圳拥有华为、平安、腾讯、万科、恒大等7家全球500强企业，其中华为、腾讯和大疆创新已成长为国际知名的科技公司。深圳拥有世界领先的高科技产品的制造能力，如手机、可穿戴设备和高端医疗器械，为世界各地的人们创造了科技改变生活的体验。

（四）从乡村小镇到国家经济技术"动力厂"

在城市地位和影响力方面，深圳一直是中国城市发展和世界进步的领头羊。第一，深圳通过扩大和复制原先在全国其他地区的试点改革，直接推动了全国市场经济体制的建立和全面开放。深圳的成功经验和发展理念激励着中国和全世界创新发展思维。第二，深圳创造的财富有相当一部分以税收的形式流向政府，以工资的形式流向农民工，支持了国民经济的增长、腹地的发展和千家万户的兴旺繁荣。2018年，深圳市辖区一般公共预算收入达9.1亿元，居中国内地城市首位。这一收入占全国总收入的5%。第三，随着深圳经济的进一步发展，深圳的产业规模不断扩大，并向周边地区和腹地城市转移，直接带动了深圳经济的腾飞。第四，随着经济发展和技术创新，深圳培养了数以百万计的技术人员、企业家和创新创造者，其中一些人回到家乡或其他地区，带动了更多地区的发展创新。2017年，深圳市根据《专利合作条约》（PCT）申请的专利占全国总量的43.1%，连续14年成为中国PCT专利最多的城市。

改革开放以来，中国内地城市由1978年的193个增加到2018年的650多个，城镇由2000多个增加到约2万个。从20世纪80年代深圳等沿海地区的五个经济特区，到新建更多的经济区和试验区，中国在这方面取得了举世瞩目的成就。深圳在经济基础、生产要素、历史文化、环境容量等方面与许多其他城市不尽相同，但这座城市却创造了经济奇迹，实现了经济、社会和环境的可持续高速增长和快速转型。

三　理论框架

本节以经济增长理论和发展经济学的理论框架为基础，结合中国城市发展的独特变量和全球化的特点，总结出中国城市发展经济学的驱动力、机制和模式。中国城市设计与崛起的四大引擎是：(1) 制度创新；(2) 非农产业集聚；(3) 全球分工；(4) 城市治理。这些引擎相互作用，推动着中国的城市崛起，并塑造着城市面貌。

基础的市场经济体制改革，规范了经济主体的权利和责任以及资源生物配置方式，为城市的崛起提供了基本动力和条件。跨国企业带来的全球分工为这一过程注入了外部活力。由于农村剩余劳动力的流入，非农部门的聚集加快了这一进程。市政府的城市治理和财政为城市的崛起提供了独特的动力（图1-5）。

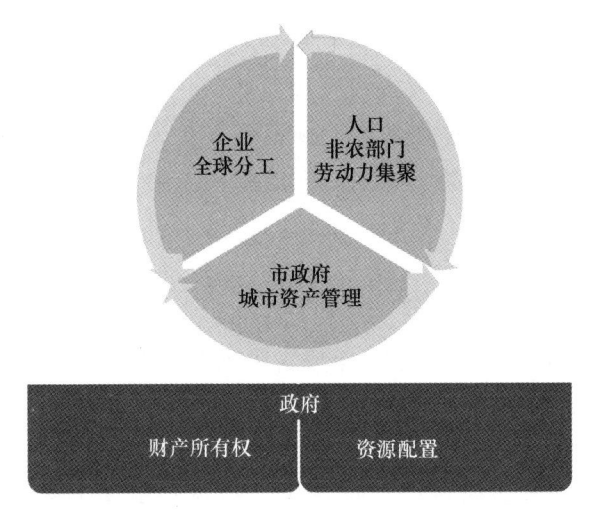

图1-5　中国城市发展的经济模式

总体而言，四大引擎有着共同的影响：市场经济的改革为其他三个引擎释放力量创造了条件和动力；农村剩余劳动力引擎与跨国企业和市政府一起向其输送能源；跨国企业必须与农村剩余劳动力和城市政府协同工作；城市政府只有与农村剩余劳动力和跨国企业相结合才能发挥作用；市场经济改革吸引了全球资本、技术和市场，加上中国农村剩余劳动力以及土地和营商环境的创建，共同推动了中国工业化和城市化的快速发展。

这些引擎在不同阶段对城市转型升级起着不同的推动作用。农村剩余劳动力首先推动城市劳动力的发展，其次是来自全球企业的资本，再次是地方土地和环境，最后是人才和劳动者。

准确地说，四个引擎之间的相互作用遵循一般规律，但由于不同城市的实际情况不同而表现出特殊性。深圳实行了经济特区制度并率先进行了改革。一方面，其市场经济和全球化水平迅速提高。在发展初期，深圳跨越了农村工业化和小规模城市化阶段，直接进入了以跨国企业为动力的外向型发展阶段。深圳的城市化是由外向型工业化推动的。另一方面，资源稀缺和成本飞涨迫使深圳绕过依靠土地和资本拉动的阶段，直接进入以高端人才为主导的创新驱动型经济增长阶段。

四 深圳的成功之路

从1979年到2019年的40年间，遵循城市发展规律，深圳充分发挥四大发展引擎的相互作用，创造了从传统农业小渔镇崛起为全球科技中心的奇迹。

（一）劳动密集型产业发展：从底层到全球产业链（1979—1992年）

1979年至1992年，深圳经济特区处于起步阶段。与香港的加工贸易和补偿贸易、来自中国内地的人口流入和大规模的土地开发，推动了深圳城市化和工业化的巨大发展，深圳也因其快速发展闻名全国，并加入了全球产业链。这一时期的主要驱动力是劳动力和制度创新，这一时期的特点是经济体制创新、人口流入、基础设施建设、劳动密集型和外向型经济发展。四大引擎之间的相互作用如下。

1. 改革开放和政治试点改革为深圳的快速发展创造了制度条件

在中国改革开放的大背景下，深圳以市场经济原则为指导，成功摆脱了计划经济枷锁，通过建立经济特区，在价格、支付、土地和住房、基础设施建设、劳动就业等制度改革方面采取了大胆举措。

1987年，深圳市政府颁布了中国第一个关于鼓励科技人员创办民营科技公司的暂行条例，该条例鼓励拥有专利或管理专长的高科技人才成为股东。现任华为总裁任正非抓住机遇，创立了华为公司，该公司已跃居为世界领先企业。早在20世纪80年代，深圳就出台了《1999—2000年深圳科技发展规划》，制定了扶持高新技术产业的政策。

2. 香港企业大规模的产业布局为深圳经济快速增长创造了有利条件

伴随着全球产业结构调整，香港企业打破了产业链，并以加工和补偿贸易的形式向深圳引进劳动密集型产业链，在推动资本、技术和管理专业知识转移的同时，将深圳打造成为加工高地。1992年起，深圳开始大力发展制造业。加工和补偿贸易使深圳从底层进入全球产业价值链。起初深圳主要生产初级工业产品，加入全球价值链后，深圳转向先进的电子和信息产业，这一关键的转折点为深圳走向技术创新以及高端技术产品制造铺平了道路。

3. 外来人口的流入为深圳的快速发展提供了劳动力

1979年，2万名工程师派往深圳，开启了劳动力大量流入深圳的进程。1989年，100万农民工来到深圳。1979年，全市在岗职工仅13.95万人，1992年达到175.9万人。15—59岁的劳动力比例从1982年的58.4%增加到1990年的88%。然而，1990年的抽样调查显示，受过高中及以下教育的劳动力占劳动人口总数的65%。劳动力特别是外来务工人员，流向深圳的非农就业岗位，他们是深圳发展劳动密集型的加工和补偿贸易的中流砥柱。来自世界各地、不同背景的"深圳人"勇于进取、敢于冒险，他们为文化包容性和创业精神注入活力，为深圳人开拓创新、远见卓识的精神埋下种子。

4. 城市基本的软硬件环境为深圳的快速发展提供了条件

深圳市政府利用与香港毗邻的优势,在税收、土地、金融、对外贸易等方面充分发挥优势,创造了低成本的商营商环境。同时,充分发挥土地使用补偿和住房建设创新制度的作用。借助土地财富,深圳得以大规模进行土地开发和城市基础设施建设,为城市发展创造了空间载体。同时,地方政府利用外资,采取市场化的城市开发经营方式,港口、码头、供电、道路、电信等基础设施快速而高效地建成。城市环境的快速改善吸引了外来投资和劳动力的流入,共同推动了城市的发展。

在此期间,深圳率先改革开放,为公共框架、人力资源和企业发展提供了远比其他城市优越的动力和条件。同时,深圳努力吸引农村大量剩余劳动力流入和外商投资技术项目集聚,实现了爆炸式增长和发展初期的目标,发展规模也初步形成。

(二)资本密集型发展阶段(1993—2002年),深圳上升到全球产业链的中下游

1993—2002年,深圳进入了创业新阶段。随着城市基础设施和功能的改善,深圳迅速提升了工业化和城市化水平,从全球产业链的底部上升到中下游。在这一阶段,资本和制度创新是促进发展的主要因素,市场经济建设、劳动力持续流入、配套设施建设和外向型发展方式转变是这一阶段的主要特征。四大发展引擎之间的相互作用如下。

1. 社会主义市场经济的建立,为当地发展和吸引外资提供了驱动力

深圳充分发挥改革开放试点的有利条件。到1997年,深圳建立了中国第一个社会主义市场经济十大体系,包括建立现代企业制度、深化国有资产管理体制改革、商业流通体制改革、完善劳动力市场、建立产权交易市场、金融体制创新等。20世纪90年代和2001年,深圳先后出台了《关于进一步扶持高新技术产业发展的若干规定》和《关于加快发展高新技术产业的决定》,这些文件为促

进科技发展和建设多个高新技术产业园区制定了政策，为高新技术产业发展创造了优质的服务体系。

2. 电子信息产业转移为深圳快速发展转型提供了条件

这一时期，全球电子信息产业结构调整，为深圳将劳动密集型加工补偿贸易升级为资本密集型和技术密集型先进制造业提供了投资、技术和广阔的国际市场。深圳的电子和电信设备制造业因此迅速扩张，推动深圳上升到全球产业链的中下游。由于跨国公司的投资和技术引进，高科技产业、现代物流和金融服务业开始蓬勃发展。2012年，通信设备、计算机及其他电子设备制造业占规模以上工业总产值的56.1%，比1993年增长25.3个百分点。高新技术产业产值达1.29万亿元。其中，具有自主产权的高新技术产业产值占61.0%，比2000年提高10.8个百分点。

3. 不断涌入的劳动力和不断完善的经济结构为深圳的快速发展和转型提供了人力资源条件

就业人数从1992年的17.59万人增加到2002年的771.2万人。只有小学或以下学历的人口比例显著下降，受过高等教育的人数激增。无永久居留权的人口大量迁出城市，这一群体的人口增长率从1994年的28%下降到1995年至2000年的10%左右。同时，深圳取消了国籍、居留权、身份和组织关系等限制，努力吸引高端人才、科研机构和教育机构，在不增加额外费用的情况下使深圳获得了高端生产要素，为其产业转型升级提供了重要的生产要素支撑。

4. 基础设施的改善为深圳的快速发展和转型创造了环境条件

地方政府继续引进外资，依靠土地出让增加财政收入，完善各种配套基础设施和城市主要功能。深圳城市治理能力的增强，满足了其高速发展的需求，吸引了投资和人才涌入。2002年，深圳建立了现代化的通信网络，平均每100人有54部固定电话和120部移动电话。同时，公共设施建设良好，全市建成区面积495.3平方公里，经济特区168.1平方公里。人均绿地面积为149万平方米，生活污水处理率提高到61%，平均环境噪声水平维持在56分贝。深圳于2000年获国际花园城市奖，2001年获中国人居环境奖。

综上所述，深圳率先建立的社会主义市场经济体制，为地方政府、人力资源和企业发展提供了优越的动力和条件。该市软硬件环境的不断改善吸引了大量技术劳动力和技术项目投资的流入。技术密集型投资和全球市场的到来，推动了深圳经济持续高速增长和经济快速转型升级。全球投资是这一时期中国经济发展和转型的主要动力。

（三）飙升的土地成本迫使深圳经济转型（2003—2012年）并向全球产业链的中端迈进

从2003年到2012年，由于经济转型，深圳需要调整政策。一方面，随着改革开放在全国范围内展开，现代化建设进入新时期，深圳不再享受制度和政策的红利。另一方面，深圳在环境开发四个方面的优势已经消失，即土地和空间、能源和水资源、不断增长的人口以及环境容量。深圳已进入经济减速的转型阶段，经济发展依靠创新驱动。土地成本上升和资源稀缺成为这一时期的主要驱动力。在这种新背景下，地方产业进入了全球产业链从中下游向中上游的过渡阶段。四大增长引擎的相互作用如下。

1. 深圳通过"走出去"增强了城市吸引力，获得了新优势

一方面，随着社会主义市场经济体制在全国范围内建立，改革开放的全面展开，深圳不再享有制度创新的红利。另一方面，国内外企业所得税按25%的税率统一征收，深圳经济特区曾享有的优惠政策宣告终结。正因如此，深圳开始探索制度创新。在基本制度层面上，深圳致力于与国际先进城市接轨，深化行政改革，建立服务型政府，并打造鼓励创新的宽容氛围。在产业政策方面，深圳规划战略性新兴产业蓝图，出台了鼓励生物、互联网、新能源、新材料、文化创新、新一代信息技术等相关产业发展的政策，这些新制度和政策为创新要素的集聚和高新技术企业的发展创造了条件。

2. 民营高科技企业的本土发展形成了产业集群，推动了强势产业转型

一方面，由于成本上升和国际市场萎缩，先前面向国际市场的资

本密集型产业失去了优势。另一方面，利用引进的知识和技术，一些地方企业快速壮大，并形成产业集群。这些幸存下来的企业通过模仿和创新成为重要的市场参与者。随着城市从旧的经济增长引擎转向新的增长引擎，经济增速略有放缓，国内生产总值平均年增长率为16.8%。尽管如此，深圳的高科技产业发展迅速，金融服务业一直居全国前三，以供应链、物流和电子商务为代表的现代物流业和文化产业蓬勃发展。

3. 通过改善结构来减缓劳动力的流入，支持经济转型

一方面，就业人数从1993年的422.3万增加到2012年的771.2万，2017年为943.3万。劳动力的涌入速度减缓。另一方面，劳动力素质稳步提高。拥有大学文凭的人口比例从2000年的8.38%增加到2010年的17.8%，平均受教育年限从2000年的9.77年增加到2009年的10.81年。更重要的是，深圳市民由来自世界各地的人们组成，他们勇于进取，富有冒险精神，思想开放，推动了创新文化的形成，掀起了一波又一波创业热潮。

4. 土地资源优势消失迫使深圳培育创新新动能

在经历了此前的高速增长后，深圳可供开发的土地持续减少，土地成本继续飙升。人均淡水量仅为全国平均水平的1/4，深圳成为中国严重缺水的七个城市之一。人口膨胀加剧了城市环境污染、交通拥堵、公共安全恶化等问题。为解决这些问题，深圳市鼓励市场竞争，制定并实施了企业准入制度，迫使高污染、高能耗行业进行转型和搬迁。另外，深圳继续完善城市基础设施和生态环境，以吸引高端产业。

在这一时期，地方政府通过推动企业走创新驱动的快速增长新道路，解决了制度和政策红利消失以及环境容量的瓶颈等问题。另外，深圳肩负起试行新做法和带头发展的使命，积极探索创新体制和政策，以开辟产业转型升级新道路。同时，这个移民城市培育了创新文化，出口型经济带来的知识和技术外溢，以及因地制宜的创新借鉴，推动着深圳逐渐在转型变革的阵痛中迈向创新驱动发展。

（四）创新驱动发展阶段（2013—2018 年），迈向全球产业链上游

2013 年至 2018 年，深圳成功进入创新驱动发展阶段。随着城市基础设施和功能的改善、软硬件环境的建立以及创新生态的强化周期，深圳开始向全球产业链的中上游延伸。在这一时期，人才和创新机构为发展的主要引擎。创新经济体系、创新资本化和创新人才的聚集和结合，以及配套的基础设施和良好的生活环境是这一时期的主要特点。四大引擎之间的相互作用如下。

1. 鼓励技术创新的制度创新为深圳增添了活力和吸引力

在制度层面，自 2013 年以来，深圳在建立高水平的社会主义市场经济体制、构建服务型政府、发展自主创新机构和打造资源节约型和环境友好型社会等四个方面进行了试点举措和实践，开始了更高水平的创新。在政策层面，政府出台了鼓励创业和投资的制度和措施，吸引各类专业人才，并为技术创新建立了系统的政策体系。创新的制度和政策激励了市场主体进行创新，加快全球创新资源在深圳的集聚，使深圳形成了新创新产业集群，进一步吸引了全球资源。

2. 创新投资推动了高科技产业的快速增长，深圳迈向全球产业链的上游

支持技术创新的金融部门持续完善，大批新兴民营科技公司涌现。私人股本行业蓬勃发展。2017 年，深圳注册私募股权公司 4377 家，占全国总数的 1/5，总计管理基金达 12143 只，估值约为 1.7 万亿元人民币。风险投资不断上涨。2012 年至 2017 年，国家级高新技术企业增加 3.9 倍，总计达 11230 家。增加值由 2012 年的 4135.24 亿元攀升至 2017 年的 7359.69 亿元，年均增长 12.2%，在国内生产总值中的份额提高到 32.8%。民营科技公司的投资促进了民营高科技企业的增长，进一步助力企业向高端市场转移并走向全球。2013 年至 2017 年，研发支出年均增长 14.9%，在国内生产总值中的份额从 2013 年的 3.67% 增长到 2017 年的 4.35%，研发支出居世界前列。在此期间，2000 多家深圳公司在全球 120 多个国家和地区投资。华为、中兴、中集、比亚迪等拥有自主产权的企

业，在技术创新、生产外包、业务拓展和营销服务等领域，已在全球建立了业务网络。深圳真正迈向全球价值链的上游。

> ## 案例1-1：吴勇谋：从打工仔到服务机器人行业领跑者
>
> 在过去40年的经济腾飞中，深圳见证了一个又一个关于个人和城市的成功故事。深圳勇艺达机器人有限公司创始人、总裁吴勇谋也与深圳一同成长。从一名打工仔到人工智能领域的企业家，他是商界人士在深圳这块沃土上取得成功的传奇范例。
>
> **从打工仔起家**
>
> 吴勇谋，1977年出生，在深圳发展并取得了成功。
>
> 1993年夏天，高中毕业生吴勇谋从老家福建晋江来到深圳，带着仅有的200元钱，开始了一场改变人生的创业冒险。他第一份工作是当搬运工，一个月后，他去了一家工厂当学徒工，开始学习无线电传输模拟信号技术。他还帮助一位日本师傅做一些琐碎的工作，这位师傅在工厂负责车间管理和技术，阅历丰富。吴勇谋无微不至地照顾着他的起居生活，也因而赢得了师傅的好感。师傅把他知道的所有东西都教给了吴勇谋，从包括手机生产流程、工厂管理流程、手机部件知识和企业文化等。由于受教育程度低，吴勇谋不得不从高等教育的初级内容学起，并向师傅请教技术。他起得很早，一直工作到深夜，连续三年，他几乎没有周末或假期。经过四年的不懈努力，他从一个学徒晋升为高级经理，月工资从200元涨到2000多元。
>
> **初次创业**
>
> 1997年，吴勇谋用打工挣来的2.8万元作为本钱，来到深圳寻找创业机会。凭借积累的专业知识，吴勇谋获得了第一笔订单——制造精密支架组件。从做精密支架组件起步，吴勇谋经营的产品种类越来越丰富，并取得了人生的第一笔财富。1997年10月，他创办了深圳勇艺电子科技有限公司（简称"勇艺电子"）——一

家手机原始设备生产商，20岁的吴勇谋实现了当老板的梦想。第一年，勇艺电子就赚了100万元。2004年，吴勇谋完成了人生的第一个亿元目标。2005年，公司销售额达数亿元，职工人数扩大到几千人。吴勇谋创办了勇艺达工业园，并收购了天彩控股有限公司——一家专业生产运动摄像机和智能硬件的公司。吴勇谋的投资使天彩控股公司迅速发展，天彩控股公司牢牢占据全球运动相机出货量第一的位置。

创业波折

生意场上总是波澜起伏。2008年的金融风暴，给吴勇谋的手机生产企业造成巨大冲击。制造手机功能部件的工厂面临技术升级。订单量萎缩，工厂规模不得不从5000名员工减至1000人，四家工厂不得不关闭。吴勇谋的创业历程面临严峻的挑战。

瞄准创新重新起步

2014年，吴永谋敏锐地察觉到人工智能的广阔前景，创立深圳勇艺达机器人有限公司，并聘请了最优秀的工程师进行服务机器人的研发。2016年底，勇艺达机器人有限公司凭借其卓越的技术实力和快速反应能力脱颖而出，赢得了LG公司价值数百万美元的制造服务机器人订单。从那以后，公司在市场上稳固了地位。随后的几年里，勇艺达机器人有限公司继续在机器人研发方面投入巨资，组建了一支200多名工程师的研发团队，申请了200多项专利，其中75项是发明专利。该团队还创造了一系列优秀的服务机器人产品，使公司成为服务机器人领域的领军者。

从制造手机到运动相机，再到机器人研发，在深圳市推进产业转型升级技术创新的关键时期，吴永谋成功完成了转型。千百万像吴勇谋一样富有进取心的企业家，以敏锐的商机意识和强大的执行力，实现了个人理想和人生价值，他们的努力也推动着这座城市的变化和发展，他们的成功故事彰显了深圳人的进取心、冒险精神、企业家精神和创新精神。

案例 1-2：康佳——从一家原始设备生产商到控股公司和产业平台

康佳是中国改革开放后成立的第一家合资电子制造商。在改革开放的前沿——深圳，康佳见证了这项政策带来的显著成就，也实现了企业的宏伟目标。康佳已经从起初的家电制造商，成长为一家控股公司，通过投资、收购和兼并提供跨行业的产业平台。

第一家中外合资电子企业

1979年3月15日，广东省华侨农场管理局与香港港华电子公司在北京签署了《光明华侨电子厂合作协议书》。随后，归侨侨眷职工在光明华侨畜牧场开始来料加工收录音机机芯。第一年，该厂实现净利润83万元，利用外资打响了第一炮。11月6日，按照中共中央领导的指导方针，同年12月签署了《广东省光明华侨电子工业有限公司合资经营协议书》。中国第一家合资电子企业应运而生。

从给定材料加工到成为原始设备制造商（OEM）

1980年5月，光明华侨电子厂在深圳经济特区沙河工业区投产，主要生产录音机、彩电、音响、计算器、电子仪表等电子产品。创立初期，这家工厂意识到，如果单纯地替别人做贴牌生产，只能赚取低廉的加工费，在市场上永远只能受制于人，于是决定给自己的产品取一个名字——康佳。1980年5月21日，这一天被正式规定为康佳诞生日。那一年，康佳生产录音机机芯30.4万套，创汇112万元，净利润83万元。

从原始设备制造商到独立品牌持有者

随着康佳录音机在市场上声名鹊起，该公司瞄准了一个技术含量更高的新兴产业——彩电制造，并通过先替港方生产彩电机芯的方式来积聚技术和资金，最终于1987年12月31日取得了国家机电部颁发的最后一张内销彩电生产许可证，实现了产业的全面升级。1990年，康佳成立了一个技术开发中心，成为该行业先锋。1992年，康佳A、

B股同时上市,其后康佳回购香港港华的股份,变身为国有企业。1993年,康佳北上,收购黑龙江省牡丹江电视机制造厂,成立"牡康",创造了著名的"牡康模式",开始了全国版图的扩张。1997年,康佳被评为中国优秀品牌,在深圳和广东省尚属首次。20世纪90年代是中国消费主义觉醒的时期,康佳抓住机遇,凭借低廉的价格在中国市场站稳了脚跟。1999年,康佳占据了中国彩电最大的市场份额,成为深圳第一家估值超过100亿元的本土企业。

战略升级和轻资产发展

从2007年开始,彩电行业出现了液晶显示屏。各大电视厂商加大了研发投入,科技公司也纷纷进军彩电制造业,导致彩电行业重新洗牌。当时,康佳未能及时做出反应,其家电制造陷入衰退。同时,由于管理层的频繁变动,公司管理受到波及,直接导致了2015年创纪录的收入损失。公司年度财务报表显示,康佳上市公司股东净亏损高达12.57亿元,收入同比下降2488.32%。企业凝聚力、员工士气、产品规划策略和运营效率均受到严重影响。

康佳重新组建了一个高级管理团队,并调整了产品结构。经过一年多的努力,公司终于扭转了亏损。同时,面对彩电行业的最新发展,在国家经济转型重组和创新驱动发展的推动下,公司开始寻求转型,将自己打造成一家资产轻量化控股公司,成为多个行业的平台。康佳明确了发展目标,将科技与工业、城市化相结合,以消费电子产品为业务基础,逐步向战略性新兴产业升级,并向科技产业园、互联网、供应链管理拓展。科技产业园、产品与业务、平台服务、投融资四大产业集群形成并协调发展。随着对高科技公司的收购和投资,康佳在建立新的增长势头和实现多元化业务扩张方面取得了稳步进展。

案例1-3:蛇口工业区——深圳改革创新的前沿

深圳蛇口工业区是中国第一个实施改革开放政策的工业区。著名的口号"时间就是金钱,效率就是生命"诞生于此。蛇口工业区一直是深圳改革创新的前沿。原占地面积1.24平方公里,现已逐步扩大到10.85平方公里,聚集了从事加工和补偿贸易的企业,诞生了中国招商银行、平安集团、华为等全球500强企业。2014年,该工业区被列入广东自贸区,有望引领新一轮改革开放。

蛇口模式——改革开放的"试管"

蛇口工业区诞生于1979年,起初为一片荒地。这是中国内地第一个出口加工工业区,被称为改革开放的"试管"。实际上,中国的经济改革是从这里开始的。1990年以前,蛇口工业区在人事、财务、资产、治安等方面具有自主权,并有权进行制度创新和改革试点。这是全国首家实行公务员录用制度、奖金制度、工程招投标实践、商品房租赁制度、社会保障制度、股份制等改革措施的区域。蛇口试点后,其实践和制度推广到深圳等全国各地。这些改革被称为蛇口模式,影响深远。

追求高端产业发展,重塑蛇口

1990年,深圳市南山区成立,蛇口工业区抓住了这一历史性机遇,并提议归还应该属于政府的权力,以便其能够专注企业管理。该区开始发挥新角色的作用,基于先前的发展,蛇口区无法继续依靠劳动密集型的产业结构来发展。1995年,蛇口区开始了大规模的工业调整。经过改革后,蛇口区撤出了对100多家从事低附加值劳动密集型产业的公司的投资,并探索向产业链中上游发展的规划。到2002年,经过几轮工业整合,蛇口工业区重新定义了业务结构,形成了以房地产和物流为核心产业,高科技和工业园区服务为主要业务线的新产业格局。

产业结构升级与创新驱动发展

2003年至2013年,蛇口工业区出台了一系列推动产业升级的措施。此前的中低端企业被迁出,为新的规划和改造腾出空间,着力打造全球500强及其他研究机构的研发中心。2009年,蛇口工业区投资600亿元,以构建以互联网信息、技术服务和文化创新为主导的高端产业结构为主要目标,对蛇口工业区进行了改造。2010年,"蛇口网谷"应运而生,逐步聚集互联网企业、物联网、

> 电子商务企业，形成了产业转型平台。
>
> **建设自贸区，探索深化改革之路**
>
> 2014年12月26日，作为国家发展战略的一部分，蛇口被列入自由贸易区。仅13.4平方公里的蛇口，又一次站在了中国改革开放的前沿，该区域面临着通过创新从第二产业升级到第三产业。招商局集团以其独特的优势，将蛇口打造为21世纪海上丝绸之路的桥头堡、枢纽港和起点站，成为深圳湾区必不可少的门户。蛇口正努力打造国际枢纽港、城市转型升级和金融发展三大战略平台。纳入自由贸易试验区后，蛇口将实施全国其他自由贸易区的法治建设和金融创新，这两大举措也是蛇口未来竞争力最强源泉。通过加大体制创新、国际枢纽港建设、城市转型升级、金融发展等方面的力度，蛇口力争成为中国独特的自由贸易区，探索新模式，为国家改革开放做出新贡献。今后，蛇口将不再是单一的工业区，而是一个具有鲜明特色的自由贸易区，一个既适合商业又适合居住的全新商业区。其产业将涵盖航运物流、金融和证券、房地产、酒店业、工业制造业和高科技产业等，业务遍及中国、香港和海外市场。蛇口将再次站在中国改革的前沿。

3. 创新人才不断壮大，创新能力不断释放，成为发展的核心引擎

2012年至2017年，深圳市就业人数由771.2万人增加到943.3万人，增幅有所放缓。但随着深圳市引进和培养的人才的增加，深圳专业人才总数已超过510万人，占常住人口总数的40.7%。与此同时，地方研究机构和教育机构迅速扩大。2017年，深圳市科研机构4296家，是2012年的7.1倍，年均增长47.9%。孵化创新的重点实验室达到1688个，是2012年的2.2倍，年均增长17.3%。2018年，高等学校数量为12所。在良好的创新环境下，众多创新人才释放出巨大的创新活力。2017年，深圳共申请PCT专利2万多件，是2012年的2.5倍，排在美国、日本等国之后列第四位。

4. 深圳建立创新型城市特色基础设施和生态环境，吸引创新要素，支持创新驱动发展

深圳在继续推动高污染、高能耗、低生产率企业转型转移的同时，优先营造创新的硬件环境。一是建设智慧城市，建立高效集约化的信息基础设施支撑体系、信息共享和大数据应用体系。二是建设生态友好型城市。2014 年，深圳市出台《推进生态文明、建设美丽深圳的决定》。根据文件精神，到 2020 年，深圳将建成国家生态文明示范城市和美丽中国典范城市，启动针对大气环境、水环境和绿色城市景观的三大举措。2017 年，万元国内生产总值能耗和水耗继续下降，分别为全国平均水平的 1/3 和 10/1，PM 2.5 浓度降至每立方米 26 微克，将努力把深圳建设成为人均公共绿地面积超过 17 平方米的园林城市。良好的环境有效地吸引和留住了创新人才，并助力了复杂创新活动的开展。

在这一时期，深圳通过成功实施向创新驱动发展的转型，进一步创造和培育创新经济的制度和政策以及生态环境的新优势，吸引了全球投资、人才和技术等高端创新要素的集聚，使创新技术与产业参与实体相结合，实现了更大规模、更高水平的创新驱动型经济发展。

综上所述，深圳由渔村向科技中心跨越式发展的根本动力是：不断深化的对外开放，为大量流入和有效利用外部生产要素创造了条件。持续的制度优势吸引外部资源进行发展和创新，为生产要素的组合和动力的释放创造了条件。硬件环境的改善为城市的发展和创新创造了条件。深圳通过积极参与并充分利用激烈的市场竞争，使自身和市场主体不断演进和升级。

五　经验与启示

深圳既没有资源，也没有生产要素，却在 40 年的时间里，实现了从一个偏远的乡村小镇到全球技术中心、从农业小镇到制造业强市的跨越式发展。从生产要素驱动的数量快速增长的发展阶段，到

经济减速、增长引擎换挡的转型阵痛，再到创新驱动、高质量发展的阶段，深圳展示了一个城市如何融入全球价值链、从底层走向高层的全过程，成为全球同行城市提升竞争力的榜样。深圳的经验对中国和其他追求未来发展的城市，对世界城市特别是发展中国家的城市，具有极高借鉴意义。

（一）以持续的制度创新为导向，培育新的优势，增强吸引力和辐射力，为进一步发展创新创造动力和条件

在全球化时代，各种发展资源是流动的，但不同城市所特有的制度环境是固定的。一个城市通过不断改善制度环境，降低制度交易成本，提高发展效益，可以激励市场主体发展创新，吸引更多的外部生产要素。深圳率先探索以市场为导向的一级经济体制，并继续率先探索完善社会主义市场经济体制，然后与国际城市接轨，最后实现了支持创新驱动型经济的制度创新。在每一个阶段，深圳都领先于内陆城市一步，因此，即使与国际城市相比，深圳在制度方面的表现也始终更胜一筹。创新使深圳能够不断吸引外来投资和生产要素，进行发展和创新，并为发展和创新创造出新的资源和生产要素。

（二）深圳一直深化改革，吸引并充分利用中国内地、香港和世界的生产要素、市场和产业

1979 年，深圳经济特区成立。20 世纪 80 年代，深圳开始向海外投资者开放市场，允许外国企业和海外华人以及香港和澳门同胞投资和创办工厂。优惠政策和较低的商业成本吸引了大量海外产业涌入，为城市发展出口导向型产业和"走出去"奠定了产业基础。20 世纪 90 年代，深圳进一步深化改革，允许国内外市场主体自主决策、公平竞争。中国采取果断行动吸引外资，并迅速完成了工业化。21 世纪初，深圳突出国际化城市建设，在制度和标准上向国际领先城市看齐，这对集聚高端资源和生产要素具有重要意义。2010 年后，深圳鼓励本土企业"走出去"，在全球范围内拓展业务，实现了向产业价值链上游转移的目标。中国有句古话："人无外财不富，马无夜草不肥。"深圳利用国际分工、全球资本、技术和市场优势，开放对外市场，这是深圳成功实现跨越式发展的关键。

（三）集聚生产要素，创造良好环境，选择适宜产业，为深圳的可持续发展和创新创造了条件和路径

一方面，移民在深圳培育了一种创新文化，由于这些有进取心和冒险精神的移民，深圳具有平等、包容的环境和浓厚的创新文化。另一方面，全球产业转移为深圳引进了创新产业。20世纪80年代，产业转移的重点是电子信息产业，作为高科技产业，其产业链横跨全球。从这个角度看，该产业迁至深圳是必然趋势，为深圳的创新发展提供了机遇和初始条件，这也决定了深圳不断创新的方向。

（四）政府在应对外部压力方面发挥了微妙作用，引导市场发挥了决定作用，推动深圳迈向全球产业链的上游

总体而言，经济的初步发展在创造有利条件的同时，也带来了困难和压力。一个城市是保持可持续增长和转型，还是走向停滞或衰退，关键在于政府的意识、能力和行动。深圳在以下几个方面取得了成功：一是地方政府不断开拓创新，利用已有的经验和条件，不断发展新优势，以取代逐步消失的旧优势。政府承担着探索改革新做法的责任，必须推动创新发展。此外，创新文化和深圳所积累的经验，使创新的效益迅速增长，推动了进一步创新。二是政府积极运用市场力量，鼓励优胜劣汰，市场主体面对资源稀缺、成本飞涨带来的压力、困难和问题，必须进行转型、搬迁和升级。

（五）作为发展的前沿，深圳积累的经验和实践，可供全国其他地区参考，实现共同富裕

一方面，通过建立经济特区，中国试点并修改完善了各种发展规划，为全国其他地区效仿其成功模式提供了有利条件，同时避免了在全国范围内展开仓促且不成熟的计划的风险。另一方面,在同一集中资源探索发展、转型和创新,以市场为主导、政府为引导,扩大成功模式的做法,符合发展规律,也是国家发展的重要途径。深圳的发展和成功经验的推广已经证明了这一点。

第二章　城市融资、企业融资和创业融资

一　介绍

深圳位于中国广东省南部，与香港接壤。这座城市在很短的时间内迅速发展起来，全市面积由1979年经济特区成立时的3平方公里扩大到近2000平方公里。1980年深圳建成中国第一个经济特区后，迅速从一个沉睡的边陲小镇崛起成为一个现代化的大城市，在工业化、现代化、城市化的历史上留下了浓墨重彩的一笔。

从1979年到2019年，深圳从一个3万多人口的边境小镇一跃成为一个拥有1000多万人口的大都市。2019年，人口约为1212万，主要通过城乡移民增长。深圳已成为一座繁荣、时尚、创新、和谐、美丽的城市，在世界工业化、城市化和创新史上创造了多个第一。

金融业作为深圳经济的支柱，占全市GDP的15%。深圳作为一个超过25年的经济特区，有丰富的经验可供借鉴。深圳有灵活高效的管理体制，其体制改革始终引领中国其他地区，直接推动了中国经济的增长。[①]

深圳在基础产业结构方面也具有优势。近年来，中国大力推进产业结构调整，高新技术产业已成为中国制造业的支柱产业。近三年来，高新技术产品产值占全市工业总产值的比重年均增长2.5个百分点，2017年达到48%，高于全国其他特大城市。深圳在计算

---

① Shenzhen, "City Information", May, 2018.

机产品、通信设备、光纤通信设备、互联网设备、数字音视频产品、生物制药、高科技医疗器械等新兴产业占有较大的市场份额。物流业发展迅速,已成为全市制造业和整个经济的重要组成部分。[①]

本章涵盖了城市金融发展、工业发展和基础设施等一系列话题。第一节介绍了市政财政的概念,接着介绍了中国地方政府财政的现状和面临的挑战。其次,介绍了深圳在财务规划和管理方面的责任,并简要概述了深圳的收支模式。下一节讨论从不同来源筹措资本支出的问题,即拥有收入资源、政府转移、私营部门、借贷以及资本市场。此外,本章还将回顾市政当局为获得发展资金而采取的创新方法。最后,本章简要总结了中国城市财政存在的问题和经验教训。

二 中国市政财政概述

对市政财政的定义有很多种,但总的来说,"市政财政"是指市政府对财政收支所作的决定,这些决定涉及市政府使用的税收和政府间转移支付的收入来源。它们还包括从运营收入和借款中为基础设施融资的方式,以及对开发商和公私伙伴关系的收费。在大多数情况下,市政当局在筹集自身资源方面总是面临挑战,继而采取银行借款、在基础设施发展方面结成伙伴关系、吸引外国投资等举措。综上所述,一个市政当局要想取得成功,就必须寻找创新的方式为其发展提供资金,而这正是深圳作为开拓者脱颖而出的地方。

在亚洲开发银行的一份文件中,张和李明确阐述了中国地方政府财政的主要问题:到 20 世纪 90 年代,财政体制改革没有向市政

---

① Beijing Review, "Shenzhen Faces New Challenges", August 26, 2003, Beijing Review. com – Special – Shenzhen 30 years on. http://www.bjreview.com/special/2010 – 08/26/content_ 294280. htm Retrieved 12th February 2019.

当局或城市化的融资需求做出任何让步。① 除了沿海富裕省份中少数受青睐的城市外，现行的收入分配制度并没有为城市提供足够的资源，使其能够在维护城市设施的同时，提供教育、医疗、社会福利和养老金等沉重的服务。此外，禁止市政当局借贷，即使是用于资本支出，这使得为基础设施融资变得困难重重。尽管存在这些限制，由于政治领导人愿意另辟蹊径，采取其他举措，保障了城市既能获得所需资源，又能为公民提供福利服务，城市因此能够快速增长和发展。

随着经济的发展，中国的市政财政已经严重依赖预算外的资源和借贷。除了收取使用费和对各种服务征收税外，市政府还利用国有资产创收补充预算。土地是政府的主要资产。随着城市化进程的加快，土地价值不断提升，土地已成为预算外收入的最大来源。2010年，地级（二线）城市土地出让金收入约占财政综合收入的35%，而税收收入仅占30%。除了销售收入外，市政当局还大量从土地和相关活动中征税——财产税、财产交易契税、建筑和房地产公司的流转税，等等。为了给公共投资融资，市政府主要依靠两个来源：土地收入和借款。由于禁止直接借款，他们必须利用融资平台。这些地方政府融资平台公司作为市政部门下属的企业，负责协调和资助供水、污水、道路和公用设施连接等设施的建设。20世纪90年代初地方政府融资平台公司首次在上海试点，现已在所有城市推广，这些平台在帮助地方政府实现世界一流水平的基础设施投资方面发挥了重要作用。通常，地方政府融资平台公司利用各种市政资产，包括预算内和预算外收入作为股权和抵押品，筹集和捆绑银行贷款和其他融资。随着城市化进程的加快，土地日益成为地方政府融资平台公司的主要资产。

张、李还阐明，今天的中国市政金融是在过去30年中经历了数次试验发展起来的，在这30年里，中国经济经历了三个转变：从社会主义计划经济向市场经济、从农业社会向城市工业社会、从世界上

---

① Zhang, Q. and S. Li, "Key Issues of Central and Local Government Finance in the People's Republic of China", ADBI Working Paper 620, Tokyo: Asian Development Bank Institute, 2016.

最贫穷的经济体之一到中等收入国家。这些转变推翻了原有的社会和经济组织，催生了新的社会和经济组织。由于中央政府忙于处理国家经济衰退带来的财政危机，市政当局只能自力更生来应对不断变化的环境。在这场旋涡中，市政府面临着巨大的压力，他们需要一个新的社会安全网来取代国有经济下的社会安全网，并完善基础设施以应对快速的经济增长和不断涌入城市的移民。

他们审时度势、通时合变。采取的第一种策略是限制城市服务的享有资格，以减少对服务的需求增长，20世纪50年代建立的居住登记制度（户口）为限制新移民提供了一种方便、可靠的机制。另一种策略是削减预算、寻找资源，市政府在这方面表现出色。这种将权力下放的做法推动了中国的城市化和发展的同时，也产生了一些消极后果。首先，对土地的高度依赖风险大，且缺乏可持续性。众所周知，土地价格波动大，土地收入不适合作为地方财政的支柱。土地租赁期为40—70年，作为一种耗竭性资源，沿海地区的城市几乎已没有土地可供出售。其次，土地和地方政府融资平台公司的相互作用导致了二者的过度利用。不断扩大的资源渠道削弱了市政府的预算限制，助长了挥霍性、低效的投资活动。再次，对预算外资源的依赖导致了市政预算的分散，加大了宏观经济调控的难度。收入由不同机构和地方政府征收。信息渠道较为分散，且报告不够全面。最后，分权决策和高层的良性忽视，导致社会两极分化加剧，只有拥有城市户口的人口才能享有教育、医疗、社会福利和养老金等重要而昂贵的公共服务，这使得2亿多人口沦为城市的"二等公民"[1]。

三 深圳经济增长

中国社科院发布的《2016年中国城市竞争力报告》显示，深圳在"整体经济竞争力"方面位居内地第一。深圳也被视为中国最重

---

[1] Zhang, M. S., Liu, Z. L., Jin, W. and Van Dijk, M. P., "For CO_2 Emission Trading in China, Can the Market Become a National One, Four Years after Creating Seven Local Markets?", *American Journal of Climate Change*, Vol. 7, 2018, pp. 218–235.

要的高科技研发和制造基地之一,同时也是世界第三大集装箱港口和中国第四大机场的所在地。深圳的人均 GDP 位居广东省第一位(表 2-1)。①

表 2-1　　　　　　　　　深圳主要经济指标

经济指标	2016		2017	
	总计	增长率	总计	增长率
国内生产总值(亿元)	1949.26	9.01	2243.84	8.81
人均国内生产总值(元)	167411	3.71	183127	4.01
增加值产出				
-第一产业(亿元)	0.71	-0.61	1.85	52.81
-第二产业(亿元)	778.05	8.01	926.68	8.81
-第三产业(亿元)	1170.49	9.81	1315.30	8.81
工业增加值产值2(亿元)	719.95	7.01	808.76	9.31
固定资产投资(亿元)	407.82	23.6	514.73	26.2
社会消费品零售总额(亿元)	551.28	9.8	601.62	9.1
通货膨胀(消费物价指数,百分比)	—	2.4	—	1.4
出口(亿元)	1568.04	-4.5	1653.36	5.5
进口(亿元)	1062.66	-4.2	1147.79	7.9
利用外资(亿美元)	6.732	3.6	7.401	9.9

资料来源:深圳信息,2018。

深圳市政府在财务规划和管理方面负有许多责任。国家法律要求市政当局平衡预算,除非预算条例或理事会通过后续决议授权,否则不允许支出。然而,有时情况并非完全如此。市政府负责理事会的全面财政管理,必须制定和维持预算执行标准。市政府还负责批准借款和其他融资,包括完善融资资本。理事会负责建立和利用

---

① Zhiyuan Yuan, Xinqi Zheng, Lulu Zhang and Guoliang Zhao, "Urban Competitiveness Measurement of Chinese Cities Based on a Structural Equation Model", In Sustainability, 22 April 2017 MDPI, 2017.

财务报告制度和标准。理事会负责建立现金资产的投资和管理政策。最后，选择并批准独立会计师进行年度独立审计。深圳多年来审计账单一直表现良好，体现了出色的财务管理。

四　预算过程

预算的编制经历了以下周期。

（一）准备

理事会制定预算日历，讨论来年的目标、需求和前景。然后，设置一些参数供员工发出请求。理事会一般在初期注重关于提供服务的重大规划和方案。值得一提的是，其收入和支出必须均衡——扣除对基金余额的贡献或使用。

（二）收支

在编制预算时，理事会首先从人员（工资、福利——这是最大的一项）、业务（办公用品、公用事业、合同）和资本（计算机、车辆等）等支出着手。市政当局的收入来自税收、营业执照、使用费、罚款和没收以及投资。由于土地一直归国家所有，土地和财产收入明显缺失，这在中国较为常见。

（三）预算核定

年度预算必须通过法定条例。预算案通过前必须举行公开听证会，以便所有预算都包含在内。

（四）财务控制和报告

理事会负责确保每月报告的编写和信息的准确性。此外，理事会还利用每月报告、总分类账和总分类账交易报告监测各部门的支出。独立的年度审计也十分必要。理事会必须每年接受和审查审计，并接受公众监督。然而，这一体制仍然存在一些弱点，如一些重大决定仍然是在预算过程之外做出的。加强问责机制，强化财政综合纪律，是下一阶段改革面临的挑战。

五 概况

在积极方面，深圳的预算责任得到了严格负责的落实。为了微调这一进程，深圳已经进行了频繁的改革。以下是值得注意的几点。

首先，立法者在地方预算/预算改革中的地位有所上升。深圳市财政支出在完善立法机关在预算编制过程中的作用方面已经相当成功。1995年，中华人民共和国常务委员会设立了计划与预算监督委员会，负责审查和监督政府预算。2000年，计划与预算监督委员会被提升为独立委员会，称为计划、预算和监督特别委员会（SCPBS）。

早在1997年，深圳立法机关就把部门预算改革作为提高立法者在预算编制过程中作用的"突破口"。因此，在过去十年中，立法机关一直是推行和改善部门预算改革的动力。[1]

其次，由于深圳市政府年复一年的廉洁审计，其绩效评估一直有效而全面，成为政府绩效审计的榜样。深圳早在2001年就出台了《深圳经济特区审计条例》。2004年，扩大了绩效考核范围，出台了政府投资项目审计条例。近年来，政府绩效评估年度报告陆续向社会公布。[2]

在消极方面，以下为一些意见。深圳以及中国其他地方政府的预算编制过程和预算本身存在一些问题。正如Wong C.所指出的，无论是中央政府还是地方政府都存在着一些薄弱之处，主要存在于以下几个方面。第一，资本预算与经常预算分开编制。第二，预算外支出居高不下，且无记载。几乎所有的基础设施投资都是由预算外供资，缺乏透明度和记录；一些决策者的税收支出，未在预算中

---

[1] Howard A Frank, "Public Financial Management", Taylor and Francis in Public Administration and Policy/119. ISBN 13-978-2849939366, 2006.

[2] Ref, China Performance Budgeting Assessment, WWW/wpqr4. adb. or. Asia Pacific cop.

报告；许多中央政府的专项拨款在年底到达，数额难以预测。这意味着如果市政局成功获得项目分配，则必须持有大量资金储备。①第三，收入预测较为薄弱，并与增长目标挂钩，而不是与经济基本面挂钩，负债报告不够全面甚至缺乏。②

六 收入与支出

深圳市财政来源具有多样性，有的来自中央政府（收入共享），有的来自自身渠道。总体而言，收入共享并不能提供所需的全部资金；深圳自身取得的收入大于从中央财政获取的收入。一份对财务报告的回顾显示，近年来收入年均增长3%—10%。2012年至2016年的收入和支出见表2-2。

表2-2　　2012—2016年深圳市财政收支情况　　（万元）

年份 项目	2012	2013	2014	2015	2016
地方政府收入	17929.886	22312100	27698077	36908610	41028880
地方政府一般预算收入	14820800	17312618	20827326	27268543	31364923
1. 税收	13299766	14989200	17548398	22722315	24888827
增值税	4210150	4232223	4798432	6846839	3639382
企业税	2697311	2884159	3450200	4649574	5695240
个人所得税	1391188	1384659	1684918	2239807	3047503
2. 非税收入	1521034	2323418	3278928	4546228	6476096
特别方案收入	382587	444215	487301	1562019	3823354
行政事业单位收费	398482	546072	910550	438659	279760
罚款收据	209042	177672	267880	303057	249007

---

① World Bank, "China: National Development and Sub-National Development", New York, 2002.
② Christine Wong, "Budget Reform in China", *OECD Journal on Budgeting*, Vol. 7, No. 1, 2007, pp. 1608-7143.

续表

年份 项目	2012	2013	2014	2015	2016
政府基金收入	3109086	4000482	6870751	9640067	9663957
L.G. 预算支出	18792934	20521394	26283153	38644225	46247931
L.G. 一般预算支出	15690071	16908280	21661841	35216708	42110429
教育	2461343	2877280	3294137	2885520	4147269
科技	792651	1329814	945707	2143182	4035240
文化、体育、传媒	328388	329433	580070	527260	547942
社会保障与就业	667785	784985	738828	845801	1054524
医疗保健	1052925	1069185	1576028	1505974	2012739
节能	1080036	1419861	1352999	1083493	1402415
城乡社区	1998352	2217321	2458768	4656457	5584938
农业、林业、水运	446591	614196	566042	441526	612541
交通运输	1000381	1116493	2938739	10445932	4508921
政府基金	3102863	3613114	4621312	3427517	4137502

资料来源：深圳市网站及市报。

笔者使用市政府而非地区的 2017 年数据，追踪了此年度收入与支出的差额。据市政府记录，2017 年全市一般公共预算收入 2086.8 亿元，比 2016 年增长 10.0%，加上杂项转移支付收入 1283.2 亿元，实现总收入 3370 亿元。全市一般公共预算支出 2361.5 亿元，增长 3.7%，加上转移支付 905.5 亿元，支出总额 3267 亿元。最后，3370 亿元的财政收入超过了 3267 亿元的支出，财政运行良好。[①] 这是由于深圳市采取了创新的筹资方式，以及审慎的财务管理。

（一）收入

深圳大部分收入来自各种各样的税收、非税收来源和中央政府

---

① Shenzhen city, *Report on the Draft of the Final Accounts of Shenzhen in 2017*, August 2018.

的拨款。随着城市的活力迸发和城市化进程加快,各种来源的收入逐年增加。税收收入范围包括国内增值税、营业税、土地增值税、城市维护建设税、资源税、城市土地使用税、印花税、个人所得税、企业所得税、关税、农牧业税、占用耕地税等。

1. 税收

根据 2017 年的数据,全市税收收入达到 14.7 亿元,比上年增长 3.9%。其中,增值税(含"现金改革")548.1 亿元,下降 11.5%,主要受综合改革和减税影响;企业所得税 456.7 亿元,增长 17.0%;个人所得税 201.6 亿元,增长 15.5%;土地增值税 146.5 亿元,增长 19.4%。

2. 非税收入

全市非税收入 610.8 亿元,增长 5.8%,其中特别收入 372.1 亿元,行政事业性收费收入 20.6 亿元,罚没收入 24.9 亿元,国有资产(资源)使用收入 124.4 亿元,其他收入 68.5 亿元。

3. 政府间财政和其他转移收入

全市中央财政转移支付收入 12833 亿元,上下两级结算收入 408.4 亿元除外。其他收入主要来自政府性基金和金融性股票基金,共计 424.7 亿元。总体上,全年结余 123 亿元,发展较为良好。这些资金为公共服务均等化提供了财政基础,这也表明地方政府过度依赖转移支付。政府向机构的转移支付提高了基本的公共服务能力,赋予了公民平等享有公共服务的机会。然而,有时财政支出并不透明、不稳定,监管力度薄弱。此外,对政府转移的过度依赖使机构几乎没有自主权。

(二) 市政开支

城市地方花费巨资提供服务,包括卫生、教育、社会服务、基础设施、文化和体育、安全和环境保护。综上所述,与中国其他城市相比,深圳在服务方面表现出色,创造了一个可持续的生活环境。在 2017 年的统计中,300 亿—500 亿元集中在五个重点领域:城乡社区支出最高(497 亿元),比 2016 年预算增长 200.2%,用于城乡社区管理、公共设施、环境卫生、工程建设等领域和行业主管部门的支出;① 其次是住房供应，达 381.1 亿元，增长 34.8%，用于保障性住房、房改等活动支出;交通运输紧随其后，支出达 302.4 亿元，下降 31.0%，用于公路、水路、铁路运输、航空运输、公共汽车补贴和其他活动。

100 亿元至 180 亿元范围内的支出主要在以下几个领域:科技 172 亿元;教育 147.7 亿元;节能环保 105 亿元。这清楚地表明了深圳对技术、教育、科学和环境问题上的重视。一般公共支出 106.9 亿元，增长 21.7%;资源开发 122.2 亿元，下降 72.1%;

对其余各行业的支出均低于 100 亿元。具体表现为:公共安全支出 97.1 亿元，增长 22.9%;社会保障和就业支出 92.6 亿元，增长 143%;医疗和计划生育支出 94.5 亿元，增长 36.5%。

最后，对外援助支出 61.2 亿元，增长 61.3%;其他支出 54.2 亿元，增长 198.3%;商务服务业支出 42.3 亿元，下降 72.7%。农林水支出 31.1 亿元，下降 5.2%;监察等财政支出 11.0 亿元，下降 48.3%。其余市政支出不足 10 亿元。

上述支出反映了这座城市的良好运转，拥有现代化的设施、充足的交通基础设施、医疗和教育设施以及现代化、智能化的增长。然而，尽管情况如此乐观，随着越来越多的人涌向城市，市政当局和大多数市政当局一样，也面临着满足不断增长的服务需求的财政挑战。主要的挑战是对巨额的资本开发资金的需求上涨，但深圳大胆采取创新方式，迎头赶上，取得了令人瞩目的成绩。这是下一节的主题。

七 深圳市资本开发融资

本章回顾了深圳市的收入和支出模式，然后概述和讨论了深圳市工业和基础设施发展所采用的传统和创新融资模式。随着传统融资模式弊端和风险的逐渐显现，中国地方政府越来越重视创新融资模式。财政困难迫使地方政府依赖土地租赁、政府投资公司等融资

---

① Christine Wong,"Budget Reform in China", *OECD Journal on Budgeting*, Vol. 7, No. 1, 2007, pp. 17.

模式，但这些融资渠道稳定性低、风险大、可持续性差。因此，除了采用创新的收入渠道外，中国地方政府正在采取创新措施，提供公共服务，如发行地方政府债券、建立公私合作伙伴关系（PPP）和中央政府转移支付。深圳市为促进发展而采取的创新战略，已让深圳成为中国乃至亚洲许多地方政府羡慕的对象。首先，我们来看一看深圳工业增长的速度，创新在为上述增长中所发挥的作用，以及创新产业从市政府获得的支持。

八　工业增长及其融资

据《城市信息》（2018年5月9日）显示，早在2008年，深圳第三产业GDP占比就已超过50%。2017年，第三产业占比为58.6%。总体而言，深圳有四大支柱产业：高新技术产业、金融业、现代物流业和文化创意产业。以高新技术产业为例，其总增加值由2010年的3059亿元增加到2017年的7359亿元，年均增长13.4%

"自主创新"一直被视为深圳发展的基石。2016年，深圳整体研发支出占其GDP的比重达4.1%，明显高于2.1%的全国平均水平。从PCT国际专利申请总量和万人发明专利拥有量来看，深圳在中国所有大中型城市中排名第一。深圳还被视为几个高科技领域的前沿，包括4G技术、DNA测序、超材料和3D显示。

2016年，深圳有3791家企业被认定为国家高新技术企业，全市高新技术企业总数达到8037家。在这些新认定的企业中，54%的企业从事电子信息系统的开发，18%的企业专注于先进制造和自动化，其余28%的企业分布在其他六个技术领域——生物技术和新医药、新能源和节能、资源与环境、航空航天、新材料与高新技术服务。

深圳的"创客"人口近年来也持续增长，目前已有数千家创新企业活跃在深圳，其中包括柴虎创客空间、童心制物和深圳矽递科技有限公司。此外，中兴通讯、华为技术、腾讯、苹果公司等一批全球知名高科技企业在深圳设立了研发中心或地区总部。

除了制造业,深圳正迅速成为一个金融中心,中国最大的两家银行的总部都设在深圳。深圳证券交易所(简称"深交所")与上海证券交易所一样,为全国性的交易所,深交所共有1700多家上市公司,其中包括创业板上市公司。深交所综合指数由500只上市股票组成,市值超过3000亿美元。于2019年推出的深圳—香港证券交易所将推动跨境交易,并可能为投资者创造更多机会。

政府希望把深圳打造成为一个与香港实力相当的金融中心,通过把深圳的前海划为具有特殊权利和特权的金融中心,进一步加强香港与内陆的密切合作,促进现代服务业的创新和发展。最重要的是,前海通过放宽资本账户限制,对中国货币(人民币)国际化给予特殊自由,这样香港银行将能够向前海的内地企业发放商业人民币贷款。①

九 产业化融资

深圳的融资创新被誉为举世闻名的成功案例。深圳工业快速增长的部分原因是该市采取了创新的城市融资战略,以及为吸引工业落户而出台的激励措施和优惠政策。马克·莫比乌斯指出,深圳是中国金融创新的试验区。深圳自20世纪80年代被确定为经济特区以来,一直大力实施改革开放政策。在发展初期,深圳为吸引国际直接投资出台了许多优惠政策。加工贸易行业(加工材料,组装零部件,然后出口最终产品到海外市场)20世纪90年代在深圳很受欢迎,因为深圳毗邻香港。许多香港实业家将生产过程转移到深圳,寻求更低的生产成本。香港企业为深圳带来了先进的管理理念、新的经营方式等,这些间接影响有利于深圳的经济增长和对其他外国跨国公司的吸引力。香港的企业已经成为创新者,吸引了投资,培育了深圳的商业环境,使外资企业更容易在中国地区开展业

---

① Mark Mobius,"Shenzhen: A City On The Move",*Franklin Templeton Investments*,2016.

务。外商投资的繁荣引发了国内投资，吸引了来自内地其他地区的大量资金流入深圳，涵盖房地产、物流、金融业等领域，而香港仍是深圳最大的国际直接投资来源。截至 2010 年年底，深圳香港企业约 42000 家，香港国际直接投资 600 亿美元，占外资企业总数的 80%，占深圳国际直接投资的 2/3。

除了香港的贡献外，深圳市政府积极推行优惠政策，吸引外国公司设立总部。2007 年，深圳市政府颁布了《关于加快总部经济发展的若干意见》，规定凡在深圳设立总部或迁往深圳的公司，将在融资、用地、人力资源等方面得到政府支持，并享受相关程序简化的待遇。在大量外资和新技术的推动下，深圳培育出华为技术、中兴通讯、比亚迪、腾讯、招商银行、平安保险等全球性企业。改革开放的引领作用，尤其是中央政府批准的深圳前海深港现代服务业合作区，推动深圳成为中国金融创新试验区。

深圳市政府还提供了各种优惠政策，促进金融创新。在保险业方面，2008 年 10 月，深圳市政府出台了《深圳市总部企业认定办法（试行）》和《关于加快发展深圳总部经济的若干意见实施细则（试行）》，为今后 5 年内在深圳开设或迁往深圳的企业提供 50 亿元奖励。这一优惠政策是中国人寿向深圳转移的直接原因。[1][2]

除了优惠政策外，保险公司将总部迁至深圳的原因还包括良好的投资环境和独特的制度创新，这有利于保险业务的发展。深圳市政府支持保险业创新发展，使深圳成为中国保险创新发展的重要试验田。[3]

另一个有利因素是深圳与香港地理位置接近，两地人才流动频繁，深圳金融业得以向香港的先进金融实践学习借鉴。[4][5]

---

[1] Tong S., Shanghai: Aspirations and Reality, and Implications for Hong Kong, 2009.
[2] Zhao, Simon Xiaobin; Lao, Qionghua; Neo Ying Ming Chan, "The Rise of China and the Development of Financial Centres in Hong Kong, Beijing, Shanghai, and Shenzhen", *Journal of Globalization Studies*, Vol. 4, No. 1, May 2013.
[3] Ibid..
[4] Tong S., Shanghai: Aspirations and Reality, and Implications for Hong Kong, 2009.
[5] Xiao, J., "The Movement of Insurance Companies Headquarters: What are the Attractiveness of Shenzhen?", *The Economic Observer*, 2010.

此外，为了吸引海外投资和更多外国公司进驻深圳，深圳已经启动了一系列举措，旨在增强深圳的商业友好性。这些措施包括精简行政要求，在营业执照审批、经营标准、政府采购和融资渠道等方面，将决策权下放。最终目的是让海外投资者安心，确保在进入市场前后，能够享有与国内企业相同的权利。

总的来说，深圳主要针对三个方面做出了改变：第一，采取措施欢迎海外投资进入以前被禁止的领域；第二，根据《中国制造2025》深圳行动计划，寻求外资投入制造业领域；第三，根据CEPA框架，深圳和香港之间的合作也将进一步深化。[①]

十　国际直接投资与深圳转型

国际直接投资（FDI）在中国特别是深圳有着悠久的历史。史蒂夫·奥尔森（Steve Olson）认为，中国政府决定开放国际直接投资，促使了深圳市从一个沉睡的渔村转型。如果说世界上有哪个城市可以说是由国际直接投资建成——不论是在字面意义上或比喻上，深圳当之无愧。深圳的国际直接投资规模和数量之大令人叹为观止。1979年是转折之年。当时中国和西方国家的发展差距拉大，中国领导人意识到必须着手实施改革开放计划，推动中国的经济发展。吸引国际直接投资是当务之急。第一个重大举措是在深圳和其他三个城市设立经济特区。鉴于毗邻高度国际化的香港，在深圳设立经济特区是必然趋势。

经济特区的构想很简单。经济特区将享有前所未有的灵活性，放宽劳动法和价格管制，允许中外合资企业，公开招标基础设施合同，并向外国直接投资者提供税收优惠和其他的优惠待遇。初衷是吸引香港及外国公司，以建立所需的基础设施，发展轻工业和出口能力。香港公司之所以特别重要，是因为它们与内地有着深厚的文化联系，以及它们在国际贸易中积累起的经验、人脉和敏锐的专业知识。

---

① HKTC Research, "Shenzhen Looks to Woo Foreign Investment Through Improved Business Environment", 22 May 2017.

1992年，改革事业得到进一步推动，邓小平著名的"南方谈话"巩固了国际直接投资的中心地位，加快了改革步伐，推动深圳进一步迈上了发展的阶梯。这些年来，重点开始从出口加工转向高科技，而国际直接投资通常以向当地合作伙伴转让技术和在本地进行越来越多的研发为条件。1996年，深圳高新技术产业园区成立，吸引了英特尔、IBM、东芝和三星等多家领先的国际公司。①

随着深圳经济的跨越式增长，深圳的许多有形基础设施和住房都是通过国际直接投资提供的。1980年至1990年，中央和地方财政用于深圳市物质建设的资金投入分别只有1.4%和13.1%。其余大部分是由国际直接投资伙伴提供的，主要来自香港。②

截至2014年年底，深圳共吸引外商投资项目5.8万多个，实际使用金额650亿美元。国际直接投资对深圳经济的影响巨大。2013年，已经进行的和正在进行中的国际直接投资和外商投资企业约占深圳GDP的41%，就业的42%，出口的48%。深圳外商投资企业的贸易业绩占全市GDP的1/5。似乎这些数字本身不够惊人，应注意的是，这些数字不包括服务部门或国际直接投资通常带来的各种溢出效益，比如技术转让、管理经验传授和生产率的提高。

关键产业部门的数据更为惊人，外商投资企业在一些领域占全部或几乎全部收入，如天然气生产和供应（100%）、石油加工（97%）、汽车制造（81%）和通用机械制造（78%）。资料显示，2016年利用外商直接投资6732美元，2017年为7401美元，增长9.9%。

深圳利用国际直接投资的经验不仅引人注目，而且具有很强的指导意义。中国政府基本上把深圳作为一个实验室，在那里进行关于国际直接投资的吸引力、管理和影响的真实实验。这些实验的结果和意义是显而易见的。如果管理得当，国际直接投资对发展中经济体来说必将是革命性的改变。深圳从一个沉睡的渔村到全球大都

---

① HKTC Research, "Shenzhen Looks to Woo Foreign Investment Through Improved Business Environment", 22 May 2017.

② Michael Enright, Edith Scott, David Dodwell, *The Hong Kong Advantage*, Oxford University Press, May 22, 1997.

市的惊人转型，是一个既真实又具有说服力的故事。①

十一　深圳创业融资

深圳是初创企业的理想创新中心。这座城市是金融科技中心，被比作硅谷。深圳的发展在一定程度上主要是市政当局的财政援助以及自筹资金的结果。深圳是大中华地区最具企业家精神的城市，其初创企业具有高增长潜力的创新思想。香港中文大学的一项调查显示，16%的人口工作在初创企业，自2009年以来增长了3倍。调查者表示，根据一项大学的联合调查，在创业方面，深圳已经超过香港和台北。2016年年中，深圳每100名成年人中就有16人从事早期创业活动，而2009年不到5人，增加了2倍多。2016年，中国的平均水平为10%，略高于台北的8%。与2009年相比，深圳成立3—42个月的新企业增长了284%，老牌企业的普及也增长了389%。值得注意的是，尽管深圳的创业率在上升，但中国其他地方的创业率却在下降。

由香港中文大学金融工程中心、香港浸会大学商学院、香港大学商学院、深圳社会科学院和萨凡塔斯政策研究所（Savantas Policy Research Institute）联合进行的《全球创业观察2016—2017深港报告》指出，近年来，香港和深圳的创业支持生态系统经历了爆炸式的增长。②

传统上，初创企业要想取得成功，需要资金、客户、产品、竞争和合适的团队。如今深圳提供了所有这些元素。除了政府为互联网和技术初创企业提供巨额资金和补贴外，还有很多风险投资家为初创企业提供资金。很多企业也自筹资金。杂志《SMB World》亚洲研究指出，金融支持的主要来源是企业家自己的储蓄。在深圳，

---

① Stephen Olson, "FDI data, Guangdong, Shenzhen", https://www.ceicdata.com/en/china/foreign-direct-investment-capital-utilized-prefecture-level-city/cn-fdi-utilized-guangdong-shenzhen 28 January 2019.

② SMB World Asia Editors, *Entrepreneurship in Hong Kong and Shenzhen on the rise: Study*, 17.2.2017.

家族在新企业融资中的作用仍然十分重要,银行也起到了支持的作用。随着创业率的提高,研究团队还发现,城市中非正规部门的文化也在不断发展。深圳的投资普及率高达成人人口的20.5%。事实上,深圳的非正规投资者是本次研究中最慷慨的群体之一,其贡献为76.112美元。这项研究还记录了投资模式的巨大变化。2009年,个人倾向投资于家庭成员,但到2016年,朋友和邻居已成为首选。

创业热潮可能与深圳相对宽松的新业务贷款有关。深圳的银行通常对初创企业青睐有加,因为它们正在寻找传统业务所缺乏的盈利机会。深圳市政府为银行提供补贴,为初创企业提供贷款。深圳的创客空间实际上是为有创意的年轻企业家提供大型孵化器(提供合作空间、指导、营销和资金支持),他们专注于ICT硬件和软件开发(3D打印、机器人、无人机、连接设备、移动应用程序和物联网),其发展和资金由活跃在房地产、金融、建筑或物流领域的控股公司提供支持。这些公司可以培养有创造力的企业家,提供商业培训、种子基金以及后期发展阶段的投资资本。实际上,深圳创客空间的优势在于整合了强大的金融投资能力,为新业务提供资金。这将使深圳对寻求资本资金和负担得起的制造业的全球创意专业人才具有吸引力。深圳拥有全国第二大证券交易所。

十二 企业融资

深圳市一直积极鼓励和资助对工业发展感兴趣的企业家。例如,据报道,2015年,深圳市设立了22亿美元的基金,用于帮助本地上市公司。[①] 深圳市有关部门设立了150亿元人民币的专项基金,用于帮助上市公司应对质押风险和提高流动性。此外,一位市场内部人士告诉一财全球,深圳中小企业融资担保集团和深圳市高新投集团有限公司共同设立了100亿元人民币的基金,鲲鹏股权投资管理有限公司则设立了50亿元人民币的基金。

---

① Yang Jiao, Wang Yufeng and Jiang Yan, Shenzhen authorities set up USD 2.2bil in Funds to assist local listed firms (Yicai Global), 2018.

市政府还开始制订一项计划，帮助20多家在过去两个月里面临股权质押和融资压力的中国上市公司。各地还成立了一个专项工作组，由来自10个部门的领导人牵头，协调解决上市公司控股股东面临的股权质押风险。

十三　创新生态系统融资

本土企业是深圳城市创新生态系统的关键缔造者，深圳拥有丰富的资源，90%以上的研发，包括人员和资金，都是由企业产生的，而大学和研究机构也是强有力的创新者。自2008年深圳成为中国第一个国家级创新型城市以来，深圳为发展高等教育和科研机构配置了更多的资源。目前，深圳有56个国家级创新平台。深圳与清华大学合作，在深圳设立了清华大学研究所、深港产学研基地（北京大学香港科技大学深圳研修院）、深圳虚拟大学园等研究机构，它们已成为知识和技术的持续输送来源。①

　　这是一个地铁站发展规划的案例，左边是标准分区编码，右边是深圳新的分区编码。以前，开发土地用于运输以外的用途是不可能的（灰色）。现在，分区法允许混合使用（按主要土地使用类型着色）。②

通过基础创新计划，深圳正在大力支持国家研发基础设施的建设，包括国家重点实验室、国家工程实验室、国家工程研究中心和中国最佳实践案例研究国家基因库。深圳现在具备了实施宏伟的国家战略研发项目的理想条件。深圳在新开发的研发基础设施的基础上，正在推进信息技术、基因工程和干细胞研究等领域的自主创

---

① World Economic Forum, "China's Innovation Ecosystem", 2016 Creating a city innovation ecosystem through education and technology infrastructure, White Paper.
② 资料来源：Wanli Fang 和 Lulu Xue 的研究以及世界资源研究所罗斯可持续城市中心的图表。

新。创新中介机构是深圳创新生态系统的另一参与者。这些机构包括孵化器、专业服务公司、技术咨询公司、行业协会和招聘机构。创新中介机构提供的信息交流、决策咨询、资源配置、技术服务和技术评估等服务,使创新者和企业家能够更快地降低风险,实现技术的商业化。现在,深圳已成为华南地区举足轻重的创新中心。

十四 创新资源

据蔡健介绍,深圳实施了多项招纳贤才的措施。[①] 截至2015年年底,"孔雀计划"已吸引59支创新研发团队进驻深圳和广东。根据该计划,共有1219人被认定为高水平的外国专业人员。仅在2015年,该计划就吸引了18个专门从事生物、制药、生命科学、软件、电信、微电子和新能源等领域的研发团队。其中,二维材料光电器件是中国新兴的研究领域。深圳还采取措施,通过扶持地方大学和提高奖励和服务来吸引和留住人才。2015年,深圳的研发支出总额占国内生产总值的4.05%。市、区财政安排研发经费209.3亿元,用于支持创新、通用和核心技术。156个战略技术项目启动。根据深圳市政府的规划,到2020年,当地研发支出总额将达到国内生产总值的4.25%。除了鼓励企业加大研发投入外,政府还将提供额外资金。此外,政府还将成立一家专注于高科技、创新和创业活动的投资公司,以推动本地风险资本市场的发展。

十五 基础设施融资创新

本节的重点是"创新"基础设施融资机制。基础设施的资金通常来自特别评估、开发费用、储备金、一般借款、赠款和财产税(与运营支出不同,运营支出仅由赠款、使用费和财产税提供资

---

① Cai Jian, "China City Innovation Ecosystem: Shenzhen's Perspective", White Paper, *World Economic Forum*, 2016.

金）。创新的融资机制包括传统机制的任何变化（如以特定来源的收入而非一般市政收入作为担保的借款，或根据项目所在地而非全市范围而变化的开发费用）或任何相对较新的、还未在中国社区推广的机制（如停车场税或车辆登记税）。融资机制创新通常涉及对地方法规和行政安排的修改，但也可能需要更为深远的改变，如修改省级立法或融资安排。

传统上，中国用于基础设施融资的金融工具包括公共资金（包括年度预算、国债和其他金融资本）、债务融资（通过银行和其他金融机构筹集的资金和债券）、内部积累（未分配利润），其中大部分都不能满足不断增长的资金需求。在本节中，笔者将介绍深圳为应对快速城市化而采用的一些创新方式，这些方式为深圳的许多基础设施项目提供了资金，其中包括土地价值获取、公私合作和债券。由于资金有限，深圳转向其他地方政府融资渠道。地方政府投资工具（LGIVs）一直是首选渠道，但这些渠道中有许多缺乏适当的管理和透明度，中央政府最近已采取行动限制其使用。土地交易融资也很重要，但是，高质量土地供应的限制、土地价格未来的不确定性以及这一公共财政改革议程导致的城市化进程的扭曲引发公众担忧。

（一）深圳交通发展与土地价值获取

薛等人认为，传统上，中国城市的大规模城市交通基础设施的资金有两个来源：土地开发权的出售和银行贷款。[①] 然而，这些不仅给城市政府带来了财政负担，而且导致了代价高昂的城市扩张。最近，深圳成功地尝试了其他方法来克服这些重大挑战。深圳的经验表明，利用土地价值为交通基础设施融资，也可以为中国城市的可持续公共交通引导开发（TOD）提供机会。

深圳是中国第一个采用铁路加物业（R+P）LVC 模式作为基础设施建设融资创新方式的城市。这种模式利用公共部门、运输公司和开发商之间的伙伴关系，协调新的运输站和邻近房地产开发项目

---

① Xue, L. L., Fang, W. L., "Rail Plus Property Development in China: The Pilot Case of Shenzhen", *Working Paper*, Beijing: World Resource Institute, 2015.

的规划和融资。在深圳,政府在地铁项目的初期使用传统的财政(市政预算和银行贷款),然后在地铁扩建阶段项目成本增加了10倍后,转向更具创新性的融资方式。灵活的风险和利润分享安排确保政府和各地铁公司分担成本和收益。①

有证据表明,这是一个双赢的结局:地铁站步行距离内的平均房价在400米时上涨了23%,在600米时上涨了17%。这说明了居民从增加无障碍设施和房地产开发商增加收入中获得的附加值,这些开发商已向R+P系统支付了公共交通基础设施的资金。这清楚地表明了,土地价值是可以创造、分享和再投资的,并促进了城市基础设施投资的良性循环(图2-1)。

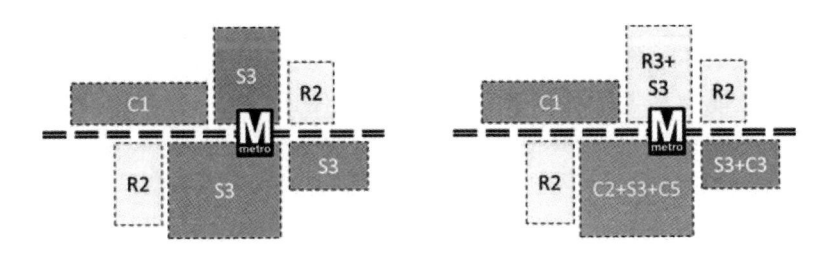

图2-1 综合运输和土地价值获取

(二) 为未来铺路

深圳的成功对中国其他城市影响深远。如果深圳能够在同样的监管和立法环境下成功实施R+P模式,其他中国城市也可以效仿。然而,R+P模式的成效并不会立竿见影。深圳实施可行的解决方案花了十多年时间,香港也花了大约十年的时间才开始获利。如果没有蓬勃发展的房地产市场、成熟的资本市场、有能力和有意愿的私营部门,以及更重要的是——对新方法持开放态度的强烈政治意愿,变革是不可能实现的。考虑到中国以交通为导向的可持续发展的需要,领导人应重视深圳的成功和R+P模式带来的机遇。

---

① Xue, L. L., Fang, W. L., "Rail Plus Property Development in China: The Pilot Case of Shenzhen", *Working Paper*, Beijing: World Resource Institute, 2015.

十六　利用地方政府金融平台

如本章前面所述,根据法律规定,中国地方政府不得从金融市场借款,因此它们一直依赖地方政府金融平台(LGFPs)为其城市基础设施发展提供资金;深圳已经用这些平台为城市的发展提供了大量资金,并取得了一些成功。尽管这些平台很好,但它们易受房地产市场波动的影响。

地方政府融资工具(LGFVs)是指中国地方政府及其部门和机构通过财政拨款或资产注入等方式设立的履行政府投资项目融资职能的经济实体。地方政府融资工具是地方政府旺盛的投资需求、有限的财政能力和狭窄的融资渠道共同作用的结果。它们的起源、发展和运作模式揭示了中国国家资本主义在地方一级不可忽视的一面。[1]

(一)与地方政府融资工具相关的主要问题和风险

明确地说,地方政府融资工具"以地换贷"模式的持续运行取决于两个前提条件,即土地供应不受限制和地价不断上涨。但这两种情况在现实世界中都无法持续满足,即使是在深圳,因为它被传统的土地持有所包围。一旦土地供不应求,或更可能出现地价下跌,地方政府融资平台的举债能力将急剧下降。而考虑到地方政府融资工具的大部分债务是通过"借新还旧"的周期来偿还的,其借新资金的能力急剧下降极有可能导致资金链断裂,从而引发违约。

(二)运用债券加强基础设施建设

如前所述,为满足深圳不断增长的城市人口的需求的巨额基础设施融资,单靠深圳市政府是远远不够的。特别是考虑到广泛

---

[1] Liao Fan, "Quench a Thirst with Poison? Local Government Financing Vehicles' Past, Present and Future", *Columbia Law School*, 2019.

的公共制约因素，深圳一直在寻求私营部门融资来缩小融资缺口。① 2014年5月，中国推出了一项计划，允许10个地方政府（浙江、江苏、江西、宁夏、山东和广东以及青岛、北京、上海和深圳）发行市政债券。在此之前，地方政府在法律上不允许借钱或为债务寻求外部融资。然而，由于地方政府支出融资缺乏直接、合法的选择，借贷并没有被阻止，而只是将借贷转移到了中国的影子银行部门。允许地方政府直接发行债券的转变是为了消除风险更高的影子银行做法，同时更好地进行监管。

为了刺激经济，中央政府允许地方政府在2009年、2010年和2011年发行年限额2000亿元人民币的债券。2011年，上海、浙江、深圳和广东是首批发行地方政府债券的试点地区。试点省市发行的政府债券为三年期、五年期固定利率债券。发行地方债券大幅提升了地方政府对基础设施建设的投资能力。深圳在建设其庞大的现代化基础设施方面，充分利用了债券和公私伙伴关系。2014年，10个试点省市自行偿还地方政府债券。

案例2-1：深圳国际低碳城项目

深圳国际低碳城（ILCC）是中欧可持续城市化伙伴关系（CEUPSU）的一个示范项目，也是了解创新融资形式的一个有趣例子，其具体目的是以环境、社会和经济可持续的方式实现这一目标。在更广泛的意义上，城市投资和融资平台以及公私合作伙伴关系（PPP）是深圳国际低碳城使用的两种金融工具。采用一种广泛的公私伙伴关系，其中利益相关者的参与是关键，通过平衡各利益相关者的利益避免了社会冲突。特别是统筹深圳村域规划，通过"地铁+物业"安排资金，为其他城市在城市更新和社区改造资金筹措、居民如何与开发商分享城市发展利益等方面提供

---

① Yan、Song, "Infrastructure and Urban Development: Evidence from Chinese Cities", Lincoln Institute, Chapter 2, https://www.lincolninst.edu/sites/default/files/pubfiles/infrastructure-urban-development-chinese-cities_0.pdf.

> 了可复制、可操作的范例。这些财政安排的结合有助于深圳国际低碳城实现可持续城市化的三重底线。深圳国际低碳城通过促进低碳转型实现环境可持续，通过居民和村民参与实现社会可持续，通过资金来源多样化实现财务可持续。从深圳国际低碳城获得的融资经验为其他城市提供了实践经验，对调整体制和组织安排，为创新融资活动创造有利条件具有重大意义。

在债券方面，深圳还支持公私合作发展基础设施。这些模式很受欢迎。此前，2015年中央政府出台了19项与公私合作伙伴关系相关的政策，旨在规范公私合作伙伴关系的发展，促进各种投融资活动。PPP融资模式可以弥补传统融资方式的不足，缓解财政和金融压力。但与政府合作关系的不确定性仍然是制约PPP模式发展的一个因素。PPP模式确实为市政当局提供了一个稳定和可持续的收入来源，供市政委员会在城市内进行市政建设和提供公共服务、交通和生态环境保护。

PPP模式将基础设施建设与运营结合起来，以更低的成本和更高的质量提供更多的基础设施。深圳在城市基础设施建设方面，采取多种形式的公私合营，调动了各界人士的积极性，增强了该市投资基础设施建设的能力。研究表明，PPP模式是一种利益共享、风险共担的合作模式，需要地方政府和企业的充分合作。该模式为市政府提供了更多的基础设施建设融资渠道，提高了市政府的公共服务能力，一定程度上提高了市政府在生态环境保护方面的支出能力。

十七　生态城市及其融资

中国经历了快速的城市化进程，但同时也伴随着严重的环境问题。因此，中国已经开始发展各种生态城市、低碳城市和其他类型的可持续城市。这些可持续举措的大规模推广，以及这些项目较高的成本，需要中国政府投入大量资金。确定用于资助生态建设的财务工具包已成为一个关键问题。在此背景下，笔者选取了中新天津生态城（SSTEC）和深圳国际低碳城（ILCC）作为研究对象，对其建设融资方式进行了比较。到目前为止，两者都被视为成功的案例。研究结果表明，这两个案例在两个关键方面存在差异。首先，深圳国际低碳城开发了一个模型，比中新天津生态城少了来自中国中央政府和外国政府的财政和其他支持，因此，对于一些不能够获得国家支持的项目，深圳国际低碳城提供了灵感来源。其次，通过在国际资本市场发行债券，中新天津生态城在中国的各种可持续举措中独树一帜，而规划整个村庄和"地铁+物业"模式是深圳国际低碳城的独特做法。最后，笔者提出了一个通用的融资模型，该模型不仅考虑了经济回报，还考虑了社会和环境影响，以促进未来以更结构性的方式进行融资。

（一）绿色金融

绿色金融是指为支持环境改善、缓解气候变化和提高资源利用效率的经济活动提供的金融服务，包括环保、节能、清洁能源、绿色交通、绿色建筑等领域的项目投融资活动。[1][2][3][4]

中国的绿色金融已经在7个城市进行了试点，深圳也是其中之一，7个城市的效果不尽相同。目前7个试点地区中，湖北市场成交量最大，深圳市场成交量最活跃，重庆、天津市场成交量相对较小，几乎停滞不前。各试点市场的碳排放补贴价格也各不相同：北京、深圳的碳排放补贴价格为40—50元/吨，其他5个试点市场的

---

[1] Jiping Zhou, et al., *Research on the Development of Green Finance in Shenzhen to Boost the Carbon Trading Market*, IOP Conf. Ser.：Earth Environ. Sci. 81 012073.

[2] Zhan, C., de Jong, M.,"Financing Sino－Singapore Tianjin Eco－City：What Lessons Can Be Drawn for Other Large－scale Sustainable City－projects?", in Sustainability 2017.

[3] Zhan, C., de Jong, M.,"Financing Low Carbon City：The Case of Shenzhen International Low Carbon City", J. Clean. Prod, 2018, pp. 180, 116－125.

[4] Changjie Zhan, Hans de Bruijin and W. Martin de Jong,"Funding Sustainable Cities：A Comparative Study of Sino－Singapore Tianjin Eco－City and Shenzhen International Low－Carbon City", *Article in Sustainability*, Vol. 10, No. 11, 2018.

碳排放补贴价格在 10 元/吨左右。①

（二）深圳市碳市场发展现状

深圳作为全国 7 个碳交易试点市场中同时具备碳交易和金融中心功能的 3 个城市之一，作为中国经济体制改革的前沿，碳排放市场建设居全国前列，交易实践和管理经验丰富。深圳碳排放限额约 3000 万吨，交易量近 900 万吨，流动性比率为 30%，远高于同期北京、上海碳交易市场。②

深圳市场交易活跃度高，主要得益于三个方面：一是深圳作为第一个碳交易试点地区市场运行时间长，企业意识强；二是深圳碳交易补贴总量最小，在 7 个试点市场中为 3000 万吨，但覆盖面最大——有 845 家企业主体；三是深圳市场从一开始就对机构和个人投资者开放，没有准入限制。③

然而，尽管取得了一定的成绩和经验，深圳碳交易市场仍存在一些问题。特别是目前深圳碳市场只交易单一产品，其碳价格低于世界主流碳市场水平，远低于国家发改委测算的有效控制排放价格，深圳市政府在促进企业减排方面的角色有待改进。

深圳要运用绿色金融手段支持节能减排绿色项目，通过扩大碳排放市场广度、增加碳衍生产品多样性、增加碳交易市场厚度等途径，加强碳交易市场的市场活跃度，努力成为区域碳排放中心和国际绿色金融中心。发展绿色金融带动深圳碳市场的政策建议包括：制订绿色金融发展规划和推进方案；建立碳评估程序；降低金融机

---

① Zhang, M. S., Liu, Z. L., Jin, W. and Van Dijk, M. P., "For CO_2 Emission Trading in China, Can the Market Become a National One, Four Years after Creating Seven Local Markets?", *American Journal of Climate Change*, Vol. 7, 2018, pp. 218 – 235.

② Beijing Sinocarbon, "Annual Report of China Carbon Market in 2014", Sinocarbon, Innovation and Investment Co., Ltd., Beijing, 2014.

③ Jotzo, F., "Emissions Trading in China: Principles, Design Options and Lessons from International Practice", *Centre for Climate Economics and Policy* (CCEP), Crawford School of Public Policy, Australian National University, Working Paper, No. 1303, 2013.

构参与碳交易市场的门槛,有序探索碳衍生品。①

(三) 土地出让和土地租赁

最后,地方政府也大胆通过土地出让来筹集资金。市政当局试图以尽可能低的价格获得尽可能多的土地,然后要么以市场价格出售土地,将其用作基础设施贷款的抵押品,要么以低于市场价格向战略投资者(主要是外国投资者)提供工业发展用地。②

尽管市政当局有能力提供新的城市土地供应,但土地租赁是一种过渡基础设施融资战略。可供出租的土地最终将耗尽。作为土地租赁的先驱,深圳15年来一直在积极拓展城市边界。深圳城市用地租赁的销售价格大大超过了其从农民手中购买的价格,通常高达100倍。到目前为止,进一步扩张或新的土地租赁的潜力几乎已经耗尽。事实上,深圳的资产管理公司已经转向在中国内地其他城市地区买卖土地使用权,以此继续利用其创业技能从土地交易中获取收入。相比之下,作为基础设施融资工具的土地租赁在中国其他地区正加速发展。③

十八 结论和经验教训

在这一章中,我们见证了一个沉睡的小村庄是如何通过行政法规和实践的改革,再通过对已有资源的精心管理,迅速发展成为一个现代化可持续发展的城市。

在经济发展方面,过去几年,深圳的经济增长一直超过中国一

---

① Changjie Zhan, Hans de Bruijn and W. Martin de Jong, "Funding Sustainable Cities: A Comparative Study of Sino – Singapore Tianjin Eco – City and Shenzhen International Low – Carbon City", *Article in Sustainability*, Vol. 10, No. 11, 2018.

② Fu, Somerville, Gu and Huang, "Land Use Rights, Government land Supply, and the Pattern of Redevelopment in Shanghai", *International Real Estate Review*, Vol. 2, No. 1, 1991, pp. 49 – 78.

③ George E. Peterson, "Land leasing and Land Sale as an Infrastructure – Financing Option", World Bank Policy Research Working Paper 4043, November 2000, USA.

线城市，在创新和经济转型方面树立了良好的声誉。20世纪80年代，深圳从一个小村庄到经济特区经过了漫长的摸索，现在已成为生物技术、互联网、新能源、新材料、信息技术和文化创意产业等创新驱动产业的中心，2019年这些产业合计增长20%，占深圳GDP的40%。

此外，深圳已成为中国创新的热点。深圳已成为中国关注的中心，因为当局将其视为经济转型和财富积累的榜样，而深圳顶住了内地其他大部分地区经济增长放缓的经济逆风。

除了作为国家的创新中心之外，如果深圳与香港联手，很可能在未来十年取代上海成为中国的全球金融中心。虽然上海市场以大型国有企业为主，但深圳更能代表规模较小、较年轻的民营企业，多家房地产开发商的总部也设在深圳。这座城市是民营经济增长的温床，催生了100多万家民营企业，其中包括一些中国最大、最热门的企业，如互联网巨头腾讯控股、电信等。

之所以取得上述成功，是因为深圳市政府多年来在发展筹资方式上不断创新。深圳还着力进行了几项改革，以促进该市的发展，并为吸引当地和国际投资者出台了许多激励措施。如今，深圳可以选择自己想要的国际直接投资。该市在鼓励和资助对工业发展感兴趣的企业家方面也给予了大力支持。

随着城市化的快速发展，对基础设施和其他服务的需求也随之增加。迄今为止，深圳已超越传统的资金来源，大胆采取创新战略，如发行市政债券、外商直接投资、项目融资、利用地方政府平台、公私合作伙伴关系、特殊机构和税收激励融资等。深圳是中国第一个通过地铁+房地产模式获取土地价值作为基础设施建设资金的城市。深圳在这方面的成功对中国和发展中国家的其他城市都有深远的影响。所有这些举措都应成为中国乃至世界的榜样，特别是对非洲、亚洲和拉丁美洲新兴低收入国家。

第三章　现代经济增长、经济特区与工业化

一　简介

深圳是一座由无数传奇故事编织而成的年轻城市，是中国改革开放的领头羊。40年前，深圳大胆突破传统计划经济体制的束缚，形成了较为完善的社会主义市场经济体制和机制，建立了较为完善的城市治理体系和法治框架。深圳实施大胆创新，不断转型升级，形成了经济高发展水平的创新驱动格局，走上了快速增长和生态文明的新道路。在1980年之前，深圳的GDP占香港的0.2%；而在2017年，深圳GDP为2.24万亿元人民币，与香港持平。人均国内生产总值2.7万美元，第二产业、第三产业比值为6∶4，高新技术产业和金融业分别占33%和13.6%。深圳在这么短的时间内实现了从农业经济向知识经济和信息经济的转变，这在世界史上是绝无仅有的。深圳已成长为中国五大最重要的经济、贸易、金融和创新发展中心的代表城市之一。

二　文献综述

深圳的经济发展引起了众多学者的兴趣，他们对深圳的发展模式进行了无数次的探讨。于军认为，深圳在经济转型和产业升级上形成了5个特点：(1) 制造业向服务业转型；(2) 服务业与制造业

融合发展；（3）制造业以创新和品牌化为主，而不是低成本；（4）传统服务业向现代服务业升级；（5）依靠出口导向型经济的国内和国际市场。①樊纲还提出了五个优先事项：让更多的农村居民融入城市生活，完善城市管理体制，促进经济模式由外向型向开放型转变，进一步深化体制改革，促进深圳香港经济一体化、社会和谐、稳定高效。②易永胜认为，面对市场是自主创新的基础，企业是自主创新的关键；产业转型升级是自主创新的动力；率先形成创新体系是自主创新的环境；活力政策指导是深圳自主创新的保证。③孙长学认为，深圳经济特区应着力加强现代产业体系建设，完善收入分配制度和激励机制，推进新一轮全面开放和区域协调发展政策，建设智慧幸福城市和一流软环境，不断引领下一步改革探索。④本章主要探讨了五个具有代表性的故事。

三 深圳提高了增长质量，加快了产业升级，但增速放缓

1980年至2016年，深圳GDP年均增长率约为20%，但从图3-1可以直观地看出，深圳的长期增长率持续下降。深圳与全国年均增长率的差距正在缩小。1980年至1985年的平均差距达到40个百分点。1990年至1995年为20个百分点。自2010年以来，一直是2个百分点。

在过去的40年中，深圳的经济增长有10年左右的中长期，这一阶段不是规律性的，但有迹可循，大约三年为一个金融周期。深

---

① Yu Jun, "Shenzhen: Transformation and Upgrading", *China Opening Journal*, No. 2, 2013, pp. 24-27.

② Fan Gang, "Another 30 Years of Prosperity for Shenzhen in Strategic Choice", *China Opening Journal*, No. 1, 2011, pp. 7-11.

③ Yi Yongsheng, "Shenzhen's Independent Innovation and Leading Experience", *Special Zone Economy*, No. 10, 2012, pp. 29-31.

④ Sun Changxue, "The Structural Reform Exploration of Shenzhen Special Economic Zone and its Demonstration Value", *Reform*, No. 5, 2018, pp. 18-26.

$y=16.12\ln(x)+66.881$
$R^2=0.7386$

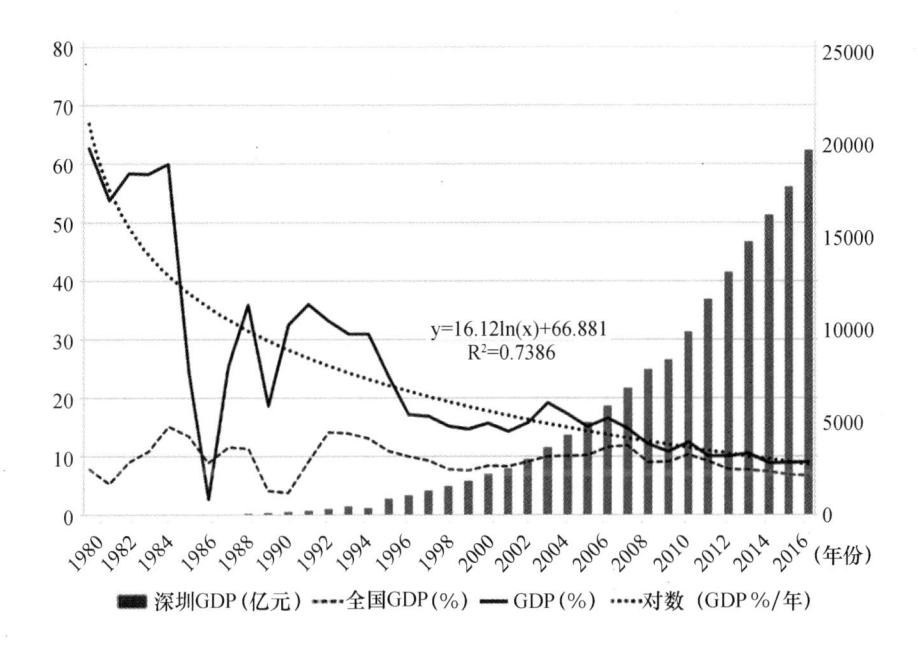

深圳GDP（亿元）　　全国GDP（%）　　GDP（%）　　对数（GDP%/年）

图 3-1　1980—2016 年深圳 GDP 年均增长率

资料来源：深圳统计局《深圳统计年鉴》。

圳的经济开放度极高，经济调整期也不同于全国，一般提前一两年。深圳经济经历的几次重要转型，基本上都发生在中长期周期的后期，这些转型开创了结构调整和产业升级的新高潮，促使深圳走上了由低到高、逐步加快的产业升级之路。①

深圳经济的第一次重大转型大致发生在 1985 年。经过计划经济时代的快速增长和经济特区成立前几年市场经济价差的拉大，深圳开始了快速工业化和城市化的进程。"国内投资为主，生产以加工组装为主，产品以出口为主。" 深圳加入全球分工体系已成为最简明的政策诉求。低成本的土地和劳动力和香港形成了以前的商店和工厂中心的周边关系。以 OEM 为代表的深圳加工贸易企业已成为支撑深圳回归高速增长的核心力量。这是深圳彻底突破传统计划经济

---

① Tang Jie, "New Norms Route of Growth and Support: Case of Shenzhen", *China Opening Journal*, No. 6, 2014, pp. 11–18.

体制，推进市场化改革的时代。深圳尝试建立系统的市场经济体制，创建深圳证券市场，主导利率信贷改革，改革土地拍卖制度，对港口、机场、公路等城市基础设施建设采取多种投资方式。①

深圳第二阶段改造始于 1995 年，历时约 10 年。在当年特区优惠政策的同时，普拉特·惠特尼集团公司也对沿海政策持开放态度。1995 年，包括深圳在内的中国经济特区实质上是没有特殊政策支持的经济特区。除了重大制度改变外，深圳还建成了深圳—汕头高速铁路。深圳机场大规模运营的完成，也成为企业重新进行合理新选址的驱动因素。深圳企业纷纷离开深圳，寻求更好的发展机遇，如加工贸易企业大规模进入东莞，引发深圳经济新一轮衰退。深圳经济已从加工贸易转向模仿创新。无论是汉语语境中的"山寨"现象，还是英语语境中的"抄袭"，都描绘出没有核心研发竞争力的核心产业化过程和对大规模生产能力的模仿。毫无疑问，山寨现象是发展中国家学习的重要途径。如果不是山寨式生产，如今深圳可能仍处于分散加工贸易阶段。深圳企业已完成从山寨生产进入专业化、差异化产品生产阶段的转变。深圳的许多著名品牌诞生于黄金时代。②

深圳的第三次转型几乎与第二次转型交替进行。2003 年前后，深圳经济陷入新一轮衰退。主要原因是深圳利用全球红利的优势进行人口红利，并在沿海地区迅速推广。山寨现象从深圳转移到全国。深圳迫切需要引进新的生产方式，实现新的更高水平的创新增长。这是新一轮升级，需要坚实基础和全面整合。这是一个从专业化加工装配向专业化制造、协同创新的升级过程。如今，深圳并不以其庞大的大型企业而闻名——这是北京和上海的特点，深圳的特点是小企业众多。大中型企业之间存在着复杂的网络型供应链关系。以华为为代表的深圳大型企业不断提升全球创新地位。中小企业进入一流大企业的供应链，分享着大企业的创新成果，但获得和保持供应商的资格是一个充满竞争的生存之路；多家企业竞争，只

---

① Li Hao, Shenzhen work anthology, Central Party Literature Press, 1999.
② Tang Jie, Dai Qun, Li Zhanjie, et al., "Theoretical Research on Shenzhen's Economic Growth", *China Special Economic Zone Research*, No. 0, 2010, pp. 13 – 43.

有一家能够脱颖而出。各参与公司必须提出最佳解决方案，击败对手，获得供应商资格。因此，这不是一个单向创新共享或传统大企业依靠垄断地位淘汰中小企业的过程，而是一个协同创新的过程，是分工与创新、创新深化分工、分工推动创新的持续创新的过程。

2010年前后，深圳开始了新的创新驱动转型。公共研发平台、公共信息平台、公共创新服务平台等有效公共产品供给快速增长，再加上企业创新能力的日益强大，深圳开始走向全球创新的前沿，从世界著名的模仿者到著名的创新温室，① 深圳形成了以市场需求为基础，产学研相结合的自主创新模式。利用互联网平台、云计算、大数据模型等新技术，依托科技型龙头企业，形成了45个产学研联盟以培育这一模式。现有基础研究、应用研究和产业化相结合的新型研发机构共70家。新一轮创新转型的最大特点是深圳已经开始了发明+创新的进程，知识与思想创造、基础科学与产业创新的结合越来越紧密。

新技术、新产业和新思想已经取代物质资本投资成为经济增长的主要来源。深圳经济发展的头20年，全社会固定资产投资率平均在50%以上，然后逐渐下降。2010年以来的平均投资率已降至23%。下一代无线通信技术、基因测序分析与设备制造、新材料、新能源汽车、显示技术等领域已成为全球领先的创新能力。根据国际专利申请的五年累计数量，深圳香港已成为日本东京横滨之后的世界级区域创新集群。②

在创新中转型，提高经济素质，不断增强协同创新能力。图3-2显示了联合国知识产权组织网站公布的《2017年世界创新报告》中主要国家的国际专利申请情况。深圳的数据来自深圳市知识产权局的年度报告。2007年，中国内地向国际知识产权组织（WIPO）申请的PCT国际专利数量位居第七，在2017年位居世界

---

① "Jewel in the crown: What China can learn from the Pearl River Delta?", The Economist, 2017-04-08.

② The Global Innovation Index 2017: Innovation Feeding the World, is the result of a collaboration between Cornell University, INSEAD and the World Intellectual Property Organization (WIPO) as co-publishers, and their Knowledge Partners.

第二，三年内可能超过美国世界知识产权组织预计成为世界第一（图3-3）。届时，中国在专利保护期内的国际专利存量很可能在2030—2035年超过美国成为世界第一。2004—2017年，深圳的专利申请量从开始331件，增加到2万多件，超过德国和韩国，略低于法国伊纳里的总量。在2016年国际专利申请排名中，有4家公司申请了4项以上的专利，中国有4家公司，共计10651项，排名第一（图3-4）。其中，前三名企业分别超过美国前五名和日本前七名（国家知识产权统计局）。特别值得一提的是，深圳以分工为核心的创新体系，显示出巨大的协同创新能力。以华为为代表的十家大型创新型企业，专业化、大型化的专利申请量约占国际专利申请量的50%。与企业共生的中小型创新型企业的国际专利申请又占50%。

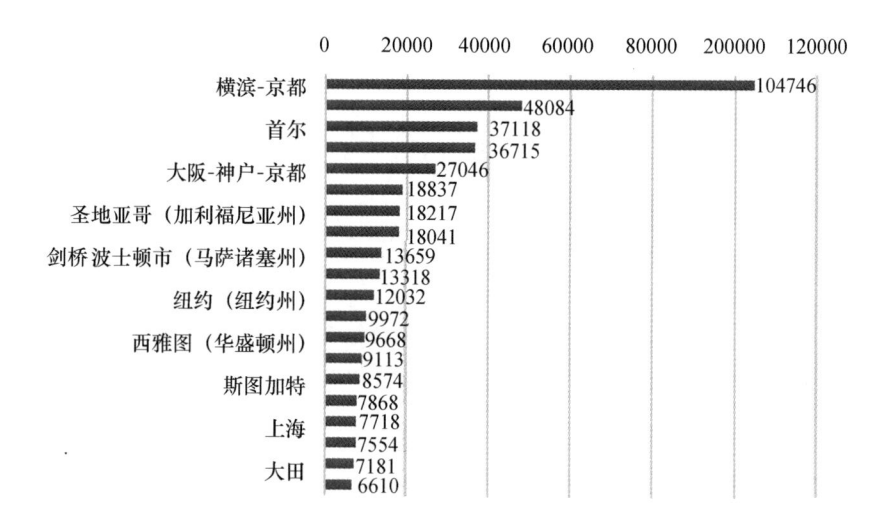

城市	专利数
横滨-京都	104746
	48084
首尔	37118
	36715
大阪-神户-京都	27046
	18837
圣地亚哥（加利福尼亚州）	18217
	18041
剑桥波士顿市（马萨诸塞州）	13659
	13318
纽约（纽约州）	12032
	9972
西雅图（华盛顿州）	9668
	9113
斯图加特	8574
	7868
上海	7718
	7554
大田	7181
	6610

图3-2　2012—2017年世界前20大城市专利中心

资料来源：康奈尔大学、欧洲工商管理学院、世界知识产权组织（2018）：2018年全球创新指数。

深圳的自主创新不仅体现在高新技术产业的高速增长上，更体现在传统产业的重大转型上。例如，深圳服装业的发展始于钉扣和缝制袖子。经过30年的发展，这里已经成为一个时尚基地，占据了中国女装生产的半壁江山。服装计算机集成制造系统（CIMS）、

第三章 现代经济增长、经济特区与工业化　73

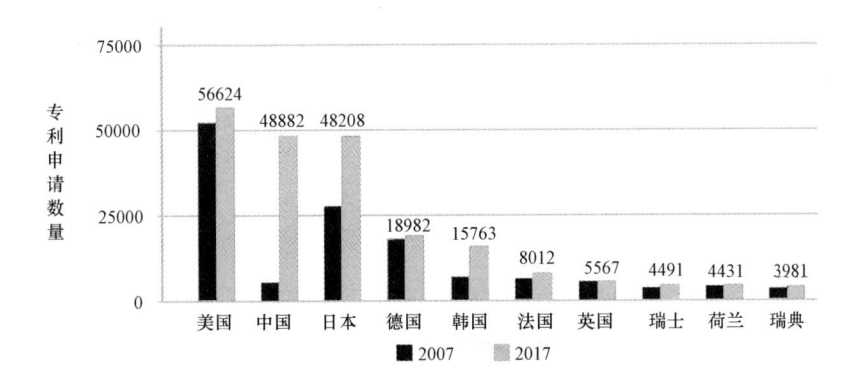

图 3-3　2007 年和 2017 年主要国家国际专利申请情况

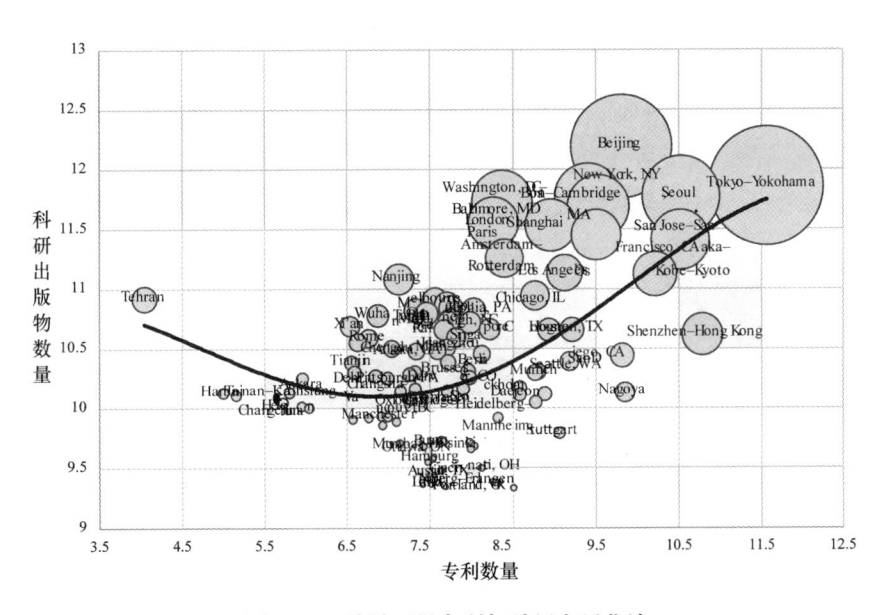

图 3-4　世界百强专利与科研出版业绩

资料来源：康奈尔大学、欧洲工商管理学院和世界知识产权组织（2018）：2018 年全球创新指数。

PAC 可编程控制、数码喷墨打印技术、计算机测色配色等最新技术的应用，以及一大批服装设计团队的加入，极大地促进了服装企业的品牌开发和产品设计,以及生产水平和能力,完成了从 OEM 到 ODM 的重大转变,最终以自己的品牌和技术与时尚产业紧密分工。深圳也是全国第一个被联合国教科文组织授予"设计之都"称号的城市,拥有近 5000 家工业设计机构。深圳数百个设计项目获得了"红点奖"和"IF 设计奖"等世界顶级设计奖(图 3 – 5)。

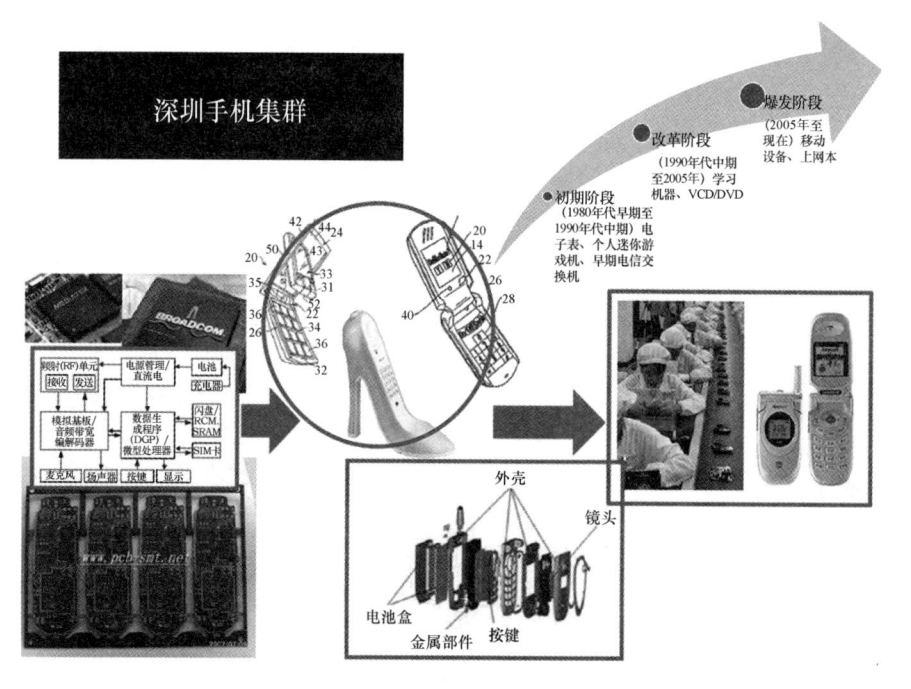

图 3 – 5 深圳手机集群从组装到制造创新不断升级

四 深圳经济开放度高,市场经济发展良好

健全的市场机制是激发创新、增强经济活力的最重要的制度保障。市场机制有三个核心功能。第一,市场经济能够提供合理的激励机制。市场经济和计划经济完全不同,计划经济没有激励机制。在市场经济条件下,企业的最大受益是激励机制。第二,市场是一种信号发现机制。当大家都说计划经济是一种不可实现的经济机制

时，事实上，任何个人或组织都无法收集到资源配置的全部信息。当不可能以很高的成本收集完整的信息或某些信息时，综合经济计划本身就是一个悖论。市场经济的最大特点是，每个人都可能发现可能是有用的信息，虽然有些观点可能不完善，从不同角度看也可能不准确。这些信息激励企业创新，激励公司和个人发掘新信息。第三，市场机制是一种可衡量的机制。资源配置是否有效？获得的信息是否准确？这些必然会反映在产品的市场价值上。

改革开放前，深圳率先建立了中国市场经济框架体系，对深圳的创新发展起到了关键支撑作用。例如，深圳率先改革中国土地使用制度，实行国有土地所有权与特定经营主体使用权分离，实行经营性土地使用权出让招标拍卖制度；全面推行住房制度改革，实现住房商品化。在金融方面，深圳引进了一批外资银行，建立了招商银行、深圳发展银行等区域性股份制银行，并建立证券交易市场；建立面向国际市场、按照国际惯例和市场机制运行的对外贸易体制，形成一套适应市场经济发展的对外贸易体制和组织形式；较早建立"人才市场"，面向国家，实现人才的自由任用和自由流动。通过一系列市场化改革，深圳逐步建立和完善了资本市场、技术市场、人才市场、产权交易市场、信息市场等体系，拥有了国内外商品、劳动力、资本。企业和技术等生产要素提供了自由流动、相互融合的场所和舞台，为市场机制在创新活动中发挥基础性作用提供了关键保障。当然，需要使市场机制合法化，因为在脆弱的法律环境中难以积累生产要素，且经济和创新活动的效率将降低。

目前，深圳上市公司数量占全国的7.9%，利润占全国的11%；深圳上市公司控股股东：国有控股19.5%；民营控股76.1%；外商投资2.9%；其他1.5%。从表3—1可以得出深圳市劳动就业分布、创业者数量和企业人均从业人员数量，这是深圳市场化程度较高的鲜明证据。经济发展程度越高，企业竞争越激烈。1980年，深圳市劳动者总数约15万人，其中企业从业人员约5万人，国有企业从业人员占82.7%，非从业人员占2/3，平均从业人员180人。2000年，总劳动力达475万人，从业人员93.4万人，国有企业从业人员占33.2%。企业家从830人增加到近11万人，从业人员平均44人。2016年，深圳劳动力总量926.4万人，从业人员442.6万人，企业从业人员比例下降到9.4%。乡镇就业不再统计，个体工商户约占就业总量的一半。不难看出，2000—2016年深圳劳动力就业的显著变化是，从业人员增加了450万人。深圳企业已经走过了规模化、标准化的过程。具有3∶1补给的传统城镇是主要特征。农村就业逐步收窄，国有企业从业人员比重下降到9.4%；就业总量比重下降到5%以下。1980年深圳创业者830人，1990年接近2万人，2000年约11万人，目前已超过150万人。公司的平均员工人数已降至6人，与纽约大致持平。这些数据都表明了深圳是典型的创业之都。

表3–1 深圳市劳动力就业与分配情况、企业人数和企业平均员工数量

年份	劳动力总数（万人）	企业员工（万人）	国有企业员工（万人）	企业份额（%）	国有企业份额（%）	企业数量（人）	劳动力平均人工数（人）
1980	14.9	4.05	32.9	82.7		830	180
1985	32.6	22.7	16.8	69.6	74.0	6853	48
1990	109.2	55.4	50.5	50.7	91.2	19827	55
1995	298.5	88.8	40.2	29.7	45.3	70785	42
2000	475.0	93.4	31.0	19.7	33.2	107457	44
2005	576.3	165.4	35.9	28.7	21.7	209443	28
2010	758.1	251.1	46.6	33.1	18.6	360912	21
2016	926.4	442.6	41.8	47.8	9.4	150455	6

资料来源：《深圳统计年鉴2017》。

一项典型的市场调查发现，80%的创新来自客户和合作伙伴，这说明了市场分工在创新中的基础性作用。这是因为高度发达的市场意味着市场有足够的专业分工与合作和发达的产业链。2018年，深圳高新技术企业超过1万家，在所有城市中仅次于北京。境内外上市公司374家，居全国城市首位。深圳在创新产业方面取得了突

出成绩，聚集了一大批不同行业、不同学科、不同规模的企业集团开展协同创新。作为广东—香港—澳门大海湾地区的核心城市，深圳可以整合大量的社会产品和研发资源、创新资源和共同创新技术。通过合作，供应商甚至竞争对手在不同行业间迅速扩散，形成了一股浪潮。一轮产业创新升级的浪潮与其说是大企业的创新，不如说是企业集团的无数协同活动。创新已成为深圳企业在市场竞争条件下的自觉行为。市场经济的发展水平决定了创新发展的潜力，创新提升了深圳企业的竞争力和生存能力。

深圳市政府还积极探索小政府、大社会的管理体制，开展了8项体制改革和4轮行政审批制度改革。审批事项由1091项减少到391项，政府服务综合效率不断提高。同时，深圳市政府财政资金已从竞争性、营利性行业撤出，集中用于基础设施建设和公用事业项目，为高新技术产业发展提供了良好的外部环境。20世纪90年代中期以来，深圳市政府将自主创新的主动权和话语权交给了企业主体，加快了高新技术产业发展对社会中介组织的服务功能，政府成为自主创新环境的营造者。这也成为深圳成功创新的关键。

五 创新求生存，依托产业链协同，聚集创新创业能量

发达的市场经济体制和分工是产业不断升级的基础。根据史密斯的理论，分工被认为是经济增长的源泉。这种分工的作用，不仅是指内部技术分工对提高劳动生产率的作用，还包括工业分工、不同工业部门的分工、国际分工和迂回生产过程的增加从而带动经济规模的扩大。深圳经验的理论逻辑是，通过对外开放和参与国际分工，深圳获得了知识溢出和外商投资及技术许可方式的推广。通过"引进—学习—改进—创新"模式，深圳本土企业逐步发展了工艺技术、工业制造技术和专业技术的专业劳动力队伍；这些专业化劳动力在随后的赶超必学阶段模仿创新，并实现了原创创新，形成一支新的专业化劳动力队伍。随着劳动数量和种类的增加，内生的专

业化分工正在深化和细化，这些子行业和产业将吸引更多的企业，加速市场竞争和创新活动，从而形成新的产业，并完善、带动经济增长。该理论对内生增长理论的扩展是，不同于后者的人力资本的同质性，本章所见的专业劳动力差异将为落后地区提供某些新兴产业的比较优势。它们可以跨越静态比较优势，实现规模收益不断增加。

深圳有许多突出品质，其中最突出的是在城市每一角落弥漫的创业精神。创业创新，催生新的产品，创造新的企业。优秀企业的成长是一个坚持不懈的过程，只有不断创新，才能在市场竞争中生存。创新型城市是创新型国家的核心，是不断创造企业家的过程。100名创新创业者推动100名创新创业者继续前进的结果是边际收益不断增加的过程。中等收入陷阱是创新边际收益递减的陷阱，世界上高收入国家陷入边际收益递减陷阱的案例有很多。

需要注意的是，竞争和生存并不是单个企业孤独追求的过程。相反，产业集群中众多专业创新企业的竞争构成了产业链的协同效应。许多企业在多领域、多层次、多环节创新，协同创新导致资源重组和有效再配置，是新兴产业崛起的根源。深圳无人机产业集群的最新崛起，是竞争生存、协同创新的经典案例。准确性的简单表达是，无人机是基于AI技术和材料技术、精密处理技术、动力电池技术、控制技术和数字移动通信技术的新兴产业。缺乏产业链中的核心关键技术，没有任何一家公司可以独立生产无人机。

首先，深圳有很多纤维材料公司。在加工贸易时代，从加工鱼竿、羽毛球拍、网球拍到高尔夫俱乐部，随着产业的逐步升级，出现了一批生产无人机机身、机壳和主要结构件的细分企业。其次，无人机精密零部件制造企业作为航空铝的后处理子行业，起源于低端航空模型件、手机外壳、消费电子外壳、机器人零件等。深圳手机制造业在模仿创新时代崛起。据不完全统计，进入21世纪后，产值已达6亿—8亿，出口占70%—80%。随着智能手机时代的到来，传统的低端手机产业迅速衰落，成为典型的产能过剩行业。与无人机制造业的协同效应和精密制造能力的提高是相关企业获得新一轮创新增长的机会。同样，特种塑料行业为无人机生产提供外壳、螺旋桨和低成本消耗品。锂聚合物电池产业是手机生产的基础，也是深圳的传统优势产业。无人机从悬停状态达到最大速度，其用时越短，对电池瞬时功率增加的要求就越高。因此，动力电池的能量密度远高于手机电池，体积能量密度或质量能量密度是传统手机电池厂商转型生存的关键。不同领域、不同环节的不同技术方案的竞争，造就了深圳无人机产业的崛起。不断扩大的产业集群也为数百家相关企业提供了更多的市场需求。值得一提的是，微电机是无人机的关键部件，磁性材料是微电机生产的核心材料，具有用量小、价值高、创新难度系数高等特点。一家企业将付出更高的代价，承担更大的风险。深圳市政府没有预见到无人机产业的崛起，但深知微伺服电机是机器人产业发展的核心技术。深圳大力支持磁性材料在公共服务和研发领域的研发，推动了深圳汽车产业升级。

六 改革开放让创新成为深圳名片

从简单的装配分工到专业化分工，深圳不断从大型制造业向研发业转型升级，市场竞争压力加大。没有创新就会惨遭淘汰，必须在创新方面取得成功。企业往往处于亏损状态，这就要求政府在提供创新公共产品方面发挥作用。政府在其中发挥保护公共产品作用的清单很长，但核心点非常明确。

一是鼓励企业创新，促进科技创新中心与产业技术创新中心的超空间合作。以下四个特点是深圳创新最显著的方面：90%的研发机构、90%的研发人员、90%的研发支出、90%的研发成果来自企业。但自20世纪90年代中期以来，深圳坚持鼓励、支持和资助企业设立研发机构，并推动与高校和科研机构建立长期的研发合作关系。这是2004年以来深圳国际专利申请爆炸式增长的重要制度因素。如今，深圳申请的每100项国际专利，其中12项是与北京合作完成的。[①] 因为北京和深圳已经成长为全球重要的工业创新中心，

[①] Results in 2017 Program Highlights 2018, Francis Gurry, Director General, World Intellectual Property Organization (WIPO) Briefing for Ambassadors, 22 March 2018.

因为深圳、北京的科学发现已经成为工业技术创新的前沿理论基础，科技创新中心地位进一步增强。

二是推进市场主导型企业创新。以北京为代表的全国乃至世界的科技创新如何与深圳企业的创新活动相结合，或者为什么北京的科研成果大量进入深圳，而不是其他城市？核心不是政府行为的差异，而是政府行为差异导致的市场主导创新成果的差异。科研成果产业化始于市场合理定价的"惊人飞跃"。知识就是力量，个人知识产权的高回报将刺激更多的知识发现。企业需要降低创新成本和风险，并希望支付更低的知识产权费用。Walras的"拍卖"市场均衡不能解决知识产品定价问题。事实证明，政府不能对高风险、高决策的创新活动定价，这是专业化风险投资产业集群的使命。从全球角度来看，创新活动最活跃的领域是风险资本最集中的领域。中国内地最活跃的创新投资城市高度集中在北京、深圳和上海。

三是创新法治基础。市场经济的本质是契约制度，契约制度是创新所依赖的最重要的公共产品。签订合法合同并有效执行，市场经济才得以运行。没有合同的可执行性和公平执行，就不可能产生广泛的创新活动。如果一家公司创造了知识产权，而另一家公司剽窃了知识产权却毫无惩罚，那么公司的创新积极性势必下降。合同可以在法治的基础上履行，而不是依靠政府的行政管理。政府对消除行政垄断的承诺是对创新的最大支持。如果有问题，找到市场就是法治，找市长反而会导致政府的不当干预。深圳市政府20年来建立了完善的风险投资和股权投资体系，形成了威慑性的知识产权保护体系，充分发挥了市场经济对资源配置的决定性作用。

1995年7月，深圳市确定了以高新技术产业为先导的转型战略，开始实施一系列扶持高新技术产业发展的政策措施。[①] 1997年9月，深圳市明确提出建立技术风险投资体系，该体系于1998年11月正式启动，以启动风险资本立法程序，将英文"Venture Capital"的风险资本翻译为风险资本投资，并确定知识产权可以以合法形式成为权益资产。2000年10月，《创新投资暂行规定》被制定为法

[①] Li Zibin, *Increase the Advantages of Innovation and Move Towards Modernization: Li Zibin's Work Collection in Shenzhen*, China Financial & Economic Publishing House, 2000.

律。2003年深圳市人大常委会通过的《深圳市创新投资条例》，包含了若干重要的理论和前瞻性的制度突破，为深圳创新投资产业的发展奠定了法律基础。《风险投资企业管理暂行办法》为风险投资企业提供了有益的立法参考。2012年9月，深圳在积累了10年实践经验后，颁布了修订后的《深圳经济特区创业投资条例》。[①]

四是建立与市场支持相适应的产业政策体系。2006年，深圳提出了支持"非共识创新"的口号，[②] 这是一个影响深远、充满哲学意蕴的口号，也是一个引起人们质疑的政策主张。问题在于，政府支持非共识创新的基础是什么？共识不能是创新。人类历史上大多数重大科学发现和工业技术创新都经历了一个从被怀疑到获得共识的过程。创新不能是带着光环的神话，必须符合科学发现的一般规律。政府不能确定谁能在创新中取得成功，也不能明确谁是创新者，但政府可以引导创新者和企业了解产业技术创新的科学基础，遵循创新的科学规范，掌握相关领域的创新进展和前人研究成果。对于已经进行的创新探索，无论成功与否，都可以为未来可行的技术路线指明方向。在市场竞争条件下，合理的政府行为需要明确科研和产业创新的支持方向，从多方面评估创新团队的创新能力和组织的有效性。确定方向、评估创新能力和指定赢家之间最大的区别在于，创新是基于市场竞争和对市场参与者的有效激励。通过在资源配置中发挥基础性作用，市场最终将决定谁是赢家。只有这样，才能更好地发挥政府的作用。2006年以来，深圳市继续努力探索建立鼓励创新的环境，制定合理有效的支持创新的政策法规，建立了科学家和创新创业者相互依赖的评价体系。

打造湿地效应，支持战略性新兴产业发展。湿地是自然界最具活力的生态系统，具有极其丰富的物种多样性。湿地经济活动是一个公平、公正、公开的市场竞争环境。只要政府不加干预，市场竞

---

① Tang Jie, "Promote the Development of Venture Capital Industry from the Source of System Construction", Shenzhen Evening News, July 24, 2016, http://wb.sznews.com/html/2016-08/10/content_3591650.htm.

② Refer to the Shenzhen Municipal Party Committee and the Shenzhen Municipal People's Government's Decision on Implementing Independent Innovation Strategy to Build a National Innovative City (Shen Fa [2006] No.1).

争就能决定谁是创新的赢家。市场竞争中不会有永远的创新赢家。深圳制定实施了一系列卓有成效的产业政策，为促进产业转型升级发挥了重要作用。通过案例分析，本章观察了以产业规划为基础的产业政策与市场机制的相容性，以及产业是如何按照市场原则进行转型升级。2010年，深圳提出了"深圳质量"转型发展的理念，制定了更加严格的限制产业发展清单，实施了更加积极集约的发展政策，促使企业迅速调整产业结构。2012年第一季度，深圳经济增速骤降至5.8%，低于全国和全省平均水平。但深圳仍坚持方向，经济增长势头不减。[①] 2013年，深圳启动了生命健康产业规划及相关产业政策，明确提出，要建设干细胞库等重大医疗基础设施，建立个体化细胞治疗的临床疗效和安全性评价体系。[②] 2018年，深圳完成了干细胞库建设和第一个国家免疫细胞质量检测实验室建设。细胞技术创新不能从实验室技术、跨中间过程、质量控制等方面进行，人体使用的细胞产品必须经过监管部门批准，并进行严格的第三方质量检验。美国食品药品监督管理局和中国食品药品监督管理局明确规定，细胞产品的应用必须经过严格的质量检测：一是细胞类型和来源的检测；二是安全性检测，细胞来源是否有传染病，制备过程是否有污染；三是疗效检验，细胞作为一种药物，临床应用能否达到治疗的目的。中国细胞产业的发展明显落后于美国、欧洲和日本。细胞制备标准和质量标准的缺乏是细胞产业发展受阻的重要原因。由此可见，有效的产业政策可以弥补产业发展过程中的关键缺陷。只要不违背市场竞争性获取资源的原则，产业政策就有利于资源配置在市场机制中的作用。

---

① Xu Qin, "Breaking the development of 'ceiling' with reform", Interview, Shenzhen Special Zone Daily, Mar 12, 2014, http://www.huaxia.com/gdtb/gdyw/szyw/2014/03/3787620.html.

② Shenzhen Municipal People's Government, "Notice of the Shenzhen Municipal People's Government on Printing and Distributing the Shenzhen Life and Health Industry Development Plan (2013 – 2020)", 2014. Shenzhen Municipal People's Government website, January 8, 2014, http://www.sz.gov.cn/zfgb/2014/gb865/201401/t20140108_2301119.htm.

七 加大改革开放力度，形成创新激励和竞争生存创新体系

20世纪90年代中期，深圳提出发展高新技术产业，但深圳高校和科研机构很少。深圳做了两件事：一是"政策洼地"吸引人才聚集深圳。由于20世纪90年代初第一批高新技术企业的成功，深圳形成了更适合高新技术产业发展的"政策洼地"。当时，一大批在内地无法独立开发的研究机构和技术开发人员南下。深圳成立了电子信息企业，90年代形成了数十万科技人员的大规模创新资源转移。二是深圳积极构建产学研相结合的创新体系。如果说创业者的到来启动了深圳科技创新的引擎，那么深圳相对完整的自主创新体系的目标，就是以企业和市场为导向，与政府、产业、研发紧密结合，推动深圳的持续创新，这是创新的不竭动力。创新体系的建立对深圳高新技术产业的发展有几个重要作用：一是克服市场失灵和组织失灵，降低创新企业的不确定性和风险，增强企业的投资和动力；二是进行技术改造，市场衍生，孵化高新技术企业，促进科技成果转化；三是增加专业劳动的数量和类型，为深化和细化分工奠定基础。

2013年，深圳市新认定国家高新技术企业591家，累计3000余家；重点实验室、工程中心、公共技术平台等创新载体176家，累计955家；社会研发投入超过500亿元，占国内生产总值的比重提高到4%，超过了发达国家的平均水平。深圳在科技创新领域实现了"四个90%"现象，即90%以上的研发机构设在企业，90%以上的研发人员集中在企业，90%以上的研发资金来自企业，90%以上的服务发明专利来自企业。高新区的创业和创新环境进一步优化，形成了比较完整的创新创业服务链，包括国际技术创业平台、风险投资服务广场、虚拟大学园区、深港产学研基地，以及国家集成电路设计深圳产业化基地等服务机构。

科技人才资源是技术创新的基础。大中型企业科技活动从业人

员由 2005 年的 57200 人增加到 2012 年的 257000 人，增长 3.5 倍。截至 2013 年年底，深圳市专业技术人员有 1216300 人，其中具有中级以上技术职称的专业技术人员 392100 人。到 2013 年，共有 3033 名高级专业人员获得认证。深圳大学城每年培养研究生 6000 余人，已成为系统、全面培养和引进高素质人才的重要地方院校。

深圳相对完善的技术服务中介是推动创新的重要桥梁。例如，通过在深圳设立创业板和中小企业董事会，公司的融资渠道将得到扩展；深圳高新区服务中心将通过引入风险投资基金、经纪投资银行和非上市业务单位、产权交易等方式，建立深圳高新区创业投资服务广场。评估、会计、律师事务所和担保、信贷、专利服务中介机构落户，为处于不同成长阶段的中小微技术企业提供多层次、立体化、全过程的融资服务。

政府制定的产业政策是深圳创新体系的重要组成部分。技术的不确定性、市场的不确定性、股权分配的不确定性和政策环境的不确定性，以及市场机制的不完善，都需要一定程度的政府干预。因此，在后发展国家或地区，政府可以通过政策规划、政府采购、财政等多种形式，影响和引导创新活动的作用和效率。深圳市颁布了《深圳经济特区企业技术秘密保护条例》《深圳经济特区无形资产评估管理办法》《深圳市企业奖励技术开发人员暂行办法》《深圳市科技研发资金管理办法》《关于进一步支持高新技术产业发展的规定》等规定，编制了科技发展规划、高新技术产业发展规划、战略性新兴产业振兴发展规划，以及未来的产业发展政策。深圳市政府还投资 30 亿元设立了创业投资引导基金，解决了创业期融资难的问题。深圳还设立了战略性新兴产业专项基金，支持生物、互联网、新能源等战略性新兴产业。通过财政资金和杠杆作用，引导更多的社会资本进入全社会的研究创新领域。

为保持深圳未来"创新驱动模式"的增长，深圳提出推进法治化、国际化的市场化改革，建立具有国际竞争力、规范有序的市场经济和法治经济，充分发挥市场在资源配置中的作用，提高资源配置效率，增强创新活动激励机制的决定性作用。深圳提出以打造"深圳品质"为导向，继续推进创新驱动发展战略，通过加强自主研发提升品牌价值，实施品质优先，促进深圳产业不断升级发展。深圳将加强科技领域市场化、法治化、国际化的制度化建设，通过产学研创新合作模式，构建具有国际竞争力的开放自主创新体系。为此，深圳提出构建一流的人才教育培训体系，支持相关教育专业和基础研究设施的建设，提升专业人才培养、基础研究和原创创新水平。

第四章　城市增长与城市规划：
面对人口增长的挑战

一　介绍

深圳在短短 40 年内由小村庄快速成长为大都市，成为城市发展的独特案例。令人印象深刻的人口和经济发展，是依靠政府规划推动、维持和调节的成功结果。① 通过特区经济体制，门户开放政策致力将临近香港的深圳打造成为经济新趋势的"窗口"、内地人才的"训练基地"和中国改革的"试验田"。② 为了实现这一目标，深圳成为中国第一个采用资本主义世界式的发展、市场和规划做法的城市，这再次体现了深圳的独特性。③

正如吴和唐所言："作为引进外资、科技的试验田，［深圳］在融入世界经济的努力中一直走在前列，特别是自 20 世纪 80 年代中期以来。"④ Shen 和 Kee 称，与广州的情况类似，深圳的成功主要与

---

① Shen, Jianfa and Gordon Kee, "Shenzhen: Innovation and Governments' Roles in Reform and Development", In *Development and Planning in Seven Major Coastal Cities in Southern and Eastern China*, Cham: Springer International Publishing, 2017.

② Shenzhen Museum, "The History of Shenzhen Special Economic Zone", Beijing: People's Press (in Chinese), 1999.

③ Zacharias, John and Yuanzhou Tang, "Restructuring and Repositioning Shenzhen. China's New Mega City", *Progress in Planning*, Vol. 73, No. 4, 2010, pp. 209 – 249.

④ Ng, Mee K. and Wing – Shing Tang, "The Role of Planning in the Development of Shenzhen, China: Rhetoric and Realities", *Eurasian Geography and Economics*, Vol. 45, No. 3, 2004, pp. 190 – 211.

其集聚能力和对外贸易、人员流动等方面有关。① 但其成功的特点在于创新过程、行政结构和实践以及政府对解决发展问题的积极参与，这对于推动城市从典型的社会主义的中央计划经济、"资源约束"经济向现代资本主义、"需求约束"经济体制的演变至关重要。② 对中国来说，这是一个前所未有的经济和社会改革体制，也是促进城市发展的合理政策，吸引了私人利益相关者，促进了城市的爆炸性发展。总体而言，正如Ng所说："考虑到人口规模、空间发展和各种经济参数的增长，深圳特区的试验是非常成功的。"③

城市规划在维持和推动城市经济增长和城市景观改造方面发挥了重要作用，与社会经济和政治环境齐头并进。④ 总体规划及其发展战略使扩张和土地利用合理化，⑤ 后者在城市发展中发挥着突出作用。⑥ 随着时间的推移，这些发展战略需跟上城市发展变化的需求，从早期的经济特区巩固，到扩大前城市的乡县，再到强化深圳在地区和世界上的角色。这些需求，加上全球和中国其他地区日益激烈的竞争，正如Ng所言，深圳在"整合社会经济和空间规划上，表现卓越"⑦。根据城市的社会和经济需求来规划空间扩张，确实像中国典型做法。然而，深圳的创新之处在于以一种新的方式进行社会经济和空间规划，即促进经济增长和市场发展。规划者通过实践

---

① Shen, Jianfa and Gordon Kee, "Shenzhen: Innovation and Governments' Roles in Reform and Development", In *Development and Planning in Seven Major Coastal Cities in Southern and Eastern China*, Cham: Springer International Publishing, 2017.

② Ng, Mee K. and Wing-Shing Tang, "Theorising Urban Planning in a Transitional Economy: The Case of Shenzhen, People's Republic of China", *The Town Planning Review*, Vol. 75, No. 2, 2004, pp. 173–203.

③ Ng, Mee K., "City Profile: Shenzhen", *Cities*, Vol. 20, No. 6, 2003, pp. 429–441.

④ Ng, Mee K. and Wing-Shing Tang, "Theorising Urban Planning in a Transitional Economy: The Case of Shenzhen, People's Republic of China", *The Town Planning Review*, Vol. 75, No. 2, 2004, pp. 173–203.

⑤ Shen, Jianfa and Gordon Kee, "Shenzhen: Innovation and Governments' Roles in Reform and Development", In *Development and Planning in Seven Major Coastal Cities in Southern and Eastern China*, Cham: Springer International Publishing, 2017.

⑥ Ibid..

⑦ Ng, Mee K., "City Profile: Shenzhen", *Cities*, Vol. 20, No. 6, 2003, pp. 429–441.

学会了这种史无前例的方法，随着时间的推移，他们逐渐从中央计划系统的专有领域转移到了更加本地化的计划制订过程。①

在以下各节中，笔者将概述城市规划的主要阶段，以及自经济特区成立以来，城市规划是如何支持城市发展的。接着将集中讨论一些与人口增长相关的核心问题，这些问题是城市扩张的特征，如移民、城市化和城市集中，并提到一些特定的流动人口（如游客）。之后，笔者将讨论可持续规划的主要原则以及提高城市人口生活水平的相关需要。

二 规划与城市演变

自1980年特区成立以来，城市规划所描绘的深圳开发设计一直在不断演变。从中央计划经济的逐步过渡也涉及城市规划本身的过程，真正的现代制度是在80年代末和90年代随着深圳市城市规划和土地管理局的成立（1989）、《深圳城市规划条例》（1998）的颁布和深圳市城市规划委员会的成立逐步建立起来的（1999）。②

如前几篇论文所述，随着时间的推移，可以确定该过程的三个阶段。这些阶段最明显的共同点之一是城市总体规划与五年规划之间的紧密联系，这意味着城市规划与城市社会经济之间有着紧密的联系。③

第一阶段从1980年经济特区成立到1985年。早期的挑战是从传统农业经济转型，以工业主要是高科技和资本密集型产业为基

---

① Ng, Mee K. and Wing‐Shing Tang, "The Role of Planning in the Development of Shenzhen, China: Rhetoric and Realities", *Eurasian Geography and Economics*, Vol. 45, No. 3, 2004, pp. 190–211.

② Shen, Jianfa and Gordon Kee, "Shenzhen: Innovation and Governments' Roles in Reform and Development", In *Development and Planning in Seven Major Coastal Cities in Southern and Eastern China*, Cham: Springer International Publishing, 2017.

③ Ng, Mee K., "City Profile: Shenzhen", *Cities*, Vol. 20, No. 6, 2003, pp. 429–441. Ng, Mee K. and Wing‐Shing Tang, "Theorising Urban Planning in a Transitional Economy: The Case of Shenzhen, People's Republic of China", *The Town Planning Review*, Vol. 75, No. 2, 2004, pp. 173–203.

础，建立一个能够吸引外商投资的现代化城市。同时，发展商业、农业、住房和旅游等多个领域。但是，这一早期阶段吸引外商投资的领域主要集中在房地产开发和低附加值的劳动密集型产业。与此同时，深圳国内投资大幅增长，中央作为投资主体作用突出。Ng 和 Tang 认为，主要是由于缺乏完善的基础设施和法律，以及潜在的外国投资者动力不足。①

第二阶段是从 80 年代中期至 90 年代中期，主要通过出口和吸引国际直接投资来提振经济，高科技产业和服务业的作用日益重要。深圳实施了一系列行政改革，促进了国际直接投资的实际增长。同时，针对城市发展有用的渐进土地分配开始引起人们对其稀缺性的质疑。

随着时间的推移，其他城市也开始经济增长，深圳已不再是中国的"例外"。因此，深圳"别无选择，只能努力成为一个榜样"，以巩固其在中国其他城市和世界的地位。自 20 世纪 90 年代以来，规划文件一直强调要将深圳打造为世界级城市的愿景。规划者加强了高科技产业和服务业的作用，注重土地的战略利用、交通和基础设施的发展。经过多年的规划，第十个五年计划（2001—2005）将可持续性、生活质量和环境保护引进经济增长。无论是在中国还是在世界范围内，深圳在可持续发展和环境保护方面的努力得到了普遍认可。

扎卡赖亚斯（Zacharias）和 Tang 的作品采用了互补的视角，描述了城市规划是如何影响土地利用的。②

根据 1986 年的第一个总体规划，深圳及其经济特区的早期发展是沿着"集群线性"模式进行的，在这种模式下，经济特区将沿着交通走廊开展一系列集群发展，由西向东依次为南山区、福田区、罗湖区、盐田区。城市被划分为"综合性"自给自足的

---

① Ng, Mee K. and Wing – Shing Tang, "Theorising Urban Planning in a Transitional Economy: The Case of Shenzhen, People's Republic of China", *The Town Planning Review*, Vol. 75, No. 2, 2004, pp. 173 – 203.

② Zacharias, John and Yuanzhou Tang, "Restructuring and repositioning Shenzhen. China's new mega city", *Progress in Planning*, Vol. 73, No. 4, 2010, pp. 209 – 249.

"城市群"①，这点在今天也可以看到。这一理论基础与中国城市传统的核心—外围发展模式相反。② 深圳的规划还考虑了基础设施的发展，以及将不同区域分配到城市扩展的特定功能。

在随后的几年里，随着综合交通基础设施的完善，深圳也随之发展。行政调整也促进了原经济特区及其周边城市用地的增长。③ 1993 年，宝安、龙岗两县成为区。新的综合规划于 1996 年完成，将原来特区的发展模式扩展到新的地区，推动建立一个连接城市不同地区的多轴网络结构。尽管经济特区和非经济特区之间以前的划分不复存在，但二者的经济和城市景观仍有所不同。④ 控制发展是主要的目标，因为这一进程比第一个总体规划中预期的更加混乱。然而，开发控制并没有如规划者所期望的那样成功。

2004 年深圳又推出了《深圳 2030 城市发展战略》的总体规划。深圳努力吸取以往经验教训，克服阻碍进一步发展的主要"四个困难"。其中两个指的是有限的资源，如土地⑤和城市用水，另外两个困难是过度拥挤和环境恶化。这一战略意味着增加城市不同地区的专业化，并提升深圳在香港、东莞、广州和惠州地区的影响力。该战略希望促进建立一个两中心+五分中心⑥的多中心城市发展模式，

---

① Ng, Mee K., "City Profile: Shenzhen", *Cities*, Vol. 20, No. 6, 2003, pp. 429 – 441.

② Zacharias, John and Yuanzhou Tang, "Restructuring and repositioning Shenzhen. China's New Mega City", *Progress in Planning*, Vol. 73, No. 4, 2010, pp. 209 – 249.

③ Shen, Jianfa and Gordon Kee, "Shenzhen: Innovation and Governments' Roles in Reform and Development", In *Development and Planning in Seven Major Coastal Cities in Southern and Eastern China*, Cham: Springer International Publishing, 2017.

④ Shen, Jianfa and Gordon Kee, "Shenzhen: Innovation and Governments' Roles in Reform and Development", In *Development and Planning in Seven Major Coastal Cities in Southern and Eastern China*, Cham: Springer International Publishing, 2017. Ng, Mee K. and Wing – Shing Tang, "Theorising Urban Planning in a Transitional Economy: The Case of Shenzhen, People's Republic of China", *The Town Planning Review*, Vol. 75, No. 2, 2004, pp. 173 – 203.

⑤ Land Shortage has Always Been One of the Major Constraints to the City Expansion. Ng, Mee K., "City profile: Shenzhen", *Cities*, Vol. 20, No. 6, 2003, pp. 429 – 441.

⑥ Zacharias, John and Yuanzhou Tang, "Restructuring and Repositioning Shenzhen. China's New Mega City", *Progress in Planning*, Vol. 73, No. 4, 2010, pp. 209 – 249.

促进活动和服务的集聚。

继第三次城市规划成功后,2010年深圳又启动了《深圳2040城市发展战略》。深圳再次面临与土地利用和经济发展有关的问题,但深圳正通过重视家庭、健康、教育、文化和社会来提高城市发展的可持续性。①

三 人口与移民

控制发展一直是深圳城市规划者关注的核心问题之一。移民和新劳动力对城市经济发展至关重要。但是,不加选择和不受控制的增长可能会给城市造成巨大的损失,因为城市可能不如预期的那样容易适应,城市结构不足以应对外来人口的流动。结果,城市空间、住房和就业机会以及为人口提供的服务可能出现短缺。在世界上人口最密集的城市周围,贫民窟的大量出现是在缺乏适当政策的情况下,快速增长的人口自我组织的反应。众所周知,生活在边缘环境下易滋生社会排斥和犯罪等,这也印证了对人口膨胀有关的社会经济现象进行管理的必要性,以便减少和/或避免对公民生活质量的威胁。

深圳人口爆炸式增长是其发展过程的特点。官方数据显示,1980—2016年,深圳常住人口增长3477%,2016年人口总数达近1200万人,其中就业人口占77.8%。② 然而,从Ng和Tang对不同规划浪潮的经济建设来看,③ 尽管中国的控制政策在限制城市增长

---

① Shen, Jianfa and Gordon Kee, "Shenzhen: Innovation and Governments' Roles in Reform and Development", In *Development and Planning in Seven Major Coastal Cities in Southern and Eastern China*, Cham: Springer International Publishing, 2017.

② SSB (Shenzhen Statistics Bureau and NBS Survey Office in Shenzhen), *Shenzhen Statistical Yearbook*, Beijing: China Statistics Press, 2018.

③ Ng, Mee K. and Wing-Shing Tang, "The Role of Planning in the Development of Shenzhen, China: Rhetoric and Realities", *Eurasian Geography and Economics*, Vol. 45, No. 3, 2004, pp. 190–211.

方面总体上是有效的，但实际人口增长始终超过了五年规划的目标。①

随着空间发展压力的显著增加，计划人口和预期人口间的不匹配产生了广泛影响。对基础设施和人口服务投资需求上涨就是其中之一。有限的土地面积和遵守中央政府五年人口目标的需要是下一步工作的关键。吴和唐举例说，从1986年到90年代初，罗湖区经济特区中心区的发展推动了规划者在福田区分配新的居住区。这种人口流动导致了交通压力加大，环境问题和水资源的短缺。②

除了数量方面外，随着时间的推移，与人口构成有关的社会影响也随之显现。深圳是一个流动人口比例巨大的城市。根据国家统计局③的数据，2016年，67.7%的常住人口没有登记。④ 这一比例随着人口的增长而增加，从1980年的3.6%增加到1990年的59.1%和2000年的82.2%。自21世纪初以来，这一比例在2016年下降到67.7%。尽管中国的户口制度只允许注册公民在其居住的城市获得教育、社会和医疗服务，但这一比例还是发生了变化。显然，从这些数字可以得出结论，登记政策并没有阻止来自国内农村地区的移民。

深圳虽然是中国人均GDP最高的城市之一，但低收入人口所占的比重很大，且大部分为移民。⑤ 移民的生活状况成为深圳爆炸式城市化的一部分。在开放政策实施之前，城乡二元结构是功能性的，城市创造了工业和服务业的发展，农村创造了粮食生产。农村

---

① Deng, Xiangzheng, Jikun Huang, Scott Rozelle and Emi Uchida, "Growth, Population and Industrialization, and Urban Land Expansion of China", *Journal of Urban Economics*, Vol. 63, No. 1, 2008, pp. 96 – 115.

② Ng, Mee K., and Wing – Shing Tang, "The Role of Planning in the Development of Shenzhen, China: Rhetoric and Realities", *Eurasian Geography and Economics*, Vol. 45, No. 3, 2004, pp. 190 – 211.

③ SSB (Shenzhen Statistics Bureau and NBS Survey Office in Shenzhen), *Shenzhen Statistical Yearbook*, Beijing: China Statistics Press, 2018.

④ In the last years there has been a slight decline in non – registered population, whereas the permanent one has increased.

⑤ Cox, Wendell, "The Evolving Urban Form: Shenzhen", New Geography, May 25, 2012, http://www.newgeography.com/content/002862 – the – evolving – urban – form – shenzhen.

地区是贫困人口集中的地区。① 1978 年改革开放后,农村人口向城市迁移已成为城市发展的主要因素,② 给城市环境带来了越来越大的压力。通常,在大城市中心,当快速城市化发生时,低收入人口住房需求刺激了贫民窟或棚户区的开发。在中国,这一现象的出现并不是因为制度约束。面对外来务工者的压力,深圳在邻近的传统村落开始扩张"城中村",随着时间的推移,这些村落逐渐融入城市。这些往往是唯一可负担得起的住房机会。除了快速城市化和农村移民收入较低的因素外,租住公共住房的障碍也促进了"城中村"的发展。③ 随着流动人口的增加,许多以前的村民把房屋由家庭住房改为出租房屋。与此同时,未经授权的建筑也有所增加。尽管政府努力对这一现象进行管制,但此类非法房屋的无节制开发仍在继续。④ 在许多情况下,这些现象导致了社区的发展,在这些社区中,家庭控制着住宅、非公共土地,并发展了平行商业。

与中心城区相比,城中村具有零散的特点,居民平均受教育水平较低,以前居住于此的人们由于户口原因而无法获得城市福利服务。⑤ 城市规划对这些集聚区的调控影响,以及城市扩张控制的有效性,仍然是一个问题。较高的犯罪率、较差的生活条件以及城中

---

① Wang, Ya P., Yanglin Wang, Jiansheng Wu, "Urbanization and Informal Development in China: Urban Villages in Shenzhen", *International Journal of Urban and Regional Research*, Vol. 33, No. 4, 2009, pp. 957 - 973.

② Shen, Jianfa, Kwan - yiu Wong, and Zhiqiang Feng, "State - sponsored and spontaneous urbanization in the Pearl River Delta of South China, 1980 - 1998", *Urban Geography*, Vol. 23, No. 7, 2002, pp. 674 - 694.

③ Wang, Ya P., Yanglin Wang, Jiansheng Wu, "Urbanization and Informal Development in China: Urban Villages in Shenzhen", *International Journal of Urban and Regional Research*, Vol. 33, No. 4, 2009, pp. 957 - 973. Wong, Tammy and Geerhardt Kornatowski, "Domination and Contestation in the Urban Politics of Shenzhen", *disP - The Planning Review*, Vol. 50, No. 4, 2014, pp. 6 - 15.

④ Ng, Mee K., "City profile: Shenzhen", *Cities*, Vol. 20, No. 6, 2003, pp. 429 - 441. Wang, Ya P., Yanglin Wang, Jiansheng Wu, "Urbanization and Informal Development in China: Urban Villages in Shenzhen", *International Journal of Urban and Regional Research*, Vol. 33, No. 4, 2009, pp. 957 - 973.

⑤ The New Urbanization Plan 2014 - 2020 aims to reform the hukou system in China and adopt more flexible policies. See Cheshmehzangi (2016) and Hong'e (2018).

村融入城市环境的速度较慢,都是亟待解决的关键方面。① 这也是房地产开发商、政府官员和规划者对城中村非正式发展方式持否定态度的原因。但从另一个角度看,城中村对移民来说是唯一的住房机会,也是房东取得租金的一种渠道。尽管高新技术产业在城市经济中日益重要,但劳动密集型产业仍然占相当大的比重。因此,城中村在接纳对城市经济增长有具体贡献的低技能劳动人口上也发挥着关键作用。

四 城市化、城市集中与城市扩张

深圳爆炸式的人口增长是近几十年来最著名的城市人口数据之一。②《世界城市化展望》预测,今天55%的城市化人口比例将在2050年增加到68%。③ 格拉泽认为,这一进程标志着从贫困向繁荣的逐步过渡。④ 同时,如果适当的政策不能解决诸如不平等、犯罪、污染、疾病和拥挤等现象,人口增长对城市生活条件可能产生巨大的消极影响。

城市化与经济增长密切相关。从一些统计数据可以看出各国城市化的积极影响:正如亨德森所报告的,⑤ "平均而言一个国家城市化率与人均GDP(均取对数)之间的简单相关系数约为0.85"⑥。城市化

---

① Wang, Ya P., Yanglin Wang, Jiansheng Wu, "Urbanization and Informal Development in China: Urban Villages in Shenzhen", *International Journal of Urban and Regional Research*, Vol. 33, No. 4, 2009, pp. 957 – 973.

② UN – Habitat. *Draft strategic plan 2014 – 2019 of the United Nations Human Settlements Programme*, 2013, https://unhabitat.org/un – habitats – strategic – plan – 2014 – 2019/.

③ UN (United Nations), *World Urbanization Prospects: The 2018 Revision*, 2018, . https://esa.un.org/unpd/wup/Publications/Files/WUP2018 – KeyFacts.pdf.

④ Glaeser, Edward L., "Cities, Productivity and Quality of Life", *Science*, Vol. 333, No. 6042, 2011, pp. 592 – 594.

⑤ Henderson, J. Vernon, "The Urbanization Process and Economic Growth: The So – What Question", *Journal of Economic Growth*, Vol. 8, 2003, pp. 47 – 71.

⑥ Alonso, William, "The Economics of Urban Size", *Papers in Regional Science*, Vol. 26, No. 1, 1971, pp. 67 – 83.

还意味着更高的发展水平和生活满意度,① 这比以 GDP 为代表的单一经济指数更具广泛的概念。然而,城市化本身并不足以维持城市人均 GDP 增长所带来的生产力,② 城市化是人口从农村向城市转移的过程。劳动力从第一部门逐步转移到第二和第三部门为这一过程的特点之一。经济政策只能通过影响部门构成和收入来产生间接影响。

与城市化不同,城市集中对经济增长具有影响力,这是政策制定者和城市规划者均可操控的因素。活动聚集产生规模经济,从而提高生产力,提高公民的财富。城市集中现象及其影响使马尔萨斯主义关于人口与增长之间关系的经典观点得以克服。这个经典理论预测,一方面,出生率增加和死亡降低可以增加人口,进而增加财富积累。③ 另一方面,由于边际生产率下降,人口增长将对人均收入产生负面影响,因为增加的人口将增加资源消耗。从长远来看,人口数量会总体平稳。

自 19 世纪以来,全球人口爆炸性增长以及人均收入的增长与这种观点相矛盾。马尔萨斯理论适用于典型的人力资本和技术有限的经济体,如那些以农业为基础的经济体。然而,人口增加和城市化进程加快导致的人口密度以马歇尔集群的形式上升,是现代城市经济的特征。这导致专业化,人力资本的提高和对基于知识的活动的更多投资,而这些活动不断增加的回报反过来又通过提高生产力促进了经济增长。与此同时,由于人口增长限制了城市为每个公民提供资源,自然资源使用收益的减少可能会产生相反的效果,导致巨大的社会成本,如犯罪、交通拥挤和传染性疾病。④ 这种权衡的总

---

① Glaeser, Edward L., "Cities, Productivity and Quality of Life", *Science*, Vol. 333, No. 6042, 2011, pp. 592 – 594.

② Henderson, J. Vernon, "The Urbanization Process and Economic Growth: The So – What Question", *Journal of Economic Growth*, Vol. 8, 2003, pp. 47 – 71. Davis, James C., and J. Vernon Henderson. 2003.

③ Sato, Yasuhiro, and Kazuhiro Yamamoto, "Population Concentration, Urbanization, and Demographic Transition", *Journal of Urban Economics*, Vol. 58, No. 1, 2005, pp. 45 – 61.

④ Wheaton, William C. and Hisanobu Shishido, "Urban Concentration, Agglomeration Economies, and the Level of Economic Development", *Economic Development and Cultural Change*, Vol. 30, No. 1, 1981, pp. 17 – 30.

体结果取决于这两种影响中哪一种占上风。① 具体地说，这产生了城市规模的可变收益。②

在第三节中，笔者指出了移民对城市发展的重要性。不受控制的流动促进了城中村的发展，这些地方的生活条件比城市中的其他地区差得多。经济学家的共同观点是，当移民可以自由流动时，城市可能将变得更加低效。移民可能产生负面影响，却不一定为相关代价买单。同时，他们会与当地人争夺土地和服务等城市资源。③ 总体结果是私人回报可能高于社会回报。④ 因此，适当的移民和融合政策是克服相关社会问题的关键因素。当然，政府在这方面的作用至关重要，对城市规划具有重要意义。随着人口的增长，两难的选择是：是促进集聚和城市密度（具有相关的优势和成本），还是支持跨空间的扩张（与集中活动相比，设施提供的效用更低）。⑤ 考虑到现有的土地限制，深圳的选择显而易见——倾向于前一种模式。

五　土地利用

在一些城市，社会经济模式对空间的使用产生了巨大影响。旧的和新的活动以及居民的需求已大大改变了城市景观。如前所述，深圳是中国社会经济因素驱动下的城市之一。在这方面，施奈德（Schneider）和伍德科克（Woodcock）结合遥感数据、空间格局指

---

① Fujita, Masahisa, *Urban Economic Theory: Land Use and City Size*, Cambridge: Cambridge University Press, 1989. Becker, Gary S., Edward L. Glaeser and Kevin M. Murphy, "Population and Economic Growth", *The American Economic Review*, Vol. 82, No. 2, 1999, pp. 145-149.

② Albouy, David, Kristian Behrens, Frédéric Robert-Nicoud, Nathan Seegert, "The optimal distribution of population across cities", *Journal of Urban Economics*, 2018, https://doi.org/10.1016/j.jue.2018.08.004.

③ Ibid..

④ Mazumdar, Dipak, "Rural-urban migration in developing countries", In *Handbook of Regional and Urban Economics*, Volume 2, Edwin S. Mills, eds., Amsterdam: Elsevier, 1987.

⑤ Albouy, David, Kristian Behrens, Frédéric Robert-Nicoud, Nathan Seegert, "The optimal distribution of population across cities", *Journal of Urban Economics*, 2018, https://doi.org/10.1016/j.jue.2018.08.004.

标和统计人口普查数据,研究了来自不同国家的25个城市的扩张率和城市化模式。① 他们确定了四个主要类别,即扩张型增长、疯狂型增长、高增长和低增长城市。被分析的中国城市有广州、东莞和成都,这些城市都属于第二类——疯狂型增长。它们在相对较小的空间范围内经历了高增长率,从而拥有了较高的人口密度,它们将土地转换为城市用途的模式是零散的。与美国典型的扩张型增长城市一样,这些城市的增长也可以归因于社会经济和政治因素,而中国城市的增长则是由于"沿海地区和内陆地区在重大改革之后的经济和人口转型"②。他们还指出,在东莞和广州,土地流转率令人印象深刻,与深圳一样,其主要原因是政策决定导致国内生产总值、外国投资和贸易,以及城乡移民增加。考虑到中国的城市和社会经济规划的中心作用,以及两者之间的共生关系,这并不足以为奇。此外,邓等人以2000多个县为样本,发现社会经济因素对中国城市的单中心增长具有显著影响,尤其是增长与人口、收入和运输成本呈正相关,而与农业租金呈负相关。③

Dou和Chen利用卫星数据调查了1988—2015年深圳陆地的扩张情况,他们详细讨论了土地利用和土地覆盖的演变。④ 他们指出,城市扩张对深圳的景观变化有很大影响。这些年来,建成区面积增加了721.1平方公里,从1988年的5.63%增加到2015年的41.77%。建筑物对耕地、森林、水体的影响最大,其中耕地年均减少0.88%,森林年均减少0.35%。在"早期"(1988—1996),

---

① Schneider, Annemarie and Curtis E. Woodcock, "Compact, Dispersed, Fragmented, Extensive? A Comparison of Urban Growth in Twenty - five Global Cities using Remotely Sensed Data, Pattern Metrics and Census Information", *Urban Studies*, Vol. 45, No. 3, 2008, pp. 659 - 692.

② Schneider, Annemarie and Curtis E. Woodcock, "Compact, Dispersed, Fragmented, Extensive? A Comparison of Urban Growth in Twenty - five Global Cities using Remotely Sensed Data, Pattern Metrics and Census Information", *Urban Studies*, Vol. 45, No. 3, 2008, p. 687.

③ Deng, Xiangzheng, Jikun Huang, Scott Rozelle and Emi Uchida, "Growth, Population and Industrialization, and Urban Land Expansion of China", *Journal of Urban Economics*, Vol. 63, No. 1, 2008, pp. 96 - 115.

④ Dou, Peng, and Yangbo Chen, "Dynamic Monitoring of Land - use/land - cover Change and Urban Expansion in Shenzhen Using Landsat Imagery from 1988 to 2015", *International Journal of Remote Sensing*, Vol. 38, No. 19, 2017, pp. 5388 - 5407.

城市发展主要集中在经济特区。在"快速发展"阶段的十年中（1996—2005），城市化率主要在经济特区以外地区增长，建成区从1996年占土地的13.32%增长到2005年的32.86%。在第三个"集约"阶段（2005—2015），城市增长放缓，主要原因是城市土地资源有限。这些数字与《城市扩展地图集》①中报告的动态一致。

表4-1列出了Dou和Chen详细阐述的深圳建成区数据，以及深圳市统计局的一些官方人口和GDP统计数据。②建成区是土地的一部分，不同于森林、耕地、水体、草地和裸地。因此，该地区的住区包括所有类型的建筑物（住宅、工业、商业等）和其他建筑物，以及经过授权和未经授权的建筑物。经过早期发展，1996年至2005年，深圳的建成区扩张速度加快，超过了人口增长。在这期间，规划促进了土地扩张增长。数据显示，由于土地限制，2005—2015年建成区的增长速度有所放缓，而人口增长速度更快。从这些数字和现有的数据中，无法推断出城市集中的细节和质量。然而，有证据表明，最近一段时期城市集中度有所上升。

表4-1　　　　　　　　　人口和建筑面积

年份	人口（1000）		建成面积（平方公里）		人均GDP（元）	
	1—	（变量%）	2—	（变量%）	3—	（变量%）
1988	1201.4	…	112.45	—	6477	…
1996	4828.9	+301.94	266.04	+136.58	22498	+247.4
2005	8277.5	+7142	656.30	+146.69	60801	+170.3
2015	113787	+37.47	834.26	+27.12	157985	+159.8

资料来源：深圳统计局（2017）和 Dou, Peng and Yangbo Chen, "Dynamic Monitoring of Land – use/land – cover Change and Urban Expansion in Shenzhen using Landsat Imagery from 1988 to 2015", *International Journal of Remote Sensing*, Vol. 38, No. 19, 2017, pp. 5388 – 5407。

---

①　UN Habitat, New York University, and Lincoln Institute of Land Policy, Various years, Atlas of Urban Expansion, http://www.atlasofurbanexpansion.org/.

②　SSB (Shenzhen Statistics Bureau and NBS Survey Office in Shenzhen), *Shenzhen Statistical Yearbook*, Beijing: China Statistics Press, 2018.

深圳 GDP 的演变（表 4-1）表明，其动态可能不一定与人口和城市增长同步，这并不奇怪。尽管像格拉泽这样的作者计算出，全球城市化增长 10% 与人均国内生产总值增长 61% 相关，他承认，"一些作者质疑这一联系的因果关系，并指出最初的城市化水平与随后的收入增长既没有正面的联系，也没有负面的联系"①。

六 城市规模

人口的新需求和商业机会的增加促进了城市工厂的发展。当然，土地供应是城市发展的自然限制之一。除此之外，城市的实体扩张是否受到限制，是否有经济衰退的风险？换句话说，是否有最佳的城市规模？对于某些经济体来说，这是至关重要的一点，因为关于城市规模的担忧总是存在。在一些以前的计划经济中，城市的"规模过大"导致了城市化的限制。但是，学者们认为，理想的城市规模很难确定，并且取决于许多因素，城市的发展背景是最重要的因素之一。②

与城市规模不同，"最佳水平"的城市集中度可以使生产率增长最大化，简化邻近城市企业之间的商品和服务交换，促进创新，并减少市民在景点之间的旅行时间。换句话说，"最佳水平"的城市集中度提高了生产率。但是，任何偏离"最佳水平"的情况都会导致生产力的损失。③ 这种"最佳集中度"因国家发展水平和规模而异。具体来说，当收入达到一定水平时，它会上升，然后下降。

---

① Glaeser, Edward L., "Cities, Productivity and Quality of Life", *Science*, Vol. 333, No. 6042, 2011, p. 593.

② Alonso, William, "The Economics of Urban Size", *Papers in Regional Science*, Vol. 26, No. 1, 1971, pp. 67-83. Davis and Henderson (2003), Albouy, David, Kristian Behrens, Frédéric Robert-Nicoud, Nathan Seegert, "The optimal distribution of population across cities", *Journal of Urban Economics*, 2018, https://doi.org/10.1016/j.jue.2018.08.004.

③ Henderson, J. Vernon, "The Effects of Urban Concentration on Economic Growth", *National Bureau of Economic Research Working Paper*, No. 7503, http://www.nber.org/papers/w7503 and Henderson, 2003.

城市集中度与收入之间关系的演变方式与威廉森假设一致，威廉森假设认为，① 城市集中度的增加是早期发展阶段的典型特征，在早期发展阶段，邻近性在促进物质资本和人力资本各组成部分之间的协同作用方面发挥着关键作用。在后一阶段，交通拥堵和将经济活动扩大到邻近地区的需要可能有利于分散。最佳集中度随国家规模的增大而减小。对区域间运输的投资至关重要，因为这降低了集中度，而且这种影响随着收入的增加而增加。此外，贸易和政治权力下放都具有影响力，尽管效果不强。由此可知，收入水平较高的城市，城市集中带来的增长损失更大。②

如本节前面所述，城市化集中度是城市经济发展的关键影响因素。由此可知，城市的规模不一定与城市的增长有关。相反，重要的是城市集中度的"质量"和城市的"有效规模"③，这对于建立集聚经济、避免人口规模造成的经济衰退和社会成本至关重要。这描绘了深圳未来发展的有趣前景。在经济特区初期，深圳在与香港接壤的相对有限的地区发展。然后扩展，包括城中村的建立。自那时以来，土地供应已成为一个主要问题。加上财富的增长以及来自移民流入的压力，房屋价格急剧上涨。现在，城市规划面临重大挑战，因为持续增长意味着要重组城市空间，以限制人口密度增加带来的负面影响。新的城市规划将深圳视为多中心城市，尽管仍然偏向于成功地促进了深圳经济增长的集聚经济，但这一规划有望减轻对前经济特区的压力。

---

① Williamson, Jeffrey G., "Regional Inequality and the Process of National Development", *Economic Development and Cultural Change*, Vol. 34, No. 4, 1968, pp. 3 – 45, as reported by Davis and Henderson (2003).

② Henderson, J. Vernon, "The Effects of Urban Concentration on Economic Growth", *National Bureau of Economic Research Working Paper*, No. 7503, http://www.nber.org/papers/w7503 and Henderson, 2003.

③ Camagni, Roberto and Roberta Capello, "Beyond Optimal City Size: An Evaluation of Alternative Urban Growth Patterns", *Urban Studies*, Vol. 37, No. 9, 2000, pp. 1479 – 1496.

七 游客——特殊的流动人口

在许多城市，旅游业只是经济部门之一。然而，与其他部门不同的是，旅游使大量人口进入城市。游客前往城市的动机不尽相同，有娱乐、办公、探亲、看病等。然而，尽管来城市的目的不尽相同，但游客与居民却共享同样的空间和资源。

旅游业一直是深圳总体规划明确的目标行业之一。[1] 如今的深圳是一个顶级旅游目的地。欧睿信息咨询有限公司数据[2]显示深圳在全球最重要的国际游客目的地中排名第十[3]，是排名第二的中国城市，仅次于香港，是中国最大的吸纳国际游客的目的地。[4] 2017年，全市旅游人数超过1200万人次，年均增长3%。[5] 根据深圳统计局的数据，2016年，酒店和餐饮服务业占深圳GDP的1.8%，增长率为2.8%。[6] 然而，旅游业的总体经济影响范围较广，评估起来也更复杂，因为旅游业还包括其他部门的间接和诱发影响，如交

---

[1] Ng, Mee K. and Wing-Shing Tang, "The Role of Planning in the Development of Shenzhen, China: Rhetoric and Realities", *Eurasian Geography and Economics*, Vol. 45, No. 3, 2004, pp. 190–211.

[2] Geert, Wouter, "Top 100 City Destinations 2018", *Euromonitor International*, 2018, https://go.euromonitor.com/white-paper-travel-2018-100-cities.

[3] "Arrivals are defined as international tourists, i.e. any person visiting another country for at least 24 hours, for a period not exceeding 12 months, and staying in paid or unpaid, collective or private accommodation. Each arrival is counted separately and includes people travelling more than once a year and people visiting several cities during one trip. Arrivals encompass all purposes of visit, such as business, leisure and visiting friends and relatives." (Geert, Wouter, "Top 100 City Destinations 2018", *Euromonitor International*, 2018, https://go.euromonitor.com/white-paper-travel-2018-100-cities.).

[4] WTTC (World Travel and Tourism Council), "Travel and Tourism. City Travel & Tourism Impact", 2018a, https://www.wttc.org/-/media/files/reports/economic-impact-research/cities-2018/city-travel--tourism-impact-2018final.pdf.

[5] Geert, Wouter, "Top 100 City Destinations 2018", *Euromonitor International*, 2018, https://go.euromonitor.com/white-paper-travel-2018-100-cities.

[6] SSB (Shenzhen Statistics Bureau and NBS Survey Office in Shenzhen), *Shenzhen Statistical Yearbook*, Beijing: China Statistics Press, 2018.

通、建筑、文化和娱乐等。例如,世界旅游委员会估计,2017年,中国旅游业的直接和总贡献占 GDP 的百分比分别为 3.3% 和 11.0%,对就业的影响分别为 3.6%(直接)和 10.3%(总计)。① 这些统计数字在 2018 年都将继续上升。

深圳游客中很大一部分为商务游客。虽然深圳不是世界顶级的休闲旅游目的地,但国际游客的数量足以说明这座城市的开放程度。多年来,深圳大力投资开发休闲景点。深圳市文化广电旅游体育局报告称,今天的深圳是"中国最重要、最具商机的旅游城市之一,被视为中国主题公园和旅游创新之都"。②

游客是一种特殊的流动人口。正如阿什沃思(Ashworth)和佩吉(Page)所言,旅游业体现在城市的方方面面,这意味着同样的城市规划原则可能也适用于旅游业。③ 但是,对游客流量的管理提出了一些要求。游客的人数、到达和停留的时间、目标和空间行为截然不同,并且超出了规划者和政府的控制范围。通常,政府主要关注的是对"游客"的管理,而不是"旅游业",因为政府行为的主要目的往往是减轻游客带来的不良影响。④ 城市规划者和地方决策者的首要目标是提高当地居民的生活水平。

旅游业是全球发展最快的产业之一。深圳已成为中国最前沿的城市之一,其经济政策还涉及将城市提升为"品牌",这确实对吸

---

① WTTC (World Travel and Tourism Council), "Travel and Tourism. Economic Impact 2018. China", 2018b, https://www.wttc.org/-/media/files/reports/economic-impact-research/countries-2018/china2018.pdf.

② SMC (Shenzhen Municipal Culture, Sports and Tourism Bureau) "Travel Guide", Shenzhen Government Online, November 21, 2018, http://english.sz.gov.cn/Travel/Guide/201811/t20181121_14603381.htm

③ Ashworth, Gregory and Stephen J. Page, "Urban tourism research: Recent progress and current paradoxes", *Tourism Management*, Vol. 32, No. 1, 2011, pp. 1 – 15.

④ Lew, Alan A., "Invited Commentary: Tourism Planning and Traditional Urban Planning Theory – the Planner as an Agent of Social Change", *Leisure/Loisir*, Vol. 31, No. 2, 2007, pp. 383 – 391. Ashworth, Gregory and Stephen J. Page, "Urban Tourism Research: Recent Progress and Current Paradoxes", *Tourism Management*, Vol. 32, No. 1, 2011, pp. 1 – 15.

引来自国外的人们前来深圳起了一定的作用。① 开发当地的旅游资源②，包括有形和无形资源，是深圳在世界市场上巩固城市地位的又一举措。保持其作为世界旅游目的地的独特性和以"迪斯尼化"③的方式复制其他标准旅游模式和景点类型，如何平衡二者之间的关系，是深圳发展旅游业面临的一个重大挑战。

八 规划与寻求可持续性

尽管深圳的扩张导致了众所周知的爆炸性经济增长，但关于城市扩张导致的诸多社会问题仍然存在。如上文所述，人口和经济增长具有直接关系，除非每个公民都享有资源，才能避免经济衰退。集聚成本是集聚经济的消极一面，是"为接近其他人而付出的代价"④。这让人想起当前关于城市增长质量的争论。大城市人口爆炸性增长现象带来的经济、社会和环境方面的治理方式日益受到关注。犯罪和污染、不平等和社会排斥、拥挤和城市服务质量下降，这些只是城市作为"[除了]生产力场所和娱乐场所"的一些负面例子。⑤ 一些实践确实有助于实现这一目标，尽管规划者已经表明，一些模型独特、难以复制。

为了将城市的新需求和紧迫需求与可持续性结合起来，城市规划者在解决增长过程中的问题方面发挥着至关重要的作用。⑥ 坎贝

---

① Shen, Jianfa and Gordon Kee, "Shenzhen: Innovation and Governments' Roles in Reform and Development", In *Development and Planning in Seven Major Coastal Cities in Southern and Eastern China*, Cham: Springer International Publishing, 2017.

② Scuderi, Raffaele, "Editorial. Special Focus: Local Resources for Tourism – from Impact to Growth", *Tourism Economics*, Vol. 24, No. 3, 2017, pp. 294–296.

③ Ashworth, Gregory and Stephen J. Page, "Urban Tourism Research: Recent Progress and Current Paradoxes", *Tourism Management*, Vol. 32, No. 1, 2011, pp. 1–15.

④ Glaeser, Edward L., "Cities, Productivity and Quality of Life", *Science*, Vol. 333, No. 6042, 2011, p. 593.

⑤ Glaeser, Edward L., "Cities, Productivity and Quality of Life", *Science*, Vol. 333, No. 6042, 2011, p. 593.

⑥ UN-Habitat. *Draft strategic plan* 2014–2019 *of the United Nations Human Settlements Programme*, 2013, https://unhabitat.org/un-habitats-strategic-plan-2014-2019/.

尔模型①是最著名的可持续规划理论之一，很好地总结了城市可持续设计规划的基本原则。该理论确定了规划的三个关键优先事项，即社会公正、经济增长和环境保护。所谓的"坎贝尔三角形"将它们表示为等边三角形的拐角，其重心是可持续发展，而平等是最顶角，中心是三个维度之间的平衡点。从该点开始的任何移动都将使其更接近三角形的边之一。每一面代表两个维度之间的潜在冲突。当社会正义与经济增长和效率发生冲突时，就会由于公共利益与私人利益之间的利益分歧而引发财产冲突。经济利益可能会干扰环境保护，从而引发自然资源开发的冲突。当社会正义与环境保护形成对比时，发展冲突便凸显出来。该模型具有深刻的启发意义，因为它将可持续发展视为脆弱的条件和难以实现的目标，因为偏离均衡可能会引起冲突。

  其他撰稿人强调了城市在促进可持续发展方面的关键作用。除此之外，卡玛尼和他的合著者强调了城市不同维度之间的互动以及实现可持续发展的重要性②，这是"一个动态、平衡和适应性的进化过程，即确保平衡使用和管理经济发展的自然环境基础"③。可持续发展的城市将环境放在首位，因为这样做会在某种程度上忽略与集聚相关的协同作用。相反，三种环境——物质环境（包括建筑环境和自然环境）、经济环境和社会环境，是共存和相互作用的。在静态意义上，它们产生了正面和负面外部效应。它们平衡的动态协同进化可能会促进分配效率和地域认同（当社会环境整合经济环境时），长期分配和地域效率（经济与物质效率）以及环境公平性和地域质量（社会和物质）。"好"城市是指以利润为导向，支持各个方面长期且可持续的发展目标。应处理空间规划问题，提供足够工具来实现可持续性，

---

  ① Campbell, Scott, "Green Cities, Growing Cities, Just Cities? Urban Planning and the Contradictions of Sustainable Development", *Journal of the American Planning Association*, Vol. 62, No. 3, 1996, pp. 296 – 312.

  ② Camagni, Roberto, Roberta Capello, and Peter Nijkamp, "Towards sustainable city policy: an economy – environment technology nexus", *Ecological Economics*, Vol. 24, No. 1, 1998, pp. 103 – 118. Camagni, Roberto, Maria C. Gibelli, and Paolo Rigamonti, "Urban Mobility and Urban form: The Social and Environmental Costs of Different Patterns of Urban Expansion", *Ecological Economics*, Vol. 40, No. 2, 2002, pp. 199 – 216.

  ③ Nijkamp, Peter and Adriaan Perrels, *Sustainable Cities in Europe*, London: Earthscan, 1994, cited by Camagni et al. (1998), p. 105.

后者应为前者设定目标。①

理论表明，评价一个城市是否达到可持续、协调的发展模式②，必须考虑到几个方面，每个方面都涉及社会、经济和环境发展的三个基本领域。有几种方法可以评估一个城市是否已进入可持续发展模式。为此，有一套好的指标往往是一个重要的起点。深圳统计局提供了丰富的信息③，尽管这些信息主要涉及深圳的经济。在接下来的内容中，笔者将尝试对可持续性的一些方面进行概述。

郑等的研究试图根据中国城市的绿化程度对城市进行排名，作者估计深圳在74个城市中排名46位。④ 深圳市政府已经做出了几项努力，以减少对环境的负面影响。继2008年国务院发布《关于促进节约集约用地的通知》后，深圳率先采取新政策，改善城市环境。⑤ 深圳也是中国第一个采取碳排放交易计划的城市，以期降低碳排放强度，提高能源利用效率，该计划于2013年6月18日生效。⑥ 所有这些都与中国政府2014年3月推出的新城市化计划不谋而合，该计划旨在通过户口制度改革⑦来改善城市和社会的环境条件。从社会角度

---

① Camagni, Roberto, "Integrated Spatial Planning: Why and How?", In *Seminal Studies in Regional and Urban Economics*, Roberta Capello eds., Cham: Springer International Publishing, 2017.

② Mendola, Daria and Raffaele Scuderi, "Assessing the Beneficial Effects of Economic Growth: The Harmonic Growth Index", In *Advanced Statistical Methods for the Analysis of Large Data – Sets*, Agostino Di Ciaccio, Mauro Coli, and Jose M. Angulo Ibanez eds. Heidelberg – Berlin: Springer, 2012.

③ SSB (Shenzhen Statistics Bureau and NBS Survey Office in Shenzhen), *Shenzhen Statistical Yearbook*, Beijing: China Statistics Press, 2018.

④ Zheng, Siqi, Rui Wang, Edward L. Glaeser and Matthew E. Kahn, "The Greenness of China: Household Carbon Dioxide Emissions and Urban Development", *National Bureau of Economic Research Working Paper*, No. 15621, 2009. http://www.nber.org/papers/w15621

⑤ Lew, Alan A., "Invited Commentary: Tourism Planning and Traditional Urban Planning Theory – the Planner as an Agent of Social Change", *Leisure/Loisir*, Vol. 31, No. 2, 2007, pp. 383 – 391.

⑥ Jiang, Jing J., Bin Ye, and Xiao Ming Ma, "The construction of Shenzhen's carbon emission trading scheme", *Energy Policy*, Vol. 75, 2014, pp. 17 – 21.

⑦ Cheshmehzangi, Ali, "China's New – Type Urbanisation Plan (NUP) and the Foreseeing Challenges for Decarbonization of Cities: A Review", *Energy Procedia*, Vol. 104, 2016, pp. 146 – 152. Hong'e, Mo, "China to adopt more flexible policies for hukou registrations in cities." ECNS. cn, March 14, 2018. http://www.ecns.cn/cns – wire/2018/03 – 14/295700.shtml.

来看，可持续增长面临的主要挑战包括缩小移民和居民之间的差距，不仅在收入不平等方面，还包括获得社会福利的机会。

深圳市数据统计局显示了近段时间相关环境指标改善的数量。[①]能源的利用效率有所提高。2005—2016 年，单位国内生产总值能耗和电耗均稳步下降。同时，二氧化硫、二氧化氮、可吸入颗粒物、工业二氧化硫、工业氮氧化物等主要污染物也有所减少，但近年来工业废气排放量有所增加。此外，2011—2016 年，民用机动车的数量从 1976164 辆增加到 3225879 辆，增加了 63%，加大了尾气排放和交通拥堵的压力。交通走廊和主要干线是城市扩张的主要决定因素。鼓励公共交通形式和对不开车的激励措施将有助于减轻对环境的影响。最新的城市总体规划所设想的城市多中心发展可能会缓解一些地区的拥挤。但是，加强可持续的交通系统建设是减少私家车使用和改善环境质量的基础。

---

① SSB（Shenzhen Statistics Bureau and NBS Survey Office in Shenzhen），*Shenzhen Statistical Yearbook*，Beijing：China Statistics Press，2018.

第五章　基本服务和当地基础设施

一　介绍

当今人类面临的最大的全球性挑战包括世界人口的迅速增长、资源消耗、二氧化碳排放的不断增加，以及气候变化对全球生态平衡的影响。

尽管人类的生态足迹已经超过地球的生物容量1.7倍①，但世界人口预计将从目前的76亿（2018年），到2100年增加到112亿②，加剧资源短缺和气候变化，从而对人民生活尤其是经济脆弱国家的人民生活产生重大影响。除了政治和社会冲突外，经济因素也可能进一步助长世界范围内的移民流动。世界范围内城市化趋势的扩大和城市的迅猛发展值得特别关注。

今天，世界上已有超过50%的人口居住在城市里。到2050年，这一比例预计将增加到近70%。③ 在应对快速增长这一巨大挑战的同时，面向未来和可持续发展的城市必须比以往任何时候都要在社会、环境和经济方面保持均衡发展。社会福利，包括医疗保健、社会保障、教育和就业，直接关系到一个城市的环境和经济质量，如清洁的空气和水、适当的住房、充足的交通基础设施和稳定的

---

① https：//www.footprintnetwork.org/our－work/ecological－footprint/, accessed 23 January, 2019

② https：//www.un.org/development/desa/en/news/population/world－population－prospects－2017.html, accessed 23 January, 2019.

③ https：//www.un.org/development/desa/publications/2018－revision－of－world－urbanization－prospects.html, accessed 23 January, 2019.

经济。

为推动全球范围内城市的成功转型、实现可持续的未来发展，必须注重与生态系统息息相关的影响，满足人类的生活需要，如防止极端天气，打造安全且健康的生活环境，提供能源、粮食和交通等（图5-1）。

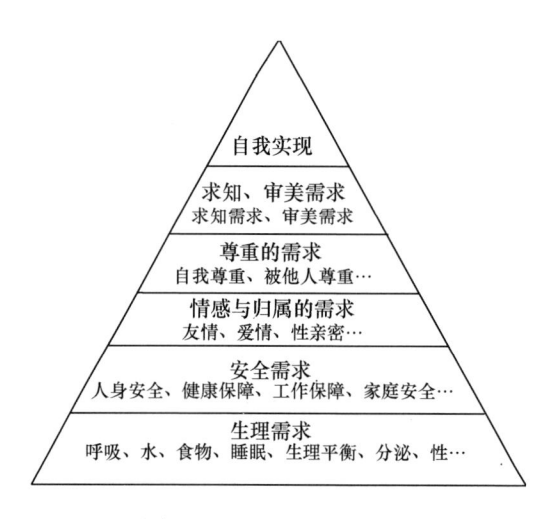

图5-1 马斯洛需求层次

自我实现

求知、审美需求
求知需求、审美需求

尊重的需求
自我尊重、被他人尊重…

情感与归属的需求
友情、爱情、性亲密…

安全需求
人身安全、健康保障、工作保障、家庭安全…

生理需求
呼吸、水、食物、睡眠、生理平衡、分泌、性…

资料来源：https://mrjoe.uk/maslows-hierarchy-needs-psychology-myth-busting-1/, accessed 27 January, 2019.

人类活动和相关基础设施系统与地球生态系统的相互作用不容忽视，包括生物圈、大气圈、水圈和土壤圈（图5-2）。为此，从根本上调整战略方向，在稳定生态系统的同时保卫人类的生活条件刻不容缓。

为了应对这些挑战，本章将着重于基本服务的可持续供应，如能源、交通运输、水和绿色基础设施等服务，旨在提高对不同城市基础设施部门重要性的认识。通过深圳与亚洲和欧洲其他城市的现状对比，提供基于指标的信息，并分析如何进一步发展城市基础设施系统以提高深圳人民的生活质量和城市的可持续性，最后将总结研究结果，为深圳成为中国南方可持续发展中心指明前景。

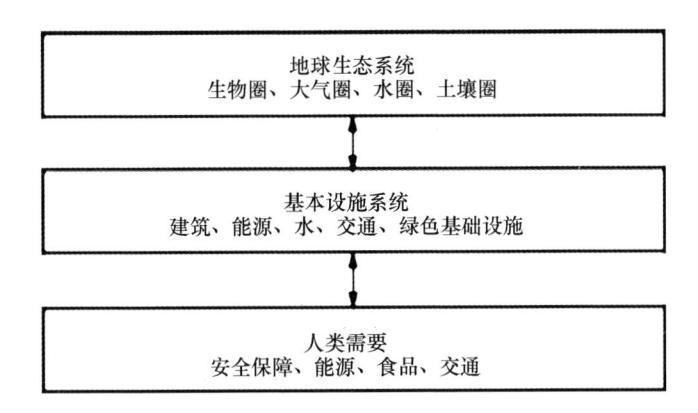

```
┌─────────────────────────────┐
│     地球生态系统              │
│  生物圈、大气圈、水圈、土壤圈  │
└─────────────────────────────┘
              ↕
┌─────────────────────────────┐
│     基本设施系统              │
│ 建筑、能源、水、交通、绿色基础设施 │
└─────────────────────────────┘
              ↕
┌─────────────────────────────┐
│      人类需要                 │
│  安全保障、能源、食品、交通    │
└─────────────────────────────┘
```

图5-2 基础设施系统、人类需求的满意程度以及与生态系统的互动

二 城市可持续发展评价指标

可持续发展在1987年联合国的《布伦特兰报告》[①]（也称《我们的共同未来》）中被定义为"在不损害子孙后代满足自身需要的能力的情况下满足当前需求的发展"。纵观本章开头提到的当前全球挑战，显然真正的可持续发展的确受到一些限制，这些都是由人类活动和由此产生的环境资源消耗、排放物和废物以及生物圈吸收废弃物的能力所造成的。虽然基本服务的提供，如能源、交通运输、水以及由绿色基础设施提供的生态系统服务，对生活在地球上的所有人来说不可或缺，但提供这些服务所需的资源消耗对城市的影响远远大于农村地区。

以深圳为例，深圳人口密度约为每平方公里6000人（2017年），是全国平均水平的41倍。[②] 由于这种大规模集中，基本需求

---

① http://www.un-documents.net/our-common-future.pdf, accessed January 27, 2019.

② http://www.szdaily.com/content/2017-05/23/content_16283983.htm, accessed January 27, 2019.

的提供严重依赖于周边地区，这种依赖性造成了城市的高度脆弱性。

此外，由于高浓度的排放物、大量的热量，以及废物和废水，建筑运作所产生的资源消耗、交通运输、生产及其他因素对于城市人口密集地区的影响更为明显。

鉴于提供基本服务的重要性，如能源、交通运输、水和绿色基础设施提供的生态系统服务，评价城市可持续发展的指标直接关系到这些服务的可持续提供，"而不损害子孙后代满足其需求的能力"①。

纵观资源消耗以及其产生的排放物和废物的现状，中国的生态足迹②目前为人均2.5 gha③，低于世界人均2.7 gha的水平，但仍大于世界1.7 gha的人均生物承载力④。如果都像中国人一样生活，我们将需要1.5个地球。

以深圳市为例，2011年深圳市人均生态足迹（2.5gha）相当于全国平均水平，人均生态承载力约为0.06gha。这意味着生态足迹大约是生态承载力的41.7倍。⑤

正如联合国人居署所称，城市是导致气候变化的主要因素。城市仅占地球表面的2%，却消耗着全球78%的能源，由于能源生产、汽车、工业和生物质利用，超过60%的二氧化碳和大量其他温室气体都

---

① http://www.un-documents.net/our-common-future.pdf, accessed January 27, 2019.

② The Ecological Footprint measures the ecological assets that a given population requires to produce the natural resources it consumes (including plant-based food and fibre products, livestock and fish products, timber and other forest products, space for urban infrastructure) and to absorb its waste, especially carbon emissions. See: https://www.footprintnetwork.org/our-work/ecological-footprint/, accessed January 27, 2019.

③ https://www.zujiwangluo.org/ecological-footprint-results/, accessed January 27, 2019.

④ A city, state or nation's bio capacity represents the productivity of its ecological assets (including cropland, grazing land, forest land, fishing grounds, and built-up land). These areas, especially if left unharvested, can also absorb much of the waste we generate, especially our carbon emissions.

⑤ G. L. Ou and S. K. Tan, "Study on Sustainable Use of Land Based on Ecological Footprint Model: A Case of Shenzhen", *Applied Mechanics and Materials*, Vols. 295-298, 2013, pp. 2551-2556.

来源于城市。①

在像深圳这样的人口密集的城市中，生态足迹和生物承载力明显失衡，资源消耗及废气废物排放需要从源头进行转变。

开始和实现向可持续发展的转变，必须考虑到生态系统及其子系统（生物圈、大气圈、水圈和土壤圈）的承载力，并对目前和未来在能源、水、原材料、土壤方面的资源需求，以及城市基础设施系统产生的污染物和废弃物进行分析。

为了给有效的城市转型战略提供坚实的基础，并就可支配的资源采取可持续的利用模式，需要对当前和未来的资源需求以及长期的资源提供能力进行详细的评估。同时，必须记录资源消耗产生的环境影响，并将其与生态系统的恢复力极限进行比较。这涉及以下基础设施系统及其与生物圈、大气层、水圈和土壤圈的相互作用。

纵观一个城市的生态足迹及其人口生产所消耗的自然资源所需的生态资产，能源消耗和由此产生的温室气体（GHG）排放是影响气候变化最重要的因素之一，威胁着生物圈以及地球上的所有生物。

因此，评价一个城市可持续性的最重要指标之一是一次能源消费和相关的温室气体排放，特别是在中国，能源生产大多以化石燃料为基础②，导致温室气体排放量居高不下。虽然这涉及工业、交通、住宅、商业和公共服务以及农业等多个部门，但本章将主要围绕建筑和交通部门的能源消耗展开。

除了能源消耗之外，饮用水的供应和处理对于人类生活，以及植物和动物的生存，也十分重要。

城市绿色基础设施（UGI）可通过遮阴和蒸散调节城市环境的微气候，并在暴雨天气时吸收雨水，因此必须把城市绿色基础设施视为推动城市可持续发展的重要驱动因素。

（一）能源供应系统

能源对于维持城市生活至关重要。粮食和货物的生产、水的供应、建筑物、基础设施和运输系统的建造和运作以及工商业活动的运

---

① https：//unhabitat.org/urban-themes/climate-change/，accessed January 27, 2019.
② https：//www.iea.org/weo/china/，accessed January 27, 2019.

转都依赖于大量能源的稳定供应。根据联合国人居署的数据，城市消耗了约75%的全球一次能源，排放了约80%的全球温室气体，其中包括城市居民产生的间接排放。①

2017年，中国全球一次能源总消费量为135.112亿公吨石油当量，目前正以2.2%/年的速度增长。② 中国的石油当量为3.132亿公吨，约占23.2%，目前正以每年30.1%的速度增长。

在中国，能源主要由煤炭（60.4%）、石油（19.4%）、天然气（6.6%）和核能（1.8%）产生。只有12%的能源是由可再生能源生产的，如水力（8.3%）和其他形式的可再生能源（3.4%），包括太阳能、风能和地热。中国二氧化碳排放量为923.26万吨，占全球二氧化碳排放量的27.6%③，人均二氧化碳排放量为7.1吨。

为了克服温室气体排放对生态系统的破坏性影响，结束城市对进口和使用矿物燃料的依赖，向可持续的能源形式过渡，如太阳能、风能、水能和地热能的开发刻不容缓。供应方的低碳技术必须与需求方的低能耗系统相结合，以减少污染和温室气体排放，从而提高城市的生活质量。

（二）交通与运输

移动使我们能够与他人互动，并满足我们的日常需求，从家到城市的各个地方，包括工作、教育、文化、购物和休闲的场所。相应的交通基础设施，包括人行道、自行车道、街道、道路和铁路，使我们能够利用非机动车辆和机动车辆四处移动、运输货物。

2010年，中国交通部门的二氧化碳排放量约占总排放量的10%④，与工业生产和其他部门相比，机动车产生的二氧化碳排放量似乎相对较低。然而，珠江三角洲交通部门的二氧化碳排放量从2000

---

① https://unhabitat.org/urban-themes/energy/, accessed 20 January, 2019.
② https://www.bp.com/content/dam/bp/en/corporate/pdf/energy-economics/statistical-review/bp-stats-review-2018-full-report.pdf, accessed 23 January 2019.
③ Ibid..
④ CO_2 EMISSIONS FROM FUEL COMBUSTION Highlights (2018 edition), International Energy Agency. Paris, France.

年的 13.1 公吨增加到了 2013 年的 74.0 公吨[1]，这也表明了降低对交通依赖的必要性。

除了日益严重的交通拥堵和尾气废物排放（包括二氧化碳、氮氧化物、颗粒物和噪声）外，还必须考虑机动车保有量的潜在增长。2015 年深圳机动车保有量为 230 万辆，平均 1000 人中拥有 296 辆机动车[2]。

考虑到对环境的影响，必须鼓励步行、骑自行车以及使用公共交通工具的出行方式，从而确保城市环境的宜居性。机动车产生的负面影响包括过度使用土地，由汽油和柴油驱动的汽车及卡车造成的噪声和污染，降低其负面影响是可持续交通政策的目标。要实现城市可持续发展，不仅需要优化交通基础设施和建筑环境，还必须改善城市绿色基础设施建设。

（三）水供应

与快速增长的大城市所面临的可持续能源供应的挑战相比，安全的饮用水的可持续供应以及废水的收集和处理同样重要。

由于城市的快速发展，特别是在亚洲等地区，建筑物和相关的交通基础设施使城市地区和周围的水系统和土壤条件发生了根本性的变化。尽管全球有足够的淡水满足每个公民的个人和家庭需求，但全球有 11% 的人口仍然无法获得安全的水资源。[3]

特别是在发展中国家人口稠密的城市地区，仍然面临着严峻挑战。例如，由于缺乏足够的卫生设施而造成的污水，导致现有水资源受到污染，从而对城市人口的健康和福祉造成严重威胁。

因此，提供清洁安全的饮用水，并通过水循环利用技术等对城市废水加以有效处理，是城市基础设施系统中至关重要的一环。

---

[1] Li, L., Structure and influencing factors of CO_2 emissions from transport sector in three major metropolitan regions of China: estimation and decomposition. Transportation (2017). https://doi.org/10.1007/s11116-017-9827-6, accessed 23 January 2019.

[2] Urban Mobility in China. Manz W., Elgendy H., Berger J., Bo hringer J., Institute for Mobility Research, Karlsruhe, Germany, 2017.

[3] https://unhabitat.org/urban-themes/water-and-sanitation-2/, accessed 20 January, 2019.

为了最大限度地减少城市地区的水足迹，这些地区通常严重依赖于从城市周围地区提供清洁用水，必须采取相应的节水措施，建立有效的净水系统。废水处理有望缓解水资源紧张，因此，必须重视废水处理，尽可能减少饮用水的消耗。[①]

在利用城市绿色基础设施提高城市生活质量方面，除了家庭用水外，水的供应和管理至关重要。没有足够的水，就不可能提供关键的生态系统服务，如冷却、遮阴以及食物供应。

（四）城市绿色基础设施

规模更大、更密集的城市必须应对日益严重的空气、噪声和水污染，更密集的城市空间，热岛以及热浪造成的更高死亡率。由于排放、生产、建筑运营和机动车辆产生的热量高度集中，城市热岛与周围人口较少的地区相比[②]，白天气温可能上升3℃，夜间气温可能上升12℃。由于深圳属于亚热带气候，其气温可能会上升，并产生负面影响，如空调费用上涨、空气污染加重和温室气体排放增加。[③] 此外，人口可能面临与高温有关的疾病和更高的死亡率，以及由于洪水和其他因素而导致的水质变差。

人口稠密城市地区的生活质量越来越依赖于城市的绿色基础设施。因为气候变化的影响，如气温升高，将对人口稠密的大城市产生巨大影响，尤其是像深圳这样位于亚热带和热带气候的城市。

城市绿色基础设施可以通过遮阴和蒸散调节城市环境的微气候，并在暴雨天气时吸收雨水，其作用不可小觑。其他因素包括促进生物多样性、提升关系人类健康的其他方面，如文化服务，包括娱乐、审美和陶冶情操等活动。虽然城市生态系统可以有效提高城市系统的可持续性和恢复力，但制定一种更广泛的办法来应对城市化

---

① Li, Wenjiang, Li, Linjun, Qiu, Guoyu, "Energy Consumption and Economic Cost of Typical Wastewater Treatment Systems in Shenzhen", *China. Journal of Cleaner Production*, Vol. 163, Supplement, 1 October 2017, pp. 374 – 378.

② https：//www.epa.gov/heat – islands, accessed January 27, 2019.

③ Ibid. .

的全球挑战迫在眉睫，因为目前城市更加紧凑化，即在保持城市规模的情况下人口密度增加，这给现有的城市绿色基础设施带来了巨大压力，导致了城市生物多样性的减少和生态系统服务质量的下降。

三　深圳的基础服务和地方基础设施：衡量成功与促进可持续发展

前几部分表明，城市基础设施系统对于城市居民的健康和生产生活至关重要，特别是在深圳等快速发展的大城市。

通过对现有城市基础设施体系现状的分析和探讨，明确目标，并制定相应的改善策略，可以为深圳迈向真正可持续发展的城市提供支撑。

将深圳的现状与中国和欧洲其他城市进行比较也是分析过程的一部分，这可以帮助在制定和实施可持续发展目标的战略方面吸取经验教训。"城市可持续发展指数"（USI）便是一个很好的例子，USI 是一个对中国城市可持续性进行评估的工具，在 2011 年中国发布了第一份关于中国城市的社会、环境、经济以及与资源相关的报告，基于社会民生、清洁程度、建成环境、经济发展和资源利用五个类别。

在 USI 报告中，2011 年深圳排名第六，2013 年排名第二，2017 年排名第一，说明了相关指标对促进面向未来的可持续城市积极发展的重要意义。

本节旨在分析可持续地提供基本服务需采用的战略、方法和技术，如能源、水和公共交通的供应，以及在诸如深圳的城市环境中创造和维持质量生活所需的相关技术和绿色基础设施。可持续地提供这些基本服务的主要目标是：尽量减少甚至避免与资源消耗、排放或土壤封闭有关的负面环境影响，最大限度地发挥绿色基础设施对城市气候和内部水流调节的积极影响。

本部分主要从能源供应、交通运输、供水和绿色基础设施四个核心方面对深圳城市基础设施的现状进行描述。

本章将深圳的数据与香港和新加坡的数据进行了比较,这两个城市的地理和气候情况与深圳相似,但政治形态与地形存在差异。除此之外,本章还提供了德国柏林的数据,以了解不同的政治、地理、文化和气候条件对资源效率及其他与可持续发展有关因素的影响。

除了与深圳气候相似外,香港和新加坡是衡量可持续发展的最好的案例,据可持续城市指数(SCI)[①]的最新报告,香港和新加坡在亚洲地区的可持续城市中分别排名第二和第一。

香港毗邻深圳,二者都位于珠江三角洲,因此在城市发展和资源利用方面存在许多相似之处。新加坡作为一个国家城市,在城市管理和资源管理方面拥有更为全面的体系。

同时,作为亚洲以外地区的一个案例研究,柏林对于揭示在不同背景下实现可持续发展的途径具有重要意义。下文对四个城市的各项相关指标进行比较,对各参数和各城市表现的客观评估将为深圳的发展提供合理化的建议。

(一) 一般信息

在比较基础设施指标之前,需要对这些城市建成环境的一些基本信息进行阐明,这些信息与城市的基础设施要求相关。进入千禧年后,四个城市的土地面积增幅较小(图 5-3)。其中,深圳土地面积最大,几乎是柏林的两倍,深圳 2016 年土地面积为 1997 平方公里,柏林 2016 年为 1106 平方公里。最小的城市是新加坡,面积仅为 720 平方公里。

虽然 2000 年至 2016 年四个城市的土地面积几乎保持稳定,但所有城市的人口增长率都相当高,特别是深圳,人口从 2000 年的 700 万增长到 2016 年的 1190 万,增长了 70%,而且根据图 5-4,深圳人口仍在急剧增长。相比之下,千禧年初,香港和深圳人口数量相似,有 670 万人,但当时只有大约 66.5 万人迁入城市。虽然新

---

① https://www.arcadis.com/en/global/our-perspectives/sustainable-cities-index-2018/citizen-centric-cities/.

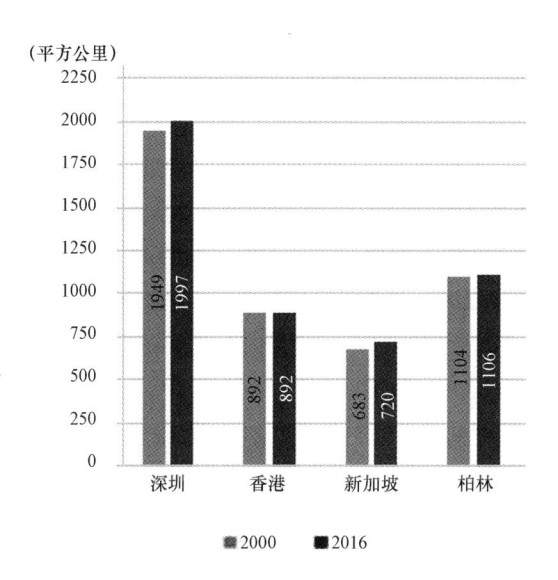

图 5-3　2000—2016 年四个城市土地面积

资料来源：《深圳统计年鉴》、《香港统计年刊》、新加坡统计局（www.singstat.gov.sg）和柏林－勃兰登堡统计局（www.statistik-berlin-brandenburg.de）。

加坡 40% 的增长率远远超过香港，人口增长量为 200 万，总人口数仅为 580 万。柏林的人口增长速度相对较慢，在这一时期，柏林的人口增长率仅为 5%，新增人口不足 20 万人。

四个城市的人口增长都导致了城市空间密度的增加。图 5-5 显示，2001 年深圳的城市密度仅为 3717 人/平方公里，略低于柏林（3799 人/平方公里）。然而，深圳在 2016 年跃升至 5962 人/平方公里，而柏林同期只有 4000 多人/平方公里。2001 年，香港和新加坡的城市密度已经很高，大约 6060 人/平方公里，而在 2004 年之后新加坡的人口增长率飙升，在 2016 年人口密度达到了 7791 人/平方公里。同时，香港的人口密度每平方公里仅增加了约 600 人，2016 年达到 6670 人/平方公里。

1. 能源供应

作为人口最多的城市，2015 年，深圳与新加坡的能源消耗分别

(千人)

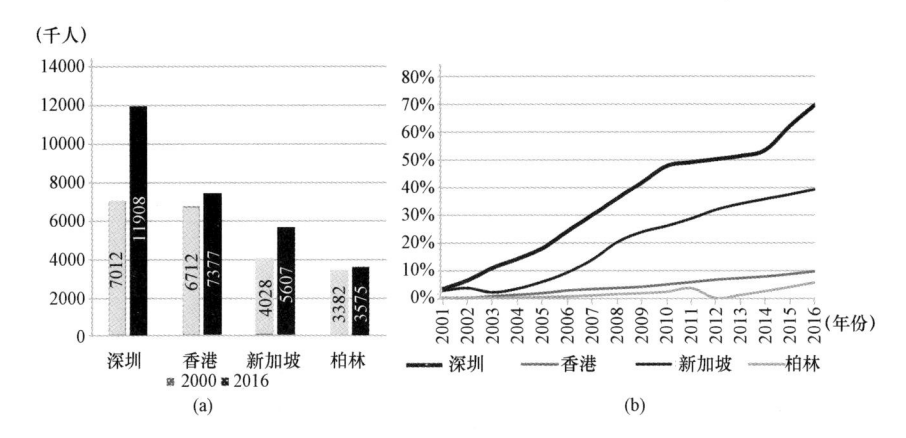

图 5-4 四个城市的人口（a）及其与 2000 年相比的增长率（b）

资料来源：《深圳统计年鉴》、《香港统计年刊》、新加坡统计局（www.singstat.gov.sg）和柏林-勃兰登堡统计局（www.statistik-berlin-brandenburg.de）。

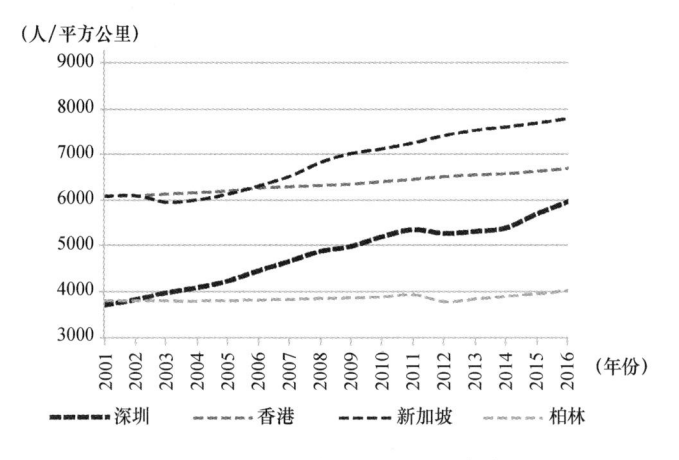

图 5-5 四个城市的人口密度

为 3910 万 TCE[①] 和 2180 万 TCE，深圳几乎是新加坡的两倍（图 5-6）。2010 年至 2015 年，深圳和新加坡的能源需求增长率高于其他城市。2015 年的一次能源消耗与 2010 年相比，柏林的能源消耗呈下降趋势，减少了超过 15 万 TCE。

---

① Tons of standard coal equivalent.

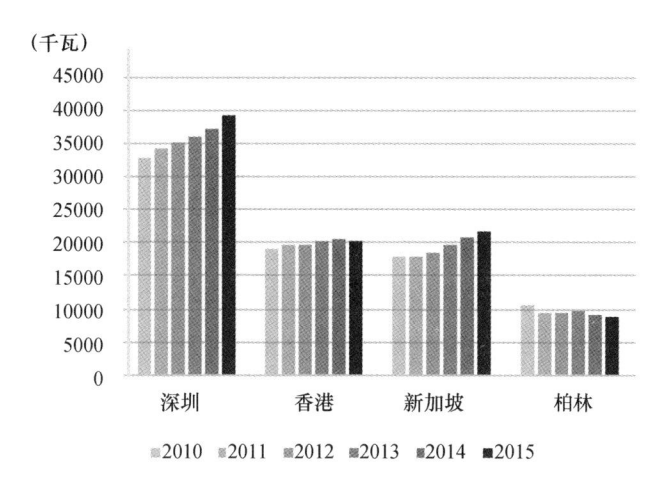

图 5-6　2010—2015 年一次能源需求

虽然一次能源需求的差异可以很容易地用这些城市总人口的差异来解释，但与单位国内生产总值的总能耗相比，情况就更清楚了（图 5-7）。2010 年，深圳消费 223 TCE/百万美元，几乎是香港、新加坡和柏林的 3 倍。2015 年，深圳单位国内生产总值的总能耗降至 149 TCE/百万美元。虽然进步明显，但同期香港和柏林仅为 63 TCE/百万美元，新加坡为 70 TCE/百万美元。

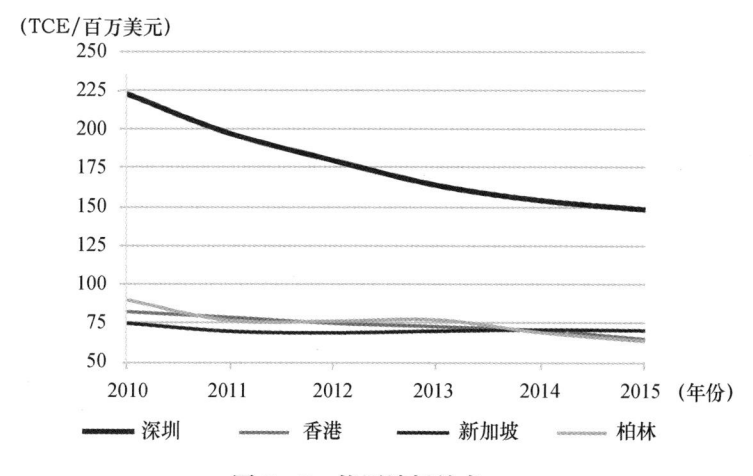

图 5-7　能源消耗效率

尽管深圳为实现国内生产总值而消耗的能源比其他3个城市多，但人均能源消耗（ECc）仍低于新加坡。2015年这两个城市的人均能源消耗（ECc）分别为3.44吨和3.94吨（图5-8）。自2012年以来，新加坡出现了异常增长的趋势，而其他城市的人均能源消耗在2013年之后有所下降。2015年，柏林居民人均能源消耗仅为2.55吨，比香港少0.2吨。

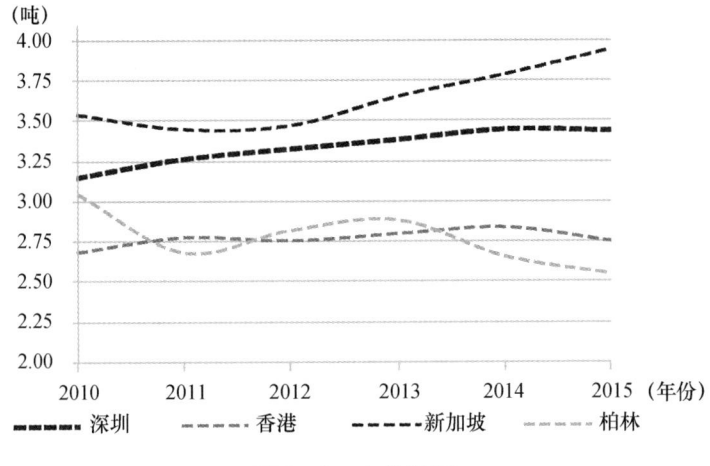

图5-8 人均能耗

资料来源：《深圳统计年鉴》、《香港统计年刊》、新加坡统计局（www.singstat.gov.sg）和柏林-勃兰登堡统计局（www.statistik-berlin-brandenburg.de）。

如图5-9所示，四个城市实现能源供应的来源不尽相同。2013年，电力占深圳总的能源消耗比例较大，其中大部分由核能①供应。香港也在一定程度上从内地进口电力资源。然而，2015年，香港的能源供应主要依赖于煤和石油，分别占47.50%和45.75%。石油是新加坡最重要的能源，2015年占63.69%；其次是天然气，占34.15%。柏林的石油（36.2%）和天然气（30.2%）的份额几乎持平；其次是煤炭（19.8%）和电力（9.8%）。柏林的可再生能源使用比例最高（4%），虽然占比不大。2015年，深圳可再生能源份额为1.1%，主要来自垃圾发电厂。

---

① Tons of standard coal equivalent.

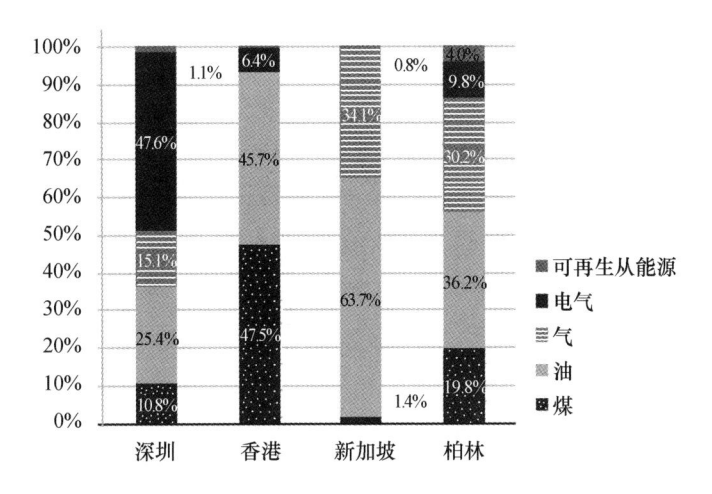

图 5 – 9 2015 年能源供应来源分配

资料来源：深圳市碳减排路径研究（Foundation, G. L. – C. D. and P. U. S. G. School, Research on carbon emission reduction route for Shenzhen 2017，Energy Foundation：http：// www. efchina. org/Reports – zh/report – 20170710 – 2 – zh，p. 156.)，深圳市能源发展"十三五"规划，《香港统计年刊》，香港机电工程署（www. emsd. gov. hk），新加坡能源市场管理局（www. ema. gov. sg）和柏林 – 勃兰登堡统计局（www. statistik – berlin – brandenburg. de）。

在 2001 年至 2016 年总用电量上，香港的能源需求较为稳定，为 450 亿千瓦时/年（图 5 – 10）。柏林的总电量也几乎稳定，约为 140 亿千瓦时。相比之下，深圳总用电量增长迅速，从 2001 年的 210 亿千瓦时增加到 2016 年的约 850 亿千瓦时。新加坡从 2005 年的约 350 亿千瓦时增加到 2016 年的 500 亿千瓦时。

与总用电量趋势类似，深圳市人均用电量从 2001 年的 487 千瓦时增加到 2016 年的 1128 千瓦时（图 5 – 11），但人均用电量明显低于香港、新加坡、柏林 3 个城市。柏林是近年来人均用电量唯一下降的城市，约 1200 千瓦时，几乎与 2001 年的水平持平。2016 年，香港人均用电量超过 1600 千瓦时，为四城市中人均用电量最高的城市。其次是新加坡，人均用电量为 1353 千瓦时。

发电量方面，2015 年深圳发电量的 46.86% 来自当地核电站，其次是天然气，占 36.75%（图 5 – 12）。2015 年，煤炭为香港电力生产的主要来源，占 65.3%；其次是石油，占 24.8%。新加坡

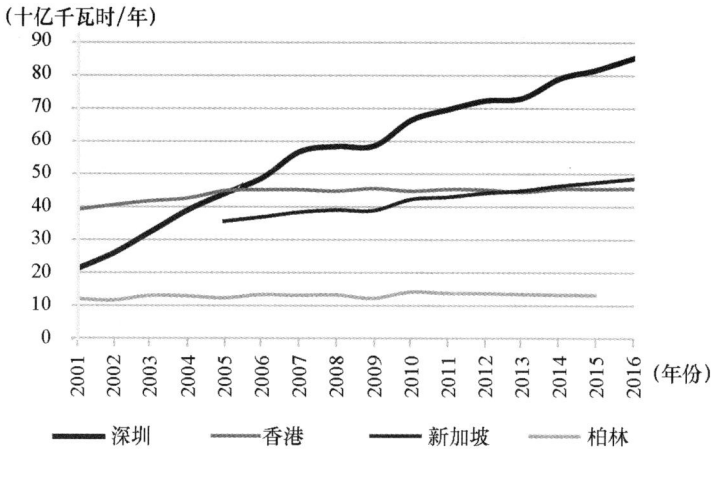

图 5-10　总用电量

资料来源：《深圳统计年鉴》、《香港统计年刊》、新加坡统计局（www.singstat.gov.sg）和柏林－勃兰登堡统计局（www.statistik-berlin-brandenburg.de）。

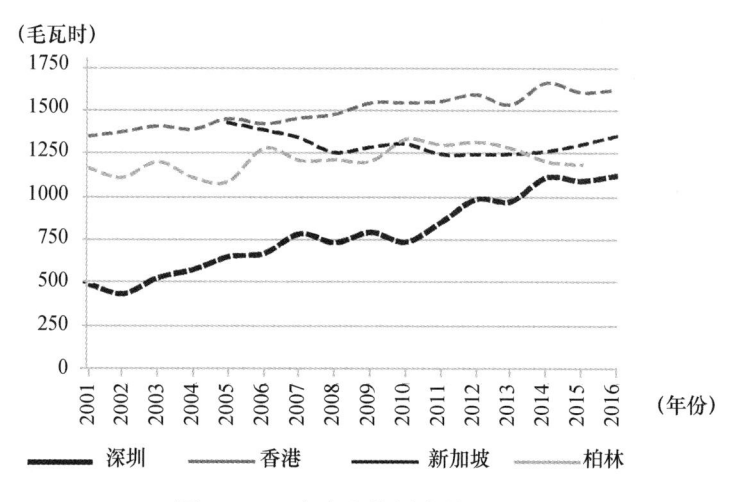

图 5-11　家庭人均用电量

资料来源：《深圳统计年鉴》、《香港统计年刊》、新加坡统计局（www.singstat.gov.sg）和柏林－勃兰登堡统计局（www.statistik-berlin-brandenburg.de）。

95.3%的电力来自天然气，剩下的大部分电力供应来自可再生能源。柏林的电力来源构成为煤炭（20.4%）、石油（36.5%）、天然气（29.6%）和可再生能源（13.5%）。在不久的将来，柏林将大力发展可再生能源，这对于减少温室气体排放来说是一个正确的方向。

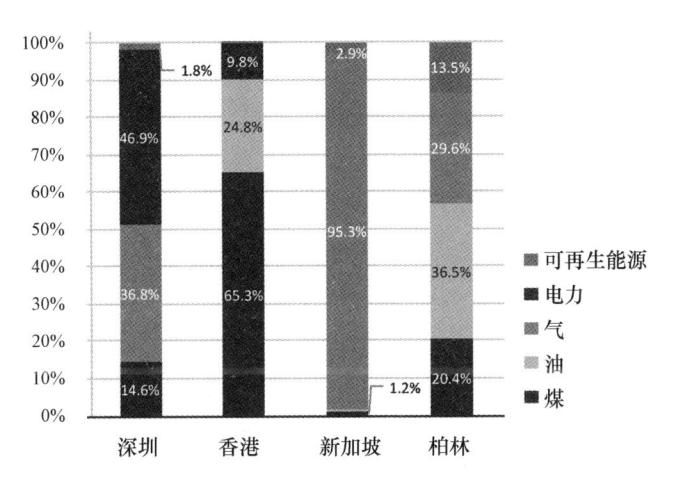

图 5-12　2015 年发电来源比例

资料来源：深圳市碳减排路径研究（Foundation, G. L. – C. D. and P. U. S. G. School, Research on carbon emission reduction route for Shenzhen 2017, Energy Foundation：http：//www.efchina.org/Reports – zh/report – 20170710 – 2 – zh, p. 156.），深圳市能源发展"十三五"规划，《香港统计年刊》，香港机电工程署（www.emsd.gov.hk），新加坡能源市场管理局（www.ema.gov.sg）和柏林 – 勃兰登堡统计局（www.statistik – berlin – brandenburg.de）。

通过对比四个城市的总电力消耗与总二氧化碳排放量可以发现，由于总能源消耗，深圳、香港和新加坡三个城市的二氧化碳排放量在不断增加，如图 5-13 所示，这意味着在减少二氧化碳排放方面效果甚微，而将绿色能源纳入整个电力生产可以降低二氧化碳排放。深圳的二氧化碳排放量最高（2013 年达 6400 万吨），新加坡（5000 万吨）和香港（4500 万吨）紧随其后。柏林二氧化碳排放量最低，约为 1800 万吨，其可再生能源在能源结构中所占份额最大。

图 5-14 显示了二氧化碳排放量与国内生产总值的关系，深圳每单位国内生产总值实际排放的二氧化碳高于其他城市。深圳的二氧化碳排放量约为 300 吨二氧化碳/百万美元，是柏林 141.47 吨的

(百万吨)

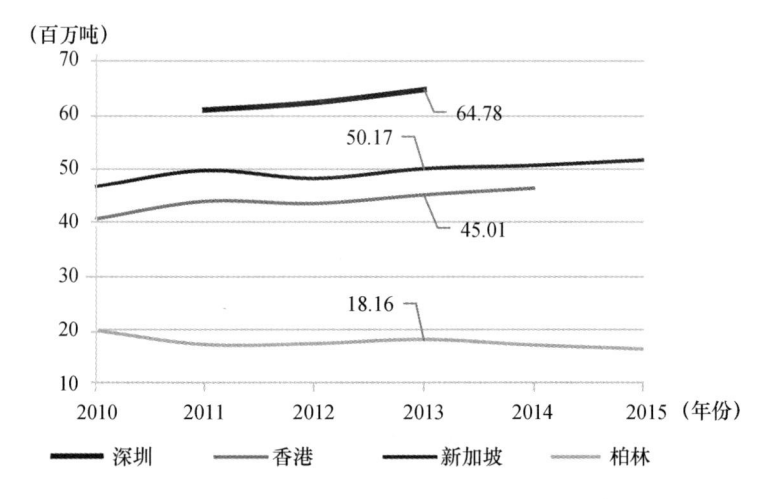

图 5 - 13 2010—2015 年二氧化碳排放总量

资料来源：深圳市碳减排路径研究、世界银行集团（https：//data.worldbank.org/indicator）、新加坡统计局（www.singstat.gov.sg）和柏林 - 勃兰登堡统计局（www.statistik - berlin - brandenburg.de）。

两倍多。然而，以人均二氧化碳排放量计算［图 5 - 14（b）］，深圳人均二氧化碳排放量为 6.09 吨，相对较低。柏林人均二氧化碳排放量为 5.31 吨。而香港则略高，达 6.24 吨。新加坡人均二氧化碳排放量远高于其他国家，2013 年人均二氧化碳排放量达到 9.29 吨。

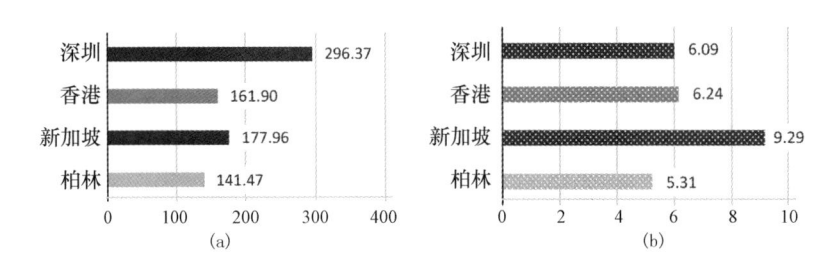

图 5 - 14 2013 年单位国内生产总值（a）和人均二氧化碳排放量（b）

资料来源：深圳市碳减排路径研究、世界银行集团（https：//data.worldbank.org/indicator）、新加坡统计局（www.singstat.gov.sg）和柏林 - 勃兰登堡统计局（www.statistik - berlin - brandenburg.de）。

2. 交通与运输

如前所述，人员流动和货物运输作为城市环境的关键一环，保障了人们获得食物、工作、教育、社会网络和其他活动的机会，如文化场所、娱乐设施和绿地。交通的重要性毋庸置疑，可以促进各种交通设施的多样化，改进城市的相关政策。

从历史上看，欧洲和亚洲城市的交通基础设施是在人们步行、骑马或使用马车的基础上发展起来的，从而形成了一个由狭窄街道组成的广泛交通网络，随着城市规模的扩大，新的交通干线应运而生。随着19世纪末有轨电车、火车等机动车辆的兴起，以及20世纪初汽车的快速增长，对街道、道路和高速公路的需求迅速改变了城市面貌。特别是在20世纪下半叶，汽车成为城市规划的主导因素，不仅导致街道和停车场的面积扩大，而且导致了油气消耗量和排放量的迅速增加。

如今，可持续的交通概念必须包括环境措施，如减少温室气体排放、空气污染和噪声，同时提供良好的环境，包括覆盖城市的绿色空间和公园。此外，还需要推广各种形式的公共交通系统，鼓励步行、自行车出行，以改善城市的空气质量，并整合绿色和蓝色基础设施以应对城市热岛效应和暴雨气候，尤其是在亚热带和热带地区。

衡量环保和健康出行程度的一个指标是所谓的交通方式划分，即使用特定交通方式的出行者所占的百分比，包括非机动车交通出行，如步行和骑自行车（主动运输），以及公共交通，如公共汽车、电车、地铁和郊区火车。交通方式划分还需考虑单独机动车辆的使用，如汽车和摩托车，这些交通工具应在特定情况下允许使用，如公共交通系统受限区域，或步行和骑自行车不合适的时候。

2000年至2016年，深圳居民采取了积极的出行方式，首选的交通方式——步行和骑自行车，占出行总量的71%（2000年）和58%（2016年）。然而，深圳的公共交通比例相当低，2000年为12%，2016年为22%（图5-15）。

相比之下，香港和新加坡是公共交通普及的模范城市，超过50%的居民将公共交通作为首选出行方式。在这一时间段，香港和

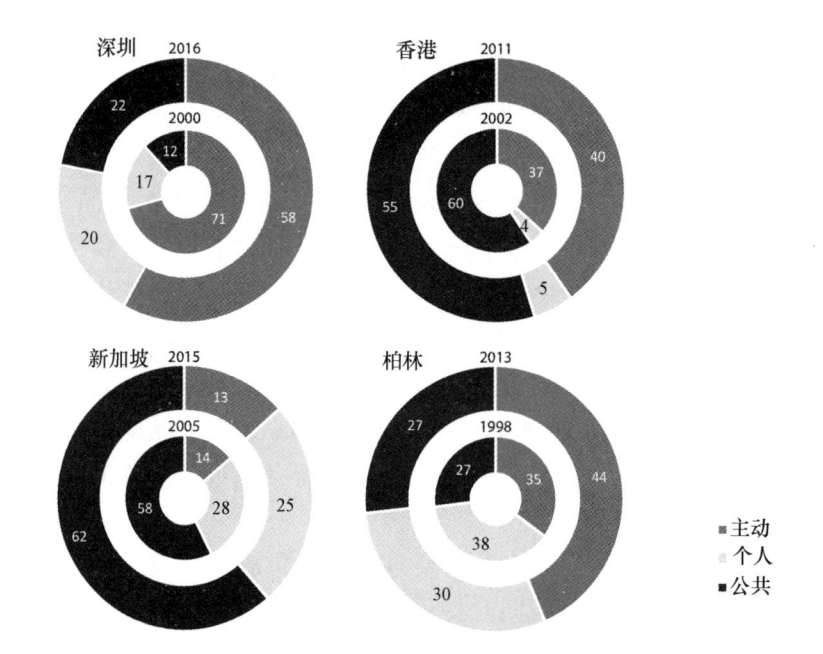

图 5-15 四个城市的交通出行模式划分

资料来源：深圳市规划局（www.szpl.gov.cn/）、《城市交通评估》。

新加坡采用私家车出行的比例分别为 5% 和 25%。

在这一背景下，值得注意的是，《2017 可持续城市流动性指数报告》[①] 将香港列为可持续流动性指数最高的城市，该报告强调了人类对于流动系统的需求及其社会、人文和环境影响（如能源消耗、污染和排放），并强调了促进经济增长的流动系统的效率和可靠性的重要性。

新加坡位居第 8，柏林位居第 22，这显示出步行和骑自行车等积极的交通方式的重要影响。1998 年，柏林的积极交通方式比例为 35%，2013 年为 44%。1998 年，柏林公共交通比例为 27%，而私人汽车的使用比例在 1998 年和 2013 年分别为 38% 和 30%，这表明

[①] https://www.arcadis.com/assets/images/sustainable-cities-mobility-index_spreads.pdf, accessed 29 January, 2019.

柏林朝可持续的交通模式发展上取得的进步。

3. 水资源供应

水塑造着城市，直接关系到人类生活的基本面。水资源短缺是世界面临的共同问题。如上所述，城市特别是高密度的城市，必须面对水资源挑战，为公民提供充足的水，同时确保水质安全、服务高效。

可持续城市用水指数（SCWI）[①] 报告评估了世界各大洲50个城市用水的弹性、质量和效率。据报告，柏林排名第4，为所有类别中表现最稳定的城市之一。新加坡位于第22位，虽然地理上较为脆弱，但新加坡在管理水泄漏、水处理和计量上表现出色。这两座城市被认为是未来成功利用水资源的模范城市。

如中国其他城市一样，深圳的自来水同样不可饮用。不过，当地政府正努力在不久的将来提供可饮用自来水。根据国家卫生标准，深圳自来水质量处于合格水平，水质低于国际放射防护委员会[②]评估的风险水平。

本章还选取另外三个供水指标来评估四个城市的现状，即总用水量（描述不同的用水需求）、家庭人均用水量（揭示每个居民在城市的用水情况）、供水份额（不仅揭示了各个城市的供水水源，而且指出了城市应对供水问题的策略）。这些指标有助于我们全面了解供水现状，并为今后发展指明方向。

如图 5-16 所示，2001 年，深圳、柏林和香港的水消耗量相似，约为 10 亿立方米。在此之后到 2008 年，只有深圳的用水量大幅增加，2016 年达 17 亿立方米。相比之下，柏林的用水量自 2000 年以来持续下降，2016 年下降到 2001 年的一半，约 5.3 亿立方米，仅占深圳用水量的 30%。2003 年到 2013 年期间，香港的用水量呈下降趋势，于 2016 年开始缓慢上升至 10 亿立方米。新加坡用水量

---

① https://www.arcadis.com/media/4/6/2/%7B462EFA0A-4278-49DF-9943-C067182CA682%7DArcadis%20Sustainable%20Cities%20Water%20Index_003.pdf, accessed 30 January, 2019.

② Hua, R. and Y. Zhang, "Assessment of Water Quality Improvements Using the Hydrodynamic Simulation Approach in Regulated Cascade Reservoirs: A Case Study of Drinking Water Sources of Shenzhen, China", *Water*, Vol. 9, No. 11, 2017, p. 825.

(百万立方米)

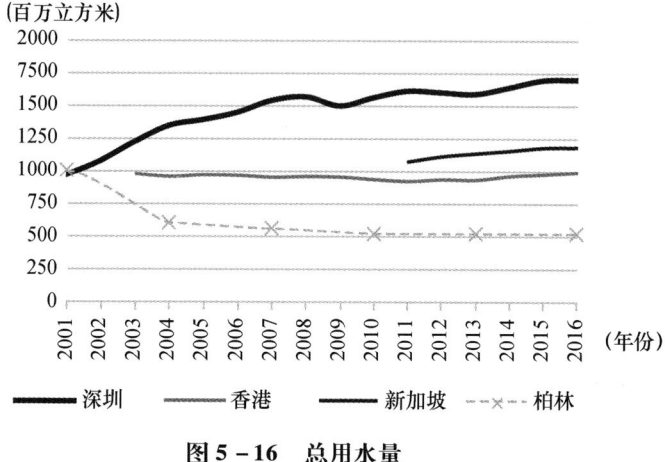

图 5-16 总用水量

资料来源：深圳市水务局（swj.sz.gov.cn），香港水务署（www.wsd.gov.hk），新加坡国家水务局（www.pub.gov.sg）和柏林－勃兰登堡统计局（www.statistik-berlin-brandenburg.de）。

也同样呈缓慢上升趋势，从 2011 年的 10.82 亿立方米增加到 2016 的 11.81 亿立方米，尽管人口数量低于香港，用水总量却高于香港。总体而言，近年来各城市用水量相对稳定。

图 5-17 显示，从 2001 年到 2016 年，深圳市家庭人均用水量（WCHc）迅速下降，并伴随一定波动。深圳在 2004 年出现了人均 90 立方米的峰值，是同期柏林 45 立方米的两倍。2016 年，深圳家庭人均用水量降至 60 立方米，仅比新加坡多 6 立方米。新加坡从 2001 年的 60 立方米持续下降至 2016 年的 54 立方米。香港的家庭人均用水量在 2008 年至 2013 年有所下降，然后在 2016 年增至 72 立方米。

根据图 5-18，深圳和香港的非生活用水占总供水量的比例远高于其他城市。特别是深圳，非生活用水比重从 2000 年的 44% 飙升至 2016 年的 81%。随着千禧后人口的激增，深圳对外来支持的依赖程度大大提高，同时深圳也开始通过采用再生水来减少水足迹，2016 年再生水占 5%，而 2000 年几乎没有再生水。2016 年，香港一半的供水来自外部，当时使用的是处理过的海水作为冲洗水和饮用水，占 21%。柏林是唯一一个水资源几乎自给自足的城市，

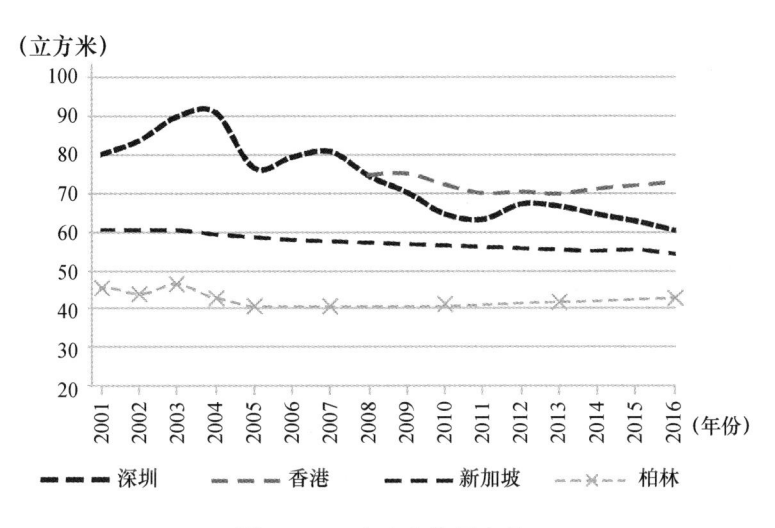

图 5-17 家庭人均用水量

只有 1% 的水来自外部，但地下水的使用比例相对较高，为 17%。新加坡在供水方面表现出色，在水循环和海水淡化①领域处于世界领先地位。新加坡是一个岛国，也是一个人口密度极高的城市，自 1965 年独立后②，新加坡面临严重的水资源短缺问题，实现水资源自给自足的愿望越发强烈。在此背景下，新加坡采取了两个主要措施来减少水足迹：一种是和香港一样进行海水淡化，但这类水主要用于冲洗。另一种是高级再生水，新加坡称之为"新生水"③，这种水采用先进的膜技术和紫外线消毒技术进行净化，水质干净，饮用安全。2016 年新加坡无非生活用水供应，地表水所占比例与深圳相同。新加坡没有从其他地区进口水，其 40% 的用水来源于再生水，30% 来源于海水淡化。此外，据政府报告，新加坡几乎所有的城市雨水都被收集并储存在饮用水蓄水池中。预计到 2030 年，新加坡

---

① https://www.pub.gov.sg/watersupply/singaporewaterstory.
② Lafforgue, M. and V. Lenouvel, "Closing the Urban Water Loop: Lessons from Singapore and Windhoek", *Environmental Science: Water Research & Technology*, Vol. 1, No. 5, 2015, pp. 622-631.
③ https://www.pub.gov.sg/watersupply/singaporewaterstory.

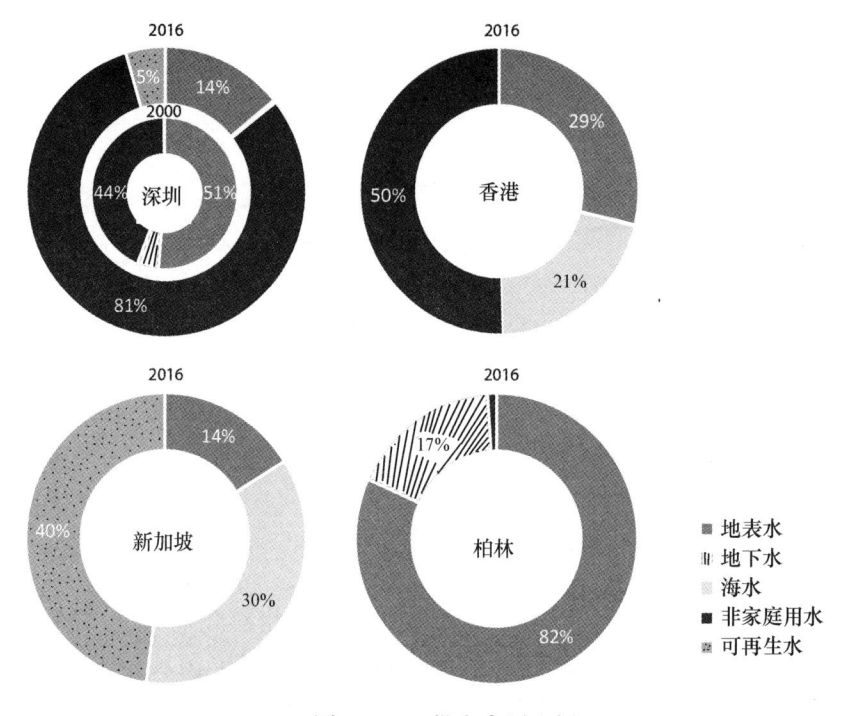

图 5 – 18 供水来源比例

资料来源：深圳市水务局（swj. sz. gov. cn），香港水务署（www. wsd. gov. hk），新加坡国家水务局（www. pub. gov. sg）和柏林-勃兰登堡统计局（www. statistik - berlin - brandenburg. de）。

新生水占供水量的比例将达到50%。在增加可利用水量方面，深圳再生水仅占5%，2016年几乎没有使用海水。

4. 绿色城市基础设施

如今，全球一半以上的人口居住在城市，这一比例仍在增加。人口密度越高，对环境的影响越大，因为人口的急剧增长需要更多的建设和交通用地，从而导致有限土地范围内绿地面积减少。在一定的城市环境中，随着绿地面积和生物多样性所占比例的降低，生态恢复力也随之降低，这对当地生态系统和区域内与生态系统有关的服务提供构成威胁。绿色城市基础设施（GUI）提供的服务包括改善温度、减少雨水径流、防洪、储存碳、减少污染、美化环境和提供娱乐服务。① 利用土地面积内的分布特征和绿地率（GAR）对绿色城市基础设施的有效性进行评估。

2016年，香港的开发建设用地面积低于30%，但绿地面积比例很大，达72%。由于动植物的生存空间得到了很好的保护，而开发区仅限于绿地内的部分区域，因此香港众多且连续的绿地面积为生物多样性提供了保障。新加坡市中心保留了大片绿地，周围为一圈建成的土地，其绿地率为56%，低于香港72%的水平。柏林和深圳的绿地率都只有45%，发达地区主要集中在中心地带，绿地分布在边缘地带。

深圳在城市东南部地区绿地连续且密集，中心散落着小块零星绿地。除了大面积的绿地和森林外，公共绿地（PGSs）也是绿色城市基础设施的一部分，包括公园、带绿地的游乐场以及路边绿地。② 公共用地及其绿地属于城市，地方政府对其的管理直接影响当地居民的生活质量。分散在城市各处的绿岛，交通便利，人员流动大，为市民提供了遮阳、呼吸新鲜空气和娱乐的场所。

图5-19显示了深圳、香港、新加坡和柏林的人均公共绿地面积（PGSs）。虽然柏林的绿地率较低，但人均公共绿地面积却是四个城市中最高的，为30.12平方米/人，几乎是深圳人均公共绿地面积的两倍，深圳为16.45平方米/人。虽然香港绿地面积庞大，但人均公共绿地面积最低，为3.37平方米。尽管新加坡对人口密度的压力加大，但人均公共绿地面积为8.74平方米，为香港的两倍。

（二）迈向可持续的未来

在快速发展的城市环境中，通过相关的地方基础设施可持续地提供基本服务是一项极具挑战性的任务。第3节对可持续提供基本服务的优势、劣势、机遇和威胁进行了分析，清晰、简明地描述了

---

① Ong, B. L., "Green Plot Ratio: an Ecological Measure for Architecture and Urban Planning", *Landscape and Urban Planning*, Vol. 63, No. 4, 2003, pp. 197–211.

② Tan, P. Y., Wang, J., Sia, A., "Perspectives on Five Decades of the Urban Greening of Singapore", *Cities* Vol. 32, 2013, pp. 24–32, doi: 10.1016/j.cities.2013.02.001.

（平方米）

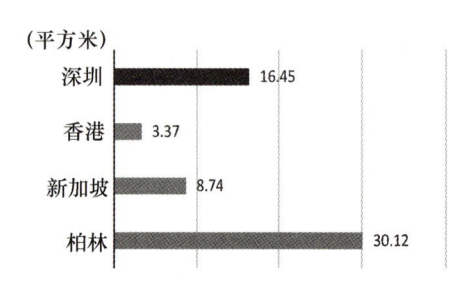

深圳　16.45
香港　3.37
新加坡　8.74
柏林　30.12

图 5-19　2016 年人均公共绿地面积

资料来源：《深圳统计年鉴》、香港规划署（www.pland.gov.hk）、国家公园局（www.npas.gv.sg）和柏林参议院环境、交通和气候保护部（www.berlin.de/sen/uvk/）。

深圳目前取得的成就和未来面临的挑战。

这一分析也有助于确定可能需要进一步发展的地区，从而提高深圳作为中国领先的可持续发展城市之一的声誉。因此，对于全球其他面临着相似的可持续发展挑战的城市来说，深圳的案例或许能提供一些参考和借鉴。

如前所述，亚洲许多城市面临着人口快速增长的共同挑战，需要更多的空间、建筑活动、能源、水、交通以及绿色基础设施。

深圳的开放空间较多，因为其土地面积在四城市中排首位。虽然深圳人口最多，但深圳的人口密度仍然低于香港，甚至低于新加坡。

在能源、交通、水和绿色基础设施等基本方面，深圳人口众多，无疑给城市和周边地区的生态环境带来了巨大的挑战和压力。

1. 能源供应

深圳人口众多，一次能源需求量远高于其他城市。与其他城市，如香港、新加坡和柏林相比，深圳在总能源消耗和排放量管理，以及能源效率提高方面面临严峻挑战。

近年来，尽管深圳人均能源消费量大幅下降，但香港、新加坡、柏林等城市单位国内生产总值总能耗仅为其 50% 左右（TCE/百万美元）。

深圳市能源基础设施和能源利用效率的提高也体现在人均能源

消耗上。2010年，深圳和柏林的人均能源消费总量（TCE/人）几乎相同。虽然柏林在接下来的5年里成功地降低了人均能源消耗，但深圳的人均能源消耗却增加了0.9 TCE/人，导致深圳的二氧化碳排放量大幅增加，因为深圳一半的能源是使用化石燃料产生的。因此，提高能源消耗效率，利用可再生能源发电对于深圳来说刻不容缓。

2. 交通与运输

在可持续的交通基础设施方面，深圳依然任重道远。自2016年以来，深圳只有22%的居民将公共交通作为首选交通工具，20%的居民开车出行。根据香港和新加坡的交通方式划分，二者的公共交通使用率分别为55%和62%。

在土地利用、防渗覆盖、资源消耗、排放、噪声和安全等方面，公共交通是城市内部最有效、最节能的交通方式。如果城郊火车、地铁和有轨电车以及公交等不同的交通方式协同良好，一些路程可采用步行和骑自行车的方式，那么公共交通将发挥更大的作用，交通网络完善的紧凑型城市就是典型案例。在这方面，香港在减少私家车出行方面卓有成效，因为只有5%的香港人口选择汽车作为出行工具，而在深圳，20%的人选择开车出行，新加坡的这一比例为25%，柏林为30%。

3. 水资源供应

珠三角两大城市供水能力均已超出负荷，特别是在深圳，近年来人均家庭用水量急剧下降，但由于人口的增长，对非家庭用水的依赖程度仍在增加。

2016年，深圳超过80%的供水来自周边城市[1]，这表明其高度依赖性。相比之下，柏林和新加坡通过多种方法保障了生活用水供应，满足了居民用水需求。

由于地表水和地下水储量充足，柏林供水充足，但新加坡正努力通过回收和循环水以及海水淡化的方式来增加当地的可用水量。深圳应增加生活供水量，抑制非生活用水需求上涨，效仿新加坡来

---

[1] Water Resources Bureau of Shenzhen (swj. sz. gov. cn), 2017.

改善水资源短缺的现状。此外,深圳可以效仿香港,采用处理过的海水作为冲洗水,这是一个低成本且有效的战略,能够减少非生活用水进口。

4. 绿色城市基础设施

在深圳,大型绿地主要位于城市东南部和北部边缘。这些地区距离市中心区相当远,市中心区绿地分布较少,散落在中心区周围。虽然新加坡和香港已设法保护城市中心区的主要绿地,但考虑到城市环境,建成区域和城市结构只能在社区周边和诸如绿色屋顶、外墙的建筑上进行优化。根据深圳市绿化系统预测[①],到2030年,深圳市人均公共绿地面积将增加到18平方米/人,所有居民距离最近的公园均在500米范围以内。因此,在深圳的这些公共空间区域,可以通过增加无障碍设施和提升空间体验来提高生活质量。

四 总结

深圳作为亚洲东南部地区经济发展最成功的城市之一,同时也是珠三角地区发展最快的城市之一,虽然成功应对了人口增长,但仍然面临着重大挑战,如向生产设施和公民提供清洁能源,以及减少对周边地区清洁饮用水供应的依赖性。随着成熟的可持续公共交通系统的进一步完善和绿色城市基础设施的加强,深圳很可能在不久的将来成为其他城市建立可持续城市基础设施系统的榜样。

---

① Urban Planning and Design Institute of Shenzhen (www.upr.cn), 2014 – 2030. Nomenclature.

第六章　环境与生态城市

一　简介

短短40年中,深圳历经了飞速的工业化和城市化进程。在这片面积为1997平方公里的土地上,人口从1979年的31万增长到2017年底的1252万多,深圳管理人口超过2000万。深圳是中国第一个实现完全城市化的城市。社会经济高速发展的同时,深圳在生态城市建设和绿色低碳循环可持续发展方面也取得了显著成绩。"深圳蓝""深圳绿"已成为城市名片,城市生态环境质量不断改善,深圳先后荣获国家园林城市、国际"园林城市"、联合国环境保护"世界500强"等荣誉称号。

然而,深圳在迅猛发展的过程中也遭遇了"城市病",如人口过剩、过度扩张和高人口密度给环境带来了巨大压力和瓶颈。这些问题主要表现在发展空间资源匮乏;地方能源资源稀缺,能源自给能力薄弱且成本高。深圳水资源紧缺问题给稳定供水带来了巨大挑战,资源、能源供需矛盾已成为制约可持续发展的重大瓶颈。

目前,深圳部分地区环境污染问题相当突出。首先,水环境污染严重,水体黑臭,治理难度大。一些近海地区污染加剧。但深圳缺少水污染防治基础设施,管道建设也不尽如人意,当地污水处理厂的运营能力超过负荷。生活垃圾激增让垃圾填埋场也面临严峻挑战。

深圳城市发展坚持人与自然和谐共处的理念,即绿水青山就是金山银山。深圳有效运用立法、政策引导、城市规划等方式,建立健全绿色发展体制机制,推动形成资源节约、环境保护型的空间格局。深圳持续推进产业结构优化升级,大力倡导绿色低碳的生产、生活方式,注重"绿色"质量经济发展。总体而言,在绿色低碳城市、智慧生态城市建设方面,深圳已取得了突出成绩。

本章首先讨论生态城市及相关概念,简要查阅了深圳生态城市规划建设的相关研究,并回顾了深圳生态城市建设过程及存在的主要问题。随后,从能源结构调整、产业转型升级、构建绿色交通体系、推进绿色建筑、倡导绿色低碳生活方式、加强低碳城市试点、政策引导与市场机制相结合等方面进行了探讨。未来,深圳将成为中国三大可持续发展试点地区之一。根据《联合国 2030 年可持续发展议程》目标,深圳已确立了短期、中期和长期的宏伟目标,并采取了多种措施和手段来推动和落实这些目标,努力为世界大城市可持续发展提供更多借鉴参考的经验。

二 生态城市与相关概念

20 世纪 70 年代,美国学者理查德·瑞杰斯特(Richard Register)在《生态城市伯克利:为一个健康的未来建设城市》一书中提出生态城市这一概念,旨在规划建设未来理想城市。随后,联合国教科文组织启动了"人与生物圈"项目,并引入了这一重要概念,引起广泛关注。1972 年 6 月 5 日,联合国召开第一次人类环境会议,通过了《人类环境宣言》,呼吁世界各国人民保护和改善环境。1987 年,世界环境与发展委员会在报告《我们共同的未来》中正式阐述了可持续发展概念。随着人们对全球气候变化等问题日益关注,许多概念应运而生,如低碳城市、绿色城市、花园城市、弹性城市、海绵城市、宜居城市、知识城市等。数年前,笔者和一些其他国际学者探讨了相关概念之间的区别和联系。[1] 有许多学者

---

[1] Martin de Jong, Chang Yu, Xinting Chen, Dong Wang, Margot Weijnen, "Developing Robust Organizational Frameworks for Sino-foreign eco-cities: Comparing Sino-Dutch Shenzhen Low Carbon City with Other Initiatives", *Journal of Cleaner Production*, Vol. 57, 2013, pp. 209-220.

研究了相关概念（*Nina Khanna*）①。由此可见，生态城市尚没有合适的定义，它与许多概念有重合之处。因此，本章并未对其概念进行严格区分，而是从宏观层面来解读生态城市概念：以最小的环境成本和最少的资源消耗来获取更多、更高质量的产出，实现人与自然和谐共处，提升城市生活宜居性，进一步满足人们物质和精神文化需求，增强人们获得感和幸福感。

关于生态城市及其相关概念方面的研究有很多。结合深圳绿色、低碳、循环利用和可持续发展，特别包括深圳生态城市规划和建设方面，这里简要地回顾了近年来与深圳密切相关的著作。

李天虹、李文凯、钱正汉指出，城市扩展对生态系统服务功能有明显影响。②石培军和余德永在基于景观城市规划与可持续发展中，对深圳环境资源和服务进行了评估。③尤何圆研究了深圳公共绿地的不平等供给。④刘林、林耀宇、王丽娜对能源配置和环境适宜性评估进行了研究，他们认为必须对地区室外和局部气候、热舒适条件进行有效评估和分析，以满足资源节约和环境友好型社会的需要。⑤黄颖、刘磊、潘晓峰以深圳——中国低碳转型中最富有活力的城市为例，运用生命周期模型对当地二氧化碳排放结构的规模进行了评估。⑥李静茹和左建等通过深圳与青岛的比较性研究，研

---

① Li Yu, "Low Carbon Eco-city: New Approach for Chinese Urbanization", *Habitat International*, Vol. 44, 2014, pp. 102–110.

② Li Tianhong, Li Wenkai, Qian Zhenghan, "Variations in Ecosystem Service Value in Response to Land Use Changes in Shenzhen", *Ecological Economics*, Vol. 69, 2010, pp. 1427–1435.

③ Peijun Shi, Deyong Yu, "Assessing Urban Environmental Resources and Services of Shenzhen, China: A landscape-based Approach for Urban Planning and Sustainability", *Landscape and Urban Planning*, Vol. 125, 2014, pp. 290–297.

④ Heyuan You, "Characterizing the Inequalities in Urban Public Green Space Provision in Shenzhen, China", *Habitat International*, Vol. 56, 2016, pp. 176–180.

⑤ Lin Liu, Yaoyu Lin, Lina Wang, Junliang Cao, Dan Wang, Puning Xue, Jing Liu, "An inTegrated Local Climatic Evaluation System for Green Sustainable Eco-city Construction: A case study in Shenzhen, China", *Building and Environment*, Vol. 114, 2017, pp. 82–95.

⑥ Ying Huang, Lei Liub, Xiaofeng Pan, "CO_2 Emissions Structure of Local Economy: A Case of Shenzhen", *Energy Procedia*, Vol. 104, 2016, pp. 86–91.

究了建筑垃圾填埋费的支付意愿。①

马丁德·容（Martin de Jong）等研究了中外生态城市活力组织框架：将深圳国际低碳城模式与其他举措进行了比较。② 展长洁等开展了生态城市和低碳城市融资研究：以深圳国际低碳城市为例，城市可持续发展融资已成为一个重大课题，尤其是在亚洲国家的建设规模上。③ 刘颖、林艳柳、傅娜、斯坦·格特曼（Stan Geertman）和范·奥尔特（Frank van Oort）研究了深圳包容性和可持续性转型：城市重建、移民和流离失所模式以及政策内涵。④

三 深圳可持续发展进程

1979年初立时，深圳的产业寥寥无几。约2000平方公里的土地上，人口仅为31万人（《统计年鉴》）。深圳GDP不足2亿元，且主要来自第一产业。深圳依山傍海，自然条件优越，但总体自然资源依然匮乏。1980年深圳经济特区成立后，曾设工业园区进行城市建设，但在90年代初，深圳主要产业为来料加工。1992年，中国改革开放总设计师邓小平先生到深圳等地考察后，城市化步伐大大加快，人口逐年快速增长。从图6-1可以看到，1992年以前，深圳每年雾霾日数不足30天；1992年以后，年雾霾日数也迅速增加，2004年达到峰值，雾霾日超过半年，长达187天。同年，深圳

---

① Jingru Li, Jian Zuo, Hong Guo, Gaihong He, Han Liu, "Willingness to pay for Higher Construction Waste Landfill charge: A Comparative Study in Shenzhen and Qingdao, China", *Waste Management*, Vol. 81, 2018, pp. 226 – 233.

② Martin de Jong, Chang Yu, Xinting Chen, Dong Wang, Margot Weijnen, "Developing Robust Organizational Frameworks for Sino – foreign Eco – cities: Comparing Sino – Dutch Shenzhen Low Carbon City with Other Initiatives", *Journal of Cleaner Production*, Vol. 57, 2013, pp. 209 – 220.

③ Changjie Zhan, Martin de Jong, "Financing Eco – cities and Low Carbon Cities: The Case of Shenzhen International Low Carbon City", *Journal of Cleaner Production*, Vol. 180, 2018, pp. 116 – 125.

④ Ying Liu, Yanliu Lin, Na Fu, Stan Geertman, Frank van Oort, "Towards Inclusive and Sustainable Transformation in Shenzhen: Urban Redevelopment, Displacement Patterns of Migrants and Policy Implications", *Journal of Cleaner Production*, Vol. 173, 2018, pp. 24 – 38.

宣布实现了全面城市化，成为中国第一座全面城市化的城市。与此同时，上到市长下到市民，环境问题引起普遍关注。

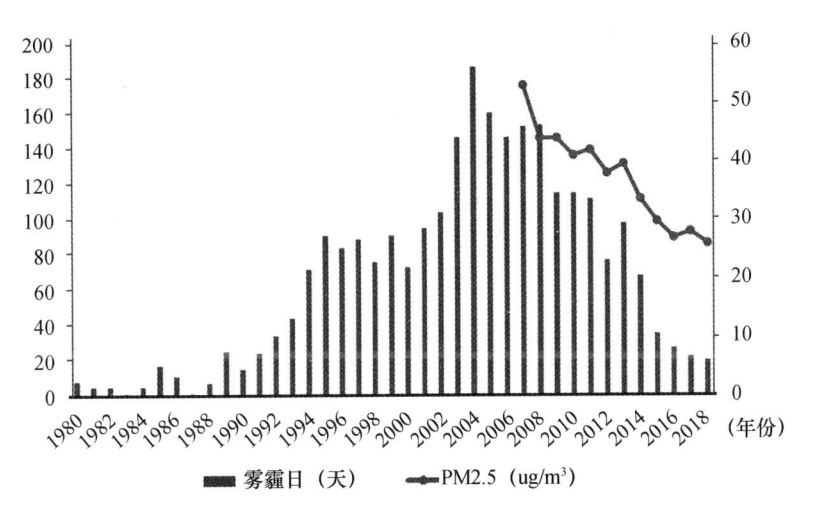

图 6-1　深圳雾霾日和 PM2.5 浓度

2017 年，深圳建成区绿化覆盖率为 45.1%，森林覆盖率为 40.04%，城市污水处理率为 96.8%。深圳已建成公园 942 个，总面积 2.2 万公顷，人均公园绿地面积 16.45 平方米。全市约有一半土地划为生态保护区。深圳现有绿道 2400 公里，生态景观林 2638 公顷；绿色建筑总面积超过 5320 万平方米，居全国第一位；深圳是全球新能源汽车最普及的城市之一，新能源汽车达 12 万辆。深圳 PM2.5 平均浓度为 $28mg/m^3$，位居全国领先地位。深圳碳排放交易所是国内首家碳排放交易所，交易活跃度与交易量均为全国第一。深圳国际低碳城已成为中欧可持续城市化合作的旗舰项目，并获得美国保尔森中心颁发的"可持续发展规划项目奖"。

四　深圳主要环境问题

除上述空气污染问题外，深圳市政府从 2004 年开始提出了

"四个不可持续问题"。当时市长的李鸿忠指出了"四大不可持续"：首先，深圳土地和空间有限，可供开发的土地面积只有200平方公里，已无法与深圳发展速度相适应。其次，即使抽干东江，深圳能源和水资源也无法支撑其快速发展。再次，就深圳目前采取发展速度模式，要实现十几亿元的GDP目标，还需要更多的劳动力，而深圳的承载力受限。最后，环境容量超出负荷，环境污染不堪重负。水污染极其严重，陆地水体的环境承载力已经耗尽。深圳清醒地意识到了环境问题（《中国改革报》2005年1月17日）。

深圳土地面积狭小，仅为1997平方公里，其中仅760平方公里可供建设。如果深圳保持每年10平方公里的开发速度，土地与人口密度和经济产出将严重失衡。20年后，深圳将没有可用土地。

深圳是中国七大严重缺水城市之一，人均可供水量仅为广东省的1/6和全国平均水平的1/5。由于深圳人口不断增加，环境负荷，水资源日益短缺。1980年深圳经济特区建成时，人口总量为33万多人。如今，深圳人口已超过1200多万，其中1026万为临时居民。人口过剩带来的一系列问题，使城市环境容量不堪重负。据深圳官方估计，如果土地匮乏和人口持续增长之间的矛盾得不到解决，或进一步恶化，深圳将陷入瓶颈，其经济将无法继续健康发展。

土地、资源、环境、人口"四大不可持续"问题，极大束缚了企业扩大再生产和结构优化升级。在土地稀缺、人口压力大、传统企业发展受限的背景下，深圳通过"三加工+一补偿"的方式，积累了第一桶"金"。深圳率先认识到必须终结传统发展模式，进行集约化、高端化转型刻不容缓。自那时起，深圳便决心要从闻名的"深圳速度"转向"深圳效益"。

五 能源结构调整与能效提升

深圳高度重视推进能源结构调整，大力推进能源基础设施规划建设，逐步提高清洁能源、外电、天然气在城市能源结构中的比重。根据2017年一次能源消费结构比，煤炭、石油、天然气和电力的比例为7.2∶27.3∶12.8∶52.7。与2010年度相比，煤炭比重由12.5%下降到7.2%，石油比重由32.4%下降到27.3%，天然气比重由10.2%上升到12.8%，电力比重由45.0%上升到52.7%。清洁能源比重比2010年提高10.3%，能源消费结构进一步优化（图6-2）。

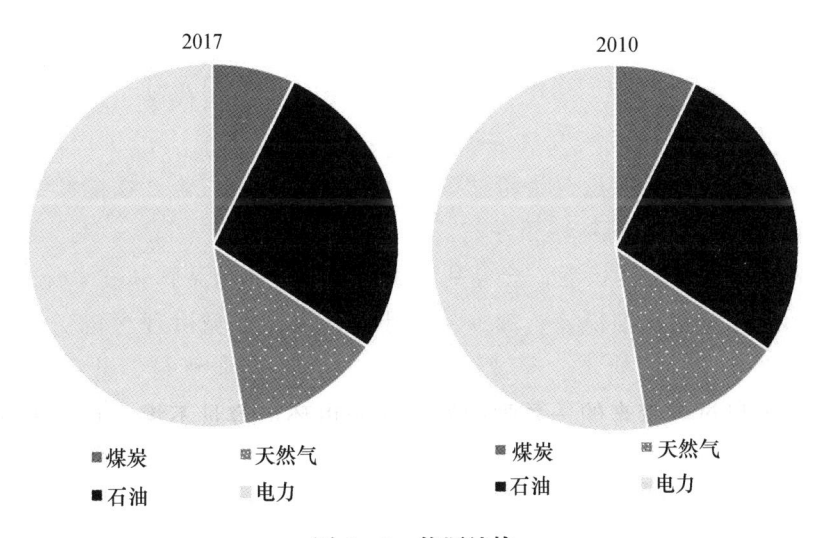

图6-2　能源结构

深圳特区建立后，由于工业化和城市化迅猛发展，电力和能源一直处于紧缺状态。截至2000年，深圳一次能源自给率不到10%，90%以上能源从内地或国外进口。除煤炭外，深圳还需大量进口燃料油和液化石油气。为解决能源瓶颈问题，深圳征求中央政府意见，首次在大鹏半岛引入中国的液化天然气试点项目。该项目耗资290多亿元，于1999年底获批，2003年底正式开工，第一阶段在2006年投入运行。从澳大利亚海底开采的天然气经加压后装至液化天然气货船，运到深圳接收站进行卸货、储存和气化。该项目是深圳能源结构调整的一次重大飞跃。此后，深圳不断加强天然气、核能、太阳能、生物质能、风能等清洁能源使用，持续提高清洁能源比重。深圳采用高效发电技术，试行碳捕集与封存方法，降低能源行业碳排放。此外，深圳还试点智能电网建设，促进可再生能源并网。

（一）大幅提高清洁能源利用率

深圳实施石油替代战略，引进天然气，拓宽天然气资源供应渠道，抓住全球能源发展的战略机遇，努力开发利用核能和可再生能源。

深圳积极引进天然气资源，大力推进西气东输2号线深圳香港分公司、西气东输2号线、深圳液化天然气应急负荷站、迭福液化天然气接收站等天然气气源项目规划和建设，形成多源供应模式。深圳天然气年供应量有望超过65亿立方米，天然气在一次能源结构中的比重有望提高至14%左右。

深圳大力发展核能，充分利用深圳核电产业的品牌和技术优势，突破传统基地规划模式，加强从工业园区向工业城市理念转变；建立以核电设计、研发、集成、服务为核心的产业集群，并以太阳能、风能等新能源和高端产业为辅能。此外，深圳还建设国家级新能源（核电）产业基地和深圳转型发展、创新发展、低碳发展的高生产率示范基地，使其成为深圳对外展示的新窗口。

深圳大力推广太阳能，所有具备必要集热条件的民用建筑必须安装太阳能热水系统。加快太阳能光电建筑一体化示范工程建设，深圳太阳能光热利用面积将超过1600万平方米，发电总装机容量达到200兆瓦。深圳积极开展太阳能空调、地源热泵等可再生能源建筑应用试点，推广安装太阳能LED、风能互补照明等新能源产品，满足城市道路和公共空间的照明需求。

加大生物质能源开发利用，深圳加快老虎坑垃圾焚烧厂二期扩建和城东垃圾焚烧发电厂规划建设。加强填埋场沼气的利用，深圳积极开展生物柴油、燃料乙醇和能源植物的研发，并适时开展生物液体燃料应用试点。目前，深圳运行的四座垃圾焚烧发电厂每天可处理生活垃圾5450吨，年发电量7亿千瓦时，排放指标达到或超过欧盟标准。同时，深圳正积极推进宝安三期、南山二期和东部环保电厂三个垃圾焚烧项目。其中，在建的深圳东部环保电厂日处理垃圾 5000 余吨。待其建成后，东部环保电厂将成为世界上最大的单体垃圾发电厂。这些项目全部完工后，深圳将对所有生活垃圾进行焚烧发电，成为中国第一个"无害化、减量化、资源化"处理所有生活垃圾的城市。

积极开展风能示范利用，结合风能资源和建设条件，深圳将研究建设风电示范项目，引领风电装备产业发展。不仅如此，深圳将根据广东省海上风电项目规划，积极开展海上风电项目可行性研究。

截至 2017 年，非化石能源占深圳一次能源消费比重为 15%，而清洁能源比重超过 90%。

（二）全面降低能源生产部门碳排放

深圳鼓励能源生产部门采用高效发电技术，开展碳捕集与封存技术应用试验，大幅降低电力行业碳排放。

加快高效发电技术研发和应用，深圳鼓励发电企业从事高效发电技术研发，对发电机组主要设备和重要的耗能辅助系统进行改造，同时注重脱硫脱磷；安装污染控制设备，提高电厂煤、气发电利用效率，降低电站电耗率和碳排放。早在 1999 年，妈湾电站 4 号机组就完成了第一批海水烟气脱硫系统的建设，也是国家环保总局示范工程。据统计，2014 年至 2017 年，深圳投入 14.23 亿元对现有燃煤电厂进行节能减排技术改造。截至目前，10 台燃煤发电机组已全部完成超低排放改造，其中 9 台通过超低排放验收，获得超低排放优惠电价。

试点能源综合集成供应模式。深圳试点户式或社区式小规模冷热电联供，结合新的城市功能区和园区，研究区域低碳能源规划，促进普通能源和可再生能源的互补发展，建立综合能源供应中心。鼓励具备必要条件的建筑物内开展天然气冷热电联供试点；鼓励在重要场馆建设储能电站，发展冰蓄冷空调和相变材料等储能形式，提高能源供应体系效率。

为减少电厂码头卸煤船柴油发电机对大气的污染，深圳能源集团股份有限公司于 2015 年开始建设妈湾电厂码头岸电设施，同时对下属运输公司运煤船岸电设施进行改造。2016 年 9 月，深圳能源集团完成了四家运营商的岸电设施改造，并于 11 月通过交接验收。经计算，港区岸电改造后每年可减少废气排放约 4000 吨，真正实现船舶废气"零排放"。据悉，该项目是国内首个成功利用低压登船的大型散货码头岸电建设项目，对深圳乃至全国推广"码头岸电"具有积极示范作用。

（三）努力提高能源利用效率

把节能降耗作为提高能源利用效率的重要载体，深圳加快结构节能、技术节能和管理节能，加强制造业、交通运输业、建筑业、事业单位等领域的节能降耗措施，降低资源能源消耗，提高能源利用效率。

加强电力、建材、制造业等重点行业节能减排管理，深圳积极采用先进且适用的节能技术改造传统产业，提高能源利用效率。到 2015 年，单位工业增加值能耗比 2010 年下降 20%，达到 0.394 吨标准煤/万元；深圳力争单位工业增加值能耗比 2015 年再下降 10%，达到 0.355 吨标准煤/万元。

电力工业节能，深圳推动火电机组技术改造，以高效、清洁的发电技术替代火电机组，降低发电能耗，降低电站耗电量；加快输变电以及配电设备技术改造和电网建设，逐步淘汰高耗能老设备，降低输变电、配电过程损耗。并推进电网简化改造水平和 20 千伏配电，加强用电侧管理，全面开展节能发电调度。

建材行业节能降耗，深圳加快玻璃工业技术改造，推广先进技术，开展玻璃窑炉余热利用技术改造。并加快淘汰陶瓷行业落后窑型，推广节能环保窑炉技术，优化燃料结构，鼓励陶瓷渣、余热回收等资源综合利用项目。

在电子设备制造方面，深圳加强电子设备制造业的能耗诊断和节能改造；加快淘汰落后、高耗能的电机、风机、水泵、注塑机、压缩机等电子设备；引导企业调整产品结构，将重点转移到低能耗、高增加值产品上；提高电子设备制造业准入门槛，严格能耗设备能耗监测。

加强重点用能单位节能降耗，加强重点单位年耗标煤 300 吨以上的节能监测，落实能源利用状况报告制度；推进能效对标，鼓励节能管理专家和能源管理体系试点。加大资金投入，引导企业开展节能技术研究，组织重点用能单位开展节能降耗服务，提高用能单位计量检测能力和标准，以及校准其能量测量设备并验证能量测量数据。

六　产业转型升级

截至2017年，深圳先进制造业、现代服务业和优势传统产业比重分别为0.1∶41.3∶58.6，形成先进制造业、现代服务业和优势传统产业协调发展的格局。高新技术、金融、物流、文化四大支柱产业增加值1.4万亿元，占市内生产总值63.4%。先进制造业实现增加值5733.87亿元，增长13.1%。现代服务业占服务业比重达70.8%，生物产业、互联网、新能源、新一代信息技术、新材料、文化创意六大战略性新兴产业增加值9183.5亿元，占市内生产总值的40.9%。深圳现已成为中国战略性新兴产业规模最大、集聚效应最强的城市之一。

（一）发展低碳新兴产业

深圳重视发展新能源、互联网、生物、新材料、文化创意、新一代信息技术、节能服务、低碳服务等低碳新兴产业；抓住低碳产业发展制高点，打造低碳发展支柱产业。

1. 新能源产业

深圳认真落实《深圳市新能源产业振兴发展规划（2009—2015年）》和深圳市新能源产业振兴发展政策，实施太阳能、核能、风能、生物质能、储能电站、新能源汽车等领域的技术创新、产业培育、开发推广、应用拓展和产业服务工程，迅速扩大产业规模，提高能源供给比例，优化能源结构。截至2015年，新能源产业产值达到2500亿元，年替代传统能源1500多万吨标准煤，二氧化碳减排2000多万吨。

2. 互联网产业

深圳加快实施《深圳市互联网产业振兴发展规划（2009—2015年）》及相关政策，加快互联网基础设施建设，大力发展电子商务、信息技术和移动互联网，努力推进互联网产业与实体经济融合，降低能源消耗。截至2015年，互联网产业产值达2000亿元。

3. 生物产业

深圳积极落实《深圳市生物产业振兴发展规划（2009—2015年）》及相关政策，以生物环保、生物能源、生物医药、生物制药、生物制造等领域为重点，加快生物环保产品生产和再生资源综合利用、环境监测、废物处理、水处理、废气处理技术及配套产品、生物柴油和燃料乙醇的使用。截至2015年，生物产业产值达到2000亿元。

4. 新型材料产业

深圳积极落实《深圳市新材料产业振兴发展规划（2009—2015年）》及相关政策，充分发挥新型材料在低碳发展中基础和导向作用。积极培育市场潜力大、技术密集、增加值高、资源消耗低、环境友好型新材料企业，支持电子信息产业转型升级，新能源、环保等低碳产业快速发展，传统优势产业转型升级，低碳产业体系核心竞争力加快提升。截至2015年，新型材料产业产值达1500亿元。

5. 文化创业产业

深圳积极落实《深圳市文化创意产业振兴发展规划（2009—2015年）》及相关政策，突出文化创意产业高端、高增加值、低碳优势。加大扶持力度，营造良好环境，大力推动创意设计、动漫游戏、数字音像、数字出版、新媒体、文化旅游、电影演艺、高端印刷、高端工业艺术等产业发展。依托高新技术，以数字内容为主体，以自主知识产权为核心，发展"文化＋技术"的文化产业新兴产业模式，增加文化产品增加值。截至2015年，文化创意产业增加值达到2200亿元，产业总产值超5800亿元。

6. 新一代信息技术产业

深圳坚持"市场导向、创新驱动、高端引领、优势凸显"原则，加强自主创新，提高行业标准，拓展应用空间，优化发展环境，促进信息技术创新的互动与融合，新兴应用扩展和新一代网络建设，促进新一代IT产业快速健康发展。截至2015年，新一代IT产业产值达1.2万亿元，年均增长率超过20%；深圳成为世界重要新一代IT产业基地。

7. 节能服务业

深圳加大对节能服务业的扶持力度，出台节能服务业发展扶持政策；鼓励技术和服务水平较高的企业采用能源管理合同模式，提供诊断、设计、融资"一站式"节能服务，对用能单位进行改革。加强服务创新、人才培养和技术研发，使节能服务产业做大做强，提高综合实力和市场竞争力；建立一批品牌知名、竞争力强的大型服务企业，推动节能服务业快速发展，建设国家节能服务业高地。

8. 低碳服务业

深圳促进碳排放统计、碳标准、碳标签、碳认证、碳金融、碳排放许可证交易等低碳服务业；鼓励企业开展碳足迹测量和产品碳认证，参与制定碳标准；鼓励金融保险机构开展碳金融（信贷）和保险业务，为低碳发展提供资金支持。探索碳排放许可证交易机制，开展碳排放许可证交易试点。鼓励国内外低碳技术研究和服务水平较高的企业落户深圳。

（二）高碳产业转型升级

深圳通过传统产业技术创新寻找突破口，加快更新改造。在能源消耗、环境等限制条件下提高碳排放准入门槛。采用清洁生产和产品碳标签，促进传统产业低碳转型升级。

（三）加快技术改造和设备更新

深圳按照《国家产业结构调整目录》和《广东省、深圳市产业指导目录》，加快淘汰落后技术、工艺和设备。提高生产效率和能源利用效率，实现产业低碳转型。加强对落后生产力淘汰工作的审查，建立落后生产力社会公告制度，定期向社会公布。

案例 6-1：深圳排放权交易所

碳交易本质上是一种金融活动，但与金融资本和以绿色技术为基础的实体经济联系更为紧密：一方面，金融资本直接或间接投资于创造碳资产的项目和公司；另一方面，不同项目和公司的减排进入碳金融市场进行交易，并发展成为标准的金融工具。

由于深圳排放量较小，国家发改委在起草第一批减排城市时，最初并未将深圳纳入其中。但由于产业结构的特殊性，深圳被列入国家试点地区。与国内其他城市相比，深圳没有重化工、钢铁、火电等大规模的二氧化碳直接排放源，而碳排放交易又是以较低成本推动节能减排的市场化手段，因此，深圳有望实现绿色低碳发展。如何通过建立市场机制，让大量"间接排放源"实现节能减排目标，将是深圳试点的意义所在。

深圳市政府高度重视该项目，成立了碳排放交易试点领导小组和办公室。市领导担任分管领导，成立了由市发改委牵头，多个政府机关组成的工作组，会同专家研究组开展广泛深入研究。

2010年9月30日，深圳排放权交易所成立，于2013年6月18日正式启动，成为"七大试点"中第一个开放市场的碳交易试点，深圳再次成为创新和改革的引领者。

2013年6月18日，深圳碳市场正式启动。这是中国乃至全世界所有发展中国家第一个真正意义上的碳市场。深圳是全国首个碳交易专项法律试点城市，也是中国第一个由地方性法规和地方政府行为构成的碳交易法律体系较为完备的试点。

截至2017年12月31日，深圳累计碳市场配额2935万吨，累计交易额9.04亿元。中国认证减排总量1105万吨，总成交额1.48亿元。深圳碳市场总交易量为4040万吨，总交易额为10.52亿元，其交易量和流动性长期处于全国领先地位。

深圳市碳排放权交易试点率先启动运行，并在筹备过程中创下数项第一：中国第一部规范碳交易的地方性法规《深圳经济特区碳排放管理若干规定》；中国第一个组织层面温室气体量化、报告和核查规范和指南；中国第一个主要采用基准法进行分配的碳交易体系；中国第一个配额博弈（如不称博弈，可称集中）分配系统；中国第一个投入使用的温室气体信息管理系统、注册登记簿系统和交易系统。深圳碳市场在碳金融创新方面创造了多项第一，并提供了全国范围内可学习和借鉴的碳金融案例，如碳资产质押融资、允许外商参与碳交易、国内外碳资产回购融资、碳债券和绿色构造矿床等。

深圳碳市场有效地提高了企业和公众减排意识。该碳市场建设和运营让越来越多的深圳企业认识到气候变化问题，认真对待企业节能减排，激励其将温室气体减排纳入生产管理和投资决策，增强了企业的社会责任感。同时，随着碳交易有关知识的宣传和推广，深圳碳市场不仅吸引了一批公益人士，也大大提高了公众对低碳生活方式和绿色出行的认识，整个社会节能减排意识都得到了提高。

（四）控制高耗能、重污染产业发展

落实新批项目管理权限联动机制和项目审批责任制。深圳严格执行项目"六个必须"要求，即项目必须符合行业政策和市场准入标准、项目审批或备案程序、用地预审、环境影响评价和审批、节能评价和资信以及安全和城市规划要求。充分借鉴能源消费标准、环境保护执法、倾销权交易、最低工资标准和社会保障，加快淘汰低端落后企业，提高行业准入门槛，实施节能准入管理，严格控制高耗能、重污染产业发展。

（五）大力推进清洁生产

扩大清洁生产规模和范围，深圳将清洁生产理念纳入产业集群基地和产业带建设进程；通过实施清洁生产，开展企业和生产基地低碳改革。高度重视建材、电镀、家电、珠宝、油漆染色、钟表等传统行业的清洁生产。对污染物排放超过国家、省、市排放标准或者污染物排放总量控制指标额定值的企业实施强制性清洁生产审查，并将清洁生产审查作为结算、扩建的约束条件之一，以及作为搬迁和享受优惠

政策的资格，在产品全生命周期内控制资源和能源消耗，降低碳排放。

（六）加快传统产业空间集聚

深圳加快传统产业集群发展，调整产业空间结构，实现合理的产业布局，缩短产品运输距离，降低能源消耗。通过不断创新，提升产业核心竞争力，提高产品质量，降低产品单位碳排放量，打造深圳低碳品牌。

（七）发展低碳都市农业

深圳立足农业低碳生态结构调整，发展具有深圳特色的现代畜牧业、水产养殖业、种植业和渔业。提高技术管理水平和产品附加值，最大限度地提高土地、水资源和能源的利用效率，降低农业生产过程中的碳排放。

七　构建绿色交通体系

截至 2017 年底，新能源汽车累计投入使用 12 万辆，其中纯电动公交车 16359 辆（目前深圳所有公交车均为纯电动）、纯电动出租车 1 万多辆（2018 年底深圳所有出租车均为纯电动），以及 3 万多辆纯电动物流车（深圳是全球新能源物流车最多的城市）。

深圳通过提高汽车能效和排放标准，努力推进交通节能减排。大力发展轨道交通、公共交通和非机动车道路交通，推广新能源汽车；建立低碳交通网络，有效降低汽车能耗，控制废气排放，实现交通碳排放逐步降低。

加强交通运输节能减排，深圳加强机动车尾气污染控制，提高车用燃料质量，提高机动车碳排放标准，加强机动车尾气监控，加快高排放汽车淘汰升级步伐；进一步提高公交车使用液化天然气等清洁能源的比例，逐步建立机动车污染监测、评价和警报系统。严格执行车辆年检制度，完善柴油车检测手段，加快淘汰老旧高耗能车辆，加强尾气检测，并依法加大对超限车辆处罚力度。确保所有车用燃料达到国家四级标准，重视加油站、油库、油罐车的油气回收利用；严格执行环保等级标识制度和车辆检修制度，减少机动车污染物排放。

优先发展公共交通，深圳实施公共交通优先发展战略，建立以公共交通为主导的交通发展模式。优化调整城市出行方式，建立以轨道交通为骨架、常规交通为网络、出租车为补充、慢行系统为延伸的综合公共交通体系，建设符合国际标准的城市公交系统。加强轨道交通与常规交通的协调，合理、有序、高效地组织火车站客流空间转移。建设畅通、便捷、高效、一体化的公交系统，显著提高公共交通参与率。到2015年，深圳建成229公里轨道交通网络，建成400公里（双向）公交专线；机动化出行参与公共交通比例达到56%，百公里油耗下降10%。到2020年，公共交通机动化出行参与率达到65%，百公里油耗下降20%。

提高汽车能效和排放市场准入门槛。深圳提高新车能效，提高排放市场准入门槛；加快改造或淘汰现有低能效汽车。严格执行轿车和轻型商用车油耗限额，限制高油耗、高污染车辆增长。

试点推广新能源汽车，深圳以建设国家级节能与新能源汽车示范推广城市为契机，加快实施《深圳市节能与新能源汽车实施方案》；试点推广新能源公交车、出租车、服务车和私家车。加快制定充电站（或充电桩）建设标准和扶持政策，加快充电站等配套设施建设。积极在盐田、龙岗、光明等地建立新能源汽车示范区，为新能源汽车大规模推广应用创造有利条件。到2015年，深圳新能源汽车达5万辆，实现年减碳5万吨；到2020年，新能源汽车有望推广至10万辆，年碳排放量将达100万吨。

案例6-2：深圳建筑科学研究院（IBR）研发办公楼（BR大楼）

本项目旨在探索低成本、软技术的绿色建筑实现模式，实现建筑全生命周期的最大节约、资源高效利用、环境保护和污染减排。

研发办公楼融合了深圳建筑科学研究院多年来的研究成果和专利技术，致力推广绿色生活和绿色办公。目前BR大楼已成为集地域特色、绿色技术、建筑艺术于一身的绿色研发办公楼。

研发办公楼位于深圳市福田区，占地3000平方米，容积率为4，覆盖率为38.5%，总建筑面积达18170平方米。建筑主体结构地上12层，地下2层。研发办公楼于2009年3月竣工并投入使用，多次获得国内外奖项。该建筑已实现最初目标，达到国家绿色建筑评价标准三星级和能源与环境设计先锋（LEED）金级要求，工程总造价4000元/平方米。这座建筑带来了显著社会效益。经初步计算分析，整栋楼建筑面积1.8万平方米，每年可节约运营费用150万元。与传统建筑相比，可节约电费145万元、水费5.4万元、标准煤610吨，减少二氧化碳排放1600吨。研发办公楼为全社会节能减排事业贡献巨大。

研发办公楼充分利用当地自然条件，且并非每一项绿色技术都需耗资。办公楼建筑通过"本土化"和"精益化"设计原则和适宜的设计方法与技术，实现绿色节能。

据资料显示，研发大楼以因地制宜的理念，整合利用了约40项绿色技术和措施，充分挖掘了自然生态环境对"绿色建筑"的价值。

研发办公楼已经变为花鸟鱼儿的聚集地，楼内有许多巧妙的设计。每个花坛和喷泉似乎都藏着一个秘密。以F1的喷泉和空中花园为例，它不仅是建筑景观，更是一个"人工湿地"——再生水处理系统将整栋建筑产生的污水转化为"再生水"，经生物处理后用于冲厕。再生池内喷泉系统也取代了空调系统的冷却塔，池底安装了透明玻璃，将自然光引入地下室花园。每一滴落在研发办公楼上的雨水都会收集起来，用以整个大楼的立体绿化灌溉。

绿色建筑本就应该生机勃勃。研发办公楼可自行发电，污水、垃圾可自行回收利用。同时，建筑外观也不是纯玻璃和混凝土，而是一件"天然外衣"。研发办公楼西侧，设计师设计了一个盾形花架，里面摆满了各种藤蔓和鲜花，爬满了整面墙。春天时，这些植物就成了大楼里亮丽的绿色装备，阻挡大楼吸收城市热量。

花台上花草常年盛开，招蜂引蝶，鸟儿甚至会在这儿筑巢安家。

除了立体绿色"天然外衣"，研发办公楼"人造外套"也颇具特色。该建筑低层外墙采用一次成型、整体安装的中空水泥纤维挤压板，不仅环保，而且强度大、重量轻，还可以抗地震和火灾，具备隔音效果。这种材料可作为室内外装饰面，省去了传统装饰的烦琐工作，节省了大量材料，同时也倡导了简单材料美学。

研发办公楼每年可节约运营成本120万元。由于低成本、高效率、本土化的绿色建筑技术综合应用，研发办公楼综合成本仅为4300元/平方米。大楼以深圳一栋普通高层写字楼造价，达到了三星级绿色建筑标准。通过运行数据分析，与深圳同类型办公楼相比，研发办公楼空调能耗降低63%左右，照明能耗降低71%左右，常规能耗降低66%左右，总能耗降低了大约63%。按此计算，研发办公楼每年可节约电能约1094.4万千瓦时。由于屋顶上安装了太阳能光伏系统，系统运行第一年发电量为7.56万千瓦时，占建筑年用电量的7%。仅电费下调一项，研发大楼每年可节省约117万元。在节约用水方面，由于该建筑采用再生水和雨水循环系统，每年可节约用水5180吨。扣除再生水系统运行费用后，每年可节约1.5万元。非传统用水利用率为52%，远远超过国家绿色建筑评价标准中40%这一最高标准。

作为本土化、低成本绿色建筑，研发办公楼得到了社会强烈认可。无论是国内还是海外的绿色建筑，在大多数人看来更像"奢侈品"。国内绿色建筑造价成本往往超过10000元/平方米，更不用说发达国家那些价格高昂的绿色建筑，高成本让绿色建筑变成了人们既向往却又遥不可及的目标。研发办公楼的广泛认可度与接受度主要在于其造价适中（4300元/平方米）。很多参观者说，在听到研发办公楼成本时，他们想让自己大楼也"绿"起来。

资料来源：深圳建筑研究所提供信息。BR Building是深圳建筑研究院（IBR）研发办公楼。

加快行人和自行车交通系统建设，深圳开展火车站周边慢行基础设施规划建设，实现地铁、公交延伸服务。结合深圳绿道建设，推进慢行通道及配套设施建设，积极营造城市慢行系统氛围。深圳建成约200公里的自行车网道，提高市民休闲时间质量。研究公共交通系统需求、实施条件、限制条件和可行性，逐步建立公共自行车系统。

加强交通组织管理。深圳通过完善道路交通网络、交通信号和交通信息平台建设，建立和完善智能交通管理系统。建立交通行业能耗和污染排放统计监测制度；制定有效措施，加强交通需求控制，提高机动车通过率，降低车辆空转时间，减少废气排放。

八 推广绿色建筑

深圳严格执行《深圳经济特区建筑节能条例》《公共建筑节能设计标准实施细则》等法律法规，确保新建建筑100%符合节能要求。到2015年，绿色建筑在全部新建建筑中比重达到40%，2020年将达到80%。建立绿色建筑全生命周期管理理念。将绿色低碳理念融入建筑勘察、设计、施工、运营、物业管理、拆迁全生命周期。研究建立具有深圳特色的绿色调查、绿色设计、绿色施工、绿色评价、绿色运营、绿色物业等绿色建筑标准体系。

案例6-3：深圳市盐田区创建生态系统生产总值（GEP）评估体系

2015年，深圳市盐田区首次在中国引入城市GEP。GEP是生态系统生产总值的英文简称，是指生态系统为人类福祉提供产品和服务的总经济价值。与更关注经济系统运行状态GDP不同，GEP则强调生态系统运行状态对生态环境的"价签"。GEP为"美丽中国"提供了量化依据，使区域发展同时向GDP和GEP"双核算、双运行、双提高"的模式转变。该系统为国家生态文明试点示范区增添了亮点,深圳荣获"2015 中国政府创新最佳实践"奖。盐田区城市 GEP 核算体系由三个层次的指标组成:两个一级指标:"自然生态系统价值"和"人居生态系统价值";11 个二级指标,包括生态产品、生态调控、生态文化、大气环境维护和改善、水环境维护与改善、土壤环境维护与改善、生态环境维护与改善、声环境价值、固体废物合理处置、节能减排、环境卫生;28 项三级指标,包括人类可直接利用的粮食、木材、水资源等,水土保持、固碳制氧、间接向人类提供空气净化等生态调节功能,源于生态景观的文化和服务功能,以及与水、气、噪声、矿渣和碳减排,污染物排放减少等有关指标。

好的计算制度必须既全面又具体。因此,指标具有普遍性,农村和城市共设置 28 项指标,但具体核算项目可能有所不同。例如,鉴于面临环境污染治理这一巨大挑战,盐田港主要核算项目可设置为节能减排。

推广新建建筑节能标准,深圳所有新建建筑将执行建筑节能标准。鼓励新建建筑实行建筑节能标识制度。发展绿色建筑,推进绿色建设。以保障性住房为突破口,推进住宅建设产业化和一次性装修,开展住宅性能和零部件认证,培育住宅产业现代化示范基地和项目,加快建设住宅产业。努力降低新建、改建建筑能耗。

对现有建筑进行节能改造,实施《深圳市既有建筑节能改造实施方案》,编制能耗统计;开展能耗审计、节能宣传和能耗检测。动员各区各部门、各单位结合城市改造、大型公共建筑改造,建立既有建筑节能改造项目数据库,建筑立面和屋面改造以及抗震住宅的实施,全面推进既有建筑节能改造,促进建筑低碳改造。

开展建筑技术创新,深圳鼓励发展和使用新建筑技术、新材料和新设备。鼓励发展高性能新型墙体材料和玻璃幕墙材料。大力发展高性能建筑能源设备,特别是建筑空调能源设备和动力设备。鼓励企业编写施工工艺和施工方法。

促进可再生能源的应用,深圳在公共建筑、市政工程和高端住宅建筑方面实施太阳能光伏建筑一体化示范工程。在公共建筑、办公建筑、工业区（园区）、宾馆、企业、住宅等具备必要条件的新建建筑和既有建筑屋顶安装太阳能光伏系统和太阳能热系统，引领太阳能产品应用及相关产业发展。

对事业单位用能设备进行节能改造，淘汰高能耗、高污染设备，推广应用节能设备和新能源产品。严格执行节能管理，建立能耗统计和监测平台，提高能源利用效率，减少事业单位碳排放。

推进事业单位节能改造，重视空调、照明和电力系统、供暖系统、办公设备、电梯、风机、水泵等的节能改造，推广清洁能源；加强日常节能管理，对政府办公楼和大型公共建筑进行节能减排监测、绩效考核和审计；加强服务车能耗管理，加强节水节材力度，完善政务信息系统建设。推广无纸化办公，严格执行夏季26℃空调控制标准。

推广节能照明产品，深圳正逐步淘汰大型公共建筑中白炽灯泡和高压汞灯，推广高效节能、技术成熟的LED灯、T5灯和三色稀土荧光灯。至2015年底，全市70%主要道路安装或采取了交替照明或智能照明调光等节能灯措施，实现了照明节能30%。

九　倡导绿色低碳生活方式

积极开展土地日、地球日、水资源日、能源日、公共交通日、无车日、节水运动、减塑运动、1小时停电等低碳活动，增强公众低碳意识。例如，2010年3月，深圳开展了"绿行动，绿种子"绿色出行、"深圳低碳年"等一系列活动，所有市民都参与了"地球一小时"活动。据深圳市供电局实时统计，停电一小时内，深圳节约了3.39万千瓦时电量，相当于13.56吨标准煤。

城市是市民的家，放松对城市生活不可或缺，城市需要一个相对放松和悠闲的氛围。漫步街头，慢节奏犹如放慢了的镜头，让人们重新领略那些曾忽视的景观，品味城市四季变幻，感受到城市的悠闲与优雅。深圳慢行交通系统不仅让出行更加便捷，而且将城市的人文景观有形地连接起来，成为城市文化休闲的延伸品。富有特色地域景观、地域文化、商业文化和公共文化服务网络由此有机连接和整合，使慢行成为人们的休闲选择，这也是城市慢行交通系统的本质。城市慢行系统关键在于路线的选择，在快节奏的城市里，人们可以放慢步伐、舒展心情，这展现出城市舒适悠闲的一面。

纵观盐田的慢行生活，这儿不仅有曲折的海岸线，还有253公里错开绿道慢行交通网络，沿途景色丰富，是深圳市民体验盐田生活最佳场所。同时，全区分布有6000辆公共自行车，让市民能在300—500米范围内享受慢生活的舒适，这是盐田区给广大市民带来的绿色福利。

十　政策引导与市场机制整合

发展之初，深圳吸引了一大批"两高一低"企业（高能耗、高污染、低效益）。如龙岗河和坪山河流域聚集了大量重污染企业，产值共计138.6亿元，税收21.2亿元，分别占全流域的12.5%和7.8%。但是，这些企业产生了整个流域61.5%的工业废水和47.7%的工业化学氧。产业呈现出明显"高碳"特征，产业布局"零散、无序、低端"。全市现有各类工业园区900多个（不含高新区、保税区），工业园区总面积超过150平方公里。不过，每个园区面积都相当小，其中74%的园区面积不足10公顷，平均容积率只有1.0。

深圳面临瓶颈制约，空间、资源、人口、环境等方面压力加剧，传统经济发展模式已无法适应，这就要求淘汰和转移落后产业，降低高碳企业排放，为传统产业转型和新兴产业发展腾出空间。

深圳很早已意识到高投入、高能耗发展模式难以为继；因此，深圳加快推进产业转型升级，始终把节能减排作为低碳发展的重要载体。深圳把产业结构优化作为低碳发展重要支撑，以较低资源消耗和环境成本，构建了深圳高质量增长新路径。

淘汰传统企业必须慎重，因为这是一项关乎社会和经济的决定。毕竟，这些企业在深圳早期发展过程中做出了巨大贡献。因此，必须认真、科学地确定产能淘汰标准。标准既不能过高，因为这会有损大批企业和职工，影响经济发展长期动力；也不能过低，影响碳排放降低效果，阻碍转型发展。

案例6-4：深圳国际低碳城综合示范效应

深圳多年来坚持绿色低碳发展实践为低碳城市规划建设奠定了良好的基础，为实现低碳发展和升级提供了良好基础。2012年，深圳国际低碳城作为中欧可持续城市化合作旗舰项目正式启动。国际低碳城坚持低碳、智慧城市的核心理念，规划建设"四个区域"，即气候友好型城市试点区、低碳新兴产业集聚区、低碳生活方式引领区、低碳国际合作示范区。国家低碳综合开发试点，目前已进入全面建设阶段。

深圳国际低碳城位于生态环境良好、经济发展相对落后地区，城市建设粗放，基础设施薄弱。深圳国际低碳城旨在探索适合城市发展相对落后地区跨越式低碳发展模式，以多规则协调手段推进产业与城市一体化建设，引导产业升级转型向低碳发展方向发展，采用国内外资源创新市场化的机制和体系，为国家新型城镇化和低碳绿色发展寻找路径和试点。

建设过程中，深圳国际低碳城摈弃了大规模拆迁的建设理念，尊重现有条件，化腐朽为神奇。低碳城积极开展当地生态诊断，对现有企业进行全面碳核查，编撰低碳城市指标体系，对低碳城市土地拍卖、项目准入、开发等碳指标进行控制。建立碳排放监测公共平台，对企业碳排放进行监测、管理、监督和评价；创建社区共享模式，探索社区、校园、公园公共设施共享模式。

2014年，深圳国际低碳城成为全国十大新型城镇化示范城之一，并获得中国国际经济交流中心和美国保尔森研究所联合主办的"2014年可持续发展规划项目奖"，这是中国唯一一个获此殊荣的项目。低碳生态城（区）规划专家对其低碳发展模式的优势、参考性和可借鉴性给予了高度肯定。2015年，深圳国际低碳城入选首批国家低碳城市（镇）试点城市，在8个试点城市中排名第一。

深圳国际低碳城自启动以来，低碳城所在的坪地街道总产值由2013年的65.45亿元增加到2017年的109.25亿元，年均增长11.3%；工业总产值由2013年的182.37亿元增加到2017年的102.37亿元，年均增长9.4%；单位GDP碳排放强度下降12.67%。自国际低碳城建立以来，坪地街道并没有因低碳城建设和产业转型而出现经济下滑，相反，其经济增长稳定。

2013年6月17日至18日，首届低碳城市论坛在此举行，至今已成功举办6届，在国内外产生了巨大反响，来自50多个国家和地区约6000多名嘉宾出席了该论坛。中国最早碳市场诞生于此；由联合国工业发展组织监督的全球可再生能源领先技术"蓝天奖"在这里颁发；全国低碳技术博览会也在这里举行。低碳城市论坛已成为展示中国应对气候变化成效的重要窗口和探索全球低碳领域前沿课题、分享智慧、开展务实合作的重要平台。

（一）产业政策指导

根据国家产业结构调整指导目录和本地区发展实际，深圳制定了产业结构调整优化和产业指导目录，从能源消耗、排放、质量安全等方面科学界定高污染行业和高环境危害产品标准。例如，由于水资源短缺，深圳将万元GDP用水量作为产业指导目录核心指标，要求通信设备、计算机及其他电子设备制造业每增加万元产值，用水量不超过4立方米。宝安区禁止新建化工、印染、电镀、电路板等高能耗、高排放、高污染项目，新企业必须采用无毒、低污染原材料，并采用先进的生产工艺代替剧毒材料和落后生产工艺，从而实现资源高效利用和循环利用。2008年以来，深圳通过加强固定资产投资项目审批备案工作，实行新批项目管理权限联动机制和项目审批问责制度。

（二）运用市场价格杠杆

高能耗、高污染、高排放企业由于利润低，通常对成本投入非常敏感。深圳利用水、电、气、最低工资等价格杠杆效应，逐步提高低端企业经营成本，用"看不见的手"把这些低端企业从市场淘汰。深圳对高耗能行业淘汰和限制性企业进行全面排查，公布企业名称，实行动态管理，严格执行差别化水、电、气价格。深圳对能耗超过现有单位产品能耗（电耗）的企业，实行非户籍计划超限额累计提价措施；加大收费力度，提高排污费。深圳率先建立了反映全国水资源稀缺性的水价机制，采取原水和自来水价格联动调整模式，不断优化原水、自来水和再生水价格关系。此外，深圳最低工资标准由 2009 年 1000 元提高到 2015 年 2030 元，实现"7 年翻番"，继续保持全国最高水平。深圳提高劳动密集型企业劳动成本，迫使低附加值企业转型。通过引导低端制造业环节有序外迁，深圳取消、撤销和清理了 10 万多家低端企业，为新兴产业和高端产业发展创造了宝贵空间。

（三）发挥金融信贷激励作用

绿色信贷是环境保护部、中国人民银行、中国银行业监督管理委员会为遏制高耗能、高污染产业盲目扩张所推出的一项新信贷政策。其核心是对违反产业和环境政策的企业和项目进行信贷控制，将企业环境保护作为商业银行批准贷款必要条件之一，发挥金融促进环境保护作用。通过建立健全绿色金融政策措施，深圳严格控制银行资金对落后产业的支持，加快淘汰"两高一低"产业。

深圳环保局与金融系统开展合作，签署了《企业环保信息提供与信息查询服务协议》，将违反环境保护法的企业信息纳入金融机构企业信用基础信息数据库。金融机构将停止向违规企业提供贷款，直至整改完成。据不完全统计，深圳停止向 100 多家违反环境保护法企业提供 50 亿元贷款，有效打击了环境保护违法行为。根据政府颁布的《深圳市重点污染企业环境保护信用管理办法》，深圳将对电镀、电路板、印染等行业的高污染企业和重点、大排量排污企业进行环保信用评价。2012年，760家重点污染企业中，绿卡企业159家，蓝卡、黄卡、红卡企业分别为420家、141家、40家。对红卡企业，除责令限期改正外，环境保护行政主管部门可以予以关闭、拒发环境保护专项资金补助或建议绿色信贷合作银行停止向企业提供贷款。环保总局相关措施极大地激励了产业链上下游企业改进工艺和设计，提高了环保标准。

（四）技术改造促进传统企业升级改造

促进产业转型升级并不一定表示要淘汰传统产业。深圳在推进产业升级改造的同时，同样注重传统产业绿色低碳发展，力争将传统产业规模和效益提升至新高度。以时尚消费行业为例，深圳坚持优质品牌、优质企业、优质产品"三个质量"原则，以品牌建设为核心，工业设计为指导，深圳赋予传统服装、黄金、珠宝、玻璃、家具等行业以独特文化价值。这样一来，企业创意和设计能力得到了增强，产品附加值得到了提升，传统先进产业向时尚消费产业转变得到了不断推动与支持。转型后，70%以上企业将营业额5%以上用于研发，成功打造了1个世界名牌、41个中国名牌、30个广东名牌。深圳黄金珠宝行业包括46%全国著名黄金珠宝品牌，而深圳占国内女装时尚市场份额已达60%。

技术改造是企业利用新技术、新工艺、新设备、新材料、新设计，改造和改善现有设施和工艺条件，实现内涵式发展的投资活动，也是实现节能减排的重要途径。长期以来，深圳家具、钟表等传统产业发展模式相对粗放，这些行业产品缺乏技术含量，工艺水平低，易受诸如日益激烈市场竞争的外部环境变化影响。深圳每年支持企业技术改造项目有100多个，加快了黄金、服装、钟表等城市产业改造和机械模具数字化装备改造。

据不完全统计，5年来，深圳累计投入升级改造资金200多亿元，通过财政资金或贴息等方式吸引社会投资3000多亿元。另外，深圳将清洁生产理念引入产业集群基地和产业带建设进程，有力促进了建材、电镀、家电、珠宝、印染、钟表等传统产业集群化发展。深圳对18个老工业区进行升级改造，建成工业设计、汽车电子等16个特色工业园区。深圳对污染物排放超过国家、省、市排放标准或超过污染物排放总量控制指标的企业实施强制性清洁生产审查,将清洁生产审查作为结算、扩建约束,重新安置和享受优惠政策资格条件之一,并在产品整个生命周期内控制资源和能源消耗,以降低其碳排放。

下 篇

Chapter 1   The Global Value Chain in Shenzhen and the Pearl Delta Region

Introduction

Shenzhen is known as the Silicon Valley of China, and analysts say that it may soon be even more significant, since it combines not only software, as in its American relative, but also hardware capabilities. Shenzhen is the home of major Chinese corporations, such as Huawei, a global electronic conglomerate; Tencent, an internet company that has WeChat and QQ; BYD, an electronic and automaker giant; BGI, a company working on life science and genome research; DJI, a company producing drones and aerial technologies; SenseTime, working on Artificial Intelligence.

How did a small village in 1979 become a global technological hub? This chapter explains the ascent of Shenzhen in terms of opening-up, finance, governance and policy. More important is that this fast development has been made while monitoring urban planning and expansion, combining productive capacities with urban expansion in novel ways.

Stylized Facts

According to the Global Urban Competitiveness Report 2018 – 2019 jointly released by the Chinese Academy of Social Sciences and the United Nations Human Settlements Programme, UN-Habitat, Shenzhen ranked fifth in the world in terms of economic competitiveness, and by country, China topped the ranking. The Global Innovation Index 2017 released by several agencies, including the World Intellectual Property Organization (WIPO), showed that Shenzhen was the second largest innovation cluster worldwide, after Tokyo and ahead of Silicon Valley. In four decades from 1978 to 2018, Shenzhen has risen from a poor remote fishing town to a global innovation metropolis and emerged from the bottom of the world's industrial chain to a leading position. Shenzhen has made world history with its rapid development. Its evolution is represented in the following aspects.

From an agricultural town with poor infrastructure to a modern metropolis

In terms of urban built area and environment development, Shenzhen used to be a small town with an area of 3 square kilometers in 1978, which was expanded to 390 square kilometers in 1979 and 1,997 square kilometers in 2010. Before the reforms and opening-up policy, Shenzhen was a barren wasteland. After 40 years it is now covered by green lands and well urbanized. Before the establishment of Shenzhen City and in the early days, Shenzhen had barely any infrastructure. Now, it has the world's foremost infrastructure as a global urban centre. By 2017, there were eight metro lines with a total length of 285 kilometers, making Shenzhen one of the top 10 global cities in terms of subway length in operation. Shenzhen is connected to more than 36 overseas cities by air. The handling capacity of Shenzhen Port has grown to 25.2 million TEUs (twenty-foot equivalent unit) containers per year, becoming the second largest port in the world for five consecutive years.

From a small town with 20,000 residents to a metropolis of tens of thousands of people

In terms of urban population and social development, Guangdong Province and its Baoan County saw thousands of residents flee to Hong Kong before the reform and opening-up. In 1978, the population of Shenzhen Town in Baoan County was about 25,000. In 1979, Baoan County was converted to

Shenzhen City, with a permanent population of 314,000. Over the following 40 years, millions of young people and college graduates have migrated to Shenzhen. In 2018, the registered permanent residents stood at 15.2283 million, and the number of actual population served by local government exceeded 20 million. The urbanisation rate was 100 percent. In 2017, the number of talents of various types exceeded 5.1 million, accounting for 40.7 percent of the total permanent population. In 2017, the average age of the permanent population was 32.5 years, and the main labour forces aged 15 to 44 accounted for 76 percent. At the same time, urban residents' disposable income per capita rose from 1,915 yuan in 1985 to 52,938 yuan in 2017, a 27.6-fold increase in 32 years, registering an annual growth rate of 10.9 percent (Figure 1-1).

From a small fishing town to a global technological centre

In terms of urban industrial and economic development, its GDP soared from 196 million yuan in 1979 to more than 2.2 trillion yuan, increasing 11223 fold over 38 years with an average annual growth rate of 22.4 percent. During the same period, GDP per capita grew from 606 yuan to 183,100 yuan, an increase of 301 times with an average annual growth rate of 11.2 percent. In 2019, Shenzhen's GDP hit 2.69 trillion yuan, overtaking Hong Kong for the first time (Figure 1-2 and 1-3) 2625.

From 1979 to 2017, Shenzhen's total export volume grew from USD 9.3 million to USD 244.221 billion, up by 9,565-fold with an annual growth rate of 27.3 percent over the last 38 years. In 1978, Shenzhen was a small traditional agricultural and fishing town. In 1979, it started to engage in processing and small production trades, that is, processing materials or given samples and assembling components.

In 2018, it became a regional financial centre, China's economic centre, and a global technological innovation centre. Starting from a handful of small-scale cotton mills and farming machinery maintenance and repair workshops, Shenzhen has grown rapidly to having 3.2 million burgeoning business

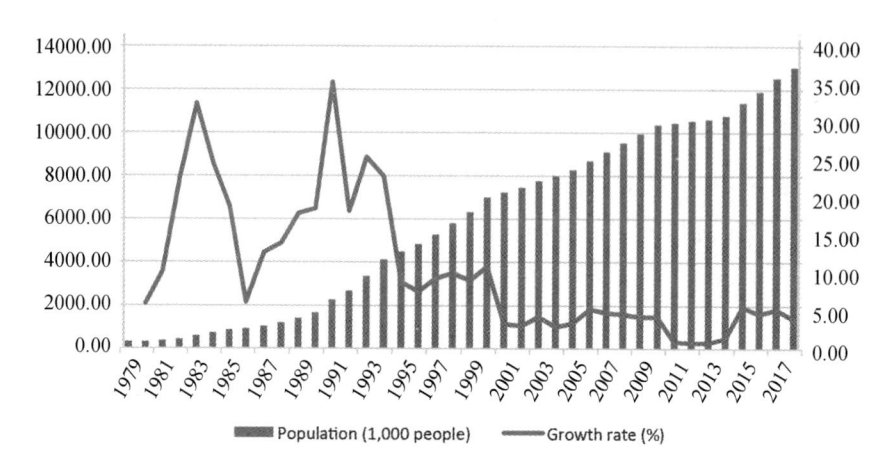

Figure 1-1: Population and its growth of Shenzhen 1979—2017

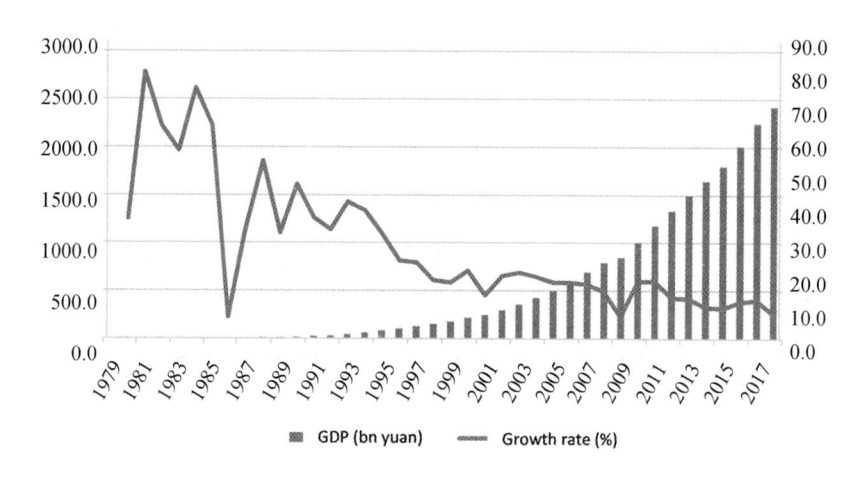

Figure 1-2: Shenzhen's GDP and growth rate (1979—2017)

entities, among which 1.88 million are enterprises and 12,000 are state-level high-tech enterprises. In 2017, the city produced 381,230 times more microcomputer equipment than in 1983, and 4,260 times more integrated circuits than in 1983. All the products are of high technology value. Shenzhen is home to seven Global Top 500 companies such as Huawei, Ping'an, Tencent, Vanke and Evergrande. Huawei, Tencent and DJI have grown into internationally reputable tech companies. The city is capable of manufacturing

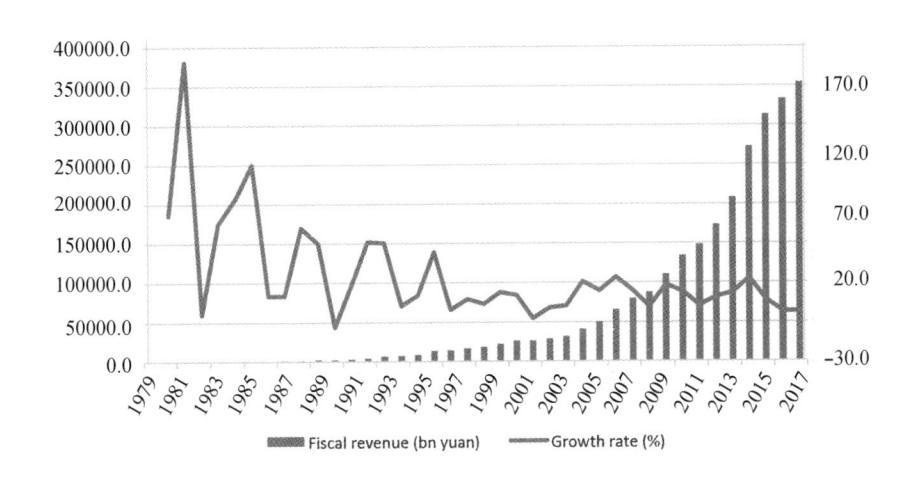

Figure 1-3: Shenzhen's fiscal revenue and its growth rate (1979—2017)

world-leading high-tech products, such as mobile phones, wearable devices and high-end medical apparatus and instruments, enabling people across the world to experience the exciting life created by technologies.

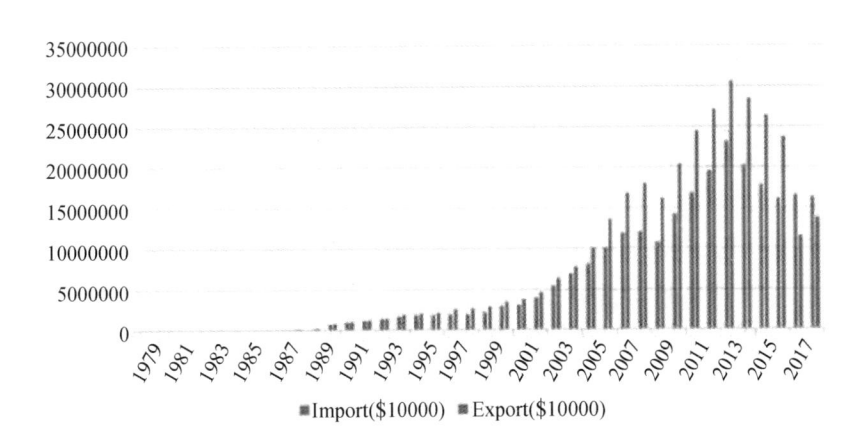

Figure 1-4: Shenzhen's export and import (1979—2017)

From a small country town to a national economic and technological powerhouse

In terms of city status and influence, Shenzhen leads the development of Chinese cities and spearheads the progress of the whole world. First, Shenzhen has directly pushed the establishment of a national system of market economy and opening up on all fronts by expanding and replicating the original reforms that were then piloted in other regions across China. The city's successful experience and development philosophies have inspired China and the entire world to change their mentality regarding development. Second, a substantial part of wealth created by Shenzhen goes to the government in the form of taxation, and to migrant workers in the form of wages, supporting national economic growth, development of the hinterland and the prosperity of millions of households. In 2018, revenues from the general public budget of urban areas under Shenzhen's administration reached 910 million yuan, ranking first among cities of the Chinese mainland. This revenue accounted for 5 percent of the national total. Third, as Shenzhen's economy grew further, its industries expanded and were transferred to neighbouring regions and hinterland cities, directly spurring their economic take-off. Fourth, with its economic development and technological innovation, Shenzhen has fostered millions of technicians, entrepreneurs and innovation makers, some of whom went back to their hometown or other regions, driving the development and innovation of more areas. In 2017, patents filed according to the patent cooperation treaty (PCT) by Shenzhen accounted for 43.1 percent of the national total, making it the city filing the most PCT patents in China for 14 consecutive years.

Since the introduction of the reform and opening-up policy, the number of China's mainland cities has grown from 193 in 1978 to more than 650 in 2018, and towns from more than 2,000 to some 20,000. From the five Special Economic Zones in coastal areas including Shenzhen in the 1980s to more new economic zones and experiment zones, impressive achievements have been made. Shenzhen does not parallel many other cities in terms of economic foundation, production factors, historical culture, and environmental capacity, but it still created an economic powerhouse and realised sustainable high-speed growth and rapid transformation in economy, society and environment.

Theoretical Framework

Based on the theoretical frameworks of economic growth theory and development economics, this research incorporates the unique variables of China's urban development and the characteristics of globalization and concludes with the driving forces, mechanism and model of China's urban development economics. The four engines that interact in the design and rise of cities in China are: (1) Institutional innovation, (2) the gathering of non-agricultural sectors, (3) the global division of labour, and (4) city governance; those are forces that compete with each other in deciding the rise of cities and shaping the urban landscape of China.

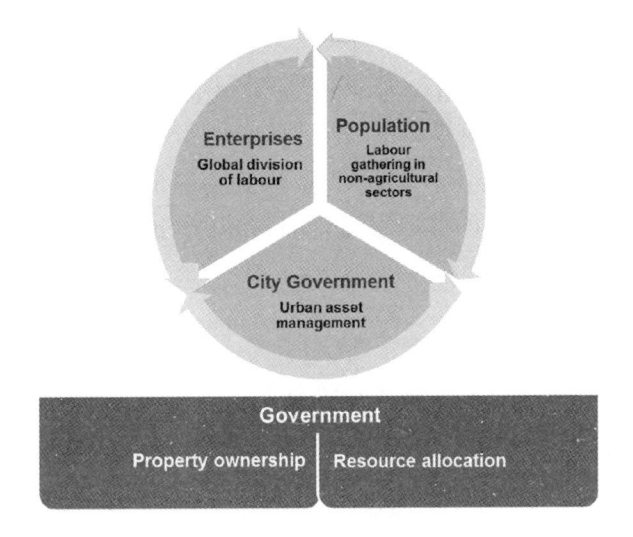

Figure 1 – 5: Economic model of Chinese urban development

As a base, the reform to establish a market economy formalises the rights and responsibilities of economic entities and the way of resource allocation, providing basic momentum and conditions for the rise of cities. The global division of labour brought by multinational enterprises injects external vitality into the process. The gathering of non-agricultural sectors as a result of the inflow of rural labour surpluses accelerates the process. City governance and finance by the municipal governments provide unique power for the rise of the cities (Figure 1 – 5).

In general, the four engines have a joint impact: the reform to establish a market economy creates conditions and driving forces for the other three engines to unleash their power; the engine of rural labour surpluses transmits to its energy in tandem with multinational enterprises and city governments; multinational enterprises have to work in tandem with the rural labour surpluses and city governments; the city government can play its role only when combined with the rural labour surpluses and multinational enterprises; the reform to establish a market economy attracts global capital, technologies and markets, and the unlimited supply of China's rural labour surpluses, land and business environment, which jointly prompt rapid industrialization and urbanization in China.

The engines play different roles at different stages to promote the transformation and upgrading of cities.

Rural surplus labour first powers the development of urban labour, then it is powered by capital from global enterprises, then by local land and environment, and lastly by talents and people.

Precisely, the interplay between the four engines follows a general law, but due to different realities in different cities, it shows particularities. Shenzhen implemented a special economic zone system and took the lead in reform. On the one hand, its market economy and globalisation level were enhanced rapidly. At the early stage of development, it jumped over the stage of rural industrialisation and small-scale urbanisation straight into the stage of export-oriented development fuelled by the engine of multinational enterprise. The urbanisation of Shenzhen was driven by export-oriented industrialisation. On the other hand, resource scarcity and soaring costs forced development to by pass the stage where the economy is driven by land and capital and move into the stage of innovation-driven economic growth where high-end talents play the leading role.

Analysis of the Success of Shenzhen

Over the 40 years from 1979 to 2019, following the laws of urban development and giving full play to the interaction of the four development engines, Shenzhen has created a miracle in which a traditional small agricultural and fishing town has risen to a global technological centre.

Labour-intensive development: joining the global industrial chain from the bottom (1979 – 1992)

From 1979 to 1992, the Shenzhen Special Economic Zone was in its early days. The processing and compensation trade with Hong Kong, the inflow of population from the Chinese mainland and the large-scale land development enabled Shenzhen's urbanisation and industrialisation to expand drastically. Shenzhen made its name across the country due to its speed of growth. It also joined the global industrial chain. In this period, the dominating driving forces were labour and institutional innovation. This stage featured innovation in the economic system, an inflow of population, infrastructure construction and the development of the labour-intensive and export-oriented economy. The interplay between the four engines is shown as follows.

Reform and opening up and political trials in Shenzhen create institutional conditions for its rapid growth

Against the backdrop of China's reform and opening up, Shenzhen managed to unshackle the chain of planned economy guided by market economy principles and took bold measures in reforming the systems of pricing, payment, land and housing, infrastructure construction and labour employment by establishing a special economic zone.

In 1987, the Shenzhen Municipal Government issued China's first "Interim Provision concerning Encouraging Technology Personnel Starting

Private Technology Companies". The document encouraged high-tech talents with patents or management expertise to become shareholders. Ren Zhengfei, now chief executive officer of Huawei, took the opportunity and founded the company, which has grown to be a world-leader. As early as the 1980s, Shenzhen issued the "Shenzhen Science and Technology Development Plan 1999 – 2000", formulating policies supporting high-tech industries.

The large-scale industrial layout by Hong Kong businesses creates favourable conditions for Shenzhen's rapid growth

Amid global industrial restructuring, enterprises from Hong Kong broke down industrial chains and brought labour-intensive chains to Shenzhen in the form of processing and compensation trades, turning Shenzhen into a processing powerhouse as they pushed the transfer of capital, technology and management expertise here. In 1992, Shenzhen began to liberalize manufacturing. The processing and compensation trade enabled Shenzhen to join the global industrial value chain from the bottom. In the beginning, it mainly manufactured primary industrial products. The global value chain Shenzhen joined was for advanced electronic and information industry, and then Shenzhen chose a pivotal starting point for its path toward technological innovation and making high-end tech products.

The inflow of migrants provides labour force conditions for Shenzhen's rapid growth

In 1979, 20,000 engineers were dispatched to Shenzhen, starting the process of massive inflow of labour forces to the city. In 1989, one million migrant workers went to Shenzhen. In 1979, the number of people on the payroll in the city was only 139,500, and the figure reached 1.759 million in 1992. The share of the labour force between 15 and 59 years old increased from 58.4 percent in 1982 to 88 percent in 1990. However, a 1990 sample survey showed that the labour force with high school education and lower accounted for as high as 65 percent of the total labour population. Labour force, especially the migrant workers, flowed to Shenzhen for non-agricultural jobs. They provided the most critical condition for the city to develop labour-intensive processing and compensation trade. "Shenzhen people" from across the world and of different backgrounds were enterprising and adventurous. They injected the genes of cultural inclusiveness and entrepreneurship in Shenzhen and sowed seeds for local people to be original and visionary.

The basic hardware and software urban environment provide conditions for Shenzhen's rapid growth

On the one hand, Taking advantage of its proximity to Hong Kong, Shenzhen Municipal Government went to great lengths for and gave full play to favourable policies in terms of taxation, land, finance, and foreign trade and created a low-cost business climate. On the other hand, it gave full scope to the institutional innovations of compensation for land use and housing construction. With wealth from land, the city was able to launch large-scale land development and urban infrastructure construction, creating the spatial vehicle for urban development. At the same time, the local government used foreign investment and adopted a market-oriented approach to urban development and operation. In this way, infrastructure projects like ports, wharves, power supply, roads and telecommunication facilities were established in a fast and efficient manner. The rapid improvement of the urban environment attracted the inflow of foreign investment and labour forces, which combined to push the city to develop.

During this period, Shenzhen took the lead in reform and opening up, providing the public framework, human resources and business development with far better powers and conditions than other cities. At the same time, it managed to attract the massive labour surplus in rural areas and foreign investment for technology projects to gather in the city and realized exploding growth and the goals in the early stage of development. The development scale also took shape.

Capital-intensive development stage (1993 – 2002), moving up to the lower medium position of the global industrial chain

In 1993 – 2002, Shenzhen entered a new stage for entrepreneurship.

With improved urban infrastructure and functions, Shenzhen rapidly upgraded industrialisation and urbanisation. It climbed from the bottom to the lower middle position of the global industrial chain. At this stage, the dominating factors fostering development were the capital and institutional innovations. The distinctive features of this stage are the building of a market economy, continuous inflow of labour forces, the construction of supporting facilities and the transformation of export-oriented development. The interplay between the four development engines is shown as follows.

The establishment of the "socialist market economy", provided indigenous development power and attraction for foreign investment

Shenzhen gave full play to its favourable conditions as a pilot for reform and opening up. By 1997, it established a socialist market economy featuring ten systems, the first of its kind nationwide. They include the establishment of the modern corporate system, deepening reform of the management system for state-owned assets, the reform of commerce circulation system, the improvement of the labour market, the establishment of a property trading market and institutional innovation in the financial sector. In the 1990s and 2001, Shenzhen issued "further regulations concerning Supporting High-Technology Industries" and "the decision concerning Accelerating the Development of High-Technology Industries". The documents formulated a set of policies for promoting the development of science and technology and building several high-tech industrial parks, creating a high-quality service system for the development of high-tech sectors.

The transfer of electronic and information industries provided conditions for Shenzhen's rapid development and transformation

In this period, the global restructuring of electronic and information industries provided investment, technologies and a vast international market for the city to upgrade labour-intensive processing and compensation trade to capital-intensive and technology-intensive advanced manufacturing. As a result, the manufacturing of electronic and telecommunication devices expanded rapidly in Shenzhen, moving the city up to the lower middle position of the global industrial chain. Thanks to spillovers from multinational companies' investment and technology, the locally grown high-tech industries, modern logistics and financial services began to thrive. In 2012, the manufacturing of telecommunication devices, computer and other electronic devices accounted for 56.1 percent of the gross industrial output above the designated size, up by 25.3 percentage points from 1993. The output of high-tech industries totalled 1.29 trillion yuan. Among them, the value of high-tech industries with independent property rights accounted for 61.0 percent, 10.8 percentage points higher than 2000.

The constant influx of labour forces and improving structure provided human resource conditions for Shenzhen's fast growth and transformation

Payroll employment figures expanded from 0.1759 million in 1992 to 7.712 million in 2002. The population with only primary school education or lower dropped significantly, whereas the number with college education surged. People without permanent residency moved out of the city in large numbers, and the population growth rate of this group declined from 28 percent in 1994 to around 10 percent between 1995 and 2000. At the same time, Shenzhen eliminated restrictions of nationality, residency, identity and organisational affiliation among them to attract high-end talents, research institutions and educational facilities, enabling Shenzhen to obtain high-end factors of production without incurring extra expenses. Shenzhen obtained significant production factor support for its industrial transformation and upgrading.

The improved infrastructure created environmental conditions for Shenzhen's rapid development and transformation

The local government continued to bring in foreign investment and increased fiscal revenue from land sales in a bid to improve a wide range of supporting infrastructure and primary city functions. As a result, the city's governance capacity was enhanced, satisfying the demands of its high-speed development and attractiveness for investment and talents. In 2002, Shenzhen established a modern traffic network. There were 54 landline phones and 120 mobile phones for every 100 people. At the same time, public facilities had been well-built. The built-up area citywide reached 495.3 square kilometers, and the special economic zone was 168.1 square kilometers. The green space per capita was 14.9 square meters. The treatment rate of domestic sewage expanded to 61 percent. The average ambient noise level was maintained at 56 dB. Shenzhen received the International Garden City Award in 2000 and the China Human Settlements and Environment Award in 2001.

In conclusion, the socialist market economy system Shenzhen built first provided better powers and conditions than other regions for local government, human resources and business development. The increasing promotion of the hardware and software environment of the city attracted massive inflows of skilled labour and investment for technology projects. The incoming technology-intensive investment and global market fuelled continuous high-speed economic growth and rapid economic transformation and upgrading of Shenzhen. Global investment was the major driving force for its economic development and transformation during this period.

Soaring land cost forcing economic transformation (2003 – 2012) and moving up to the middle of the global industrial chain

From 2003 to 2013, Shenzhen had to adjust its policies due to radical economic transformation. On the one hand, with the reform and opening up carried out nationwide and the modernisation drive entering a new era, Shenzhen no longer enjoyed the institutional and policy dividends. On the other hand, its advantages in four aspects of the development environment had disappeared. They were land and space, energy and water resources, the rising population, and the capacity of the environment. Shenzhen had entered a transformation stage where the economy slowed down, and innovation gained momentum to spur development. The dominating driving force in this period was the rising cost of land and scarcity of resources. Under this new scenario, local industries entered the transitional stage from lower and middle level to the middle and higher end of the global industrial chain. The interplay of the four growth engines is shown as follows.

Shenzhen added new strengths by going global to increase the level of attractiveness of the city

On the one hand, as the socialist market economy system was established nationwide and the reform and opening up on all fronts came into being, Shenzhen no longer had the dividends generated by institutional innovation. On the other hand, the corporate income tax for domestic and foreign enterprises was unified at a rate of 25 percent, ending the last preferential policy given to the Shenzhen Special Economic Zone. Because of this, Shenzhen began to explore new institutional innovation. At the basic institutional level, it kept in alignment with practices of leading international cities to deepen administrative reform, establish service-oriented government and encourage innovation while tolerating failures. In terms of industrial policies, it mapped out blueprints for strategic emerging industries and introduced policies to boost bio-industry, as well as Internet-related sectors, new energy, new materials, culture and innovation and a new generation of information technology among others. These new institutions and policies created conditions for the gathering of innovation factors and the growth of high-tech businesses.

The indigenous growth of private high-tech businesses formed industrial clusters and pushed challenging industrial transformation

On the one hand, due to the rising cost and contraction of the international market, the previous capital-intensive industries oriented towards the international market lost their advantages. On the other hand, utilizing the spillover of knowledge and technologies, some local enterprises multiplied and formed an industrial cluster. They survived and became significant market players by imitation and innovation. As the city shifted gear from old economic growth engines to new ones, it saw a slight slow-down of the economy, with the GDP growing 16.8 percent annually on average. Despite this, high-tech industries in Shenzhen grew rapidly, the financial service sector consistently occupied the top three positions nationwide, modern logistics represented by supply chain, logistics and e-commerce thrived, and cultural industries boomed.

Slowing down the influx of labour forces with an improving structure supported economic transformation

On the one hand, the figure for payroll employment rose from 4.223 million in 1993 to 7.712 million in 2012. The figure for 2017 was 9.433 million. The influx of the labour force slowed down. On the other hand, the quality of the labour force was improving. The share of the population with college diplomas increased from 8.38 percent in 2000 to 17.8 percent in 2010. The average years of schooling grew from 9.77 years in 2000 to 10.81 years in 2009. More important, Shenzhen citizens were made up of people from across China and the world who were enterprising, adventurous and open-minded, so shaped a culture of innovation, inspiring waves of people to start up businesses and undertake entrepreneurial adventures.

Disappearing advantages in terms of land and resources forced Shenzhen to foster new momentums of innovation

After previous high-speed growth, Shenzhen saw an ongoing decline in land available for development. The land cost continued to soar. The per capita freshwater volume was only one-fourth of the national average, making Shenzhen one of the seven Chinese cities with a severe water shortage. The ballooning population aggravated city issues like environmental pollution, traffic congestion, and worsening public safety. To address them, Shenzhen encouraged market competition and formulated and implemented rules on company entries, forcing the high-polluting and high energy-consumption industries to transform and relocate their businesses. On the other hand, Shenzhen continued to improve its urban infrastructure and ecological environment to attract high-end industries.

In this period, the local government addressed the disappearance of institutional and policy dividends and the bottleneck of environmental capacity by forcing businesses to take a new path of fast growth driven by innovation. On the other hand, Shenzhen assumed the mission of piloting new practices and spearheading development. It explored innovative systems and policies to forge a new road for industrial transformation and upgrading. At the same time, the innovation culture fostered in the formation of a migrant city, the spillover of knowledge and technology brought by the export-oriented economy, and the innovation based on imitation in line with real conditions enabled Shenzhen to gradually move toward innovation-driven development in the throes of transformation.

The stage of innovation-driven development (2013 – 2018), moving up to the high reach of global industrial chain

From 2013 to 2019, Shenzhen successfully entered the stage of innovation-driven development. With the improving urban infrastructure and functions, the building-up of institutional software and hardware environment, and the reinforcing cycle of innovation ecology, Shenzhen began to move up to the middle and upper reach of the global industrial chain. The dominating development engines in this period have been talent and innovative institutions. The period is characterized by the gathering and combination of an innovative economic system, innovative capitalization, and innovative talent, as well as supporting infrastructure and a favourable living environment. The interplay between the four engines is shown as follows:

Institutional innovation that supports technological innovation adds powers and attractiveness to Shenzhen

At the institutional level, the city has started a higher level of innovation since 2013 by implementing trial measures and practices in four aspects of establishing a high-level socialist market economy system, service-oriented government, institutions for independent innovation and institutions for energy-saving and environmental-friendly society. At the policy level, the government introduced institutions and measures to spur business start-ups and investment, attract various professionals, and build systematic policies for technological innovation. Innovative systems and policies motivate market entities to engage in innovation, and accelerate the gathering of global innovation resources in Shenzhen so that the city forms a new innovative industrial cluster that further attracts global resources.

Innovative investment enabled rapid growth of high-tech industries, moving Shenzhen to the upper reaches of the global industrial chain

The supporting financial sector for technological innovation continues to improve, spurring mushrooming private tech companies. The private equity industry has boomed. In 2017, Shenzhen had 4,377 registered private equity firms, accounting for one-fifth of the national total. The firms managed 12,143 funds with a valuation of 1.7 trillion yuan. Venture capital was on the rise. From 2012 to 2017, the number of state-level high-tech enterprises increased 3.9 fold, reaching 11,230. The added value climbed from 413.524 billion yuan in 2012 to 735.969 billion yuan in 2017, registering an annual growth rate of 12.2 percent. Its share in GDP was elevated to 32.8 percent. The investment of private tech firms bolstered the growth of private high-tech enterprises and further supported them to move up market and go global. From 2013 to 2017, R&D expenditure rose by 14.9 percent annually. Its share in GDP grew from 3.67 percent in 2013 to 4.35 percent in 2017, leading the world in R&D expenditure. In this period, more than 2,000 Shenzhen-based companies invested in more than 120 countries and regions worldwide. Companies holding independent property rights like Huawei, ZTE, CIMC and BYD, had established business networks across the globe in area of technological innovation, production outsourcing, business expansion and marketing services. Shenzhen genuinely moved to the upper reaches of the global value chain.

Innovative talent continues to grow and unleash capabilities of innovation to be the core engine of development

From 2012 to 2017, payroll employment in Shenzhen grew from 7.712 million to 9.433 million, registering a slowing down in the rate of increase. However, with more talent brought in and cultivated by the city, the total number of professionals in Shenzhen exceeded 5.1 million, accounting for 40.7 percent of the total permanent residents. At the same time, local research institutes and education Facilities expanded rapidly. In 2017,

Shenzhen had 4,296 research institutes, 7.1 fold the level of 2012, registering an annual growth rate of 47.9 percent. Key laboratories incubating innovation reached 1,688, 2.2 times that of 2012, registering an annual growth rate of 17.3 percent. Schools of higher learning numbered 12 in 2018. In a favourable environment for innovation, the large volume of innovative talent unleashed massive energy of innovation. In 2017, Shenzhen filed more than 20,000 PCT patents, 2.5 times that of 2012, ranking fourth after countries including the United States and Japan.

Case 1: Wu Yongmou—from a migrant worker to forerunner of service robots

Over the past 40 years of an economic take-off, Shenzhen witnessed one success story after another about individuals and the city. Wu Yongmou, founder and president of YYD Robo Co., Ltd., grew up with Shenzhen. From a migrant worker to an entrepreneur in the sector of artificial intelligence, he is a legendary example of how business people achieved success in this fertile land of Shenzhen.

Starting as a migrant worker

Wu Yongmou, born in 1977, grew up with Shenzhen and made his fortune in the city.

In the summer of 1993, Wu Yongmou, a high school graduate, came to Shenzhen from his hometown of Jinjiang, Fujian Province, with only 200 yuan, embarking on an entrepreneurial adventure that changed his life. The first job he had was as a porter. One month later, he was working as an apprentice in a factory, starting to acquire knowledge of radio transmission analogue signal technology. He also helped the Japanese master with some trivial work. The master was in charge of workshop management and techniques in the factory and had extensive experience. Wu Yongmou took care of his master in a meticulous way, and thus found favour in his eyes.

The master taught Wu everything from mobile phone production process to plant management procedure, knowledge of mobile phone components and corporate culture. Due to his poor education, he had to teach himself the primary level of higher learning and learned techniques from the master. He got up early and worked until late at night. For three years in a row, he barely had weekends or vacation. Thanks to the unremitting efforts of four years, he was promoted to a senior manager from an apprentice, and his monthly salary rose from 200 yuan to more than 2,000 yuan.

First entrepreneurial endeavour

In 1997, Wu Yongmou, with the 28,000 yuan he earned as a migrant worker as the initial capital, went to Shenzhen seeking entrepreneurial opportunities. Relying on his accumulated professional knowledge, Wu won his first order—manufacturing precision bracket components. Starting from this product, he gradually diversified the range of production, and made the first fortune of his life. In October 1997, he founded Shenzhen Yongyi Electronics Co., Ltd. to engage in OEM production of mobile phones. Wu Yongmou, at 20, realised his dream of becoming a boss. In its first year, Yongyi Electronics earned 1 million yuan. In 2004, Wu earned 100 million yuan for the first time in his life. In 2005, the sales revenue amounted to several hundred million yuan, and the company expanded to employ several thousand people. Wu established Yongyida Industrial Park and bought shares of Tiancai Holding Co., Ltd., a company that specializes in making sports cameras and intelligent hardware. Wu's investment enabled the rapid growth of Tiancai, which is firmly established as a sports camera maker with a massive shipment volume.

Entrepreneurial setback

Business prospects are unpredictable. The financial turmoil in 2008 severely hit Wu's mobile phone factory. The factory manufacturing functional components for mobile phones required technological upgrading. As a result, the order volume shrank, and the factory scale had to be reduced from 5,000 employees to 1,000. Four factories had to be shut down. Wu Yongmou was confronted with a daunting challenge in his entrepreneurial adventure.

Starting again with innovation

In 2014, Wu Yongmou was keenly aware of the promising prospect of artificial intelligence and established YYD Robo Co., Ltd. He recruited the best engineers for R&D of service robots. At the end of 2016, YYD Robo Co., Ltd., with its excellent technical strength and rapid response capabilities, stood out from its rivals and won the bid of a multi-million-dollar order of manufacturing service robots from LG. Since then, the company established its stronghold in the market. Over the following years, YYD Robo Co., Ltd. continued to invest heavily in robot R&D. It established an R&D team of more than 200 engineers, who have filed more than 200 patents, 75 of which are invention patents. The team also created a range of outstanding service robot products, making the company a leader in the field of service robots.

From manufacturing mobile phones to sports camera, and then robot R&D, Wu Yongmou succeeded in business transformation. The background was the pivotal period when Shenzhen advanced technological innovation for industrial transformation and upgrading. Millions of enterprising business people like Wu Yongmou fulfilled their personal ideals and life values with an acute sense for business opportunities and high quality of execution. Their endeavors also pushed the city to change and evolve. His story of business success is indicative of the outlook of Shenzhen people who are aggressive, risk-taking, enterprising and innovative.

Case 2: Konka—from an OEM factory to a holding company and industrial platform

Konka is the first joint venture electronic maker established after China's reform and opening up. In Shenzhen, the frontline of the reform and opening-up, Konka witnessed the remarkable accomplishment the policy brought, and achieved major goals itself. From a pure home appliance maker at the beginning, Konka has grown to be a holding company offering an industrial platform across industries via investment, acquisition and merger.

The first joint venture in electronics manufacture

On March 15, 1979, Guangdong Provincial Administration of Overseas Chinese Farm signed an agreement with Hong Kong Wah Electronics Co., Ltd. on jointly establishing Guangming Overseas Chinese Electronics Factory in Beijing. Following that, returning overseas Chinese and their families worked in processing tape recorders with given materials and samples. In the first year, the factory made a net profit of 830,000 yuan, becoming the first Chinese company using foreign investment to succeed. On November 6, in line with the guiding principles of the central leadership of the Communist Party of China, the joint venture agreement on Guangdong Guangming Overseas Chinese Electronic Industry Co., Ltd. was signed in December the same year. China's first joint venture electronics enterprise came into being.

Processing with given materials and being an Original Equipment Manufacturer (OEM)

In May 1980, Guangming Overseas Chinese Electronics Factory was put into operation in Shahe Industrial Area of the Shenzhen Special Economic Zone, mainly making recorders, colour TV sets, sound sets, calculators, electronic meters and other electronic products. In the beginning, the factory was aware that it could earn only marginal commissions and be controlled by others in the market if it remained an OEM forever. Therefore, it named its products Konka. Thus, May 21, 1980, was made the birthday of Konka. In that year, Konka manufactured 304,000 sets of movements for tape recorders, earning foreign exchanges of 1.12 million yuan and a net profit of 830,000 yuan.

From an OEM to an independent brand holder

As Konka recorders made its name in the market, the company aimed at an emerging industry with higher technology content——colour TV set making. First, it accumulated technology and capital by processing movements of colour TV sets for Hong Kong partners. On December 31, 1987,

China's ministry of machinery and electronic industry then granted Konka permission to manufacture colour TV sets for the domestic market. The company thus achieved an overall business upgrade. In 1990, Konka established a technology development centre, becoming the first company in the sector to do so. In 1992, Konka went public on both China's A and B shares. Later, it bought out the shares of Hong Kong Kong Wah and turned itself into a state-owned enterprise. In 1993, Konka expanded northward and purchased Mudanjiang River TV Sets Manufacturing Factory in Heilongjiang Province. It launched another brand of Mukang and began to expand nationwide. In 1997, Konka was recognized as an outstanding Chinese brand, the first of its kind in Shenzhen and Guangdong Province. Seizing opportunities in the 1990s, a time of awakening Chinese consumerism, Konka built its foothold in the Chinese market with the strength of its low prices. In 1999, it took up the largest market share of colour TV sets in China and become the first locally grown company in Shenzhen with a valuation exceeding 10 billion yuan.

Strategic upgrading and pursuing asset-light development

Starting in 2007, the colour TV industry saw the emerging of liquid crystal display (LCD) screens. Major TV makers increased inputs on R&D, and tech firms also made forays into the colour TV set manufacturing sector, causing the industry to reshuffle. At that time, Konka failed to respond promptly, and its home appliance making went into a recession. At the same time, its management was unstable, suffering from frequent changes of officers. The immediate result was the record revenue loss in 2015. The annual financial statement of the company showed that the net loss of shareholders of Konka's listed companies was as high as 1.257 billion yuan. The revenue was down 2,488.32 percent year on year. The corporate cohesion, employee morale, product planning strategy and operational efficiency were all severely affected.

Konka re-established a senior management team and adjusted the product mix. After more than one year of effort, it managed to overcome its loss making. At the same time, in the face of the latest development of the colour TV industry, and amid national economic transformation and restructuring as well as promotion of innovation-driven development, the company began to seek its transformation to build itself into an asset-light holding company as a platform for multiple industries. It set a clear development goal, combining technology with industry and urbanization, took consumer electronics as the base of the business and gradually upgraded to strategic emerging industries and expanded to a science and technology industrial park, internet and supply chain management. Four business clusters of science and technology industrial park, products and businesses, platform service, and investment and financing have taken shape and grown in a coordinated manner. With the acquisition of and investment in high-tech firms, Konka has made steady progress towards building new growth momentum and attaining diversified business expansion.

Case 3: Shekou Industrial Zone——the frontier of Shenzhen's reform and innovation

Shekou Industrial Zone in Shenzhen was the first to implement the reform and opening up policy across China. The famous slogan, "Time is money and efficiency is life," was born here. The zone has been the frontier of Shenzhen's reform and innovation ever since. Formerly occupying an area of 1.24 square kilometers, it has gradually expanded to 10.85 square kilometers, gathering companies engaging in processing and compensation trades and giving birth to present global top 500 companies like China Merchant Bank, Ping An Group and Huawei, among others. In 2014, the zone was included in the Guangdong Free Trade Zone and is expected to spearhead a new round of reform and opening-up.

Shekou model, the "test tube" of reform and opening up

In an inhospitable wasteland, the Shekou Industrial Zone was born in 1979. It is the first processing industrial zone for exports in the Chinese mainland and was dubbed the "test tube" of reform and opening-up. In a real sense, China's economic reform started from here. Before 1990, Shekou Industrial Zone had autonomy in terms of personnel, finance, assets, and public security and the authority to pilot institutional innovation and reform. It was the first nationwide company to implement a recruitment system for government officials, bonus system, project bidding practice, commercial housing and rental system, social security system, and shareholding system and other reform measures. After the trial in Shekou, the practices and systems were expanded to Shenzhen and other regions in the country. These reforms were dubbed the Shekou model, generating far-reaching impacts.

Pursuing high-end industrial development to re-build Shekou

In1990, Nanshan District of Shenzhen was established. Shekou Industrial Zone seized the historic opportunity and proposed to return powers that were supposed to belong to governments so that it could focus on the management of businesses. The zone found its new role. Based on its previous development, Shekou could not continue to thrive with a labour-intensive industrial structure. In 1995, the zone started a massive round of industrial adjustment. After clean-up campaigns, the zone pulled out of its investment in more than 100 companies engaging in labour-intensive industries with low added value and explored moving up to the middle and upper reaches of the industrial chain. By 2002, after rounds of industrial integration, Shekou Industrial Zone re-defined its business structure, forming a new industrial landscape with real estate and logistics as the core industries and high-tech and industrial park services as the main lines of business.

Upgrading the industrial structure and pursuing innovation-driven development

From 2003 to 2013, a raft of measures was introduced to push the industrialupgrading of the Shekou Industrial Zone. Previous low-and middle-end companies were moved out to make space for new planning and renovation, which focused on R&D centres of the global top 500 and other research institutes.

In 2009, Shekou Industrial Zone invested 60 billion yuan to rebuild the zone with a primary goal of establishing a high-end industrial structure dominated by Internet information, technology services and cultural innovation. In 2010, Shekou Internet Valley came into being, gradually gathering Internet firms, Internet of Things, and e-commerce companies to form a platform for industrial transformation.

Building the free trade zone to explore the road for deepening reform

On December 26, 2014, Shekou was included in a free trade zone as part of a national development strategy. With an area of only 13.4 square kilometers, Shekou once again stood on the frontier of China's reform and opening-up. It had to upgrade itself from secondary industry to the tertiary sector via innovation. With its unique strengths, China Merchants Group aimed to build Shekou into a bridgehead, hub port and starting station along the 21st Century Maritime Silk Road, and an essential gateway for the Shenzhen Bay Area. Shekou is now building three strategic platforms of an international hub port, urban transformation and upgrading and financial innovation and development. As it was included in the free trade pilot zone, Shekou will implement the rule of law and financial innovation from other free trade zones across China. These two features are also the source of the strongest future competitiveness of Shekou. By stepping up efforts in institutional innovation, the establishment of an international hub port, urban transformation and upgrading, and financial development, Shekou strives to become the unique free trade zone in China and make a new contribution to national reform and opening up by exploring new models. In the future, Shekou will no longer be a single industrial zone. It has been redefined as a free trade zone with distinctive characteristics, as well as a brand new commercial and business district that is suitable both for businesses and residents. Its industries will cover shipping logistics, finance and securities, real estate, hospitality, industrial manufacturing and high—tech industries, among others, with businesses spreading across China, Hong Kong and overseas markets. It will once again be at the forefront of China's reform.

Shenzhen established infrastructure and an ecological environment distinctive to innovative cities to attract factors for innovation in support of innovation-driven development

While continuing to force high-polluting, high energy-consuming but less productive enterprises to transform and transfer, Shenzhen gave priority to the building of a hardware environment for innovation. First, it built a smart city, and established an efficient intensive supporting system of information infrastructure, and the system for information sharing and big data application. Second, it built an ecologically friendly city. In 2014, Shenzhen issued the decisions concerning Pushing Forward the Building of Ecological Civilization of Beautiful Shenzhen. According to the document, Shenzhen will have been established as a state demonstration city for ecological civilisation and typical beautiful city in China by 2020. It will launch three initiatives for promoting the atmospheric environment, water environment and green urban landscape. In 2017, energy and water consumption for GDP per 10,000 yuan continued to decline to one third and one-tenth of the national average. The $PM_{2.5}$ concentration dropped to 26 microgram per cubic meter. It worked to build Shenzhen into a garden city with a public green area per capita exceeding 17 square meters. The environment effectively attracts and keeps innovative talent and supports the operation of sophisticated, innovative activities.

In this period, by successfully carrying out the transformation to innovation-driven development, Shenzhen attracts the gathering of high-end innovation factors, like global investment, talent and technology, by further creating and fostering institutions and policies for the innovative economy and new advantages of ecological environment. It also enables the combination of innovative technologies and entities in industrial activities to achieve innovation-driven economic development of a larger scale and higher level.

In sum, the fundamental driving forces for Shenzhen's leapfrogging development from a fishing village to a technological centre are as follows: Ongoing deepening opening-up creates conditions for the massive inflow and effective use of external production factors. Continuous institutional advantages attract external resources for development and innovation, and create conditions for the combination of production factors and unleashing of driving engines. The improving hardware environment creates conditions for urban development and innovation, and forces the city to keep on developing and innovating. By actively participating in and taking full advantage of fierce market competition, Shenzhen forced itself and market entities to evolve and regularly upgrade.

Experience and Inspirations

With neither resources nor production factors, Shenzhen made leapfrogging development from a remote country town to a global technological centre and from an agricultural town to a manufacturing powerhouse over a period of 40 years. From the development stage featuring rapid quantitative growth driven by production factors to the throes of transformation when the economy slowed down and the growth engine shifted gears, and then the stage when innovation-driven, high-quality development was pursued, Shenzhen showcased the whole process of how a city joins the global value chain and moves from the bottom to the highest rank, making itself a role-model in promoting competitiveness for global peer cities. Shenzhen has produced experiences which are of reference to China and other cities pursuing future development, and world cities, especially those in developing countries.

First, guided by continuous institutional innovation, Shenzhen fosters new strengths to increase attraction and radiation and create powers and conditions for further development and innovation.

In an era of globalisation, various resources for development are mobile, but institutional environment, which is unique to different cities, cannot be moved. By continuously improving the institutional environment, lowering institutional transactions costs, and increasing the benefits of development, a city can motivate market entities to develop and innovate, and attract more external production factors. Shenzhen took the lead in exploring the market-oriented primary economic system, then continued to lead in exploring how to improve the socialist market economy system, then remained aligned with the practices of international cities, and then achieved institutional innovations that support the innovation-driven economy. At each stage, it stayed one step ahead of the inland cities, so the city always outperformed inland peers in terms of institutions, even compared with more and more international cities. Innovation enabled it to attract constant foreign investment and production factors for development and innovation and to endogenously create new resources and production factors for development and innovation.

Second, Shenzhen kept on deepening reform and attracted and made full use of production factors, markets and industries from the Chinese mainland, Hong Kong and the world.

In 1979, the Shenzhen Special Economic Zone was established. In the 1980s, the city opened its market to overseas investors and allowed foreign businesses and overseas Chinese as well as compatriots from Hong Kong and Macao to invest and start factories. Preferential policies and lower business costs attracted a massive influx of overseas industries, laying the industrial foundation for the city to grow export-oriented industries and go global. In the 1990s, Shenzhen furthered the reform, allowing independent decision-making and fair competition for both domestic and foreign market entities. It took decisive actions to attract foreign investment and rapidly finished industrialisation. In the early 21st century, Shenzhen highlighted the building of an international city, and kept itself aligned with leading international cities in terms of institutions and standards. This was of great significance for gathering high-end resources and production factors. After 2010, Shenzhen encouraged local businesses to go global and expand operations across the world. The goal of moving up to the upper reaches of the industrial value chain was achieved. There is an ancient saying in China, "People cannot get rich without external help, and a horse will not get fat and strong if it is not fed at night. " By opening its market to the outside world, Shenzhen took advantage of the international division of labour, global capital, technologies and markets. This is the key that enabled the city to leapfrog development.

Third, Shenzhen gathered production factors, created a favorable environment and chose the suitable industries at the beginning, creating the conditions and path for its sustainable development and innovation.

For one thing, immigrants fostered a culture of innovation in Shenzhen, which features an equal and inclusive environment thanks to those enterprising and risk-taking immigrants. They created a culture of innovation. For another, global industrial transfer brought innovative industries to Shenzhen. In the 1980s, the focus of industrial transfer was on the electronic information industry, whose industrial chain spans across the world. It was also a high-tech industry. From this perspective, it was inevitable that the industry relocated to Shenzhen, and provided a blessing and initial conditions for Shenzhen's innovation and development. This also determined the direction of Shenzhen toward continuous innovation.

Fourth, the government played a subtle role in handling external pressure and guided the market to play its decisive role, enabling the city to climb to the upper reaches of the global industrial chain.

Generally, the initial economic development generated favourable conditions but also brought difficulties and pressure for further expansion. The key to whether a city maintains sustainable growth and transformation or goes to stagnation or recession lies in the awareness, capability and action of the government. Shenzhen was successful in the following aspects: first, the local government remained enterprising and innovative and continued to develop new strengths to replace the disappearing ones utilizing previous experience and conditions. Primarily, it bore the national responsibility for exploring new practices for reform and had to move forward and produce innovation. Additionally, the culture of innovation, and the experience that it achieved, multiplying benefits from innovation, motivated it to keep on innovating. Secondly, the government actively used market forces to encourage the survival of the fittest, so that market entities had to transform, relocate and upgrade their businesses in the face of pressure, difficulties and problems caused by resource scarcity and soaring costs.

Fifth, Shenzhen accumulated experience and practice that the regions taking the lead in development could apply to the rest of the nation to move toward shared prosperity.

For one thing, by establishing a special economic zone, China piloted various plans for development and revised and improved the successful plans. In this way, the rest of the country was able to catch up by following the exemplary forerunners and their successful models, while avoiding the risks of rushing into the nationwide expansion of an immature plan. For another, the practice of achieving development, transformation and innovation in one place by concentrating resources there and then expanding the successful model with the market playing the decisive role and government playing the guiding role, is in line with the law of development and also an important approach to national development. This has been proven by Shenzhen's development and the expansion of its successful experience.

Chapter 2　Financing the City, Financing the Firms and Financing Entrepreneurship

Introduction

Shenzhen is located in southern Guangdong Province, China, and borders Hong Kong. The city has witnessed rapid growth in a very short time. The city has grown from an area of 3 square kilometers, when the Special Administrative Region was first established in 1979, to nearly 2 thousand square kilometers. After being established as China's first economic zone in 1980, Shenzhen quickly developed from a sleepy small border town into a large modern city, quite impressive in the history of industrialization, modernizing, and urbanization.

From 1979 to 2019, Shenzhen has skyrocketed from a tiny border town with a population of more than 30,000 to a metropolis with a population of more than 10 million. In 2019 the population is estimated to be 12.12 million and still growing mainly through rural urban migration. It has become a prosperous, chic, innovative, harmonious and beautiful city and has established many firsts in the history of world industrialization, urbanization and innovation in many ways.

Financial industry is the backbone of Shenzhen's economy, totalling 15 percent of the city's GDP. Shenzhen also has more than 25 years' experience as an SEZ to draw from. It has a flexible and efficient management system and its institutional reform always leads other regions in China, directly boosting its economic growth.

Shenzhen also has advantages in basic industrial structure. In recent years, it has energetically promoted industrial restructuring and hi-tech industry has become the pillar of its manufacturing sector. In the past three years, the share of hi-tech products' output value in the city's gross industrial output value increased at a rate of 2.5 percentage points annually, reaching 48 percentage in 2017, higher than in any other mega-city nationwide. Shenzhen has large market shares in rising industries such as computer products, communications equipment, optical fibre communication equipment, internet devices, digital audio and video products, biological pharmaceuticals and high-tech medical appliances. Logistics has developed rapidly, becoming an important part of the city's manufacturing sector and its entire economy in general.

This chapter covers an array of issues, dealing with the way the city finances development, industrial development and infrastructure. Section one introduces the concept of municipal finance, followed by a background on the state of local government finance in China and the challenges faced. This is followed by a background on the city of Shenzhen in terms of the responsibilities of the city in financial planning and management. Also presented here is an outline of the revenue and expenditure patterns of the city. The next section looks at financing capital expenditure from different sources, viz. own revenue resources, government transfers, the private sector, borrowing and also capital markets. Besides, there will be a review of the innovative methods the municipality has pursued to obtain money for development. Finally, the chapter provides a brief summary of the issues of municipal finance and lessons to be learnt from the city's experience.

Municipal Finance In China: An Overview

There are many definitions of Municipal finance, but by and large "Municipal finance" refers to the decisions that municipal governments make about revenue and expenditure. These decisions cover the sources of revenue in the form of taxes used by municipal governments and intergovernmental transfers. They also include ways of financing infrastructure from operating revenues and borrowing, as well as charges on developers and public-private partnerships. In most cases, municipalities always have challenges in raising their own resources and, in the end, they resort to bank borrowing, going into partnerships in infrastructure development, attracting foreign investments, and so on. All said, for a municipality to succeed it has to look for innovative ways to finance its development and this is where Shenzhen stands out as a trail blazer.

Zhang and Li, in an Asian Development Bank paper, clearly articulate the main issues in local government finance in China as follows: Through the 1990s, reforms of the fiscal system made no concessions to municipalities or the financing needs of urbanization. Except for a few favoured cities in the rich coastal provinces, the current system of revenue-sharing does not provide sufficient resources for cities to meet their heavy responsibilities in service provision, including education, health care, social welfare and pensions, alongside urban facilities. Moreover, municipalities are prohibited from borrowing, even for capital expenditures, making it difficult to finance infrastructure. In spite of these constraints, the remarkable growth and development of cities have proceeded because political leaders have been willing to tolerate a plethora of informal, backdoor solutions that enabled cities both to obtain the resources needed and to adapt to limitations on eligibility for benefits.

As it evolved, China's municipal finance has come to rely overwhelmingly on extra-budgetary resources and borrowing. Apart from charging user fees and imposing quasi-taxes on various services, municipal governments have used state assets to generate revenues to supplement the budget. And land is their principal asset. With accelerated urbanization boosting land values, land has become the biggest source of extra budgetary revenue. In 2010, receipts from land sales accounted for an estimated 35 percent of comprehensive fiscal revenues for prefectural level (second-tier) cities, compared with just 30 percent from tax revenues. In addition to sales receipts, municipalities collect a plethora of taxes from land and associated activities—property taxes, deed taxes on property transactions, and turnover taxes on construction and real estate companies, and so on. To finance public investment, municipal governments have relied mainly on two sources: land revenues and borrowing. Prohibited from direct borrowing, they have resorted to the use of financing platforms. Set up as enterprises under municipal departments, these local investment corporations (LICs) coordinate and finance the construction of facilities such as water supply, sewerage, roads, and utility hook-ups. First piloted in Shanghai in the early 1990s, these LICs now operate in all cities and have been instrumental in helping local governments achieve world-beating levels of investment in infrastructure. Typically, the LICs raise and bundle together bank loans and other financing, using a variety of municipal assets, including budgetary and off-budget revenues as equity and collateral. Increasingly, with urbanization bringing rising land values, land has become the principal asset backing LICs.

Zhang and Li continue to elucidate that municipal finance in China today grew out of ad hoc, adaptive experimentation over the past three decades, a period during which the Chinese economy was undergoing three transitions: from a socialist planned economy to a market oriented economy, from an agrarian society to an urban industrial society, and from being one of the world's poorest economies to a middle-income country. These transitions overturned pre-existing social and economic organizations, and new ones had to be created. With the central government preoccupied with the fiscal crisis brought on by the decline of the state economy, municipalities were left on their own to cope with their changing environment. In this maelstrom, municipal governments faced enormous pressures to provide a new social safety net to replace the one under the state economy, and to provide infrastructure to support the fast unfolding economic growth and the migrants flooding into cities.

They improvised. One tactic was to limit eligibility for urban services to reduce the growth in demand for them, and the system of residency registration (hukou) instituted in the 1950s provided a convenient, a mechanism for excluding the new migrants. Another tactic was to go off-budget in search of resources, and municipal governments displayed remarkable ingenuity in doing so. This decentralized approach has been instrumental in enabling China's urbanization and growth, but it has also produced some adverse outcomes. First, the current high dependence on land is risky and unsustainable. Land prices are notoriously volatile and land revenues are unsuitable as a pillar of local finance. With leases running for 40 – 70 years, land is an exhaustible resource. In the coastal regions, cities are already running out of land to sell. Second, the interplay between land and LICs has led to the overuse of both. The expanding resource envelope has softened the budget constraint for municipal governments and encouraged wasteful and inefficient investments.

Second, the reliance on extra budgetary resources has led to a fragmentation of municipal budgets that renders macroeconomic control difficult. Revenues are collected by different agencies and local governments. Information is scattered in different channels and not always reported in full. Finally, decentralized decision-making and benign neglect from the top have allowed the creation of a two-tier society where access to vital and costly public services, such as education, health care, social welfare, and pensions is open only to those with urban hukou, leaving over 200 million defacto, second-class citizens in Chinese cities.

Shenzhen Economic Growth

According to the "Report on China's Urban Competitiveness 2016", published by the Chinese Academy of Social Sciences, Shenzhen is ranked as number one in the mainland in terms of "overall economic competitiveness."

It is also regarded as one of China's most important high-tech R&D and manufacturing bases, while additionally being home to the world's third largest container port and China's fourth largest airport. Shenzhen's per capita GDP is the highest in Guangdong. (Table 2 – 1)

Table 2 – 1　　　　　Shenzhen: Major Economic Tndexes

Economic Tndexes	2016		2017	
	Value	Growth (% y-o-y)	Value	Growth (% y-o-y)
Gross Domestic Product (billion yuan)	1,949.26	9.01	2,243.84	8.81
Per Capita GDP	167,411	3.71	183,127	4.01
Added Value Output				
– Primary Industry (billion yuan)	0.71	–0.61	1.85	52.81
– Secondary Industry (billion yuan)	778.05	8.01	926.68	8.81
– Tertiary Industry (billion yuan)	1,170.49	9.81	1,315.30	8.81
Value-added Industrial Output2 (billion yuan)	719.95	7.01	808.76	9.31
Fixed-asset Investment (billion yuan)	407.82	23.6	514.73	26.2
Retail Sales of Consumer Goods (billion yuan)	551.28	9.8	601.62	9.1
Inflation (Consumer Price Index, percent)	—	2.4	—	1.4
Exports (billion yuan)	1,568.04	–4.5	1,653.36	5.5
Imports (billion yuan)	1,062.66	–4.2	1,147.79	7.9
Utilised Foreign Direct Investment (USD billion)	6.732	3.6	7.401	9.9

Source: Shenzhen City Information, 2018.

The Shenzhen municipality has many responsibilities in respect of financial planning and management. State law requires the municipality to adopt a balanced budget. No expenditures may be permitted unless authorized by the budget ordinance or by the Council via a subsequent resolution. However, at times this has not been always the case. The municipality is responsible for the overall fiscal management of the Council. It must develop and maintain budget enforcement standards. It also approves borrowing and other financing options, including financing capital improvements. Ultimately the Council is responsible for establishment and utilization of financial reporting systems and standards. The Council establishes policies for investment and management of cash assets. Finally, it selects and approves an independent public accountant to perform annual independent audits.

It is encouraging to see that Shenzhen has been receiving clean audit bills of health in most years, are flection of good financial management.

The Budget Process

The preparation of the budget goes through the following cycle:

Preparation

The Council develops the budget calendar. After this, discussions follow on the goals, needs and the outlook for the coming year. Then it sets some parameters for staff to make requests. The Council generally concentrates at the beginning on any major planning and programming for service delivery. It is worth mentioning that its revenue and expenditure must equal one another— net of contribution to, or use of, fund balance.

Revenue and Expenditure in preparing the budget, the Council starts off with expenditures that are composed of personnel (salaries, benefits— this is the biggest item of all); operating (office supplies, utilities, contracts) and capital (computers, vehicles, etc.) . Revenue of the municipality comes from taxes, business licences, user fees, fines and forfeitures and investment. Conspicuously missing is revenue from land and property, a common practice in China, as land was owned by the state until recently.

Adoption of the Budget

The annual budget must be adopted by ordinance. A public hearing must beheld before adoption of the budget. This makes the budget inclusive.

Financial Controls and Reporting

The Council is responsible for ensuring that monthly reports are prepared and that information is accurate. Further, the Council monitors departmental expenditures by using monthly reports, general ledger and, when necessary, general ledger transaction reports. Independent annual audit is required. The Council must accept and review the audit annually and this must be available to the public for review. However, some weaknesses remain. For example, important decisions are still made outside of the budget process. Strengthening accountability mechanisms and enforcing aggregate fiscal discipline constitute the challenges for reform in the next phase.

Overview

On the positive side, Shenzhen's budget responsibilities have been carried out diligently and responsibly. There have been frequent reforms to fine tune the process time and again. The following is worth noting. First, there has been a rise of the legislator in local budgeting/budget reform. The Shenzhen municipality expenditure in improving the legislature's role in the budgeting process has been quite successful. In 1995, the People's Republic of China's Standing Committee established a Planning and Budgeting Supervision Committee responsible for examining and supervising the government budget. In 2000, the PBSC was promoted as an independent committee called the Special Committee for Planning, Budgeting and Supervision (SCPBS).

In Shenzhen, early in 1997, the legislature issued the departmental budgeting reform as the "break through point" to improve the legislator's role in the budgeting process. Therefore, during the past ten years, the legislature has been a driving force to implement and improve the departmental budgeting reform.

Second, Shenzhen government's performance evaluation is effective and comprehensive as it has been getting clean audits year after year. It could serve as the role model for government performance auditing. Shenzhen put in place Shenzhen Special Economic District Auditing Regulations as early as 2001. In 2004, it expanded the scope of performance evaluation and issued regulations on auditing government investment projects. In recent years, annual reports of government performance evaluation have been presented to the public.

On the negative side, the following observations have been made. In Shenzhen, as well as in other local governments in China, there are issues with the budgeting process and the budget itself. As noted by Wong C., both in central and local government, there are weaknesses here and there. A number of criticisms have been observed. First, the capital budget is made separately from recurrent budgets; Second, Extra-budgetary expenditures remain high and unreported. Nearly all infrastructure investments are financed off budget, in non-transparent ways and poorly tracked; Policy makers continue to use tax expenditures, the costs of which are not reported in the budget; Many earmarked transfers from central government arrive late in the year and in unpredictable amounts. The matching requirement means that the Municipal Council has to hold significant reserves of funds in the event that they are successful in getting projects allocated. Lastly, revenue forecasting remains weak and pegged to growth targets, rather than economic fundamentals, and reporting on contingent liabilities is also weak to non-existent.

Revenue and Expenditure

To begin with, Shenzhen's regional municipality has diverse sources of finance, some from central government (revenue sharing) and some from own sources. On the whole, revenue sharing does not provide all the funds required. Revenue from own sources exceeds that from central government. A review of financial reports shows that revenue has been rising in recent years by between 3 – 10 percent annually. A chronology of revenue and expenditure from 2012 to 2016 is shown below (Table 2 – 2).

Table 2 – 2　　　　　Shenzhen Revenue and Expenditure
2012 – 2016 (10,000 Yuan)

ITEM	2012	2013	2014	2015	2016
Local Government Revenue	22,312,100	27,698,077	36,908,610	41,028,880	17,929,886
Local Government General Budgetary Revenue	14,820,800	17,312,618	20,827,326	27,268,543	31,364,923
1. Taxes	13,299,766	14,989,200	17,548,398	22,722,315	24,888,827
Value Added Tax	1,875,512	2,740,958	3,156,076	3,362,040	6,509,463
Corporate Tax	2,697,311	2,884,159	3,450,200	4,649,574	5,695,240
Individual Income Tax	1,391,188	1,384,659	1,684,918	2,239,807	3,047,503
2. Non-tax revenue	1,521,034	2,323,418	3,278,928	4,546,228	6,476,096
Special Programme Receipts	382,587	444,215	487,301	1,562,019	3,823,354
Charge of Administrative & Units	398,482	546,072	910,550	438,659	279,760
Penalty Receipts	209,042	177,672	267,880	303,057	249,007
Government Fund Revenue	3,109,086	4,000,482	6,870,751	9,640,067	9,663,957
L. G. Budgetary Expenditure	18,792,934	20,521,394	26,283,153	38,644,225	46,247,931
L. G. General Budgetary Expenditure	15,690,071	16,908,280	21,661,841	35,216,708	42,110,429

续表

ITEM	2012	2013	2014	2015	2016
Education	2,461,343	2,877,280	3,294,137	2,885,520	4,147,269
Science & Technology	792,651	1,329,814	945,707	2,143,182	4,035,240
Culture, Sports & Media	328,388	329,433	580,070	527,260	547,942
Social Security & Employment	667,785	784,985	738,828	845,801	1,054,524
Medical & Health Care	1,052,925	1,069,185	1,576,028	1,505,974	2,012,739
Energy Savings	1,080,036	1,419,861	1,352,999	1,083,493	1,402,415
Urban and Rural Community Affairs	1,998,352	2,217,321	2,458,768	4,656,457	5,584,938
Agriculture, Forestry and Water connections	446,591	614,196	566,042	441,526	612,541
Transportation	1,000,381	1,116,493	2,938,739	10,445,932	4,508,921
Government Funds	3,102,863	3,613,114	4,621,312	3,427,517	4,137,502

Source: Shenzhen Website and Municipal Reports.

Tax revenue

According to 2017 figures, the city's tax revenue reached 1.47 billion yuan, an increase of 3.9 percent from the previous year. Among them, value-added tax (including "cash reform") was 54.81 billion yuan, down 11.5 percent, mainly due to the impact of comprehensive reform and tax reduction; corporate income tax was 45.67 billion yuan, an increase of 17.0 percent; personal income tax was 20.16 billion yuan, an increase of 15.5 percent, and land value-added tax was 14.65 billion yuan, an increase of 19.4 percent.

Non-tax revenue

The city's non-tax revenue reached 61.08 billion yuan, an increase of 5.8 percent, of which special income was 37.21 billion yuan, administrative business fee income was 2.06 billion yuan, penalty income was 2.49 billion yuan, income from the use of state-owned assets (resources) was 12.44 billion yuan, and other income was 6.85 billion yuan.

Inter-governmental Finance and other Transfer income

The city's financial transfer income from central government was 1,283.3

billion yuan, except for the settlement income of the upper and lower levels of 40.84 billion yuan. Other income was mainly transferred from government funds and financial stock funds amounting to 42.47 billion yuan. All in all, the annual balance was 12.3 billion yuan, which is rather healthy for the city. These funds provide the financial basis for the equalization of public services, which is also indicative of the local government's over-reliance on transfer payments. Government transfer payments to the council improve basic public service capabilities and promote equitable access to them. However, at times they are not transparent or steady, and not well regulated. Furthermore, the over reliance on government transfers leaves the council with little autonomy.

Council Expenditure

Urban local authorities spend vast sums on the delivery of services that include health, education, social services, infrastructure, culture and sports, safety, and environmental protection. By all accounts, Shenzhen has done quite well in-service provision compared to other cities in China, resulting in a sustainable living environment. Of the 2017 figures, between 30 – 50 billion yuan were in five key areas viz: the highest expenditure was on urban and rural community expenditure (49.7 billion yuan), an increase of 200.2 percent from the 2016 budget. Expenditures were for urban and rural community management, public facilities, environmental sanitation, engineering construction and other fields and industry authorities. This was followed by housing provision, at 38.11 billion yuan, an increase of 34.8 percent. This was expenditure for affordable housing, housing reform and other activities; transport followed closely with 30.24 billion yuan, down by 33.0 percent. Expenditure was in the areas of highway, waterway, railway transportation, air transportation, bus subsidy and other activities.

Expenditure in the range of 10 and 18 billion yuan is spread as follows: Science and technology 17.2 billion yuan; education 14.77 billion yuan; and energy conservation and environmental protection 10.5 billion yuan. This clearly shows how serious the city is with regard to technology, education, science and environmental concerns. General public expenditure was 10.69 billion yuan, an increase of 21.7 percent; and resource exploitation was 12.22 billion yuan, down 72.1 percent.

The rest of the sectors received less than 10 billion yuan each. These were as follows: public safety expenditure 9.71 billion yuan, an increase of 22.9 percent; 9.26 billion yuan on social security and employment, an increase of 143 percent; and 9.45 billion yuan on medical and family planning, an increase of 36.5 percent.

Lastly, 6.12 billion yuan was spent as aid to other regions, an increase of 61.3 percent; other expenditure stood at 5.42 billion yuan, an increase of 198.3 percent; and expenditure on business service sectors was 4.23 billion yuan, down 72.7 percent. Agriculture, forestry and water expenditure was 3.11 billion yuan, down 5.2 percent; and expenditure on financial expenditure like supervision, 1.10 billion yuan, a decrease of 48.3 percent. The rest of municipal expenditure was less than 1 billion yuan.

The above expenditure accounts for the spectacular state of the city, with its modern facilities, adequate transport infrastructure, medical and educational facilities and its modern, smart growth. However, in spite of this rosy picture, the municipality, like most municipalities, has also been facing financial challenges to meet the ever-rising demand for services, as more and more people flock to the city. The major challenge has been capital development funding that normally requires vast sums of money, but Shenzhen has ventured to adopt innovative ways to meet the challenges head on with spectacular and proud results. This is the subject of the following section.

Financing of Capital Development In Shenzhen

Having looked at the revenue and expenditure patterns of the city, this chapter now moves on to outline and discuss both the traditional and innovative financing models adopted by the Shenzhen municipality for industry and infrastructure development. With the gradual emergence of the disadvantages and risks of traditional financing modes, local governments across China have been paying more attention to innovative financing models. Financial difficulties have forced local governments to rely on such financing models as land-leasing, and government-invested companies. But the features of these financing channels are low stability, high risk, and low sustainability. As a result, in addition to resorting to innovative revenue channels, the PRC's local governments are taking creative measures to be able to provide public services, for instance, through issuing local government bonds, establishing public-private partnerships (PPP), and transfer payments from the central government. We now look at innovative strategies that have been adopted by Shenzhen municipality to enhance development, that have made the city the envy of many local authorities across China and Asia at large. To begin with, we will look at the pace of industrial growth in Shenzhen and the role of innovation in financing said growth and the support that industry receives from the municipality.

Industrial Growth and its Financing

According to the City Information (9 May, 2018), dating back as far as 2008, the GDP share of Shenzhen's tertiary industries has exceeded 50 percent. In 2017, such industries accounted for 58.6 percent of the total. Overall, the city has four pillar industries—high-tech, financial services, modern logistics and the cultural sector. In the case of its high-tech industries, their overall value-added output has risen from 305.9 billion yuan in 2010 to 735.9 billion yuan in 2017, an average annual growth rate of 13.4 percent.

"Indigenous innovation" has long been seen as the cornerstone of Shenzhen's development. In 2016, its overall R&D expenditure amounted to 4.1 percent of its GDP, a figure significantly higher than the national average of 2.1 percent. In terms of total PCT international patent filings and invention patent ownership per 10,000 people, it ranks first among all of China's medium to large-sized cities. It is also seen as a global pioneer in several high-tech sectors, including 4G technology, DNA sequencing, meta materials and 3D displays.

In 2016, 3791 of Shenzhen's businesses were designated as national high-tech enterprises, taking the city's overall total to 8,037. Among these newly designated enterprises, 54 percent were engaged in the development of electronic information systems, 18 percent were focussed on advanced manufacturing and automation, while the remaining 28 percent were spread across six other technological sectors—biotechnology and new pharmaceuticals, new energy and energy conservation, resources and the environment, aviation and aerospace, new materials and high-tech service.

Shenzhen's "maker" population has also enjoyed continuous growth over recent years, with thousands of such businesses now active in the city, including Chaihu Maker Space, Makeblock and Seeed Studio. In addition, a number of globally-renowned high-tech enterprises have established R&D centres or regional headquarters in Shenzhen, including ZTE, Huawei Technologies, Tencent and Apple Inc.

In addition to manufacturing, Shenzhen is quickly becoming a financial centre, with two of China's largest banks headquartered there. The Shenzhen Stock Exchange (SZSE), like the Shanghai Stock Exchange, is a national exchange with more than 1,700 listed companies on SZSE, including those listed on Growth Enterprise Market (GEM) Board. The SZSE Composite Index consists of 500 listed stocks with a market capitalization of more than USD 300 billion. The Shenzhen-Hong Kong stock connection, which will facilitate cross-border trading, is expected to be launched sometime in 2019 and could open up more opportunities for investors.

The government is currently promoting Shenzhen as a financial centre to equal Hong Kong by designating Qianhai, a district of Shenzhen, as a financial centre with special rights and privileges. The purpose is to position the zone for innovation and development of modern services, in addition to fostering closer cooperation between Hong Kong and mainland China. Most significantly, Qianhai is being given special freedoms with regards to the internationalization of China's currency, the renminbi (RMB), by loosening capital account restrictions so Hong Kong banks will be allowed to extend commercial RMB loans to Qianhai-based onshore mainland entities.

Financing industrialization

Funding innovation in Shenzhen has been hailed as a success story that is known worldwide. The rapid pace of industrial growth noted above is due in part to the adoption of innovative city financing strategies adopted by the city, and inducements and preferential policies introduced by the municipality to woo industries to locate in the city. Mark Mobius has observed that Shenzhen is an experimental zone for financial innovations in China. Shenzhen has a long history in the implementation of reforms and opening up policies ahead of other cities in China, since it was designated as a Special Economic Zone in the 1980s. At the early stage of development, Shenzhen provided many preferential policies to attract FDI. Processing trade industries (processing with materials, assembling supplied components, and then exporting the final products to overseas markets) were very popular in Shenzhen in the 1990s due to its proximity to Hong Kong. Many Hong Kong industrialists moved their production processes to Shenzhen, seeking lower production costs. Hong Kong enterprises brought advanced management concepts, new modes of operation and so forth to Shenzhen. These indirect effects were beneficial for Shenzhen's economic growth and attractiveness to other foreign MNCs. Hong Kong's enterprises had become innovators, generated investment and nurtured Shenzhen's business environment, making it easier for foreign enterprises to do business in China's regions. The prosperity of foreign investment initiated domestic investment and attracted a lot of money from other parts of the mainland to invest in Shenzhen from spheres such as real estate, logistics, financial industries, etc. Hong Kong remains the largest source of FDI in Shenzhen. By the end of 2010, there were about 42,000 Hong Kong companies in Shenzhen and USD 60 billion in FDI from Hong Kong, accounting for 80 percent of the total foreign companies and two-thirds of the total FDI in Shenzhen.

Apart from Hong Kong's contribution, the Shenzhen municipal government actively conducts a preferential policy to attract foreign companies setting up their headquarters. In 2007, the Shenzhen municipal government promulgated "Some Opinions on Accelerating the Development of Headquarter Economy in Shenzhen", which states that any company that establishes its headquarters in or moves to Shenzhen will get support from the government in financing, use of land, human resources as well as the simplification of related procedures. In fact, with a lot of foreign investments and new technologies, Shenzhen itself cultivated several global corporations, like Huawei technologies, ZTE Corporation, BYD, Tencent, China Merchants Bank and Ping An Insurance. The function and role of reforms and opening-up of frontiers, moved Shenzhen forward to become an experimental zone for financial innovation in China, especially of the pilot plan approved by the central government for the development of Shenzhen-Hong Kong Modern Service Industry Cooperation Zone in Qianhai.

Internally, the Shenzhen municipal government also provided different kinds of preferential policies to promote financial innovation. For the insurance industry, the Shenzhen government issued "Measures for Accreditation of Headquarter Enterprises in Shenzhen (Trial)" and the "Detailed Implementation Rules of Several Opinions on Accelerating the Development of a Headquarter Economy in Shenzhen (Trial)" in October 2008, which provided 5 billion yuan to award enterprises that would set up or move their headquarters to Shenzhen in the next five years. This preferential policy is the direct reason for the movement of China Life to Shenzhen.

Apart from the preferential policy, one of the reasons for insurance companies to move their headquarters to Shenzhen is the good investment environment and unique institutional innovation, which is beneficial for the development of insurance businesses. Shenzhen's government supports the innovation development of its insurance industry and have made Shenzhen into a major experimental place of insurance innovation development in China.

Another favourable factor is Shenzhen's close proximity to Hong Kong, which enhances the flow of talented people between Hong Kong and Shenzhen and allows Shenzhen's financial industry to learn from Hong Kong's advanced financial practices.

Further, in a bid to woo overseas investment and attract the presence of more foreign companies, Shenzhen has initiated a series of moves designed to make the city more business friendly. These include streamlining administrative requirements and delegating decision-making to more accessible levels with regard to business licence approvals, operating standards, government procurement and finance channels. The ultimate aim is to reassure oversea investors that they will enjoy the same privileges as domestic businesses both before and after gaining market access.

Overall, three primary areas have been targeted for change: Firstly, moves are to be made to welcome overseas investment into previously prohibited sectors. Second, foreign capital is also to be sought for the manufacturing sector in line with the Shenzhen Action Plan for Made in China 2025 and third, the co-operation between Shenzhen and Hong Kong, in accordance with the CEPA framework, is also to be deepened.

Foreign Direct Investment and the Transformation of Shenzhen

Foreign Direct Investment (FDI) has a long history in China and Shenzhen in particular. Steve Olson (2016) considered that Shenzhen city was transformed from a sleepy fishing village by the decision of the Chinese government to open Shenzhen to foreign direct investment. If there is any city in the world that can be said to have been built—in both literal and figurative terms—by FDI, it is Shenzhen. The sheer size and volume of FDI into Shenzhen is breath-taking. The pivotal year was 1979. The developmental gap between China and the West had grown so immense that China's leaders recognized the need to embark upon a reform and opening-up program in order to jump-start the country's economic development. Attracting foreign direct investment was job number one. The first major initiative was to set up Special Economic Zones (SEZs) in Shenzhen and three other cities. Given its proximity to highly internationalized Hong Kong, Shenzhen was a natural choice.

The idea was simple enough. The SEZs would be given unprecedented flexibility to loosen labour laws and price controls, permit Sino-foreign joint ventures, openly tender infrastructure contracts, and provide tax benefits and other forms of preferential treatment to FDI-providers. The hope was to attract foreign companies—at the onset, principally from Hong Kong—in order to build out the needed infrastructure, and develop a light manufacturing sector and a viable export capacity. Hong Kong companies were especially important because of their strong cultural connection to the mainland, as well as their experience, contacts and savviness in international commerce.

The cause of reform was given a further boost in 1992, with Deng Xiaoping's famed Talk in South, which solidified the centrality of FDI and hastened the pace of reform, helping to push Shenzhen even further up the development ladder. The emphasis began to shift during these years from export processing to high technology, and FDI was often conditioned upon technology transfers to local partners and commitments to undertake more and more research and development locally. The Shenzhen High-Tech Industrial Park was established in 1996, and attracted a number of leading international firms, such as Intel, IBM, Toshiba, and Samsung.

As Shenzhen was growing by leaps and bounds, much of its physical infrastructure and housing was being delivered through FDI. The Central Government and local government invested only 1.4 percent and 13.1

percent, respectively, of the funds used for the physical development of Shenzhen from 1980 to 1990. Much of the rest was provided by FDI partners, principally from Hong Kong.

By the end of 2014, Shenzhen had attracted more than 58,000 foreign invested projects, with a utilized value of USD 65 billion. The impact of this FDI on Shenzhen's economy would be hard to overstate. Historical and ongoing FDI and foreign invested enterprises accounted for roughly 41 percent of Shenzhen's GDP, 42 percent of its employment, and 48 percent of exports in 2013. The trade performance of Shenzhen's FIEs accounted for a whopping one-fifth of the city's GDP. As if these figures were not amazing enough on their own, it should be noted that they do not include the service sector or the various spillover benefits that FDI typically brings such technological transfers, greater managerial expertise, and increased productivity.

The figures for several key industry sectors are even more extraordinary, with FIEs accounting for all or nearly all revenue in areas such as the production and supply of gas (100 percent), the processing of petroleum (97 percent), the manufacture of automobiles (81 percent), and the manufacture of general purpose machinery (78 percent). According to Shenzhen City Information, the utilized Foreign Direct Investment (USD) value in 2016 was 6,732 and in 2017 it was 7,401, a growth of 9.9 percent.

The Shenzhen experience with FDI is not only striking, but also highly instructive. Chinese officials essentially used Shenzhen as a laboratory in which to run real-world experiments on the attraction, management and impact of FDI. The results—and implications— of these experiments are entirely evident for all to see. When properly managed, FDI can be nothing short of transformative for developing economies. Shenzhen's astonishing transformation from a sleepy fishing village to global metropolis tells this story both eloquently and convincingly.

Entrepreneurship Financing in Shenzhen

Shenzhen is a top innovation hub for start-ups. The city is the Fintech hub and is compared to Silicon Valley. Their development is mainly a result of financial help from the municipality, in part, as well as through self-financing. Shenzhen is the most entrepreneurial city in greater China and its start-ups are well geared to deliver innovative ideas with high growth potential. A survey done by The Chinese University of Hong Kong (CUHK) shows that 16 percent of the population is engaged in start-ups, a three fold rise since 2009. She says that Shenzhen has topped Hong Kong and Taiwan's capital Taipei in terms of entrepreneurship in China, according to a joint university survey. Sixteen out of every 100 adults in Shenzhen were engaged in early-stage entrepreneurial activities in mid – 2016, more than a two fold increase from 2009, when the figure was less than five. China's average was 10 percent in 2016, slightly outperforming Taipei's 8 percent. New businesses that were between 3 and 42 months old in Shenzhen jumped by 284 percent compared to 2009. The prevalence rates of established businesses recorded an increase of 389 percent as well. It is worth noting that while entrepreneurship rates are on the rise in Shenzhen, they are declining in other places in China.

A collaborative effort by CUHK CfE, HKBU School of Business, the University of Hong Kong's Faculty of Business and Economics, Shenzhen Academy of Social Science and Savantas Policy Research Institute, the research entitled "Global Entrepreneurship Monitor (GEM) Hong Kong and Shenzhen Report 2016 – 2017" notes that in recent years, Hong Kong and Shenzhen have experienced an explosive growth in the start-up support ecosystem.

Start-ups traditionally require several things to be successful: Funding, customers, products, competition and the right team. Shenzhen offers all of these elements today. Aside from huge government funding and subsidies for the internet and technical start-up scene, there are also a lot of venture capitalists offering funding for start-ups. Much also comes from self-financing. The SMB World Asia study notes that the principal source of financial support is their own savings. The role of the family in financing new ventures is still significant in Shenzhen. Banks are also quite supportive. Aligned with higher entrepreneurship rates, the research team also found a growing culture of informal sectors developing in the city. Shenzhen recorded a high investment prevalence rate of 20.5 percent of the adult population. In fact, Shenzhen's informal investors are among the most generous of all economies in the study, with a contribution of USD 76.112. The study also recorded a dramatic change in investment patterns. While in 2009 individuals were preferably investing in family members, by 2016, friends and neighbours had become the first choice.

The rush to entrepreneurship might be linked to relatively lax lending for new business in Shenzhen. Banks in Shenzhen are generally more supportive of start-ups as they are seeking profit opportunities that are lacking in traditional businesses. The Shenzhen government has offered subsidies for banks to provide loans for start-ups. Maker spaces in Shenzhen are in effect large incubators (providing co-working space, mentoring, marketing and financial support) for young entrepreneurs with ideas. They concentrate on ICT hardware and software development (3D printing, robots, drones, connected equipment, mobile Apps and internet of things). Their development and funding are supported by holding companies that are active in real estate, finance, construction or logistics. Such companies can nurture creative entrepreneurs, provide business training, seed funding as well as investment capital at a later development stage. In effect, the strength of Shenzhen's maker spaces lies in the integration of strong financial investment capacity to fund new businesses. This will make Shenzhen attractive to creative professionals worldwide looking for capital funding and affordable manufacturing. Shenzhen holds the second largest stock exchange of the country.

Financing the Firm

The city of Shenzhen has been quite supportive in encouraging and financing entrepreneurs who are interested in industrial development. For example, it is reported that the municipality set up USD 2.2 billion in funds to assist local listed firms in 2015. Authorities in Shenzhen have set up special funds to the tune of 15 billion yuan to assist listed companies in dealing with pledge risks and boosting liquidity. Further, Shenzhen Small and Medium-Sized Enterprise Guarantee Group and Shenzhen HTI Group jointly established a CNY10 billion fund, while Kunpeng Capital set up a 5 billion yuan pot, a market insider told Yicai Global.

The municipal government has also begun formulating a plan for assisting more than 20 listed Chinese companies that have faced pressure in terms of equity pledges and financing over the last 2 months. Local authorities have also set up a special working group led by major officials from 10 departments to coordinate and resolve stock pledge risks facing controlling shareholders of listed companies.

Financing Innovation Eco System

Local enterprises are the key innovators in Shenzhen's city innovation ecosystem and the city has abundant resources. Over 90 percent of R&D, including personnel and funding, is generated by enterprises, but universities and research institutes are also powerful innovators. Since 2008, when Shenzhen became China's first National Innovative City, it has allocated more resources to develop tertiary education and research institutes. Currently, Shenzhen has 56 national innovation platforms. Collaborating with universities, Shenzhen has established the Research Institute of Tsinghua University in

Shenzhen, the PKU-HKUST Shenzhen-Hong Kong Institution, the Shenzhen Virtual University Park and other research organizations. These have become a continuous source of knowledge and technology.

> An example of development plans for a metro station, with standard zoning codes on the left and Shenzhen's new zoning codes on the right. Previously, it was impossible to develop land for purposes other than transport (coloured in grey). Now, the zoning codes allow for mixed-use (coloured by primary land use type). Source: Wanli Fang and Lulu Xue (2015) and Graphic by WRI Ross Centre for Sustainable Cities.

Through its Basic Innovation Program, Shenzhen is supporting the development of national R&D infrastructure in the city, including key national labs, national engineering labs, national engineering research centres and the China Best Practice case studies National Genebank. Shenzhen is now ideally equipped to carry out ambitious national strategic R&D projects. Building on its newly-developed R&D infrastructure, Shenzhen is promoting independent innovation in areas like IT, genetic engineering and stem cell research. Innovation intermediaries are another player in Shenzhen's innovation ecosystem. These include incubators, professional services firms, technology consultancies, trade associations and recruitment agencies. Services provided by innovation intermediaries—including information exchange, decision-making advice, resource allocation, technical service and technology evaluation—enable innovators and entrepreneurs to mitigate risks and commercialize technology faster. The city has now become a highly important innovation hub in South China.

Innovation resources

According to Cai Jian, Shenzhen has implemented a number of measures to attract talent. By the end of 2015, the "Peacock Plan" had attracted 59 innovative R&D teams to Shenzhen and Guangdong. A total of 1,219 people had been designated as high-calibre foreign professionals under the plan. In 2015 alone, the plan attracted 18 R&D teams specializing in areas such as biology, pharmaceuticals, life sciences, software, telecommunications, microelectronics and new energy. Among them, 2D Material Optoelectronic Devices is an emerging field of research in China. The city has also taken steps to attract and retain talent by strengthening local universities and improving incentives and services. Total R&D spending across Shenzhen represented 4.05 percent of its GDP in 2015. Municipal and district governments allocated a R&D budget of 20.93 billion Yuan to support pioneering, generic and core technologies. One hundred fifty six strategic technology projects were initiated. According to the Shenzhen Municipal Government plan, total local R&D spending will be 4.25 percent of its GDP by 2020. As well as encouraging companies to invest more in R&D, the government will also provide additional funds. Moreover, the government will set up an investment company focused on hi-tech, innovative and entrepreneurial activities as a boost to the local venture capital market.

Innovations In Infrastructure Financing

The focus of this section is on "innovative" infrastructure funding mechanisms. Infrastructure is usually funded from special assessments, development charges, reserves, general borrowing, grants, and property taxes (as opposed to operating expenditures, which are funded only from grants, user fees and property taxes). Innovative funding mechanisms include any variation in the conventional mechanisms (such as borrowing backed by revenue from a specific source rather than by general municipal revenues, or development charges that vary according to the location of the project rather than being applied municipality-wide) or any relatively new mechanism that is not already widely used in Chinese communities (such as a parking site tax or a vehicle registration tax). Innovation in funding mechanisms usually involves some change to local by laws and administrative arrangements, but they may also require more far-reaching changes such as modifications to provincial legislation or funding arrangements.

Traditionally, the financial vehicles China employs to finance infrastructure include public funding (including the annual budget, treasury bonds and other financial capital), debt financing (funds raised through banks and other financial institutions and bonds), inner accumulation (undistributed profits), However, most of these do not meet the ever-rising demand for funds. In this section, we look at some of the innovative ways Shenzhen has used to finance many of the infrastructure projects in the city in response to rapid urbanization. These include land value capture, public private partnership, and bonds. Due to limited funds, the city has consequently turned to alternative sources of financing local government. Local government investment vehicles (LGIVs) have been a preferred source. Many of these vehicles lack adequate governance and transparency arrangements, and the central government has recently acted to curb their use. Financing from land transactions has also been important. But limits on the supply of higher-quality land, uncertainty about the future of land prices, and distortions in the urbanization process resulting from this Public Finance Reform Agenda are causes for concern.

Transport development and land value capture in Shenzhen

Xue et al. posits that in Chinese cities, funding for large-scale urban transit infrastructure traditionally comes from two sources: sales of land development rights and bank loans. However, these approaches not only financially burden city government, but also lead to costly urban sprawl. Recently the city of Shenzhen has been successfully experimenting with alternative approaches to overcome these significant challenges. Shenzhen's experience demonstrates that financing transport infrastructure by harnessing the value of land can also be an opportunity for sustainable transit-oriented development (TOD) in Chinese cities.

Shenzhen was the first city in China to use the Rail plus Property (R + P) LVC model as an innovative way of funding its infrastructure development. This model leverages partnerships between the public sector, transit companies and developers to coordinate planning and financing of new transit stations and adjacent real estate developments. In Shenzhen, the government used traditional finance (municipal budget and bank loans) for the initial phase of its metro project and then switched to more innovative financing methods after project costs increased ten fold in the metro expansion phases. Flexible risk-and-profit sharing arrangements ensured that both costs and benefits were shared among the government and various metro companies.

The evidence of benefits suggests a win-win situation: Average home values within walking distance of metro stations increased by 23 percent at 400 metres and 17 percent at 600 metres. This speaks of the added value that residents gain from increased accessibility and increased revenues of property developers who have paid into the R + P system to finance public transport infrastructure. Here it clearly shows that land value is created, shared and reinvested, spurring a virtuous cycle of urban infrastructure investment (Figure 2 – 1).

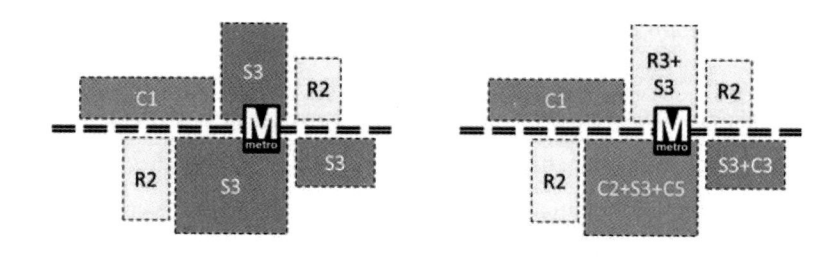

Figure 2 – 1 Integrated Transport and Land Value Capture

Paving the way for the future

Shenzhen's success has profound implications for other Chinese cities. If Shenzhen can successfully implement R + P under the same regulatory and legislative environment, other Chinese cities can follow suit. However, R + P does not offer quick wins.

In Shenzhen, it took over a decade to implement viable solutions. Hong Kong also took about a decade to make a profit. Change won't be possible without a booming real estate market, a mature capital market, a capable and willing private sector, and more important, a strong political will that is open to new approaches. Given the need for sustainable transit-oriented development in China, leaders can't afford to overlook Shenzhen's successes and the opportunities that R + P presents.

Use of Local Government Financial Platforms

As noted earlier in this chapter, local governments in China are by law not allowed to borrow from the financial market and thus they have been relying on local government financial platforms (LGFPs) to finance their urban infrastructure development; Shenzhen has used them quite a lot to finance development across the city with some success here and there. Good as they are, they are subject to the volatility of the real estate market.

Local government financing vehicles (LGFVs) are economic entities established by Chinese local governments and their departments and agencies through fiscal appropriation or injection of assets to perform the function of financing government-invested projects. LGFVs are the combined result of local governments' exuberant investment demand, limited fiscal capacity and a narrow financing channel. Their origin, development and operation model reveal an unignorable aspect of state capitalism in China—state capitalism at the local level.

Major problems and risks associated with LGFVs

To be clear, the sustained operation of the LGFVs' "land for loan" model depends on two preconditions, i. e. , unlimited supply of land and the constant rise of the land price. But neither of them can be continuously met in the real world, not even in Shenzhen, as it was surrounded by traditional land holdings. Once land is in short supply, or more probably, the land price drops, the debt-raising capacity of LGFVs will decrease sharply. And considering that a large portion of the LGFV debts are paid through the "borrow new to pay the old" cycle, the sharp decrease in their capacity to borrow new money is highly likely to result in a break of the capital chain, thus triggering default.

Use of Bonds by Shenzhen Municipality for Infrastructure Development

As indicated much earlier, financing the huge amount of infrastructure needed to meet the demands of growing urban population in Shenzhen has been beyond the reach of the municipality and governments alone. Private sector financing has been sought to close the financing gap, particularly given widespread public constraints. In May 2014, a programme was rolled out that allowed 10 local governments (Zhejiang, Jiangsu, Jiangxi, Ningxia, Shandong, and Guangdong provinces as well as the cities of Qingdao, Beijing, Shanghai and Shenzhen) to issue municipal bonds. Before then, local governments were not legally allowed to borrow money or seek outside financing for their debt. However, the lack of direct, legal options for financing local government spending did not prevent borrowing, but simply moved it underground to China's shadow banking sector. The shift to allow local governments to directly issue bonds is a move to eliminate the riskier shadow banking practices, while providing a better-regulated alternative.

To stimulate the economy, the central government allowed local governments to issue bonds with a yearly quota of 200 billionyuan in 2009, 2010, and 2011. In 2011, Shanghai City, Zhejiang Province, Shenzhen City, and Guangdong Province, were the first pilot areas to issue local government bonds. The government bonds issued by trial provinces or cities were fixed-rate bonds with a term structure of three years or five years. Issuing of local bonds profoundly upgraded local governments' investment capability for infrastructure construction. Shenzhen itself has made great use of bonds and public private partnerships in building its vast array of modern infrastructure in the city. In 2014, 10 pilot provinces and cities managed to pay back the local government bonds themselves.

Case 2 – 1: Shenzhen International Low Carbon City project

Shenzhen International Low Carbon City (ILCC) is a demonstration project of the China-EU Partnership on Sustainable Urbanization (CEUPSU) and an intriguing example for understanding innovative forms of funding with the specific aim of doing this in environmentally, socially and economically sustainable ways. Urban Investment and Finance Platforms and Public-Private-Partnerships (PPPs), in a broader context, were the two financial vehicles ILCC uses. A broad approach to PPPs is chosen in which stakeholder involvement is key and social conflicts are avoided by balancing the interests of various stakeholders. In particular, planning the village area in Shenzhen as a whole and arranging finance through "metro + property" provides a replicable and operable example for other cities in funding urban renewal and community transformation and dealing with the issue of how residents can share the benefits of urban development with developers. The combination of these financial arrangements facilitates the achievement by ILCC of the triple bottom line in sustainable urbanization. ILCC is environmentally sustainable by promoting low carbon transition, socially sustainable through resident and villager involvement, and financially sustainable through diversification of funding sources. The financing experience gained from ILCC provides practical lessons for other cities and has significant implications for adapting institutional and organizational arrangements to create enabling conditions for innovative financing activities.

Hand in hand with bonds, Shenzhen has also embraced Public Private Partnerships for infrastructure development. These models have been very popular. This followed the issue by the central government of 19 PPP-related policies in 2015, which were aimed at regulating PPP development and facilitating various investment and financing activities. PPP financing models can make up for the shortcomings of traditional financing methods and ease fiscal and financial stress. But the uncertainty in cooperative relations with government remains a factor restricting the development of PPP patterns. PPP models did provide the municipality with a stable and sustainable source of income for the Council of Shenzhen to undertake municipal construction and provide public services, transportation, and ecological environmental protection within the fragile city.

The PPP model binds infrastructure construction to its operation to provide more infrastructure at lower cost and of higher quality. Multiform public-private partnerships have been used in Shenzhen in the areas of the city's infrastructure construction to arouse the enthusiasm of people from all walks of life. This has enhanced the city's capacity to invest in infrastructure construction. It shows that the PPP model is a cooperative model that shares benefits as well as risks and requires full cooperation between local government and business. The model offers the council more financing channels for infrastructure construction, improves its public service capabilities, and to some extent enhances its spending capabilities on ecological environmental protection.

Eco Cities and Their Financing

China has undergone a rapid process of urbanization, but this has been accompanied by serious environmental problems. Therefore, it has started to develop various eco-cities, low-carbon cities, and other types of sustainable cities. The massive launch of these sustainable initiatives, as well as the higher cost of these projects, requires the Chinese government to invest large sums of money. Identifying the financial toolkits to be employed to fund this construction has become a critical issue. Against this backdrop, the authors have selected Sino-Singapore Tianjin Eco-city (SSTEC) and Shenzhen International Low-Carbon City (ILCC) and compared how they finance their construction. Thus far, both are considered to be successful cases. The results show that the two cases differ from each other in two key aspects. First, ILCC has developed a model with fewer financial and other supports from the Chinese central government and foreign governments than SSTEC, and, hence, may be more valuable as a source of inspiration for other similar projects for which political support at the national level is not always available. Second, by issuing bonds in the international capital market, SSTEC singles itself out among various sustainable initiatives in China, while planning the village area as a whole and the metro plus property model are distinct practices in ILCC. In the end, the authors present a generic financing model that considers not only economic returns but also social and environmental impacts to facilitate future initiatives to finance in more structural ways.

Green Finance

Green finance refers to financial services provided for economic activities that are supportive of environment improvement, climate change mitigation and more efficient resource utilization. It includes investment and financing activities for projects in areas such as environmental protection, energy saving, clean energy, green transportation, and green buildings.

Green finance in China has been piloted in 7 cities, Shenzhen among them, with varying success. Among the 7 pilot areas at present, the Hubei market has the largest trading volume, the Shenzhen market has the highest trading activity, and the Chongqing and Tianjin markets have relatively small trading volumes, with trading almost stagnant. The carbon allowance price of each pilot market also varies: the carbon price in Beijing and Shenzhen is RMB 40 – 50/ ton, while that of the other 5 pilot markets is around 10 yuan/ ton.

Current Development Situation of Shenzhen Carbon Market

As one of the 3 cities possessing both carbon exchange and financial centre functions in 7 national carbon trading pilot markets, and as the vanguard in China's economic system reform, Shenzhen leads the whole country in carbon emissions market construction and is highly experienced in trading practice and management. Shenzhen generates nearly 9 million tons of trading volume with about 30 million tons of carbon allowance, with a liquidity rate of 30 percent, which is far higher than that of Beijing and Shanghai carbon trading markets in the same period.

The high trading activity of the Shenzhen market mainly benefits from three aspects: firstly, Shenzhen, the first carbon trading pilot area, has a long carbon market running time and high enterprise awareness; secondly, Shenzhen has the smallest total allowance—30 million tons among the 7 pilot markets, but has the largest coverage—845 enterprises and other subjects; thirdly, Shenzhen market has been open to institutions and individual investors from the beginning, without access restriction.

However, Shenzhen carbon trading market has some problems, despite the achievements and experience obtained. In particular, only a single product is now traded in the Shenzhen carbon market, its carbon price is lower than the level of world mainstream carbon markets and far lower than the effective emission control price measured and calculated by the National Development and Reform Commission, and its role in promoting enterprises' emission reduction is to be improved.

Shenzhen should use the means of green finance to support green projects on energy conservation and emission reduction, to strengthen the market activity of carbon trading market by expanding the carbon emissions market breadth, increasing the diversity of carbon derivatives, and the carbon trading market thickness, trying to become a regional carbon emission centre and international green financial centre. Policy recommendations for developing green finance to drive Shenzhen carbon market include: Formulate the green finance development plan and promotion scheme. Establish carbon assessment procedures. Lower the threshold for financial institutions to participate in the carbon trading market and explore carbon derivatives in an orderly manner.

Land Concessions and Land Leasing

Lastly, local governments have also ventured to raise money through land concessions. The Municipalities try to acquire as much land as possible, and as cheaply as possible, then either sell it at market rates, use it as collateral for infrastructure loans, or provide it at below-market rates to strategic (mostly foreign) investors for industrial development.

Despite municipalities have the ability to create new supplies of urban land, land leasing is a transitional infrastructure-financing strategy. The supply of land available for leasing will eventually run out. Shenzhen, the pioneer in land leasing, aggressively expanded its urban boundaries for 15 years. The municipality's sale price for leasing land for urban use has vastly exceeded the purchase price it pays farmers, often by a factor as large as 100 times. By now, the potential for further expansion or new land leasing has almost been exhausted. In fact, Shenzhen's asset management company has turned to buying and selling land-use rights in other urban areas of the interior of China as a way of continuing to use its entrepreneurial skills to generate revenues from land transactions. By contrast, land leasing as an infrastructure-financing tool is gathering speed in other parts of China.

Conclusion and Lessons Learned

In this chapter, we have seen how a small, sleepy village has been catapulted to a modern, sustainable city in China through the adoption of reforms of administrative laws and practices, and secondly, through careful management of resources at hand.

In terms of economic development, Shenzhen has been outperforming China's first-tier cities in economic growth over the past couple of years, developing a reputation for innovation and economic transformation. The city has come a long way from a small village to a special economic zone in the 1980s, and now its transformation into a hub for innovation-driven industries—including biotechnology, the internet, new energy, new materials, information technology and cultural and creative industries, which together grew 20 percent last year and accounted for 40 percent of Shenzhen's gross domestic product.

Furthermore, Shenzhen has become a hot spot of innovation in China. Shenzhen has become the centre of attention in China as authorities hold it up as a role model of economic transformation and wealth accumulation that defies the economic headwinds that have slowed growth in most other parts of the mainland.

Besides being the nation's innovation hub, Shenzhen could very possibly overtake Shanghai as China's global financial centre in the next decade, if it cooperates with Hong Kong. While the Shanghai market is dominated by large state-owned enterprises, Shenzhen is more representative of smaller, younger, privately owned companies, and is the headquarters for a number of property developers. The city is a hotbed for private economic growth, spawning more than 1 million private companies, including some of China's biggest and hottest companies, such as internet giant Tencent Holdings, telecommunications.

The success noted above has come about because the Shenzhen government has been innovative in the way it has financed its development over the years. It has gone out of its way in making several reforms to facilitate development in the city and has also provided many incentives to woo local and international investors. Today Shenzhen can pick and choose whichever FDI it wants. The city has also been quite supportive in encouraging and financing entrepreneurs interested in industrial development.

With fast urbanization has come the need for infrastructure and other services. To-date, Shenzhen has gone beyond the traditional funding streams and ventured into innovative strategies, such as issuance of municipal bonds, foreign direct investments, project finance, use of local government platforms, public private partnerships, special purpose vehicles and tax incentive financing. Shenzhen municipality was the first city in China to use land value capture through the Metro plus property land model as an innovative way of funding its infrastructure development. Shenzhen's success in this approach has profound implications for other cities both in China and in the developing world. All of these actions that have resulted in one of the best planned and developed cities should be a model not only in China but the rest of the world, especially the emerging low-income countries in Africa, Asia and Latin America.

Chapter 3　Modern Economic Growth, Special Economic Zone and Industrialization

Introduction

　　Shenzhen is a young city woven from an infinite number of legendary stories, and it is the leader of China's reform and liberalisation. Forty years ago, Shenzhen boldly broke through the constraints of the traditional planned economic system and formed a relatively sound socialist market economic system and mechanism, establishing a relatively complete urban governance system and framework for the rule of law. Shenzhen has implemented bold innovation, continuous transformation and upgrading, and has formed an innovation-driven pattern of high economic development level, embarking on a new path of rapid growth and ecological civilization. Before 1980, Shenzhen's GDP was 0.2 percent of that of Hong Kong and in 2017 it was 2.24 trillion yuan, which was the same as Hong Kong. Its per capita GDP is USD 27,000, the ratio of secondary and tertiary industries was 6 : 4, and high-tech industry and financial sector accounted for 33 percent and 13.6 percent, respectively. No other city in the world has made a transition from agricultural economy to knowledge and information economy in such a short time. It has grown into a representative of China's 5 most important economic, trade, financial and innovative development centres.

Literature Review

The economic development of Shenzhen has caused many scholars to explore, and engage in countless discussions on the development model of Shenzhen. YuJun argued that Shenzhen has developed 5 features in economic transformation and industrial upgrading: (1) transformation to service industry from manufacturing industry (2) integrated development of service industry and manufacturing industry (3) manufacturing industry gives priority to innovation and branding instead of low cost (4) traditional service industry upgrades to modern service industry and (5) reliance on both domestic and international markets from an export-oriented economy. Fan Gang also presented five priorities: incorporating more rural residents into urban life, improving the urban administration system for promoting the growth pattern transition from an outward economy model to an open economy model, promoting further Shenzhen-Hong Kong economic integration and social harmony, stability and efficiency by further institutional reform. Yi Yongsheng holds the view that facing the market is the foundation of independent innovation, enterprise is the key to independent innovation; industrial transformation and upgrading is the motivation of independent innovation; taking the lead in the formation of an innovation system is the environment of independent innovation; energetic policy guidance is the guarantee of the independent innovation of Shenzhen. Sun Changxue considered that Shenzhen Special Economic Zone should focus on enhancing the construction of a modern industrial system, improving the income distribution system and incentive mechanism, promoting a new round of comprehensive opening and regional coordinated development policy, constructing a wise and happy city and a first-class soft environment to continually lead the next step of reform exploration. In this chapter, we mainly discuss five representative stories.

Shenzhen Improves the Quality of Growth and Speeds Up Industrial Upgrading but Speed of Growth Declines

The average annual growth rate of GDP in Shenzhen from 1980 to 2016 was about 20 percent, but it can be seen intuitively from Figure 3 – 1 that Shenzhen's long-term growth rate continues to decline. The gap between Shenzhen and the national average annual growth rate is shrinking. The average gap between 1980 and 1985 reached 40 percentage points. It was 20 percentage points from 1990 to 1995. Then it has been 2 percentage points since 2010.

In the past 40 years, Shenzhen's economic growth has a medium-long period of about 10 years that is not regular but has been traced. It has nested a financial cycle of about three years. Shenzhen's economic openness is extremely high, and the economic adjustment period is also different from the national ones, generally one year or two ahead of the country. Several important transformations that the Shenzhen economy has experienced have basically taken place at the bottom of the medium and long-term cycle. They have created a new boom in structural adjustment and industrial upgrading, and have embarked on a path of low-to-high, gradual and rapid industrial upgrading.

The first major transformation of the Shenzhen economy occurred roughly in 1985. After the rapid growth of the arbitrage era of the planned economy and the market economy price difference in the previous years of the establishment of the special economic zone, Shenzhen began the process of rapid industrialization and urbanization. "Domestic investment is the mainstay, production is mainly based on processing and assembly, and products are mainly exported." It has become the most concise policy claim for Shenzhen to join the global division of labour system. The low-cost land and labour force and Hong Kong form the former store-and-factory centre-peripheral relationship. The Shenzhen processing trade enterprise represented by OEM has become the core force supporting Shenzhen's return to high-speed

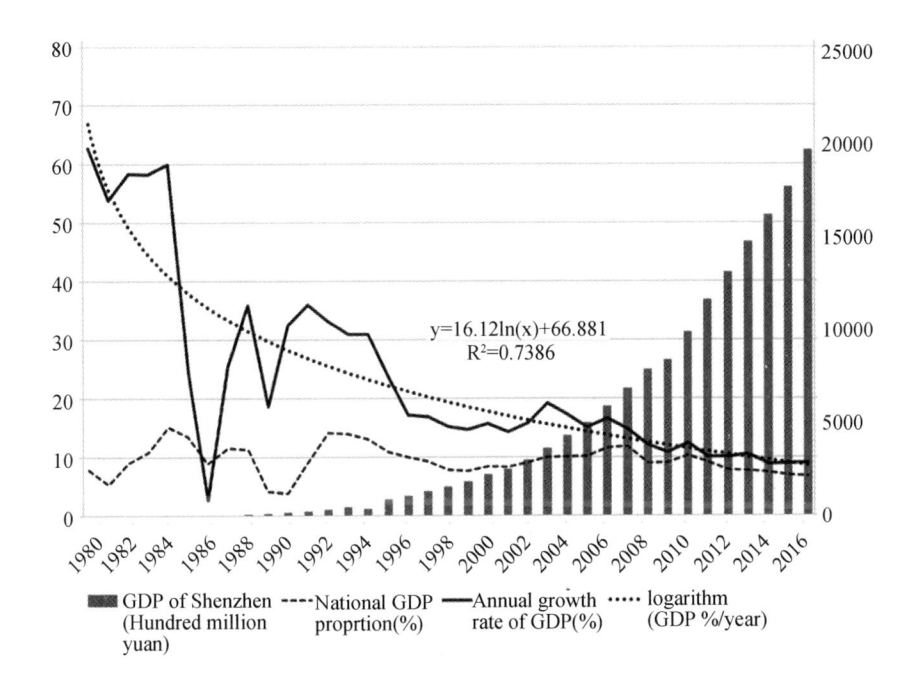

Figure 3−1: The average annual growth rate of GDP in Shenzhen (1980−2016)
Source: Shenzhen Statistics Bureau and Shenzhen Statistical Yearbook.

Chart legend: GDP of Shenzhen (Hundred million yuan); National GDP proprtion(%); Annual growth rate of GDP(%); logarithm (GDP %/year). Trend equation: $y=16.12\ln(x)+66.881$, $R^2=0.7386$.

growth. This is an era in which Shenzhen has completely broken through the traditional planned economic system and promoted market-oriented reform. It has attempted to create a systematic market economic system, created the Shenzhen securities market, led the reform of interest rate credit, reformed the land auction system, and adopted diversified investment methods for ports, and urban infrastructure construction such as airports and highways.

The second phase of the transformation in Shenzhen began in 1995 and lasted for about 10 years. Along with the SAR preferential policy of the year, Pratt & Whitney were open to the coastal policy. In 1995, the Chinese special economic zone including Shenzhen was essentially a special economic zone without special policy support. In addition to major institutional changes, the Hong Kong-Shenzhen-Shantou high-speed railway was built. The completion of the large-scale operation of Shenzhen Airport has also become a driving factor for enterprises to re-discover new and reasonable locations. Shenzhen enterprises have left Shenzhen to seek better development opportunities, such as the large-scale entry of processing trade enterprises into Dongguan, triggering a new round of recession in Shenzhen's economy. The Shenzhen economy has shifted from processing trade to imitation innovation. Whether it is the cottage phenomenon in the Chinese context or the Copycat in the English context, it depicts the core industrialization process without core R&D competitiveness and the imitation of large-scale production capacity. Undoubtedly, the phenomenon of the cottage is an important example of attending a middle school, and it is also an important way for knowledge catch-up by developing countries. No longer in cottage-style production, today Shenzhen may still remain in the stage of decentralized process processing trade. Shenzhen enterprises have entered the production process of specialized and differentiated products from cottage production. Many famous brands in Shenzhen were born in the golden age.

The third transformation in Shenzhen almost alternated with the second transformation. Around 2003, Shenzhen's economy was in a new round of recession. The main reason was that Shenzhen exploited the prevailing advantages of the global dividend for the demographic dividend, and quickly popularized and promoted it in the coastal areas. The phenomenon of the cottage moved from Shenzhen to the entire country. Shenzhen urgently needs to introduce new production methods to achieve new and higher levels of innovation growth. This is a new round of upgrades with a solid foundation and comprehensive integration. It is a process of upgrading from specialized processing and assembly to specialized manufacturing and collaborative innovation. Today, Shenzhen is not known for its large number of large enterprises. This is a feature of Beijing and Shanghai. Shenzhen is characterized by a large number of small enterprises. There are complex network-type supply chain relationships between large and medium-sized enterprises. The large-scale Shenzhen enterprises represented by Huawei are constantly improving their global innovation status. SMEs entering the supply chain of first-class large enterprises are not only sharing the innovation achievements of large enterprises, but more important, obtaining and maintaining the qualification of suppliers is a competitive survival process; many companies compete, but only one can stand out. Every participating company must propose the best possible solution to defeat the opponent to obtain the supplier qualification. Therefore, this is not a one-way innovation sharing or the process of traditional large enterprises relying on monopoly status to eliminate small and medium-sized enterprises, but a collaborative innovation process. It is division of labour and innovation, innovation deepening the division of labour, and promoting new continuous innovation.

Around 2010, Shenzhen began a new innovation-driven transformation. The supply of effective public goods, such as public research and development platforms, public information platforms, and public innovation service platforms have grown rapidly. Combined with the increasingly strong innovation capabilities of enterprises, Shenzhen has begun to move towards the forefront of global innovation, from the world-famous copycat to the famous innovation greenhouse. Entering the era of innovation, Shenzhen has formed an independent innovation model based on market demand and integrating production, education and research. Using new technologies such as Internet platform, cloud computing and big data model, and relying on technology-based leading enterprises, 45 industry-university-research alliances have been formed to cultivate this model. There are 70 new R&D institutions that integrate basic research, applied research and industrialization. Perhaps the biggest feature of the new round of innovation transformation is that Shenzhen has begun the process of invention + innovation. Knowledge and ideological creation, basic science and industrial innovation are more and more closely integrated.

New technologies, new industries, and new ideas have replaced material capital investment as the main source of economic growth. In the first 20 years of Shenzhen's economic development, on the whole society's average investment rate in fixed assets was over 50 percent, and then gradually declined. The average investment rate since 2010 has dropped to 23 percent. The next generation of wireless communication technology, gene sequencing analysis and equipment manufacturing, new materials, new energy vehicles, display technology and other fields have become the world's leading innovation capabilities. According to the five-year cumulative number of international patent applications, Shenzhen-Hong Kong has become the world-class regional innovation cluster after Tokyo-Yokohama in Japan.

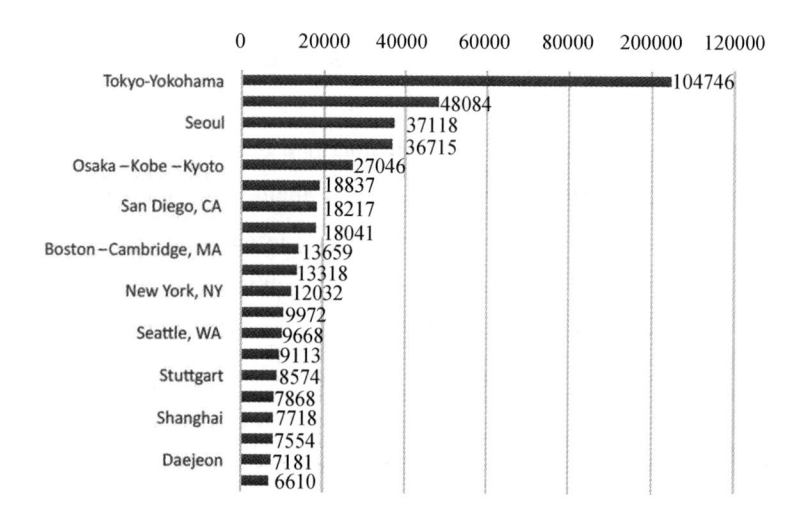

City	Patents
Tokyo-Yokohama	104746
Seoul	48084
	37118
	36715
Osaka–Kobe–Kyoto	27046
	18837
San Diego, CA	18217
	18041
Boston–Cambridge, MA	13659
	13318
New York, NY	12032
	9972
Seattle, WA	9668
	9113
Stuttgart	8574
	7868
Shanghai	7718
	7554
Daejeon	7181
	6610

Figure 3 – 2: World's top 20 city centers for patents during 5 years

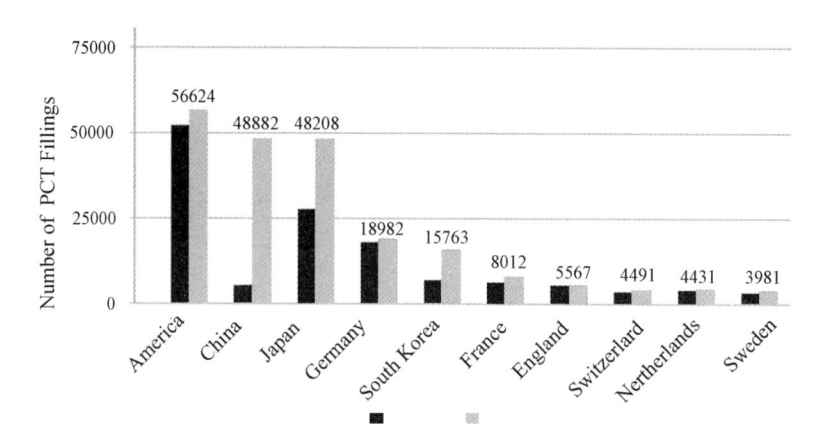

Country	2007	2017
America	56624	
China		48882
Japan	48208	
Germany	18982	
South Korea	15763	
France	8012	
England	5567	
Switzerland	4491	
Netherlands	4431	
Sweden	3981	

Figure 3 –3: Application for international patents in major countries in 2007 and 2017

Transforming in innovation, improving economic quality, and continuously strengthening the ability of collaborative innovation. Figure 3 – 2 shows the application for international patents of major countries in the 2017 World Innovation Report published on the website of the United Nations Intellectual Property Organization. The data of Shenzhen is from the annual report of the Shenzhen Intellectual Property Office. In 2007, mainland China applied to the International Intellectual Property Organization (WIPO) for the seventh largest number of PCT international patents, ranking second in the world in 2017, and may surpass the United States within three years, when it is expected by WIPO to become the world's number one (Figure 3 – 3). In time, China's international patent stock during the patent protection period is likely to surpass the United States as the world's number one in 2030 – 2035. In 2004 – 2017, the number of patent applications in Shenzhen began from 331, increasing to more than 20,000, exceeding Germany and South Korea, slightly lower than the total of France Inari. In the 2016 international patent application rankings, there were 4 companies with more than 4 patent applications, and 4 companies from China, totalling 10,651, ranking first (Figure 3 – 4). Among them, the top 3 companies exceeded the top 5 in the USA and the top 7 in Japan respectively. (National Intellectual Property Statistics Bureau.) It is particularly worth mentioning that Shenzhen's innovation system, with division of labour as the core, has demonstrated a huge ability of collaborative innovation. The ten large-scale innovative enterprises represented by Huawei account for about 50 percent of international patent applications, professional and large. International patent applications for small and medium-sized innovative companies that are symbiotic in the enterprise account for another 50 percent.

Shenzhen's independent innovation is not only reflected in the high-speed growth of high-tech industries, but also in the deep impression left by traditional industry. For example, the development of the Shenzhen garment industry started with nail buttons and sewing sleeves. After 30 years, it has become a fashion base, occupying half of China's women's garment production. The application of the latest technologies such as clothing computer integrated manufacturing system (CIMS), PAC programmable control, digital jet printing technology, computer colour measurement and colour matching, and a large number of fashion design teams has greatly enhanced the brand development and product design of apparel enterprises, their production level and capacity, and completed a major transformation from traditional OEM to ODM, and finally to the fashion industry with its own brand and technology and a close division of labour. Shenzhen is also the first city in the country to be awarded the title of "Design Capital" by UNESCO. It has nearly 5,000 industrial design institutions. Shenzhen Design has won the "Red Dot Award" and "IF Award" for the world's top design awards, with hundreds of items (Figure 3 – 5).

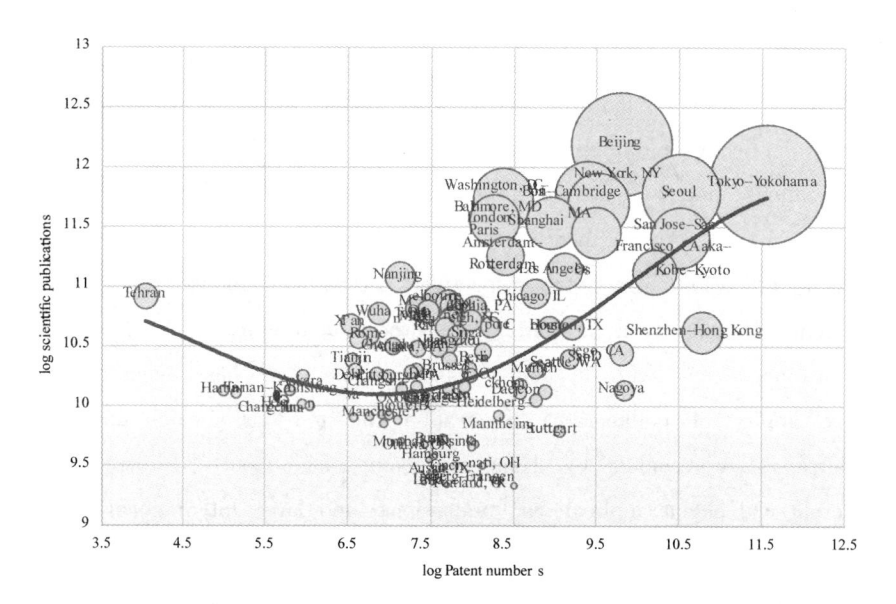

Figure 3 – 4: World's top 100 clusters patent and scientific publishing performance
Source: Cornell University, INSEAD and WIPO (2018): The Global Innovation Index 2018.

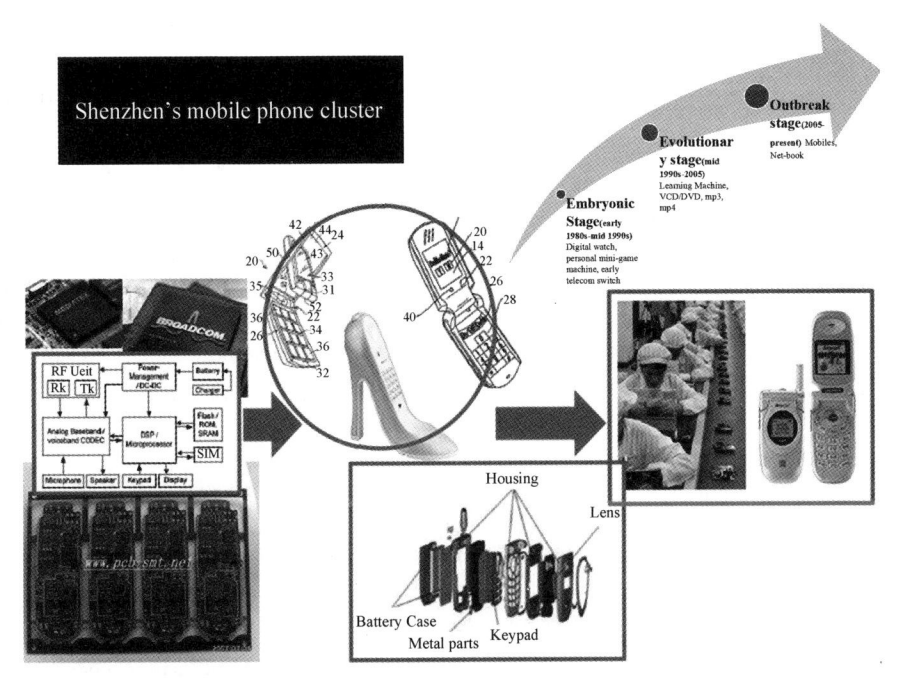

Figure 3 – 5 Shenzhen's mobile phone cluster is constantly updated from assembly to manufacturing andinnovation

Shenzhen is the City with the highest Economic Openness and good Market Economy Development

A sound market mechanism is the most important institutional guarantee for stimulating innovation and enhancing economic vitality. The market mechanism has three core functions. First, the market economy can provide a reasonable incentive mechanism. The market and the planned economy are completely different. The planned economy has no incentive mechanism. Under market conditions, the maximum benefit of the enterprise is the incentive mechanism. Second, the market is a signal discovery mechanism. When everyone says that the planned economy is an unrealizable economic mechanism, in fact, no individual or organization can collect all the information about resource allocation. When it is impossible to collect complete information or collect some information at a very high cost, the comprehensive economic plan itself is a paradox. The biggest feature of the market economy is that everyone may find that some points may be imperfect and may be inaccurate from different angles, but may be useful information. These information generates incentives for entrepreneurial innovation and motivates companies and individuals to discover new information. Third, the market mechanism is a measurable mechanism. Is resource allocation effective? Is the information obtained accurate? Finally, it will definitely be reflected in the market value of the product.

Before the reform and liberalisation, Shenzhen took the lead in establishing a framework system for the market economy in China, which played a key supporting role for Shenzhen's innovation and development. For example, Shenzhen took the lead in reforming the land use system in China, separating the national ownership of land from the rights of use of specific operators, and implementing bidding and auction systems for the transfer of rights of use of operational land; comprehensively implementing housing system reforms to achieve commercialization of housing. In the financial aspect, introducing a number of foreign-funded banks, establishing regional joint-stock banks, such as China Merchants Bank and Shenzhen Development Bank, and breaking through the resistance to create a stock trading market; establishing a foreign trade system that is oriented towards the international market, operating according to international practices, and market mechanisms, and forming a set of foreign trade systems and organizational forms that adapt to the development of the market economy; earlier establishing a "talent market", facing the country, achieving the free appointment and free flow of talent. Through a series of market-oriented reforms, Shenzhen has gradually established and improved the system of capital markets, technology markets, talent markets, property rights trading markets, information markets, etc. The specific space that Shenzhen has is domestic and foreign commodities, labour, and capital. Production factors such as enterprises and technologies provide a freely mobile, mutually integrated and grafted place and stage, providing a key guarantee for the market mechanism to play a fundamental role in innovation activities. Of course, the market mechanism needs to be legalized to ensure that in a fragile legal environment, production factors will be difficult to accumulate, and economic and innovation activities will be more inefficient.

At present, Shenzhen listed companies account for 7.9 percent of the country's total, profits account for 11 percent of the country's total; Shenzhen listed company controlling shareholders: state-owned holdings 19.5 percent; private holdings 76.1 percent; foreign investment 2.9 percent; and others 1.5 percent. The distribution of labour employment in Shenzhen, the number of entrepreneurs and the number of employees per capita of enterprises can be obtained from the table 3 − 1, which is clear evidence of the high degree of marketization in Shenzhen. The degree of economic development is the highest, and the competition for enterprises is the most intense. In 1980, the total number of labourers in Shenzhen was about 150,000, of which some 50,000 were employed by enterprises, 82.7 percent were employees of state-owned enterprises, 2/3 were non-employees, and the average number of employees was 180. In 2000, the total labour force reached 4.75 million, the number of employees was 934,000, and the employees of state-owned enterprises accounted for 33.2 percent. The number of entrepreneurs has reached nearly 110,000 from 830, and the average number of employees is 44. In 2016, the total labour force reached 9.264 million, the number of employees reached 4.426 million, and the proportion of employees in Chinese enterprises fell to 9.4 percent. Employment in towns and villages is no longer counted, and individual industrial and commercial households account for about half of total employment. It is not difficult to see that the fundamental change in the employment of labour in Shenzhen in 2000 − 2016 is that the number of employees in work has increased by 4.5 million. The Shenzhen enterprises have gone through the process of scale and standardization.

Table 3–1 Shenzhen labour force employment and distribution;
Entrepreneur numbers and enterprise per capita employees

Year	All labour force Ten thousand	Corporate employees Ten thousand	State – owned enterprise employees Ten thousand	Enterprise share (percent)	Share of state – owned enterprises (percent)	Number of enterprises	Labour force per business
1980	14.9	4.9	4.05	32.9	82.7	830	180
1985	32.6	22.7	16.8	69.6	74.0	6853	48
1990	109.2	55.4	50.5	50.7	91.2	19827	55
1995	298.5	88.8	40.2	29.7	45.3	70785	42
2000	475.0	93.4	31.0	19.7	33.2	107457	44
2005	576.3	165.4	35.9	28.7	21.7	209443	28
2010	758.1	251.1	46.6	33.1	18.6	360912	21
2016	926.4	442.6	41.8	47.8	9.4	1504255	6

Traditional towns with three to one supplement are the main characteristics. Employment in the village has gradually been narrowed, and the proportion of employees in state-owned enterprises has fallen to 9.4 percent; the proportion of total employment has fallen below 5 percent. The number of entrepreneurs in Shenzhen was 830 in 1980, close to 20,000 in 1990, and about 110,000 in 2000, currently more than 1.5 million. The average number of employees in the company has dropped to 6, roughly the same as in New York. This shows that Shenzhen is a representative city of entrepreneurship.

A typical market survey found that 80 percent of innovation comes from customers and partners, which illustrates the fundamental role of market division of labour in innovation. This is because a highly developed market means that the market has sufficient specialized division of labour and cooperation and a developed industrial chain. In 2018, the number of high-tech enterprises in Shenzhen exceeded 10,000, ranking second to Beijing among all cities. The number of domestic and overseas listed companies was 374, ranking first in the national cities. Shenzhen has attained outstanding achievements in the innovation industry, and has gathered a large number of different industries, different sub-disciplines, and different scales of enterprise groups to carry out collaborative innovation. As the core city of Guangdong-Hong Kong-Macao Greater Bay Area, Shenzhen can integrate a large number of social products and R&D resources, innovative resources and common innovative technologies. After cooperation, suppliers and even competitors rapidly spread among different industries, and a wave is formed. Then a wave of industrial innovation and upgrading is not so much the innovation of The Story of Shenzhen: Its Economic, Social and Environmental Transformation of large enterprises, but essentially the collaborative activities of the enterprise groups that cannot be counted. Innovation has become the conscious behaviour of Shenzhen enterprises under conditions of market competition. The development level of the market economy determines the potential for innovation and development. Innovation boosts the ability of Shenzhen enterprises to achieve stronger competition and survival.

  The Shenzhen government has also actively explored the administrative system of small government and large society. It has carried out 8 institutional reforms and 4 rounds of administrative examination and approval system reforms. The examination and approval items have been reduced from 1091 to 391, continuously improving the overall efficiency of government services. At the same time, the Shenzhen government's fiscal funds have been withdrawn from the competitive and profitable sectors, and concentrated on infrastructure construction and public utility projects, providing a good external environment for the development of high-tech industries. Since the mid—1990s, the Shenzhen government has given the initiative and discourse power of independent innovation to the main body of the enterprise, and has accelerated the service function of the development of high-tech industries to social intermediary organizations, becoming the builder of an independent innovation environment. This has also become the key to Shenzhen's successful innovation drive.

Innovate in Competitive Survival, rely on Industry Chain Synergy, Gather Innovative Entrepreneurial Energy

The developed market economy system and division of labour are the basis for the continuous upgrading of industry. According to Smith's theory, division of labour is considered to be the source of economic growth. The role of this division of labour not only refers to the role of internal technical division of labour in the improvement of labour productivity, but also includes the division of labour in industry, the division of labour in different industrial sectors, the international division of labour, and the increase in the round about production process thus driving the expansion of the economic scale. The theoretical logic of the Shenzhen experience is that through opening up and participation in the international division of labour, Shenzhen has gained knowledge spillover and spreads of foreign investment and technology licensing methods. Through the "introduction-learning-improvement-innovation" model, Shenzhen local enterprises have gradually developed process technology, industrial manufacturing technology and specialized technology of the professional workforce; these specialized labour forces in the subsequent follow-up and catch-up stage imitate innovation and achieve original innovation, and form a new specialized workforce, with professionals. With the increase in the number and types of labour, the endogenous specialized division of labour is deepening and refining. These sub-sectors and industries will attract more enterprises, accelerating market competition and innovation activities, which may lead to the formation of new industries, and perfect, driving economic growth. The extension of this theory to the endogenous growth theory is that, unlike the homogeneity of the latter's human capital, the difference in specialized labour as seen in this paper will provide the backward regions with comparative advantages in certain emerging industries. They can achieve the catch-up development of increasing scale returns across static comparative advantages.

Shenzhen has many fascinating qualities, the most prominent of which is the entrepreneurial spirit that vibrates in every corner of the city. Entrepreneurship and innovation create newproducts from scratch and create new enterprises. The growth of excellent enterprises is a process of never giving up. Only by continuous innovation can we survive in market competition. An innovative city, the core of an innovative country, is the process of entrepreneurs creating entrepreneurs. The result of 100 innovative entrepreneurs driving 100 innovative entrepreneurs to continue to advance is the process of increasing marginal revenue. The middle-income trap is the diminishing marginal return of innovation, and there are many cases in which high-income countries in the world fall into the marginal diminishing returns trap.

What we need to pay close attention to is that competition and survival are not the single enterprise's process of lonely pursuit. On the contrary, the competition of many professional and innovative enterprises in the industrial cluster constitutes the synergy effect of the industrial chain. Many enterprises in many fields, multi-level, multi-link innovation, collaborative innovation resulting in resource restructuring and effective re-allocation, are at the root of the rise of a new industry. Shenzhen's latest rise in the UAV industrial cluster is a classic case of competitive survival and collaborative innovation. The brief expression of accuracy is that the UAV is a new industry based on AI technology and material technology, precision processing technology, power battery technology, control technology and digital mobile communication technology. No one company can independently produce drones, and it can't produce drones without the core key technologies in the industry chain.

First of all, there are many fibre material companies in Shenzhen. In the era of processing trade, from processing fishing rods, badminton rackets, tennis rackets to golf clubs, with the gradual upgrading of the industry, a number of subdivided enterprises emerged for the manufacture of fuselage, casing and main structural parts for drones. Secondly, the UAV precision parts manufacturing enterprise, as a post-processing sub-sector of aviation aluminium, originated from low-end aviation model parts, mobile phone casings, consumer electronics casings, robot parts and so on. Shenzhen's mobile phone manufacturing has risen in the era of imitative innovation. According to incomplete statistics, after entering the 21st century, output has reached 600 – 800 million, and exports accounted for 70 – 80 percent. With the advent of the smart phone era, the traditional low-end mobile phone industry has rapidly declined, becoming a typical overcapacity industry. Synergies with drone manufacturing and improved precision manufacturing capabilities are opportunities for related companies to gain a new round of innovation growth. Similarly, it is the specialty plastics industry that provides enclosures, propellers and low-cost consumables for UAV production. The lithium polymer battery industry is the basis of mobile phone production and is also a traditional advantage industry in Shenzhen. The drone reaches its maximum speed from the hovering state. The shorter the UAV performance, the higher the requirement for instantaneous power increase of the battery. Therefore, the energy density of the power battery is much higher than that of the mobile phone battery, and the volume energy density or the mass energy density is the key to the transformation and survival of the traditional mobile phone battery manufacturer. The competition of different technical solutions in different fields and different links has created the rise of the UAV industry in Shenzhen. An expanding industrial cluster has also provided more market demand for hundreds of related companies. It is worth mentioning that the micro-motor is the key component of the UAV. The magnetic material is the core material for the production of micro-motors. It has the characteristics of small dosage, high value and high innovation difficulty coefficient. A single business will pay a higher price and bear greater risks. The Shenzhen Municipal Government did not foresee the rise of the drone industry, but knew that the micro-servo motor is the core technology for the development of the robot industry. It has given critical support to the research and development of magnetic materials in the field of public service and research and development, and upgraded the Shenzhen motor industry.

Reform and Opening Up Make Innovation the Characteristic of Shenzhen

From simple assembly and division of labour to specialized division of labour, Shenzhen's continuous transformation and upgrading from large-scale manufacturing to R&D creates a huge market competition pressure. There are pressures to be eliminated without innovation, and innovation failures must be eliminated. Businesses are often at a loss, and this requires the government to play a role in providing innovative public goods. The list of public goods in which the government plays a protective role is long, but the core points are extremely clear.

The first is to encourage enterprise innovation and promote the hyperspace cooperation between the Science Innovation Centre and the Industrial Technology Innovation Centre (Innovation). The four 90 percent features are the most notable aspects of Shenzhen's innovation, 90 percent of research and development institutions, 90 percent of research and development personnel, 90 percent of research and development expenditures, and 90 percent of research and development results are from enterprises. However, since the mid—1990s, Shenzhen has insisted on encouraging, supporting and subsidizing enterprises to establish research and development institutions, and has promoted the establishment of long-term research and development cooperation with universities and research institutions. This is an important institutional factor for the explosive growth of Shenzhen's international patent applications since 2004. Now, every time Shenzhen applies for 100 international patents, 12 of them are completed in cooperation with Beijing. Because Beijing and Shenzhen have grown into a globally important industrial innovation centre: because of Shenzhen, Beijing's scientific discovery has become the frontier theoretical basis of industrial technology innovation, and the status of scientific innovation centre has been further strengthened.

The secondis to promote market-led enterprise innovation. How do the scientific and technological innovations from the whole country and even the world, represented by Beijing, integrate with the innovation activities of Shenzhen enterprises, or why have the scientific research results in Beijing entered Shenzhen in large numbers, instead of other cities? The core is not the difference in government behaviour, but the difference in outcomes of market-led innovation resulting from differences in government behaviour. The industrialization of scientific research results began with a "thrilling leap" in rational market pricing. Knowledge is power, and the high return on personal intellectual property will spur more knowledge discovery. Companies need to reduce innovation costs and risks and want to pay lower intellectual property fees. Walras' "auctional" market equilibrium cannot solve the problem of pricing knowledge products. It turns out that the government cannot price high-risk and high-decision innovation activities, which is the mission of a specialized venture capital industry cluster. From a global perspective, areas where innovation activities flourish are areas where venture capital is most concentrated. The most active cities for innovation investment in mainland China are highly concentrated in Beijing, Shenzhen and Shanghai.

The third is to create an innovative basis for the rule of law. The essence of a market economy is the contract system, which is the most important public product on which innovation depends. The legal contract is signed, the contract can be effectively executed, and the market economy can operate. Without the enforceability of contracts and their fair implementation, it is impossible to produce a wide range of innovative activities. If one company creates intellectual property and another company plagiarizes it without penalty, no company will be willing to innovate. Contracts can be fulfilled on the basis of the rule of law, rather than government administrative controls. The government's commitment to eliminating administrative monopolies is the greatest support for innovation. If there is a problem, finding the market is the rule of law. If there is a problem, finding the mayor will lead to improper intervention by the government. The Shenzhen government has built a perfect venture capital and equity investment system for 20 years, and has formed a deterrent intellectual property protection system to give full play to the decisive role of the market economy in resource allocation.

In July 1995, Shenzhen City defined a transformation strategy with high-tech industry as the forerunner and began to implement a series of policy measures to support the development of high-tech industries. In September 1997, it was explicitly proposed to establish a technology venture investment system, which was made official in November 1998, in order to initiate the venture capital legislation process, and translate the venture capital of English "Venture Capital" into a venture capital investment, and determine that intellectual property rights can become equity assets in legal form; in October 2000, the "Interim Provisions on Innovation Investment" were enacted into law. The legislative procedure, the Shenzhen Innovation Investment Regulations passed by the Standing Committee of the Shenzhen Municipal People's Congress in 2003, which contains several important theories and forward-looking institutional breakthroughs, laid the legal foundation for the development of Shenzhen's innovative investment industry, and was the 10th National Committee of the National Development and Reform Commission in 2005. The Interim Measures for the Administration of Venture Capital Enterprises provide useful legislative references. In September 2012, Shenzhen accumulated 10 years of practice and promulgated the revised "Shenzhen Special Economic Zone Venture Capital Regulations".

The fourth is to establish an industrial policy system that is compatible with market support. In 2006, Shenzhen proposed a far-reaching slogan to support "non-consensus innovation". This is a slogan full of philosophical implications and a policy proposition that has raised questions. The challenge is, what is the basis for the government to support non-consensus innovation? Consensus must not be innovation. Most major scientific discoveries and industrial technological innovations in human history have gone through a process from being suspected to becoming consensus. Innovation must not be the myth of the so-called aura of light, and must conform to the general law of scientific discovery. The government can't determine who can succeed in innovation, and can't specify who is the innovator, but it can guide innovators and companies to understand the scientific basis of industrial technological innovation, follow the scientific norms of innovation, grasp the innovation progress in related fields, and understand their predecessors. Innovative explorations that have been carried out, whether successful or not, clarify the technical routes that are feasible in the future. Under the conditions of market competition, reasonable government behaviour is to clearly define the direction of scientific research and industrial innovation to be supported, as well as to evaluate the innovative ability of the innovation team in many aspects and effective organization. The biggest difference between determining direction and assessing innovative ability and designating winners is that innovation is based on market competition and effective incentives for market players. By playing a fundamental role in the allocation of resources, the market will ultimately determine who is the winner. Only in this way is it possible to better fulfil the role of the government. Since 2006, Shenzhen has continued to patiently and meticulously explore the establishment of an environment that encourages innovation, formulates reasonable and effective policies and rules to support innovation, and has created an evaluation system in which scientists and innovative entrepreneurs rely on both sides.

Create wetland effects and support the development of strategic emerging industries. Wetlands are the most dynamic ecosystem in nature and have an extremely rich species diversity. The economic activity of the wetland is a fair, just and open market competition environment. As long as the government does not stretch out, market competition can determine who is the innovation winner. There will be no eternal innovation winners in market competition. Shenzhen has formulated and implemented a series of fruitful industrial policies and played an important role in promoting industrial transformation and upgrading. Through case analysis, it is observed how the industrial policy based on industrial planning is compatible with the market mechanism, and industry is transformed and upgraded according to market principles. In 2010, Shenzhen put forward the concept of "Shenzhen Quality" transformation development, formulated a more restrictive list of restrictive industry development, implemented a more active and intensive development policy, and rapidly moved enterprises in industrial restructuring. In the first quarter of 2012, Shenzhen's economic growth rate plummeted to 5.8 percent, which was lower than the national and provincial average. Shenzhen still insisted on the same direction, kept pace, and did not lose momentum. In 2013, Shenzhen launched the life health industry planning and related industrial policy points. It is clearly stated that it is necessary to build major medical infrastructure such as a stem cell bank and establish a clinical efficacy and safety evaluation system for individualized cell therapy. In 2018, Shenzhen has completed the construction of a stem cell bank and the first national immune cell quality testing laboratory. Cell technology innovation cannot be carried out from laboratory technology, across intermediate processes, quality control, and cellular products used in humans must undergo regulatory approval and have strict third-party quality checks. The US Food and Drug Administration and China's Food and Drug Administration have clearly stipulated that the application of cell products must have strict quality testing: one is the detection of cell type and source; the other is safety testing, whether the cell source has infectious diseases, and whether the preparation process has pollution; the third is the effectiveness test, the cell as a kind of drug, whether the clinical use can achieve the goal of treatment. The development of China's cellular industry has clearly lagged behind the US, Europe and Japan. The lack of cell preparation standards and quality standards in the development of the cell industry is an important reason. It can be seen from this that an effective industrial policy can speed up the key shortcomings in the process of industrial development. As long as they do not violate the market principle of competitive access to resources, industrial policies are conducive to the role of resource allocation in market mechanisms.

Increase Reform and Opening Up, Form An Innovation Incentive and Competition Survival Innovation System

In the mid - 1990s, Shenzhen proposed the development of high-tech industries, but there are few universities or research institutions in Shenzhen. Shenzhen has done two things. First, "policy and depression" attracts talents to gather in Shenzhen. Due to the success of the first batch of high-tech enterprises in the early 1990s, Shenzhen has formed a "policy depression" that is more suitable for the development of high-tech industries due to market-oriented reforms. At that time, a large number of research institutions and technology developers who could not independently develop in the Mainland went south. Shenzhen established an electronic information enterprise, and in the 1990s, it formed a large-scale innovation resource transfer of hundreds of thousands of scientific and technological personnel. Second, Shenzhen has actively built an innovation system integrating production, education and research. If the arrival of these entrepreneurs initiated the motor of Shenzhen's scientific and technological innovation, then the objective of Shenzhen's relatively complete independent innovation system, which is enterprise-oriented, market-oriented, and closely integrated with government, industry, research and development, is to maintain Shenzhen's continued innovation. This is the inexhaustible motive force for innovation. The establishment of an innovation system has several important roles in the development of high-tech industries in Shenzhen: first, overcome market failures and organizational failures, reduce the uncertainty and risks of innovative enterprises, and enhance the investment in and motivation of enterprises; second, establish technological transformation. Market derivative, and incubate high-tech enterprises, to promote the transformation of scientific and technological achievements; third, increase the number and types of specialized labour, and lay the foundation for deepening and refining of the division of labour.

In 2013, 591 new national high-tech enterprises were identified in Shenzhen, amounting to more than 3,000; 176 innovative carriers including key laboratories, engineering centres, and public technology platforms were accumulated, a total of 955 in all; social R&D investment exceeded 50 billion yuan. The proportion of GDP has increased to 4 percent, exceeding the average level of developed countries. Shenzhen has achieved "four 90 percent" phenomena in the field of scientific and technological innovation, that is, more than 90 percent of R&D institutions are established in enterprises, more than 90 percent of R&D personnel are concentrated in enterprises, and more than 90 percent of R&D funds are from enterprises and over 90 percent of service invention patents come from enterprises. The high-tech zone's entrepreneurial and innovation environment has been further optimized, and it has formed a relatively complete innovative and entrepreneurial service chain, including an international technology business platform, venture capital service plaza, virtual university park, Shenzhen-Hong Kong production and research base, and National IC design Shenzhen Industrialization Base and other service agencies.

The resources of scientific and technical personnel and professionals are the basis of technological innovation. The number of people engaged in science and technology activities in large and medium-sized enterprises increased from 57,200 in 2005 to 257,000 in 2012, an increase of 3.5 times. By the end of 2013, there were 1,216,300 professional and technical personnel in Shenzhen, including 392,100 professional and technical personnel with intermediate technical titles and above. By 2013, 3,033 high-level professionals were recognized. Shenzhen University City has trained more than 6,000 graduate students every year, and has become an important local institution with systematic, all-round training and introduction of high-quality talents.

Shenzhen's relatively complete technology service intermediary is an important bridge to promote innovation. For example, through the establishment of the GEM and SME board in Shenzhen, the company's financing channels will be expanded; the Shenzhen High-tech Zone Service Centre will establish the Shenzhen High-tech Zone Venture Capital Service Plaza, through the introduction of venture capital funds, brokerage investment banking and non-listed business units, property rights transactions. The assessment, accounting, law firm and guarantee, credit, and patent service intermediaries have settled in, providing "multi-level, three-dimensional, and full-process" financing services for small and medium-sized micro-technical enterprises at different stages of growth. The industrial policy formulated by the government is an important part of the Shenzhen innovation system. The uncertainty of technology, the uncertainty of markets, the uncertainty of equity distribution and the uncertainty of policy environment, as well as the imperfect market mechanism, require a certain degree of government intervention. Therefore, in the post-development countries or regions, the government can influence and guide the role and efficiency of innovation activities through various forms such as policy planning, government procurement, and finance. Shenzhen promulgated the "Regulations on the Protection of Technical Secrets of Shenzhen Special Economic Zone Enterprises" "Measures for the Management of Intangible Assets of Shenzhen Special Economic Zones" "Interim Measures for Shenzhen Technology Enterprises for Reward Enterprises" and "Interim Measures for the Extraction and Use of Enterprise Technology Development Funds in Shenzhen", the "Regulations on Further Supporting the Development of High-Tech Industries" and other regulations have compiled scientific and technological development plans, high-tech industry development plans, strategic emerging industry revitalization development plans, and future industrial development policies. The Shenzhen Municipal Government has also invested 3 billion yuan to set up a venture capital guiding fund to solve the problem of financing difficulties in the seeding and start-up period. Shenzhen has also set up a special fund for strategic emerging industries. The government supports strategic emerging industries such as biology, the Internet, and new energy. By guiding financial funds and leveraging, it will guide more social capital into the research and innovation field of the whole society.

In order to maintain the growth of Shenzhen's "innovation-driven model" in the future, Shenzhen proposes to promote market-oriented reforms with the rule of law and internationalization, establish an internationally competitive, standardized and orderly market economy and rule of law economy, and give full play to the market in resource allocation. The decisive role of improving resource allocation efficiency and enhancing the incentive mechanism for innovation activities. Shenzhen proposed to build "Shenzhen Quality" as a guide, continue to promote innovation-driven development strategy, enhance brand value by strengthening independent research and development, and implement quality priority, and promote the continuous upgrading and development of Shenzhen industry. Shenzhen should strengthen the institutionalization of marketization, rule of law and internationalization in the field of science and technology, and build an open and independent innovation system with international competitiveness through an innovative cooperation model of industry, university and research. To this end, Shenzhen proposes to build a first-class talent education and training system, support the establishment of relevant education majors and basic research facilities, and enhance the professional talent training, basic research, and original innovation level.

Chapter 4 City Growth and Urban Planning: Encountering the Challenges of Population Growth

Introduction

The fast growth of Shenzhen from small village to metropolis in only four decades is a unique case of urban development. The impressive dynamics of both population and economy is the result of a peculiar and successful process that has been promoted, sustained and regulated by governmental planning. Through the institution of the Special Economic Zone (SEZ), near Hong Kong, the Open Door Policy set up Shenzhen as a "window" on the new trends in economics, a "training ground" for talents in the Mainland, and an "experimenting ground" for reforms in China. In order to achieve this, it was the first city in China to adopt capitalist world-type development, market and planning practices, which once more stress its uniqueness among other cities.

As Wu and Tang claim, "as the testing ground for the importation of foreign capital, science and technology into China, [Shenzhen] has been at the forefront of that country's efforts at integration with the world economy, especially since the mid – 1980s". Shen and Kee (2017) report that, similarly to what happened in Guangzhou, the success of Shenzhen is mainly related to both the capacity of agglomeration and the creation of flows in terms of foreign trade and movement of people. But the peculiarities of its success reside in the innovation processes, also in administrative structure and practices, and in the active involvement of government in addressing development. The latter has been crucial in driving the evolution of the city from a centrally planned, "resource-constrained" economy, typical of socialism, towards a modern capitalist, "demand-constrained", economic system. A system of unprecedented economic and social reforms for China, as well as appropriate promotion policies of the city, attracted and involved private stakeholders and then facilitated the city's explosive development. Overall, as Wu claims, "Judged by the growth in population size, spatial development and various economic parameters, the experiment of Shenzhen's SEZ was extremely successful".

Urban planning has played a central role in sustaining and driving the city's economic growth and the transformation of urban landscape, going hand in hand with both socio-economic and political context. Master plans and their development strategies have rationalised expansion and land use, with the latter having a prominent role in the city development. Over time, these strategies have been consistent with the changing needs and role of the city, from early SEZ consolidation, to its expansion of the former city's Counties, to the strengthening of its role in the region and in the world. These needs, along with growing competition worldwide and with other Chinese areas, have stimulated what Ng defines as " an impressive job in integrating socio-economic and spatial planning". The latter efforts to plan spatial expansion consistently with the city's social and economic needs are indeed typical of centrally planned economies like China. However, the main novelty in Shenzhen was the use of socioeconomic and spatial planning in a new way, namely, facilitating and promoting economic growth and market development. Planners have learned this unprecedented approach only by practice, gradually moving over time from the exclusive realm of centrally planned system to a more locally based formulation of plans.

In the following Sections, I will outline the main phases of urban planning and how it has supported the city's growth since the inception of the SEZ. I will then focus on some core issues related to population growth that have characterised the city expansion, that is migration, urbanization and urban concentration, with a digression on a particular floating population, like tourists. Afterwards, I will discuss the main principles of sustainable planning and the related need to improve the living standards of the city's population.

Planning and the Evolution of the City

Since the institution of the SEZ in 1980, the design of Shenzhen development as depicted by urban plans has constantly evolved. The gradual transition from a centrally planned economy also concerned the process of urban planning itself, where a real modern system emerged only in the late 1980s and the 1990s with the establishment of the Shenzhen Urban Planning and Land Administration Bureau (1989), the Regulations on City Planning of the Shenzhen Municipality (1998) and the Urban Planning Board of Shenzhen (1999).

As discussed in previous papers, over time, three phases of this process can be identified. One of the most evident elements these stages have in common is the strict relationship between urban master plans and five-year planning, which has implied a tight connection between urban planning and socio-economic aspects of city growth.

The first phase goes from the SEZ inception in 1980 to 1985. The early challenge was to build a modern and attractive city for foreign investors based on industry, mainly high-tech and capital intensive, from the formerly agricultural economy. At the same time, the city should have developed multiple specializations in commerce, agriculture, housing, and tourism. However, this early stage mainly attracted foreign investors for real estate development and low-value added labour-intensive industries. At the same time, domestic investment in the city grew significantly, with central ministries having a prominent role as investors. In Wu and Tang's view, potential foreign investors were discouraged, mainly by the lack of adequate physical and legal infrastructures.

In the second phase (mid 80s-mid 90s), planning was addressed to boost the economy through the export and attraction of foreign direct investment (FDIs), with an increasingly important role of high-tech industry and services. A series of administrative reforms were implemented. Actual growth of FDIs was the most important result of these efforts. At the same time, progressive land allocation, for uses that were functional to city development, started to pose questions as to its scarcity.

As time passed, the city of Shenzhen ceased to be an "exception" in China, as other cities also started to grow economically. Therefore, it had "no choice but to strive to be an example" in order to consolidate its position towards both other Chinese cities and the rest of the world. The ambition to make it a world-class city has characterised the planning documents since the 1990s. Planners have reinforced the role of high-tech industry and services, with particular attention on the strategic use of land, and transportation and infrastructure development. After years of planning, mainly focused on economic growth, the Tenth Five-Year Plan (2001 – 2005) introduced sustainability, quality of life and environmental protection. The city's efforts in sustainable practices and environmental protection have been acknowledged, both in China and worldwide.

A work by Zacharias and Tang adopts a complementary perspective and describes how urban planning has shaped land use.

According to the first master plan in 1986, early development of the city and its SEZ was along a "clustered linear" model, where the SEZ would have grown as a string of clusters along traffic corridors. It included, in order from west to east, the administrative Districts of Nanshan, Futian, Luohu and Yantian. This distinction can also be seen today, as the city is divided into "integrated "self-sufficient" urban clusters". This rationale was opposite to the traditional core-periphery development of Chinese cities. The plan also considered the development of infrastructures, and the allocation of different areas to specific functions for city expansion.

In the subsequent years, the city grew, along with comprehensive transportation infrastructure that facilitated its development. Administrative adjustment also promoted the growth of both the original SEZ area and its neighbouring areas within the city land. In 1993, the two Counties of Bao'an and Long gang became Districts. Completed in 1996, the new comprehensive plan extended the development model of the original SEZ to the new Districts, by promoting the building of a multiple axes network structure that would have connected the different parts of the city. Despite the former division between SEZ and non-SEZ zones ceasing to exist, the economic and urban landscapes of these two areas are still different. The main objective was to control development, as the process was more disordered than expected in the first master plan. However, development control did not succeed in the way that planners expected.

A further urban master plan named "Shenzhen 2030 Development Strategy" was launched in 2004. It tried to implement the lessons learned from the previous experience in order to overcome the main "four difficulties", which constitute obstacles to further development. Two of them are the limited availability of resources, like land and water for urban use. Overcrowding and environmental degradation are the other two. This strategy meant increasing the specialization of different parts of the city, as well as improving its role in the region with respect to Hong Kong, Dongguan, Guangzhou and Huizhou. The plan wanted to foster the building of a polycentric urban development model with two centres and five sub-centres. This would have facilitated the agglomeration of both activities and services.

A following stage of urban planning called "Shenzhen 2040 Development Strategy" was launched in 2010, following the success of the third one. It again faces issues related to land use and economic development, but now it seeks to improve city sustainability by giving importance to family, health, education, culture, society.

Population and Migration

Development control has been one core issue for Shenzhen urban planners. Migration and new labour force may be fundamental to the development of a city's economy. However, indiscriminate and uncontrolled growth can be costly to cities, as a city may not be as receptive as expected. This may happen because the city structure would not be adequate to face unexpected flows of incoming population. As a result, urban space, housing and employment opportunities, and services for population can be lacking. Proliferation of slums around the most populated cities worldwide is the self-organised response of the fast-growing population in the absence of appropriate policies. Well-known implications of living in marginal conditions, like social exclusion and crime, certainly justify the need to govern social and economic phenomena related to population expansion, in order to reduce and/or avoid threats to the citizens' quality of life.

Explosive population growth of Shenzhen has characterised its development process. Official data report that in the period 1980 – 2016, Shenzhen's permanent population grew by 3,477 percent, reaching nearly 12 million people in 2016, of which 77,8 percent are employed. However, from Ng and Tang's reconstruction of the different waves of planning, actual population growth has always exceeded the targets of five-year plans, despite control policies having been generally effective in limiting the growth of cities in China.

The implications of such mismatch between planned and expected population are different, as pressure on spatial development increases significantly. The unexpected need to increase the amount of investment in infrastructure and services for the population is one of them. Limited land surface and the already mentioned need to comply with the central government's five-year population targets are further critical aspects. As an example, Wu and Tang report that between 1986 and the early 1990s, the growth of the central part of SEZ in Luohu District led planners to assign new residential areas in Futian District. This movement of people caused an increase in traffic, as well as environmental problems and a shortage of resources like water.

In addition to merely quantitative aspects, there are other social impacts related to population composition over time. Shenzhen is a city where the population's share of migrants is massive. According to SSB, in 2016, 67.7 percent of the permanent population was non-registered. This share has grown with population, from 3.6 percent in 1980, to 59.1 percent in 1990, and 82.2 percent in 2000. Since the beginning of the 2000, it has decreased to 67.7 percent in 2016. This happened despite the Chinese hukou system, which grants only registered citizens access to education, social and health services in the city where they reside. Clearly, from these numbers, one can conclude that registration policies have not discouraged migration from internal rural areas.

Although Shenzhen is one of the wealthiest cities in China in terms of per capita GDP, the share of low-income population is large, and most of it consists of migrants. Living conditions of migrants is another aspect of Shenzhen's explosive urbanization. Before the Open-Door policy came into effect, the duality between urban and rural areas was functional, to create industry and services development in the former, and production of food in the latter. Rural areas were also those where the poor population concentrated. After the 1978 reform, rural migration to cities has become the main factor for city growth, putting increasing pressure on the urban context. Usually, in big urban centres, the development of either slums or squatter settlements is the response to the housing needs of the low-income population, when rapid urbanization takes place. In China, this has not happened due to institutional constraints. The response to migrants' pressure in Shenzhen was the expansion of neighbouring traditional villages called "urban villages", which, over time, have been progressively incorporated into the city. They often represent the only available and affordable possibilities for housing. In addition to rapid urbanization and lower income of rural migrants, barriers for rural population to rent public housing have fostered their development. With the increase of migrant flows, many former villagers have changed the function of their buildings from family houses to rentals. In parallel, there has been an increase in unauthorised buildings. Despite the government's efforts to regulate the phenomenon, uncontrolled development of such illegal houses has taken place. In many cases, this led to the development of communities where families controlled residential, non-public land, and where parallel business and commerce grew.

Urban villages have maintained their characteristics of satellite entities in relation to the central urban area, with lower average education and where formerly rural population live who are unable to gain access to the city's welfare services because of the hukou. The influence of urban planning on the regulation of these agglomerations is still an issue, as well as the effectiveness of controls on urban expansion. Higher crime rates, lower living conditions, and slower integration of urban villages into the urban context are further critical aspects. These are the reasons property developers, government officials, and planners have had a negative view of the informal way urban villages have developed. But from another angle, urban villages have been the only housing opportunities available to migrants, besides being a business for inhabitants who rent their houses. Despite the progressively increasing importance of high-tech sectors in the city's economy, labour intensive industry still constitutes a significant share of the total. For this reason, urban villages also have a key role in hosting the low-skilled working population that concretely contributes to the city's economic growth.

Urbanization, Urban Concentration, and City Expansion

The explosive population growth of Shenzhen reflects one of the bestknownfigures on urban population in the last decades. The World Urbanization Prospects forecasts that today's 55 percent share of urbanised population will increase to 68 percent in 2050. Glaeser argued that this process signals the progressive transition from poverty to prosperity. At the same time, the impact on living conditions in cities may be enormous and negative, if appropriate policies do not address phenomena like inequality, crime, pollution, diseases, and congestion.

Urbanisation is associated with economic growth. A quick look at some statistics shows how positive urbanization has been for countries: as Henderson reports, "In any year, the simple correlation coefficient across countries between the percent urbanized in a country and, say, GDP per capita (in logs) is about 0.85". Urbanization also implies a higher level of development and life satisfaction two broader concepts than the solely economic one represented by GDP. However, urbanization alone does not suffice to sustain productivity caused by an increase in per capita GDP of cities; it is the process of population moving from rural areas to cities. As such, it is characterised by a progressive shift of the labour force from the primary sector to the secondary and tertiary sectors. Economic policies can influence it only indirectly, by acting on sectorial composition and income.

Unlike urbanization, urban concentration is influential for economic growth, and it is a factor that both policymakers and urban planners can influence. Proximity of activities generates scale economies that improve productivity, and then the wealth of citizens. The phenomenon of concentration in cities and its implications allows the classical Malthusian view on the relationship between population and growth to be overcome. What this classic theory predicts is that, on the one side, an increase in wealth would have expanded population by both increasing births and reducing deaths. But on the other side, population growth would have had a negative effect on per capita income because of diminishing marginal productivity, as the increasing population would deplete resources. A stationary population in the long term would have been the final outcome.

Explosive dynamics of population growth worldwide since 19th century, along with a raise in per capita income contradicted this view. The theory of Malthus is typical of economies with limited human capital and technology, such as those based on agriculture. Instead, increased density caused by higher population and greater urbanization is what characterises modern urban economies, in the fashion of Marshall's clusters. This leads to specialization, human capital improvement and greater investment in knowledge-based activities, the increasing returns of which, in turn, foster economic growth through productivity increase. At the same time, there might be an opposite effect of diminishing returns from the use of natural resources, as the increase of population limits the city's resource availability for each citizen. This causes significant social costs, such as crime, congestion, and contagious disease. The overall result of this trade-off depends on which of the two effects prevail. Concretely, this generates variable returns to city size.

In Section 3, I pointed out how migration has been crucial for city development. Uncontrolled flows have boosted the growth of urban villages, where in many cases living conditions are worse than in the rest of the area. The common view of economists is that when migrants are free to move, cities may become inefficiently large. Migrants may both produce negative externalities, and not necessarily pay for the related cost. At the same time, they compete with locals for city resources like land and services. The overall result is that private returns may be higher than social returns. Therefore appropriate migration and integration policies are key elements to overcome the related social costs. And, of course, the role of government is crucial in this, with significant implication for urban planning. As population grows, the dilemma is between fostering agglomeration and city density, with related advantages and costs, and favouring the expansion across space with amenities providing lower utility than the one coming from concentrated activities. Given available land constraints, the choice of Shenzhen seems to be obvious and towards the former model.

Land use

In some cities, socio-economic patterns have had a dramatic impact on the use of space. Old and new activities, as well as residential needs, have changed the landscape significantly. As already mentioned, Shenzhen is one of the Chinese cities the development of which has been driven by socio-economic factors. In this regard, Schneider and Woodcock (2008) studied the rates of expansion and patterns of urbanisation of 25 cities from different countries by combining remotely sensed data, spatial pattern metrics and statistical census data. They identified four main categories, namely expansive growth, frantic growth, high growth, and low growth cities. The analysed Chinese cities are Guangzhou, Dongguan and Chengdu, and they all fall within the second category of frantic growth. They have experienced high growth rates within a relatively small spatial extent, thus determining high population density. Their patterns of land conversion to urban use have been fragmented. Along with expansive-growth cities, which are typical of the USA, their growth can be ascribed to socio-economic and political determinants, which, in the case of Chinese cities, is due to "economic and demographic transformation following significant reforms on the coast and, later, in the interior". The authors also note that in Dongguan and Guangzhou, the rate of land conversion has been impressive and, as in the case of Shenzhen, its main causes are policy decisions that have led to an increase in GDP, foreign investment and trade, as well as a rise in rural-urban migration. This is not surprising, given the central role of both, and the symbiosis between, urban and socio-economic planning for China. Also, Deng et al. (2008) found that socio-economic factors are significant for the monocentric growth of Chinese cities, using a sample of over 2000 counties. In particular, growth was positively associated with population, income, and transportation costs, whereas agricultural rents had a negative effect.

Table 4 – 1   Population and built-up area

Year	Population (1000)		Built-up area (sq. kilometers)		GDP per capita (yuan)	
	1.	(variation %)	2.	(variation %)	3.	(variation %)
1988	1,201.4	…	112.45	…	6,477	…
1996	4,828.9	+301.94	266.04	+136.58	22,498	+247.4
2005	8,277.5	+71.42	656.30	+146.69	60,801	+170.3
2015	11,378.7	+37.47	834.26	+27.12	157,985	+159.8

Source: Compiled from SSB (2017) and (2017).

Dou and Chen (2017) investigated the expansion of Shenzhen across the land during the period 1988 – 2015 by using satellite data. Specifically, they discussed how land use and land cover have evolved. They point out how urban expansion has considerably affected the change in landscape of Shenzhen. Over these years, built-up area has increased by 721.1 square kilometres, from 5.63 percent in 1988 to 41.77 percent in 2015. Building's main impact was on cultivated land, forest, and water body, of which the average yearly decrease has been 0.88 percent for cultivated land, and 0.35 for forest. In the "early age" (1988 – 1996), urban development concentrated mainly around the SEZ area. In the ten years of the "rapid development" stage (1996 – 2005), the urbanization rate increased mainly outside the SEZ area, with built-up areas evolving from 13.32 percent of the land in 1996 to 32.86 percent in 2005.

In the third "intensive" stage (2005 – 2015), there has been a slowdown in city growth, mainly due to limited urban land resources. These figures are consistent with the dynamics reported in the Atlas of Urban Expansion.

Table 4 – 1 reports the data on built-up area in Shenzhen taken from the elaborations of Dou and Chen, as well as some official population and GDP statistics from SSB (2018). Built-up area is the part of the land distinct from forest, cultivated land, water body, grassland and bare land. Therefore, settlements in this area include all the types of buildings (residential, industrial, commercial, etc.) and other structures, as well as both authorised and unauthorised ones. After the period of early development, Shenzhen's built-up area expansion rate has been greater and exceeded population growth between 1996 and 2005. In those years planning had the effect of promoting expansive growth all over the land. The figures show a slowdown in built-up area growth over 2005 – 2015 due to land limitation, whereas population rose at a faster rate. From these numbers and the available data, I cannot infer much about details and quality of city concentration. However, there is evidence of an increase in urban concentration in the most recent period.

The evolution of Shenzhen's GDP (Table 4 – 1) suggests that its dynamics may not be necessarily synchronic with the ones of both population and urban growth. This is not surprising. Though authors like Glaeser calculate that a worldwide 10 percent increase in urbanization is associated with a 61 percent increase in per capita GDP, he admits that "some authors have questioned the causality of this link and shown that initial urbanization levels are neither positively nor negatively associated with subsequent income growth".

City size

New needs of population and increasing opportunity for business have promoted the growth of the urban factory. Of course, land availability is one natural limit to city growth. Besides this, is there a limit to physical expansion of the city, after which diseconomies in the city would exceed advantages? In other words, is there an optimal city size? This is a crucial point for some economies, as sometimes there is concern as to whether cities are either too big or too small. In some former planned economies, the "excessive size" of cities led to restrictions in urbanization. However, scholars have argued that an ideal city size can be hardly identified and depends on a number of factors, and the context in which a city is inserted is among the most significant ones.

Unlike city size, an "optimal level" of urban concentration can maximise productivity growth. Proximity in cities eases the exchange of goods and services between firms, it promotes innovation, it reduces travel time for citizens between places of interest. In other words, it increases productivity. But any deviation from the "optimal" level causes losses in productivity. This "best degree" of concentration varies with a country's development level and size. Specifically, it increases with income up to a certain level, and then it declines. The way the relationship between urban concentration and income evolves is consistent with the Williamson hypothesis for which increasing urban concentration is typical of the early development stage, where proximity plays a key role in promoting synergies between the various components of physical and human capital. At a later stage, congestion and the need to expand economic activity to neighbouring areas may favour deconcentration. Optimal concentration decreases as country scale increases. Investment in inter-regional transport matters as it reduces concentration, and this effect increases with income. Also, trade and political decentralization are both influential, though the effect is not strong. By implication, growth losses from urban concentration are higher for those cities where income level is higher.

Urbanization concentration is again reported as a key influencing element of the economic development of a city, as shown earlier in this Section. A first reflection arising from this is that the size of a city is not necessarily related to its growth. What matters instead is the "quality" of urban concentration, and the "efficient size" of a city. This is crucial in order both to generate agglomeration economies, and avoid diseconomies and social costs for the population. This depicts interesting perspectives for the future growth of Shenzhen. At the early stage of SEZ, the city grew in the relatively limited area bordering Hong Kong. Then it expanded, gradually including urban villages. Land availability since then has become a major issue. Together with its growth in wealth, and the pressure from migration inflows, the price of houses has risen dramatically. Urban planning now has major challenges, as sustaining growth means to reorganize urban spaces in order to limit the negative effects of the increasing population density. The new urban plans, envisioning the city as polycentric, may succeed in this and result in putting less pressure on the former SEZ area, although still favouring the successful agglomeration economies that have fostered Shenzhen's growth.

Tourists, a peculiar floating population

In many cities tourism is only one of the economic sectors. However, unlike other sectors it allows significant flows of people to enter the city. This group is heterogeneous in terms of motivations, ranging from leisure to business, from visiting relatives to health reasons. However, it shares the same space and resources of residents, though each of the two groups may have different purposes in doing so.

Tourism has been one of the sectors explicitly targeted by Shenzhen's master plans. Today Shenzhen is a top tourist destination. Euromonitor International ranks the city tenth among the most important world destinations in terms of number of international arrivals. It is the second Chinese city in the ranking, after Hong Kong that is ranked first, and the largest Chinese destination in terms of international demand. In 2017 more than 12 million tourists visited the city with a yearly growth rate of 3 percent. According to SSB (2018), in 2016, the sector of hotels and catering services accounted for 1.8 percent of Shenzhen GDP, and reported a growth rate of 2.8 percent. However, the total economic effects of tourism are wider and more complex to assess, as they also include indirect and induced effects from other sectors, like transportation, construction, culture and entertainment, etc. For instance, WTTC estimated that, in 2017, the direct and total contribution of tourism in China was 3.3 percent and 11.0 percent of GDP, respectively. Impact on employment was 3.6 percent (direct) and 10.3 percent (total). All these statistics are expected to rise in 2018.

A large share of Shenzhen tourists is indeed composed of business travellers. Though the city is not a top world destination for leisure tourism, the number of international travellers is one further symptom of the degree of openness of the city. Over the years, the city has also invested in developing its attractions for leisure. SMC reports that today Shenzhen is "one of the most important and profitable tourist cities in China and regarded as the capital of Chinese theme parks and tourism innovation".

Tourists are a peculiar floating population. As Ashworth and Page observe, tourism is embedded in many dimensions of a city, which implies that the same principles of urban planning may apply to tourism. However, the management of tourist flows presents some criticalities. The number, time of arrival and stay, objectives and spatial behaviour of tourists may be heterogeneous and go beyond the control of planners and governments. And usually governmental actions mainly concern the management of "tourists" rather than "tourism", as often the main goal is to mitigate the undesirable impact of guests. The main reason is that urban planners and local policymakers' primary aim is the improvement of the living standards of the local residents.

Tourism is one of the fastest growing industries worldwide. Shenzhen has become one of the top cities in China at the forefront. Its economic policies have also involved the promotion of the city as a "brand", which is indeed functional to the attraction of people travelling from abroad. Exploitation of local resources for tourism, including both tangible and intangible ones, is one further step towards the consolidation of the city in the world market. The trade-off between affirming its uniqueness as a world destination, and replicating other standard tourist models and types of attractions in the fashion of a "disney fication", is one main challenge to further develop its role as an attractive destination, also for leisure tourists.

Planning and the Search for Sustainability

Despite Shenzhen's expansion leading to the well-known explosive economic growth, different questions about the social costs of city growth still arise. As recalled in Section 4 above, population and economic growth are in a direct relationship until resources are available for each citizen and diseconomies do not occur. Agglomeration costs are the negative side of agglomeration economies and "the price paid for being close to other humans". This recalls the current debate on the quality of city growth. There is growing attention to the way to govern the economic, social and environmental aspects brought by the explosive phenomena of increasing population in major cities. Rise in crime and pollution, inequalities and social exclusion, congestion and quality of urban services, are only some examples of those harmful phenomena to cities as "places of pleasure, besides being places of productivity". Best practices are indeed of help to this end, though planners have shown that some models are unique and may hardly be replicated.

Urban planners have a crucial role in addressing growth processes, in order to combine new and pressing needs of a city with sustainability. The Campbell model, one of the best-known theorisations for sustainable planning, summarizes very well the basic principles of planning for sustainable design of cities. The theory identifies three key priorities for planning, namely social justice, economic growth and environmental protection. The so-called "Campbell's triangle", represents them as corners of an equilateral triangle, the centre of gravity of which is sustainable development, with equity being the top corner. Then the centre would be the equilibrium point between the three dimensions. Any shift from that point would bring it closer to one of the sides of the triangle. Each side represents a potential conflict between two dimensions. When social justice clashes with economic growth and efficiency, it generates property conflict resulting from the diverging interests between the public good and private benefit. Economic interest may interfere with environmental protection, thus generating a conflict for exploiting natural resources instead of preserving them. When social justice and environmental protection contrast, development conflict is at stake. This model is particularly evocative, as it sees sustainable development as a fragile condition, which is also difficult to achieve, since deviating from the equilibrium may cause conflicts.

Other contributors have stressed the key role of cities in promoting sustainable development. Among others, the works by Camagni and co-authors emphasised the crucial interactions between different dimensions of a city in order to reach sustainability, where the latter is "a dynamic, balanced and adaptive evolutionary process, i. e. a process in which a balanced use and management of the natural environmental basis of economic development is ensured". A sustainable city not only gives priority to the environment, as doing this would somehow neglect the synergies related to agglomeration. Rather, the three environments, namely physical (both built and natural), economic and social, coexist and interact. In a static sense, they generate externalities, both positive and negative. Their balanced dynamic co-evolution may develop distributive efficiency and territorial identity (when social environment integrates the economic one), long-term allocative and territorial efficiency (economic with physical), and environmental equity and territorial quality (social and physical). A "good" city is a city that favours the development of all the aspects, along with long term, sustainability related objectives instead of short term, profit oriented ones. Spatial planning should be addressed to provide adequate tools in order to reach sustainability, and the latter should set the goals for the former.

Theory indicates that evaluating whether a city has reached a sustainable and harmonic development pattern has to account for several aspects, each pertaining to the three basic domains of social, economic and environmental development. There are several ways to evaluate whether a city has entered a sustainable pattern. To this end, the availability of a good set of indicators is often an important starting point. SSB provides a rich set of information, although it mainly relates only to the economy of Shenzhen. In what follows, I will try to give an overview of some aspects of sustainability.

A study of Zheng et al. attempted to rank Chinese cities according to their greenness. The authors estimated that Shenzhen was ranked 46 out of 74 cities. However, several efforts have been made by the Shenzhen government in order to reduce negative environmental effects. Following the State Council Circular on "Promoting Efficient and Intensive Land Use" in 2008, Shenzhen was the first city to adopt urban renewal policies which had a positive impact on the environment. It was also the first city in China to adopt a carbon emissions trading scheme, in order to reduce carbon intensity and improve the efficient use of energy, which came into effect on 18 June 2013. All of this coincides with the New Urbanization Plan, launched by the Chinese government in March 2014, which aims to improve environmental conditions of cities, as well as social ones, also through the reform of the hukou system. As to the latter, indeed the main challenge to sustainable growth from a social point of view concerns the divide between migrants and residents, not only in terms of income inequality, but also of the access to social welfare.

City-level statistics from SSB show how many environment-related indicators have improved over time. Use of energy has become more efficient. Both energy and electricity consumption per unit of GDP have steadily decreased during 2005 – 2016. Over the same time, main pollutants like SO_2, NO_2, PM10, industrial sulphur dioxide, and industrial nitrogen oxide have reduced. However, the volume of industrial waste gas emission has increased in the most recent years. In addition, during 2011 – 2016 the number of civil motor vehicles increased by 63 percent, from 1,976,164 to 3,225,879. The latter is not a comforting signal in terms of both vehicle emissions and traffic congestion. Traffic corridors and main arterial routes have been the main determinants of the city's expansion. Sustainable forms of public transportation and incentives for not using cars would contribute to the objective of reducing the environmental impact. Polycentric development of the city as envisioned by the most recent urban master plans may decongest some areas. But the strengthening of a sustainable transport system is basic to discourage the use of private cars and improve environmental quality.

Chapter 5　Basic Services and Local Infrastructure

Introduction

Some of the biggest global challenges mankind is facing today include the rapidly growing world population, the increasing consumption of resources as well as emissions of CO_2, and the ongoing climate change with the corresponding consequences for the global ecological balance.

While the ecological footprint of humanity already exceeds the bio capacity of our planet by a factor of 1.7, the anticipated increase in the world population from currently 7.6 billion people (2018) to up to 11.2 billion in the year 2100 will have a major impact on our living conditions as a result of scarcity of resources and aggravated effects of climate change, especially in economically weaker countries. In addition to political and social conflicts, economic aspects are likely to further contribute to the increase in migration movements worldwide. Particularly noteworthy in that regard is the worldwide increase in urbanization and the tremendous growth occurring in cities worldwide.

More than 50 percent of the world's population already lives in cities today. By the year 2050, the share is expected to increase to almost 70 percent. While dealing with this tremendous challenge of rapid growth, future-oriented and sustainable cities have to create more than ever—a balance between social, environmental, and economic aspects. Social welfare, including healthcare, social security, education, and employment, is directly related to a city's environmental and economic qualities, such as clean air and water, appropriate housing, adequate transport infrastructure, and a stable economy.

In order to advance the profound and effective transformation of cities required to secure a sustainable future on a global scale, the satisfaction of human needs, such as protection from extreme weather and the provision of a safe and healthy living environment, energy, food and mobility, has to be achieved in direct relation to the resulting impact on our ecosystem (See Figure 5 - 1).

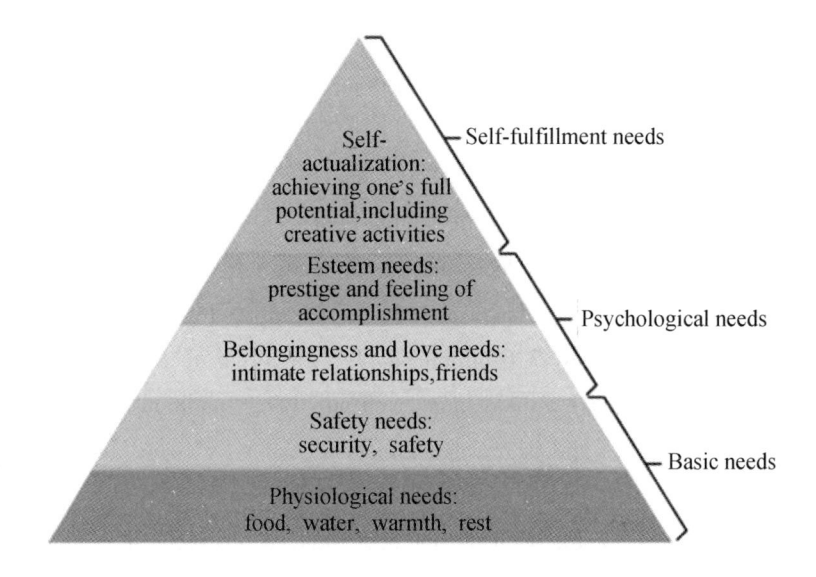

Figure 5 - 1: Hierarchy of needs (according to Maslow)

This requires attention to be paid to the interactions of human activity and the relevant infrastructure systems with the ecosystem of our planet, including our biosphere, atmosphere, hydrosphere, and pedosphere (Figure 5 - 2). In doing so, a fundamental reorientation of strategies for the sustainable safeguarding of our living conditions while stabilizing our ecosystem is imperative.

```
┌─────────────────────────────────────────────────────┐
│           Ecosystem Planet Earth                    │
│ Biosphere, Atmosphere, Hydrosphere, Pedosphere      │
└─────────────────────────────────────────────────────┘
                          ↕
┌─────────────────────────────────────────────────────┐
│              Infrastructure Systems                 │
│ Buildings, Energy, Water, Transport, Green Infrastructure │
└─────────────────────────────────────────────────────┘
                          ↕
┌─────────────────────────────────────────────────────┐
│                  Human Needs                        │
│   Safety and Security, Energy, Food, Mobility       │
└─────────────────────────────────────────────────────┘
```

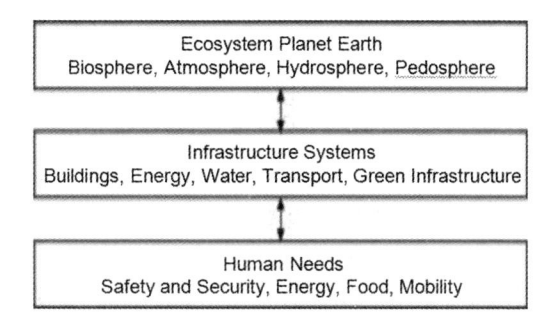

Figure 5 – 2: Infrastructure systems, satisfaction of human needs and interaction with our ecosystem

Addressing these challenges, this book chapter will focus on the sustainable provision of basic services, such as the supply of energy, mobility and transport, water, and green infrastructure. The intention of this contribution is to raise awareness regarding the importance of these different sectors of urban infrastructure, to provide information based on the relevant indicators to describe the current status of Shenzhen compared to other cities in Asia and Europe, to analyse how urban infrastructure systems might be developed further to increase the quality of life and the sustainability of Shenzhen and it will summarize the findings in order to provide a potential outlook for the development of Shenzhen towards a sustainability hub in the southern part of China.

Indicators for Evaluating the Sustainable Development of Cities

According to the Brundtland report *Our Common Future*, which was presented to the UN General Assembly in 1987, sustainable development is development which "meets the needs of the present without compromising the ability of future generations to meet their own needs". Looking at the current global challenges, which are mentioned at the beginning of this chapter, it becomes clear that truly sustainable development does imply limitations. These are imposed by human activities and the resulting consumption of environmental resources, the corresponding emissions and waste, and by the ability of the biosphere to absorb them. While the provision of basic services, such as energy, mobility and transport, water, and ecosystem services provided by green infrastructure, is essential for all humans living on the globe, the effects of the resource consumption required to provide these services is felt much stronger in cities than in rural areas.

To give an example, the population density of Shenzhen is approx. 6,000 people per square kilometre (2017), which is 41 times the national average. As a result of this massive concentration, the provision of basic needs is heavily dependent on the surrounding region, creating a high vulnerability of cities due to their dependency on the hinterland.

Furthermore, the resulting effects of resource consumption for the operation of buildings, the provision of transport, as well as for production and other needs, are felt much stronger in dense urban areas, due to the high concentration of emissions and excess heat, as well as waste and wastewater.

Due to the importance of providing basic services, such as energy, mobility and transport, water, and ecosystem services provided by green infrastructure, the indicators for evaluating the sustainable development of cities are directly related to the sustainable provision of these services "without compromising the ability of future generations to meet their own needs".

Looking at the current situation with regard to resource consumption and the corresponding emissions and waste, China's Ecological Footprint is currently at 2.5 gha per capita. This is less than the world average per capita Ecological Footprint of 2.7 gha, but still larger than the world average biocapacity available per person, which is 1.7 gha. If everybody lived like the average Chinese, we would need 1.5 Earths.

Looking at the city of Shenzhen, the per capita Ecological Footprint in

Shenzhen (2.5 gha) was equal to the national average in 2011, while the per capita ecological capacity was approximately 0.06 gha. That means that the Ecological Footprint was about 41.7 times greater than the ecological capacity.

As stated by UN Habitat, cities are major contributors to climate change. Covering less than 2 percent of the earth's surface, cities are consuming 78 percent of the world's energy and produce more than 60 percent of all carbon dioxide and significant amounts of other greenhouse gas emissions, mainly through energy generation, vehicles, industry, and biomass use.

Considering this tremendous imbalance with regard to the ecological footprint and bio capacity in densely urban environments like Shenzhen, it becomes clear that a fundamental shift is necessary with regard to resource consumption and the related emissions and waste.

To initiate and achieve a transformation towards a sustainable development, the current and future resource requirements with regard to energy, water, raw materials, soil, etc. and the resulting pollutant and waste generation of urban infrastructure systems have to be analysed and related to the limits of our ecosystem's resilience and the corresponding subsystems, such as biosphere, atmosphere, hydrosphere and pedosphere.

To create a robust foundation for developing effective strategies for the transformation of our cities to deliver a fundamentally sustainable approach with regard to the resources at our disposal, a detailed, spatially resolved assessment of current and future resource needs and the long-term existing resource capacities is required. At the same time, the resulting environmental impacts must be recorded and compared with the limits of our ecosystem's resilience. This concerns the following infrastructure systems and their interaction with the biosphere, atmosphere, hydrosphere and pedosphere.

Looking at the ecological footprint of a city and the corresponding ecological assets that its population requires to produce the natural resources it consumes, the consumption of energy and the resulting greenhouse gas

(GHG) emissions is one of the most important parameters affecting our environment with regard to climate change, threatening our biosphere, and therefore, life on our planet as we know it today.

Therefore, one of the most important indicators for evaluating the sustainability of a city is the primary energy consumption and the related greenhouse gas emissions, especially in China, where most of the energy production is based on fossil fuels, leading to high greenhouse gas emissions. While this involves a wide range of sectors, such as industry, transport, residential, commercial and public services and agriculture, this chapter will mainly focus on the energy consumption in the building and transport sector.

Next to the consumption of energy, the supply and treatment of drinking water is of particular importance for supporting our lives, including plants and animals.

As Urban Green Infrastructure (UGI) can play a major role, by regulating the microclimate of urban environments via shading and evapotranspiration, and by absorbing rain water in case of heavy rain events, this aspect has to be regarded as a driving element for sustainable cities as well.

Energy Supply Systems

Energy is of utmost importance when it comes to supporting life in our cities. The production of food and goods, provision of water, construction and operation of buildings, infrastructure and transport systems as well as the operation of industrial and commercial activities are dependent on the steady supply of tremendous amounts of energy. According to UN Habitat, cities consume about 75 percent of global primary energy and emit approximately 80 percent of the world's total greenhouse gases, In 2017, the total global primary energy consumption in China was 13511.2 million tonnes oil equivalent, currently growing at a rate of 2.2 percent/year. With 3132.2 million tonnes oil equivalent, China's share is approx 23.2 percent, currently growing at a rate of 30.1 percent/year.

In China, energy is generated mainly by using coal (60.4 percent), oil (19.4 percent), gas (6.6 percent) and nuclear energy (1.8 percent). Only 12 percent was produced by renewable energies, such as hydro (8.3 percent) and other forms of renewable energies (3.4 percent), such as sun, wind, and geothermal. As a result, 9232.6 million tons of carbon dioxide were emitted in China, which is 27.6 percent of the global CO_2 emissions1 and equals 7.1 tons of CO_2 emissions per capita.

In order to overcome the devastating impact of greenhouse gas emissions on our ecosystem and end the dependency of our cities on importing and using fossil fuels, a substantial transition to sustainable forms of energy, such as solar-, wind-, hydro-and geothermal energy is urgently needed.

Low carbon technologies on the supply side have to be coupled with low-energy systems on the demand side, reducing pollution and greenhouse gas emissions, thereby enhancing the quality of life in our cities.

Mobility and Transport

Being mobile allows us to interact with other people, and to satisfy our daily needs, getting from our homes to various places within a city, such as locations for work, education, culture, shopping, and leisure. The corresponding transport infrastructure, including walkways, bicycle lanes, streets, roads and railroads, allows us to use non-motorized and motorized vehicles to move around and to transport goods.

With a share of approx, 10 percent of the total CO_2 emissions coming from the transport sector of China in 2010, the CO_2 emissions related to motorized vehicles seem to be relatively small, compared to industry production and other sectors. However, the CO_2 emissions from the transport sector increased from 13.1 Mt in 2000 to 74.0 Mt in 2013 in the Pearl River Delta, indicating the need for controlling the growth of transport dependence.

Apart from increasing levels of congestion and environmental emissions of traffic, including CO_2, NOX, PM and noise, the potential growth of the use of motorized vehicles (MVs), with 2.3 million MVs in Shenzhen in 2015 and MV ownership (2015) of 296 MV/1,000 inhabitants has to be considered.

Alternative forms of mobility, such as walking and biking and the use of public transport have to be supported due to their environmental advantages, thereby securing the liveability of our urban environment. Therefore, a substantial reduction of the negative impact of the use of MVs, such as excessive land-use, noise and pollution caused by gas and diesel-powered cars, and trucks, must be the goal of a sustainable transport policy. As shown in section 2.4, to achieve the state of a sustainable city, not only does the transport infrastructure and the built environment need to be optimized, but also the adaptation of Urban Green Infrastructure has to be supported.

Water supply

Comparable to the challenges with regard to a sustainable energy supply of rapidly growing mega cities, the sustainable provision of safe drinking water as well as wastewater collection and treatment are equally important.

Due to the rapid growth of cities, especially in fast growing regions like Asia, the water systems and soil conditions have been fundamentally altered in urban regions and the surrounding land, due to buildings and related transport infrastructure. Although there is enough freshwater available globally to satisfy every citizen's personal and domestic needs, 11 percent of the global population still has no access to water that is safe for consumption.

Especially in dense urban areas in developing countries, we are still facing serious challenges, such as contaminated water due to the absence of adequate sanitation facilities, leading to pollution of the available water resources, thereby creating a serious risk for the health and wellbeing of the urban population.

Therefore, the provision of clean and safe drinking water and the availability of an effective urban waste water management, including water reuse technologies, are crucial elements of urban infrastructure systems.

To minimize the water footprint of urban areas, which typically rely heavily on the provision of clean water from the region surrounding the city, the creation of closed cycles, including water conservation measures and effective water purification systems, is imperative. Due to its potential to alleviate water shortage, wastewater treatment has to be regarded as an important means to reduce the consumption of drinking water where possible.

In addition to domestic use, the availability and management of water are crucial, when it comes to the use of Urban Green Infrastructure for the enhancement of the quality of life in cities. Without sufficient water, crucial ecosystem services, such as cooling and shading as well as the provision of food are not possible.

Urban Green Infrastructure

Larger and denser cities must deal with increasing air, noise and water pollution, denser urban spaces, heat islands as well as a higher mortality caused by heat waves. As a result of a high concentration of emissions, heat generation by production, building operation and motorized vehicles, the Urban Heat Island might lead to an increase in air temperatures of 3°C during daytime and 12°C during night-time, if compared to the surrounding less densely populated areas. Due to its subtropical climate, Shenzhen is likely to experience increasing air temperatures. This might lead to negative effects, such as higher air conditioning costs, air pollution and greenhouse gas emissions. Furthermore, the population might face heat-related illnesses and a higher mortality, as well as poorer water quality due to flooding and other effects.

The quality of life in densely populated urban areas is increasingly dependent on urban green infrastructure, as the effects of climate change, such as an increase in temperature, will affect large, dense cities the most, especially if located in sub-tropical and tropical climates, such as Shenzhen.

Urban Green Infrastructure (UGI) can play a major role by regulating the microclimate of urban environments via shading and evapotranspiration, and by absorbing rain water in case of heavy rain events. Other factors are the promotion of biodiversity, and other aspects directly affecting human health, such as cultural services, e. g. recreational, aesthetic and spiritual benefits. While urban ecosystems can make a substantial contribution to increasing the sustainability and resilience of urban systems, clearly there is a need to develop a much wider approach to meet the global challenges of urbanization, as the current emphasis on city compaction, i. e. increasing the population density of humans without enlarging the city borders, puts great pressure on existing UGIs, resulting in a decrease in urban biodiversity and ecosystem services.

Basic Services and Local Infrastructure In Shenzhen: Measuring Success and Fostering Sustainable Development

The previous sections have shown, that urban infrastructure systems are crucial for healthy and productive life in urban environments, especially in large, fast expanding cities, such as Shenzhen.

Through the analysis and discussion of the current situation of the existing urban infrastructure systems, the clear definition of goals, and the development of corresponding strategies for improvement, the sustainable development of Shenzhen towards a truly sustainable city can be supported.

As part of the analysis process, the situation of Shenzhen will be compared to other cities in China and Europe, allowing for lessons being learned with regard to the development of strategies for defining and implementing sustainability goals. An example of such an approach is the "The China Urban Sustainable Index" (USI), a tool for comparing urban sustainability across China, which in 2011 released its first report on social, environmental, economic, as well as resource-related aspects of Chinese cities, based on five categories, namely, social welfare, cleanliness, built environment, economic development and resource utilization.

In the 2011 version of the USI report, Shenzhen was ranked 6th, in 2013 it was ranked 2nd, and in 2017 Shenzhen was ranked 1st, demonstrating the significance of relevant indicators to enhance the positive development of future-oriented, sustainable cities.

The main aim of this chapter is to analyse the strategies, methods and technologies used for the sustainable provision of basic services, such as the supply of energy, water and public transport, and the related technical as well as green infrastructure, needed for the creation and maintenance of the quality of life in an urban environment such as the city of Shenzhen. The major goal of a sustainable provision of these fundamental services is to minimize or even avert any negative environmental impact with regard to resource depletion, emissions, or soil sealing, and to maximize the positive impact of green infrastructure with regard to a comfortable urban climate and the regulation of water flows within the city.

In this part, the status quo of the urban infrastructure in Shenzhen is described through indicators of four central aspects, which are the supply of energy, mobility and transport, water supply and green infrastructure.

In order to get a better view of how Shenzhen compares in general to its neighbours, the data obtained for Shenzhen is compared to the data of Hong Kong and Singapore, which are in a similar geographical and climatic situation, but are different with regard to their political boundaries and their topography. In addition to this, data for the city of Berlin/Germany is brought in to see how different political, geographical, cultural and climatic conditions might influence the resource efficiency and other factors relating to sustainable development.

In addition to similar conditions with regard to the local climate, Hong Kong and Singapore are the best cases for the benchmark on sustainable development, as these two cities were ranked second and first amongst sustainable cities within the Asian region, respectively, following the latest version report of the Sustainable Cities Index (SCI).

Hong Kong is adjacent to Shenzhen and both cities are located in the Pearl River Delta, thus many similarities exist in urban development and resource utilization. Singapore, a country-city, seems to offer a more comprehensive system with regard to urban administration and the management of resources.

Meanwhile, the City of Berlin, as a case study from outside of Asia, might also be highly valuable to see how very different possibilities might exist for achieving sustainable development in a very different context. In the following text, various relevant indicators for all four cities will be compared with each other, and an objective evaluation of the various parameters and the respective performance will allow for the development of rational suggestions for Shenzhen.

General information

Before comparing the indicators on infrastructure, some basic information for the built environment of these cities needs to be interpreted, which is associated with their infrastructure requirements. After entering the millennium, only a few enlargements were achieved in the land area of each city (Figure 5 -3). Among them, Shenzhen possessed the largest land area with 1997 square kilometers in 2016, which is almost twice as large as Berlin, with 1106 square kilometers in 2016. The smallest city is Singapore with 720 square kilometers.

While the land area remained almost stable in the four cities during the period from 2000 to 2016, the growth of population in all the cities is rather high, especially in Shenzhen, where the population increased by 70 percent from 7 million in 2000 to 11.9 million in 2016, and is still rising sharply according to Figure 5 - 4. In contrast, Hong Kong had a similar population to Shenzhen at the beginning of the millennium with 6.7 million people, but then only around 665 thousand people moved into the city. Although the rate of increase of Singapore was overwhelmingly greater than in Hong Kong, about 2000 percent compared to 40 percent the actual increment was only 580 thousand. Berlin illustrated a relatively slower rate of population growth with only 5 percent and fewer than 200 thousand people added to the city's

(spuare Klometas)

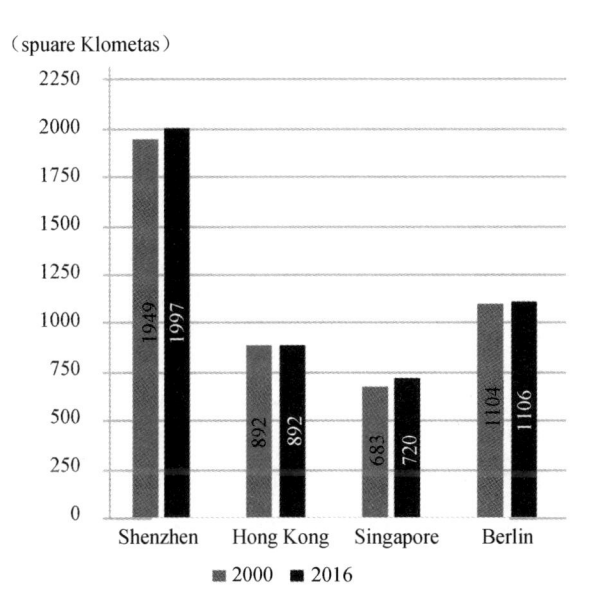

Figure 5-3: The land area of the four cities from 2000 to 2016

Source: Shenzhen Statistical Book, Hong Kong Annual Digest of Statistics, Singapore Department of Statistics (www. singstat. gov. sg), and the Office for Statistics of Berlin-Brandenburg (www. statistik-berlin-brandenburg. de).

population during this period.

The growth of population, leading to an increasing density of the urban space, is common to all four cases. Figure 5 – 5 illustrates that the urban density of Shenzhen started at only 3717 pers/square. kilometers in 2001, which was a little lower than Berlin's (3799 pers. / sq. kilometers) . However, Shenzhen jumped to 5962 pers. / sq. kilometers in 2016, while Berlin was just over 4000 pers. / sq. kilometers at the same time. Hong Kong and Singapore already had high urban density in 2001, with around 6060 pers/ sq. kilometers, while a dramatic growth rate can be observed for Singapore after 2004, which reached a population density of 7791 pers. /sq. kilometers in 2016. Meanwhile, the population density in Hong Kong only increased by approximately 600 pers. / sq. kilometers, reaching 6670 pers. / sq. kilometers in 2016.

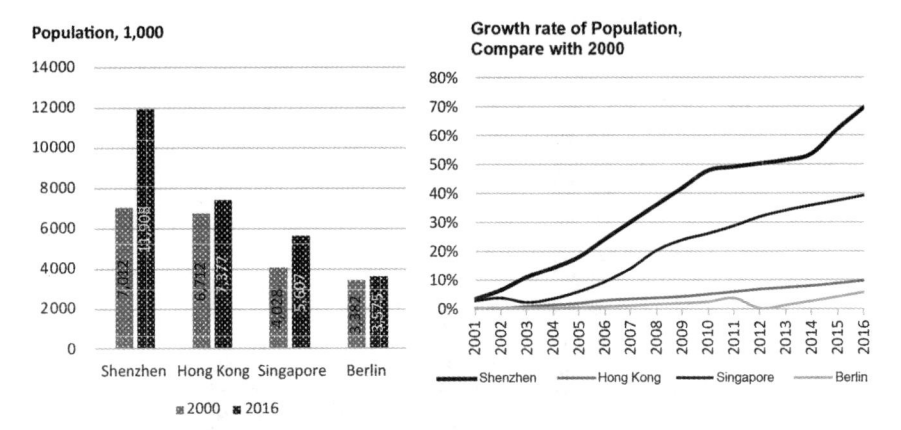

Figure 5-4: The population of the four cities (a)
and their Growth rate compared to 2000 (b)

Source: Shenzhen Statistical Book, Hong Kong Annual Digest of Statistics, Singapore Department of Statistics (www.singstat.gov.sg), and the Office for Statistics of Berlin-Brandenburg (www.statistik-berlin-brandenburg.de).

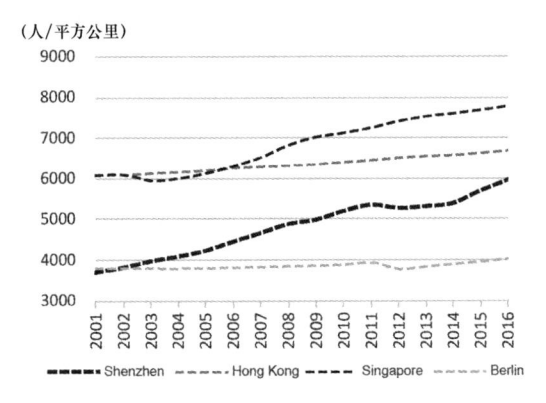

Figure 5-5: Population density in four cities

Energy Supply

As the most populous city, the energy consumption of Shenzhen reached 39.1 million TCE in 2015, which was almost twice as much as the energy requirements of Singapore, with 21.8 million TCE (see Figure 5-6). These two cities showed greater total energy consumption per unit of GDP shows a

Frgure 5 – 7). In 2010, Shenzhen consumed 223 TCE/1 million USD, which was almost 3 times the amount of Hong Kong, Singapore, and Berlin. In 2015, the total energy consumption per unit of GDP was reduced to 149 TCE/1 million USD (2015). Although this was a huge improvement, Hong Kong and Berlin required only 63 TCE/1 million USD in 2015, while Singapore reached 70 TCE/1 million USD in 2015.

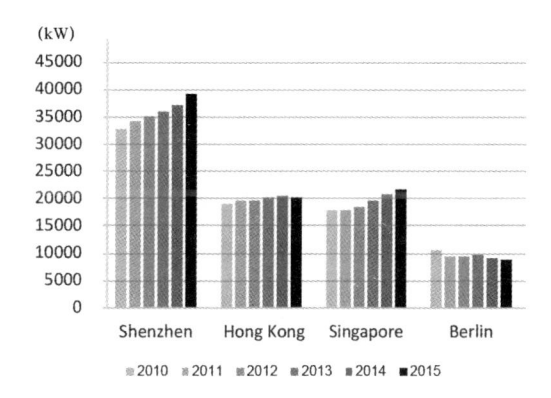

Figure 5 – 6: The primary energy requirement

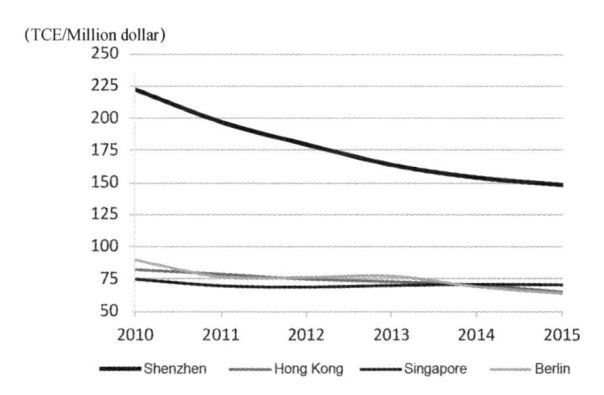

Figure 5 – 7: The efficiency of energy consumption from 2010 to 2015

Although Shenzhen consumed more energy to achieve its gross domestic product than the other 3 cities, the energy consumption per capita (ECc) was still lower than Singapore's, with ECc of 3.44 tons and 3.94 tons of SCE in 2015 for the two cities, respectively (Figure 5 – 8). An abnormally increasing trend has emerged in Singapore since 2012, while the ECc of the other cities decreased after 2013. The residents of Berlin consumed the least energy per capita in 2015, only 2.55 tons of SCE, which was 0.2 tons of SCE lower than in Hong Kong.

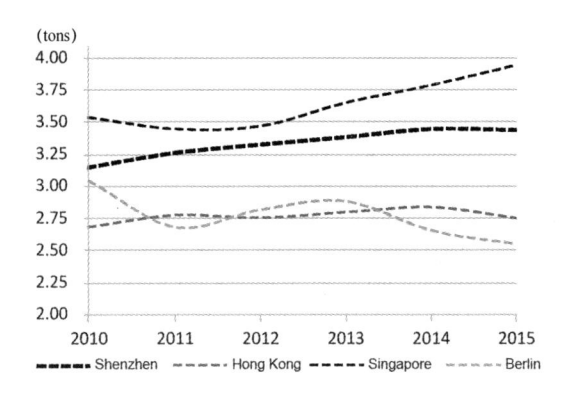

Figure 5 – 8: Energy consumption per capita

Source: Shenzhen Statistical Book, Hong Kong Annual Digest of Statistics, Singapore Department of Statistics (www.singstat.gov.sg), and the Office for Statistics of Berlin-Brandenburg (www.statistik-berlin-brandenburg.de).

As shown in Figure 5 – 9, the four cities use very different resources for achieving their energy supply. In Shenzhen, almost half of the energy consumption growth rates in energy requirement from 2010 to 2015 than others. Berlin even presented a descending tendency of energy consumption and over 1500 thousand TCE were reduced, comparing primary energy consumption in 2010 with 2015.

While the differences in primary energy requirement might be easily explained by the differences in the total population of these cities, comparing the was electricity in 2013, which was mostly provided by nuclear power. Hong Kong was also importing electricity from China's mainland to a certain extent. However, in 2015, the energy supply of Hong Kong was mainly reliant

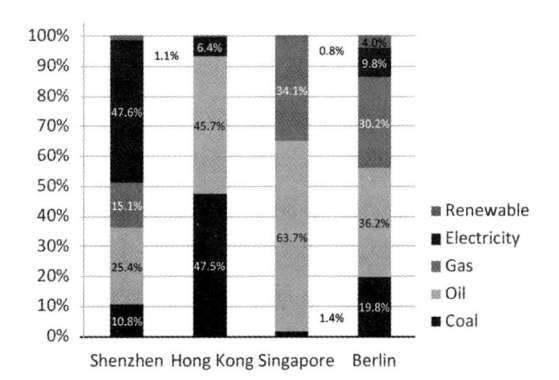

Figure 5–9: Share of energy supply sources in 2015

Source: *Research on carbon emission reduction route for Shenzhen* "The 13th five-year plan of Shenzhen's energy development", Hong Kong Annual Digest of Statistics, Electrical and Mechanical Services Department of Hong Kong (www.emsd.gov.hk), The Energy Market Authority (EMA) of Singapore (www.ema.gov.sg), and the Office for Statistics of Berlin-Brandenburg (www.statistik-berlin-brandenburg.de).

on coal and oil, which generated 47.50 percent and 45.75 percent, respectively. In Singapore, oil is the most important energy source, which accounted for 63.69 percent in 2015, followed by gas (34.15 percent). Berlin shows an almost even share of oil (36.2 percent) and gas (30.2 percent), followed by coal (19.8 percent) and electricity (9.8 percent). Berlin showed the highest share of renewable energy use (4 percent), even with only a small percentage. In that context, Shenzhen had a share of 1.1 percent of renewable energy in 2015, which came mainly from waste-to-energy power plants.

With regard to the development of total electricity consumption from 2001 to 2016, Hong Kong shows an almost constant energy need of about 45 billion kWh/year (Figure 5–10). In a similar way, this consumption in Berlin was almost constant, and was in the range of 14 billion kWh. In that context, Shenzhen illustrates a very dynamic growth rate, increasing from 21 billion kWh in 2001 to approximately 85 billion kWh in 2016. Singapore shows an increase from roughly 35 billion kWh in 2005 to 50 billion kWh in 2016.

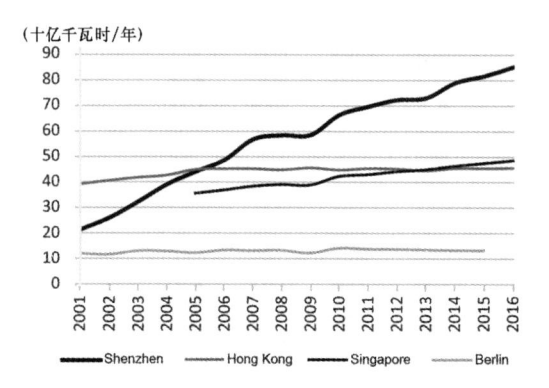

Figure 5 – 10: Gross electricity consumption

Source: Shenzhen Statistical Book, Hong Kong Annual Digest of Statistics, Singapore Department of Statistics (www. singstat. gov. sg), and the Office for Statistics of Berlin-Brandenburg (www. statistik-berlin-brandenburg. de).

Similar to the development of total electricity consumption, per capita electricity consumption of Shenzhen increased from 487 kWh per capita in 2001 to 1128 kWh per capita in 2016 (Figure 5 – 11). However, the per capita consumption was considerably lower than in the other 3 cities of Hong Kong, Singapore and Berlin, which was the only city which shows a decline in per capita consumption during recent years, settling at around 1200 kWh per capita, which is almost identical to the value in 2001. With over 1600 kWh per capita, Hong Kong had the largest electricity consumption of the 4 cities in 2016, followed by Singapore with 1353 kWh per capita.

Considering electricity generation, 46.86 percent of the electricity generated in Shenzhen in 2015 came from the local nuclear power plant, followed by the use of gas with 36.75 percent (Figure 5 – 12). With a share of 65.3 percent for Hong Kong, coal was the main source of electricity production in 2015, followed by oil with 24.8 percent. In Singapore, 95.3 percent of the electricity was generated by using gas, with most of the remaining electricity supply generated by renewable sources. For Berlin, electricity was generated by using coal (20.4 percent), oil (36.5 percent), gas (29.6 percent) and renewable energies (13.5 percent), pointing in the

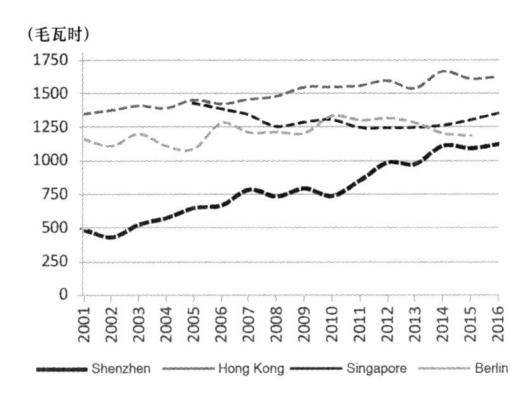

Figure 5 – 11: The electricity consumption by households per capita

Source: Shenzhen Statistical Book, Hong Kong Annual Digest of Statistics, Singapore Department of Statistics (www. singstat. gov. sg), and the Office for Statistics of Berlin-Brandenburg (www. statistik-berlin-brandenburg. de).

right direction when it comes to reducing the GHG emissions by turning towards renewable energies in the near future.

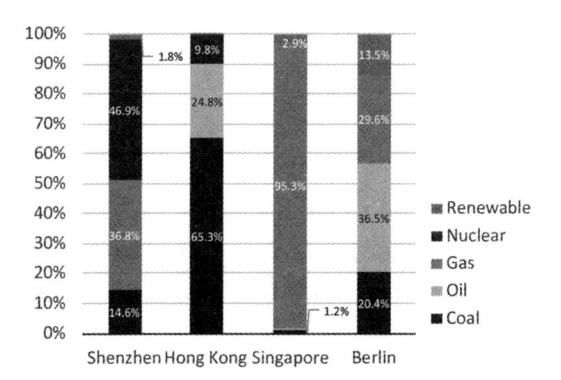

Figure 5 – 12: Share of electricity generation sources in 2015

Source: *Research on carbon emission reduction route for Shenzhen*, The 13th five-year plan of Shenzhen's energy development, Hong Kong Annual Digest of Statistics, Electrical and Mechanical Services Department of Hong Kong (www. emsd. gov. hk), The Energy Market Authority (EMA) of Singapore (www. ema. gov. sg), and the Office for Statistics of Berlin-Brandenburg (www. statistik-berlin-brandenburg. de).

Comparing the development of the total electricity consumption of the 4 cities with the development of total CO_2 emissions, it has to be noted, that the 3 cities of Shenzhen, Hong Kong and Singapore show a constant increase in CO_2 emissions, which correlates to the total energy consumption, as shown in Figure 5 – 13. That means that hardly any improvement is to be seen in reducing CO_2 emissions, which could have been achieved by integrating green energy in to the overall electricity production. Shenzhen has to be ranked first with regard to its CO_2 emission (64 million tons in 2013), with Singapore (50 million tons) and Hong Kong (45 million tons) following. Berlin, being the smallest of the 4 cities, had CO_2 emissions of roughly 18 million tons, while having the largest share of renewable energies in its energy mix.

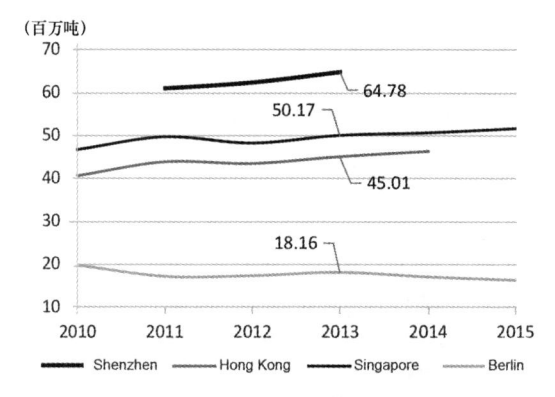

Figure 5 –13: The total CO_2 emissions from 2010 to 2015

Source: *Research on carbon emission reduction route for Shenzhen*, World Bank Group (https://data.worldbank.org/indicator), Singapore Department of Statistics (www.singstat.gov.sg), and the Office for Statistics of Berlin-Brandenburg (www.statistik-berlin-brandenburg.de).

Regarding the CO_2 emissions in relation to the GDP (Figure 5 – 14), Shenzhen actually emitted much more CO_2 per GDP unit than the other cities. With almost 300tCO_2/\$1M Shenzhen emitted more than twice as much CO_2/\$1M as Berlin with 141.47 tons CO_2 per GDP unit. However, in terms of tons of CO_2 per capita (Figure 5 – 14b), the emission of Shenzhen with 6.09 tons CO_2 per capita was relatively low. Only Berlin was lower with 5.31

tons CO_2 per capita, while Hong Kong with 6.24 tons CO_2 per capita, was slightly higher. However, the CO_2 emission of each Singapore resident was much higher than the others and reached 9.29 tons CO_2 per person in 2013.

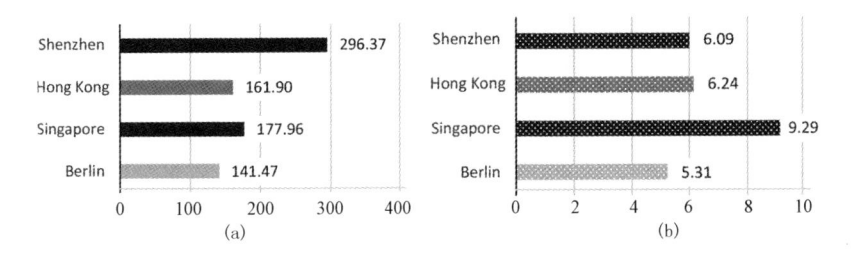

```
Shenzhen   296.37          Shenzhen   6.09
Hong Kong  161.90          Hong Kong  6.24
Singapore  177.96          Singapore  9.29
Berlin     141.47          Berlin     5.31
        0  100  200  300  400         0    2    4    6    8    10
                (a)                             (b)
```

Figure 5 – 14: The CO_2 emissions per unit GDP (a) and per capita (b) in 2013

Source: Research on carbon emission reduction route for Shenzhen, World Bank Group (https://data.worldbank.org/indicator), Singapore Department of Statistics (www.singstat.gov.sg), and the Office for Statistics of Berlin-Brandenburg (www.statistik-berlin-brandenburg.de).

Mobility and Transport

As mentioned before, the mobility of people and transportation of goods is one of the key requirements in urban environments, providing access to food, work, education, social networks and other activities such as cultural venues as well as recreational facilities and green spaces. While the need for mobility cannot be negotiated, the means for providing access to the various amenities of a city can be very diverse and depend on the policies of a city.

Historically, the transport infrastructure of European and Asian cities developed on the basis of people walking, riding or using horse drawn carriages, leading to an extensive network of narrow streets, supplemented by larger transport arteries when cities became larger. With the rise of motorized vehicles, such as trams and trains, in the late 19th century, and the rapid increase of cars in the early 20th century, the demand for streets, roads and motorways changed our cities rapidly. Especially in the second half of the 20th century, the car became the dominant factor for city planning, leading not only to a higher share of impervious surfaces for streets and parking, but also to a rapid increase in gas and oil consumption and emissions.

Today we understand that sustainable mobility concepts have to include environmental measures, such as reducing greenhouse gas emissions, air pollution and noise, while providing an attractive environment, including green spaces and parks covering the city. Furthermore, they include increasing the percentage of pedestrian and bicycle-oriented mobility, supplemented by various forms of public transport systems, allowing for the improvement of the air quality of our cities, and the integration of green and blue infrastructure for dealing with the urban heat island effect and heavy rain events, especially in sub-tropical and tropical environments.

An indicator for measuring the share of environmentally benign and healthy mobility concepts is the so-called modal split, which is the percentage of travellers using a particular type of transportation. This includes non-motorized mobility, such as walking and using a bicycle (active transportation), and public transport, such as buses, trams, underground and suburban trains. The modal split also accounts for the use of individual motorized vehicles, such as cars and motorcycles, which should be restricted to areas where public transport systems might not be available or walking and using a bicycle might not be an option for certain individuals.

Looking at the city of Shenzhen in the period from 2000 to 2016, people have chosen active forms of mobility, such as walking and cycling, which was the preferred mode of transport, accounting for 71 percent (2000) and 58 percent (2016) of trips, respectively. However, the proportion of public transit in Shenzhen was rather low, ranging from 12 percent in 2000 to 22 percent in 2016 (Figure 5 – 15).

In contrast, both Hong Kong and Singapore are the benchmark with regard to the use of public transit, since more than 50 percent of the residents selected public transit as the primary journey method. While only 5 percent of the people in Hong Kong used a private car in the given time period, that percentage was 25 percent in Singapore.

In that context it is interesting to note, that the current "Sustainable

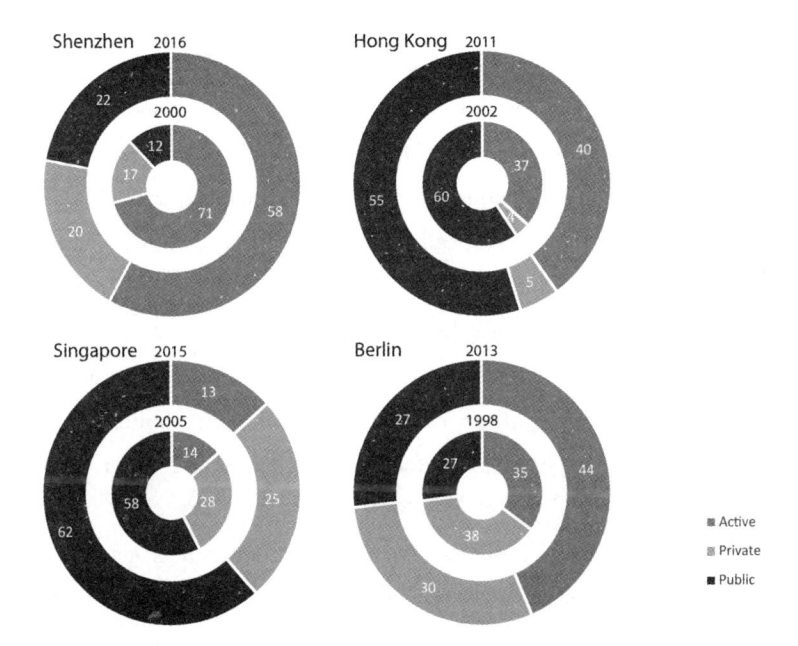

Figure 5 – 15: Modal split of the four cities

Source: Shenzhen Planning Bureau (www. szpl. gov. cn/), Assessing Urban Transport.

Cities Mobility Index 2017" ranks Hong Kong as the city with the most sustainable transport and mobility concept, addressing the needs of the people, including social and human implications of mobility systems. Other aspects include environmental impacts, like energy consumption, pollution and emissions, as well as the efficiency and reliability of a mobility system to facilitate economic growth.

With Singapore following in 8th position, Berlin was ranked 22nd, with the modal split being almost uniformly divided between active forms of mobility, such as walking and cycling, accounting for 35 percent (1998) and 44 percent (2013). Public transport accounted for 27 percent at that time, while private car use can be attributed to 38 percent of the population in 1998 and 30 percent in 2013, indicating a move towards sustainable forms of mobility.

Water Supply

Water helps shape our cities and is directly related to the basic issue of human life. The water shortage problem exists all over the world. As mentioned above, cities, especially those with high density, have to face the challenge of supplying sufficient water for the benefit of their citizens, and at the same time, the level of water security and efficiency should be guaranteed as well.

Following a report evaluating the resilience, quality, and efficiency of water usage in 50 cities across all continents of the world, named the Sustainable Cities Water Index (SCWI), Berlin occupied 4th position and was among the most consistently highperforming cities across all categories. Singapore, in 22nd place, succeeded in controlling leakage, treatment and metering, since it belongs to the area with geographic vulnerability. These two cities are considered as desirable references on harnessing water for future success.

As in other Chinese cities, the tap water in Shenzhen is not drinkable. However, the local government is currently aiming at providing drinkable tap water in the near future. According to the national health standards, the pipe water of Shenzhen is acceptable, and the quality is within the risk levels recommended by the International Commission of Radiation Protection.

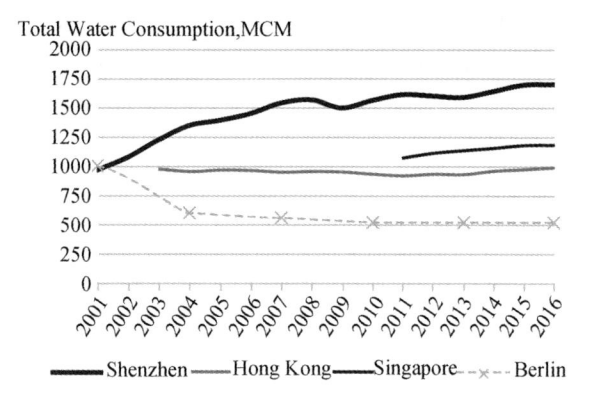

Figure 5 – 16: Total water consumption

Three additional water supply indicators are selected for assessing the current status of the four cities, namely, total water consumption, to describe

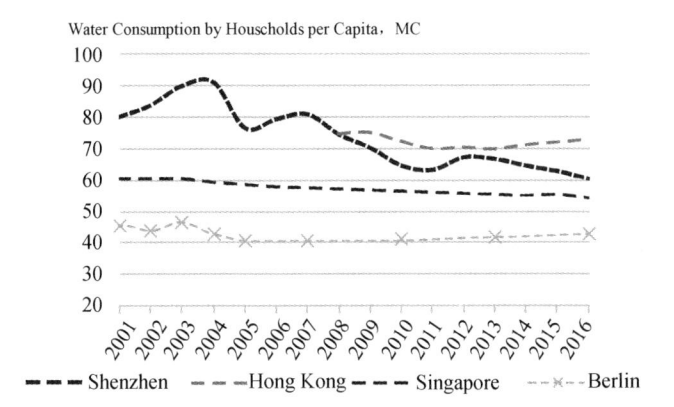

Figure 5 – 17: Water consumption by households per capita

the varying demands for water; water consumption by households per capita to illustrate each resident's water use in a city; and the share of water supply, which not only reveals the sources of water supply in each city, but also indicates the strategies applied in a city to deal with the water supply issue. The results contribute to helping us to gain an overview of our water supply reality and the potential direction we could move towards in the future.

As shown in Figure 5 – 16, the water consumption in Shenzhen, Berlin and Hong Kong is similar, around 1000 million cubic meters (MCM) in 2001. After that, only the water supply of Shenzhen increased dramatically until 2008 and then the growth rate slowed down to 1700 MCM in 2016. In contrast, the consumption in Berlin has continued to fall since the millennium and the supply of water in 2016 declined to half of the level in 2001, around 530 MCM, which is only 30 percent of the water consumption in Shenzhen. The consumption of water in Hong Kong showed a declining tendency from 2003 to 2013, and then slowly started to ascend to 1000 million cubic meters in 2016. The same weak growth as Hong Kong was also illustrated in Singapore, where consumption increased from 1082 MCM in 2011 to 1181 MCM in 2016, which is even higher than in Hong Kong, although it has a smaller population than Hong Kong. Evidently, the water consumption of each city has been relatively stable in recent years.

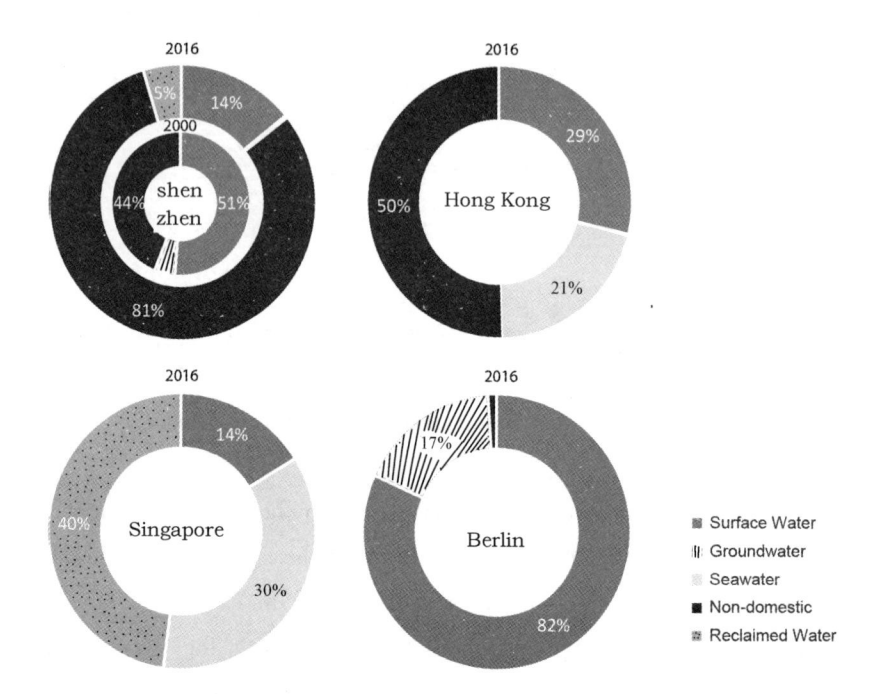

Figure 5 – 18: The share of water supply sources

Source: Water Resources Bureau of Shenzhen (swj. sz. gov. cn), Water Supplies Department of Hong Kong (www. wsd. gov. hk), Singapore's National Water Agency (www. pub. gov. sg), and the Office for Statistics of Berlin-Brandenburg (www. statistik-berlin-brandenburg. de).

Figure 5 – 17 illustrates that the water consumption for household per capita (WCHc) in Shenzhen rapidly descended with some fluctuations from 2001 to 2016. The peak value of Shenzhen appeared in 2004 with over 90 MC per capita, which is twice the level of Berlin (45 MC) in the same year. In 2016, the WCHc of Shenzhen decreased to 60 MC, only 6 MC higher than in Singapore, where WCHc declined continuously from 60 MC in 2001 to 54 MC in 2016. The WCHc in Hong Kong presented a growth trend after a short-term reduction from 2008 to 2013, and then increased to 72 MC in 2016.

According to Figure 5 – 18, the share of non-domestic water in total water supply in Shenzhen and Hong Kong is much higher than in the other cities. Especially in Shenzhen, the proportion of non-domestic water increased sharply from 44 percent in 2000 to 80 percent in 2016. With the population boom after the millennium, dependence on outside support in Shenzhen was much greater, while Shenzhen also started to minimize its water footprint by adopting reclaimed water, which accounted for 5 percent in 2016, compared to hardly any recycling water in 2000. In 2016, half of the water supply in Hong Kong came from the outside, when it used a volume of treated seawater as flushing water and drinking water, which accounted for 21 percent. Berlin was the only city almost self-sufficient in water, only 1 percent of water from outside, but the usage of underground water is at a relatively high level, taking up 17 percent. The benchmark in water supply among these cities is Singapore, which is a world leader in both water recycling and seawater desalination. As an island and also a super high-density population country-city, Singapore had a more severe water shortage problem and a stronger desire for water self-sufficiency, since it affected the country's safety after its independence in 1965. Against this background, Singapore adopted two main measures to minimize its water footprint: the first is seawater desalination, which is also used in Hong Kong but mainly for flushing water. The other one is high-grade reclaimed water, known as NEWater in Singapore, which is ultra-clean and safe to drink since it is purified using advanced membrane technologies and ultraviolet disinfection. In 2016, there was no non-domestic water and the use of surface water was the same as in Shenzhen. Instead of importing water from other regions, around 40 percent of water consumption was reclaimed water and 30 percent was desalinated seawater. Moreover, as reported by the Government, almost all urban rainwater is harvested and stored in drinking water reservoirs in Singapore. NEWater is expected to reach 50 percent of the water supply in Singapore in 2030. In terms of increasing the available water, reclaimed water in Shenzhen only accounted for 5 percent and hardly any seawater was used in 2016.

Green Urban Infrastructure

Today, more than half of the global population lives in cities and this number is still increasing. The higher the population density, the heavier the

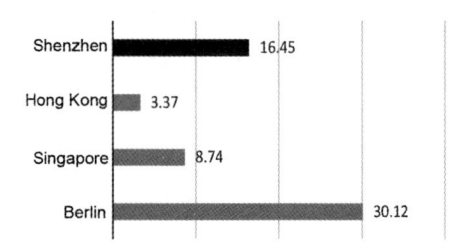

```
Shenzhen    ████████ 16.45
Hong Kong   █ 3.37
Singapore   ███ 8.74
Berlin      ███████████████ 30.12
```

Figure 5 – 19: The public green area per capita in 2016

environmental impacts, since the overwhelming population growth demands more land for construction and transport, which leads to the reduction of green areas within a limited land area. With a decreasing share of green area and biodiversity within a certain urban environment, ecological resilience also decreases. This creates a threat to the local ecosystem and the provision of ecosystem related services within that region. Services provided by the green urban infrastructure (GUI) include the amelioration of temperatures, reduction of the rainwater runoff, protection from floods, storing of carbon, reduction of pollution, improvement of the aesthetic appearance and the provision of recreational services. This effectiveness of GUI can be assessed by the distribution characteristics and green area ratio (GAR) within the land area.

  Hong Kong only possessed less than 30 percent of land area for development and construction, but left abundant area for greenery, the GAR of which reached 72 percent in 2016. Its large, continuous green area offers a wide bio-diversity, since the living space for flora and fauna is well preserved, while the developed area is confined to sections within the green land. In Singapore, a large area of green is retained in the middle of the city, surrounded by a ring of built-up land. With a GAR of 56 percent, the percentage of green area is much lower than the GAR of Hong Kong, which is 72 percent. The green area ratio of Berlin and Shenzhen is, in both cases, only 45 percent, with the developed area mainly in the centre, with the green located along the edges.

Shenzhen has a continuous and intensive green area in the south-eastern area of the city, with smaller, isolated green areas dispersed throughout the centre. In addition to large areas of green land and forests, public green spaces (PGSs) are also part of the green urban infrastructure of a city, including parks, playgrounds with greenery as well as roadside greenery. The public land with its green spaces belongs to the city, allowing the local government to directly influence the quality of life of the local residents. Green islands, dispersed throughout the city, are easily reached and accessed, and therefore, are used more frequently than more distant green land, offering shading, fresh air and entertainment space for the citizens.

Figure 5 – 19 illustrates the public green spaces (PGSs) per capita of the four cities, Shenzhen, Hong Kong, Singapore and Berlin. Although showing a lower GAR, Berlin has the largest PGSs among the four cities with over 30 square meters per capita for its residents, which is almost twice the amount of the public green space in Shenzhen, which is only 16.5 square meters per capita. Although Hong Kong has preserved a huge green area, it has the smallest PGSs per capita, which is 3.37 square meters, for its citizens. Although Singapore absorbs more stress on population density, it still has double the PGSs per capita of Hong Kong, around 8.7 square meters.

Moving Towards A Sustainable Future

The sustainable provision of basic services through the relevant local infrastructure of a rapidly growing urban environment is an extremely challenging task. Using the results of section 3, the analysis of the strengths, weaknesses, opportunities, and threats regarding the sustainable provision of basic services, provides a clear and concise picture of the current achievements and future challenges of the city of Shenzhen.

This analysis has also allowed for the identification of areas, where further development might be necessary, fostering the reputation of Shenzhen as one of the leading sustainable cities in China. Thus, Shenzhen might serve as a case study for other major cities worldwide, which are facing similar challenges in securing their future in a sustainable manner.

As pointed out earlier, the common challenge of many cities in Asia is constant and rapid growth, demanding more space, building activity, energy, water, transport as well as green infrastructure.

Open space seems to be abundant in Shenzhen, as the city possesses the largest land area of the 4 cities we have looked at. Although Shenzhen accounts for the largest number of citizens, the population density of Shenzhen is still lower than Hong Kong, and even lower than that of Singapore.

With regard to the basic requirements, such as energy, mobility, water and green infrastructure, the large population of Shenzhen certainly creates a tremendous challenge and exerts great pressure on the ecosphere of the city and the surrounding region.

Energy Supply

Due to its large population, the primary energy requirement of Shenzhen is much higher than in other cities. While it is a major challenge to manage total energy consumption and the resulting emissions, it is also a tremendous challenge to increase energy efficiency, compared to other cities, such as Hong Kong, Singapore and Berlin.

While Shenzhen has achieved a considerable reduction in its energy consumption per capita (ECc) during recent years, cities like Hong Kong, Singapore and Berlin only show about 50 percent of the Total Energy Consumption per unit of GDP (TCE/USD1million).

The need for improving the energy infrastructure and its efficiency in Shenzhen can also be seen in the energy consumption per capita (ECc). In 2010, Shenzhen and Berlin had almost the same total energy consumption per capita (TCE/capita). While Berlin succeeded in reducing its energy consumption per capita during the following 5 years, Shenzhen saw an increase by 0.9 TCE/capita, leading to a considerable increase in the CO_2 emissions of Shenzhen, as half of its energy is generated by using fossil fuels. Thus, it is critical for Shenzhen to increase the efficiency of energy consumption and move towards the use of renewable energies for producing electricity.

Mobility and Transport

With regard to a sustainable transport infrastructure, Shenzhen has still to make considerable efforts, since in 2016, only 22 percent of the residents in Shenzhen selected public transit as their main means of transport, while 20 percent use their cars. Comparing the modal split of Shenzhen with Hong Kong and Singapore, the percentage of people using public transport was 55 percent and 62 percent, respectively.

Public transit is the most effective and energy-efficient method for transporting people within the city, when it comes to land-use, impervious cover, resource consumption, emissions, noise and safety. This is even more effective, when the different modes of transport, such as suburban and urban trains, underground trains and trams as well as buses are well connected and can be easily reached by walking and biking, which is the case in compact cities with well-established transport networks. In that regard, Hong Kong has had greatest success in the reduction of private car travel, as only 5 percent of the population chooses the car as their means of transport, whereas in Shenzhen 20 percent choose to use their car, while in Singapore this share is 25 percent and in Berlin 30 percent.

Water Supply

The two major cities in the Pearl River Delta have exceeded their own capacity for water supply. Especially in Shenzhen, where household water consumption per capita has declined dramatically in recent years, the magnitude of the dependency on non-domestic support is still increasing due to the growth in population.

In 2016, over 80 percent of the water supply of Shenzhen came from the surrounding cities, indicating its high dependence on its neighbours. In comparison, Berlin and Singapore succeed in meeting their residents' needs by providing sufficient domestic water, using different methods.

While Berlin has an adequate water supply due to its local reserves of surface and ground water, Singapore is making efforts to increase its locally available water by reclaiming and recycling water, and by desalinating seawater to a high degree. That way, Singapore could be a role model for the city of Shenzhen in ameliorating the water shortage by increasing its domestic water supply and reducing the rapid growth of the demand for non-domestic water. Moreover, adopting treated seawater for flushing as in Hong Kong, could also be a low-cost and efficient strategy for reducing the import of non-domestic water.

Green Urban Infrastructure

In Shenzhen, large green areas are mainly located at the south-eastern and northern edge of the city. These areas are rather distant from the downtown district, where relatively small areas of green can be found, which are dispersed throughout the central area. While Singapore and Hong Kong have managed to preserve major areas of green in the centre of the city, benefitting the urban environment, the built-up area and urban structure can be optimized only on a neighbourhood scale and on the building level with regard to green roofs and green facades. According to the Shenzhen green system, the public green area per capita is forecast to increase to 18 Square meters/capita, with all residents within 500m of the nearest park by 2030. Therefore, the quality of life could be enhanced by increasing accessibility and the space experience in these public space areas of Shenzhen.

Conclusions

As one of the economically most successful cities in the south-eastern region of Asia, Shenzhen is also one of the fastest growing cities in the Pearl River Delta. While it has managed to deal with population growth in a successful way, it is still facing major challenges, such as providing clean energy to its production facilities and citizens, and providing clean drinking water, while being independent from its neighbouring cities. With further improvements with regard to a well-established sustainable public transport system and intensifying its green urban infrastructure, Shenzhen might well serve as a role model for its neighbours and other cities with regard to the establishment of sustainable urban infrastructure systems in the near future.

Chapter 6   Environment and Eco-City

Introduction

In less than 40 years, Shenzhen has gone through rapid industrialization and urbanization. In this land of 1997 square kilometres, the population has grown from 310,000 in 1979 to more than 12.52 million at the end of 2017, and there are over 20 million people under its management. Shenzhen is the first city in China to achieve 100 percent urbanization. While the society and economy are developing at a high speed, Shenzhen also made remarkable achievements in sustainable development of eco-city construction and green low-carbon cycle. "Shenzhen Blue" and "Shenzhen Green" have become the brightest colours in the city, and the quality of the ecological environment has continued to improve. The city has won the honorary titles of National Garden City, international "Garden City" and "Global 500" for UN Environmental Protection.

Shenzhen also encountered "urban diseases" in the process of rapid development. Overpopulation, excessive expansion and high density brought about huge environmental bottlenecks and pressures. These problems are mainly manifested in the serious shortage of space resources for development; extremely scarce local energy resources, weak energy self-sufficiency, and high costs. The scarce local water resources pose great challenges to the stability of water supply, and the contradiction between supply and demand of resources and energy has become a key bottleneck restricting sustainable development.

At present, the environmental pollution problems in some areas of Shenzhen are quite prominent. First of all, water environmental pollution is severe, with black and odorous water bodies, making treatment quite challenging. Pollution is common and severe in some offshore areas. However, Shenzhen lacks infrastructure for water pollution prevention and control, the pipeline constructions are unsatisfactory, and the capacity of local sewage treatment plants is insufficient to treat all the waste water. The sudden increase in household garbage has also raised a serious challenge for landfill.

Shenzhen's development practices adhere to the ideas of harmonious coexistence of people and nature, and establish and implement the philosophy that green mountains and waters are mountains of gold and silver. Shenzhen effectively employs means such as legislation, policy guidance and planning to establish and improve the system and mechanism of green development; it continues to promote the formation of a spatial pattern featuring resource saving and environmental protection. Shenzhen pushes forward the optimization and upgrading of industrial structures, and strongly advocates for green and low-carbon production and lifestyle to increase the green content in the quality development of the economy. Altogether, it has made outstanding achievements in the construction of a green and low-carbon city, as well as a smart and ecological city.

This chapter first discusses the concept of eco-city and related concepts, briefly examines the related research of Shenzhen's eco-city planning and construction, and reviews the process and main problems of Shenzhen's eco-city construction. Then the paper discusses the following aspects: energy structure adjustment, industrial transformation and upgrading, building green transportation system, promoting green buildings, advocating green and low-carbon lifestyle, strengthening pilot projects of low-carbon cities, and combining policy guidance with market mechanism. In the future, Shenzhen will become one of the three pilot areas of sustainable development in China. Shenzhen has proposed its ambitious goals for the short, medium and long term in accordance with the goals of UN 2030 Agenda for Sustainable Development, and it has begun to promote and implement these goals with various measures and means, trying to create reproducible and transferable experiences for the sustainable development of the world's mega cities.

Eco-City and Related Concepts

Eco-city is a concept put forward by American scholar Richard Register in the 1970s to plan and build an ideal future city (Eco-city Berkeley: Building a City for a Healthy Future). Subsequently, UNESCO launched the Human and Biosphere Project, which also introduced this important concept and attracted wider attention. On June 5, 1972, the first United Nations Conference on the Human Environment was held and the Declaration on the Human Environment was adopted, aiming at appealing to the peoples of the world to protect and improve the human environment. In 1987, the World Commission on Environment and Development formally elaborated the concept of sustainable development in its report entitled Our Common Future. With the increasing attention to global climate change and other issues, many different concepts have emerged, such as low-carbon city, green city, garden city, resilient city, sponge city, liveable city, knowledge city and so on. Several years ago, the author and other international scholars discussed the differences and connections between some related concepts. And many scholars have examined the related concepts (Nina Khanna). As can be seen, eco-city does not have a very well-recognized definition and coincides with many of the concepts mentioned above. Therefore, in the discussion of this paper, we do not make a strict distinction between the above concepts and understand eco-city from a very wide range of aspects: that is to say, to get more and higher quality output with the smallest possible environmental cost and least resource consumption, to strive for the harmonious coexistence of man and nature, to let people live in more liveable urban areas, to meet people's higher material and spiritual and cultural needs, and to have a higher sense of acquisition and happiness.

There are many works on the eco-city and the related concepts mentioned above. In combination with Shenzhen's green, low-carbon, recycling and sustainable development, especially the planning and construction of Shenzhen's eco-city, we briefly examine some recent works closely related to Shenzhen. In addition, a conceptual analysis framework is simply established for the use of this paper in the follow-up discussion.

Li Tianhong, Li Wenkai and Qian Zhenghan point out that urban expansion significantly affects ecosystem services and functions. Peijun Shi and Deyong Yu assess Shenzhen urban environmental resources and services, in landscape based urban planning and sustainable development. You Heyuan describes the unequal supply of public green space in Shenzhen. Lin Liu, Yaoyu Lin and Lina Wang consider energy allocation and environmental suitability assessments: outdoor and local climate and thermal comfort conditions in the region should be effectively assessed and analysed to meet the needs of resource conservation and environmental friendliness. Ying Huang, Lei Liub and Xiaofeng Pan take Shenzhen as an example, one of the most passionate local governments in China's low-carbon transformation, their paper uses the EIO-LCA model to evaluate the local scale of carbon dioxide emission structure. Jingru Li and Jian Zuo study willingness to pay higher landfill fees for construction waste: a comparative study of Shenzhen and Qingdao.

Martin de Jong, etc. consider developing robust organizational frameworks for Sino-foreign eco-cities: comparing Sino-Dutch Shenzhen Low Carbon City with other initiatives. Changjie Zhan conducts research on financing an eco-city and a low-carbon city: the case of Shenzhen international low-carbon city financing of sustainable urban development has become a major issue, especially in the construction scale of Asian countries. Liu Ying, Lin Yanliu, Fu Nana, Stan Geertman and Frank van Oort focus on Shenzhen's inclusive and sustainable transformation: urban reconstruction, migration and displacement patterns as well as policy implications.

Shenzhen's Sustainable Development Process

When Shenzhen was established in 1979, there were hardly any industries. On about 2000 square kilometres of land, about 310,000 people were living in Shenzhen (Statistical Yearbook). The GDP of Shenzhen was less than 200 million Yuan, mainly from the income of primary industry. Shenzhen is close to the mountains and the sea, and its natural conditions are good. Generally speaking, though, there is a lack of natural resources. After the establishment of the Shenzhen Special Economic Zone in 1980, industrial parks were set up to carry out urban construction, but in the early 1990s, the main industry was the processing of incoming materials. After Mr. Deng Xiaoping, the chief designer of China's reform and opening-up policy, visited Shenzhen and other places in 1992, the pace of urbanization in Shenzhen accelerated greatly, and the population expanded rapidly year by year. As can be seen from, before 1992, there were fewer than 30 haze days per year in Shenzhen, and after 1992, the number of haze days per year also increased rapidly, reaching the highest level in 2004, with the number of haze days exceeding one-half of the whole year, reaching 187 days. It was in this year that Shenzhen announced that it had achieved 100 percent urbanization. This is the first city to do so in China. Around this time, everyone, from mayor to citizen, began to attach importance to environmental issues.

In 2017, the green coverage rate of the built-up area in Shenzhen was about 45 percent, the forest coverage rate was about 40 percent, and the urban sewage treatment rate was about 96 percent. Shenzhen has built 942 parks with a total area of 22,000 hectares and a per capita park green area of 16.45 square meters. About half of the city's land is classified for ecological protection. Shenzhen has 2,400 kilometres of greenways and 2,638 hectares of ecological landscape forests; the total area of green buildings exceeded 53.2 million square meters, ranking first in the country; it is one of the largest cities in the world for the promotion of new energy vehicles, and has promoted 120,000 of them. The average concentration of PM2.5 is 28mg/m^3, which is at the leading level in domestic cities. Shenzhen Carbon Emissions Exchange is the first of its kind in China, with the most active transactions and highest trading volume. Shenzhen International Low Carbon City has become the flagship project of China-Europe Sustainable Urbanization Cooperation and won the "Sustainable Development Planning Project Award" from the Paulson Institute of the US.

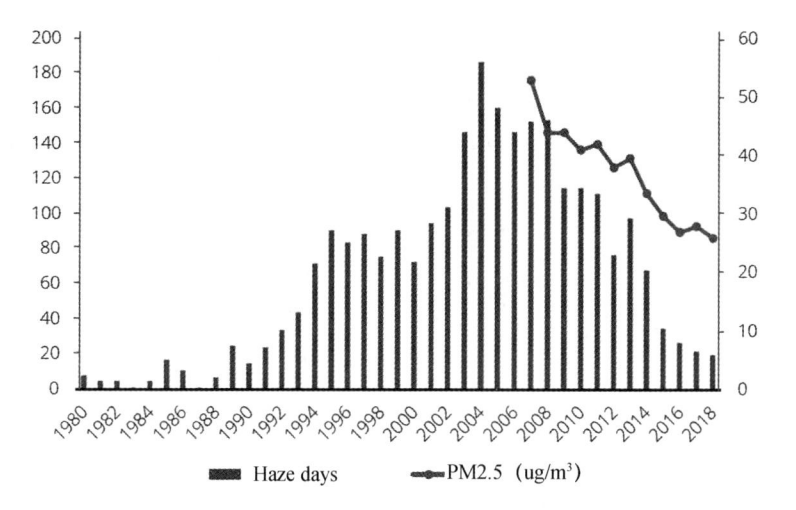

Figure 6-1: Haze days and PM2.5 concentration in Shenzhen

Shenzhen's Major Environmental Problems

Besides the air pollution issue mentioned above, Shenzhen's government has raised the "4 non-sustainability problems" since 2004. The mayor at that time (Li Hongzhong) pointed out the following non-sustainability issues: firstly, Shenzhen has limited land and space; it has only 200 square kilometers of land available for development and this area can no longer match the speed of Shenzhen's development. Secondly, Shenzhen's energy and water resources won't be able to support its rapid development, even if we dry up the Dongjiang River. Thirdly, the speed mode of development that Shenzhen currently adopts will require more labour input to realize the target of one billion Yuan of GDP, yet the city cannot bear such a heavy load and fourthly, the environmental capacity is severely overextended, the environment cannot tolerate any more pollution (not with severe water pollution; not to mention that there's no more environmental capacity left in the land water bodies). Shenzhen has a very clear understanding of its environmental problems (*China Reform News*, January 17th, 2005).

Shenzhen has a quite small land area of 1,997 square kilometers with only 760 square kilometers available for construction. If Shenzhen maintains its development speed of 10 square kilometers peryear, there will be a severe imbalance between land, the denominator, and the population density and economic output, the numerator. Shenzhen will have no land left for any purpose in 20 years.

Shenzhen is one of the 7 cities with severe water shortage in China. The average per capita water availability is only 1/6 of Guangdong and 1/5 of the national average. With the constant increasing of Shenzhen's population, the environmental load, especially on water resources, is growing rapidly. There were about 332,900 people in the area when the Shenzhen Special Economic Zone was built in 1980. Today, Shenzhen administers over 12 million people, 10.26 million of whom are temporary residents. A series of problems, derivatives of overpopulation, have damaged the city's environmental capacity. According to the estimation of Shenzhen's officials, the city will be overwhelmed if the conflict between scarce land and ever-increasing population cannot be solved or gets even worse, and in turn, the healthy growth of Shenzhen's economy will be gone.

The "4 non-sustainability problems" of land, resources, environment and population greatly restricted the expanded reproduction and structural optimization and upgrade of the enterprises. Shenzhen, the city which garnered its first pot of gold via "three processing and one compensation" with scarce land, severe population pressure and the restricted development of traditional enterprises, was the first to realize that the traditional course and expanding development mode has come to an end; and intensive and high-end transformation becomes an urgent task. Ever since then, Shenzhen is determined to transform from the famous "Shenzhen Speed" to "Shenzhen Benefits".

Energy Structure Adjustment and Energy Efficiency Improvement

Shenzhen attaches great importance to promoting the energy structure adjustment. It greatly promotes the planning and construction of energy infrastructures and gradually increases the proportions of clean energy, extraneous electricity and natural gas in the city's energy structure. In the primary energy consumption structure in 2017, the proportions of coal, petroleum, gas and electricity were 7.2 : 27.3 : 12.8 : 52.7. Compared with 2010, the proportion of coal dropped from 12.5 percent to 7.2 percent, the proportion of petroleum dropped from 32.4 percent to 27.3 percent, while the proportion of natural gas increased from 10.2 percent to 12.8 percent and the proportion of electricity increased from 45.0 percent to 52.7 percent. The proportion of clean energy was 10.3 percent higher than 2010 and the energy consumption structure continues to optimize (Figure 6-2).

After the establishment of Shenzhen City, electricity and energy have always been in short supply due to the rapid industrialization and urbanization. By 2000, Shenzhen's self-sufficiency rate of primary energies was less than 10 percent, more than 90 percent of the energies were

2017　　　　　　　　　　　2010

■ coals　　■ gas　　　　　　■ coals　　■ gas
■ petroleum　　electricity　　■ petroleum　　electricity

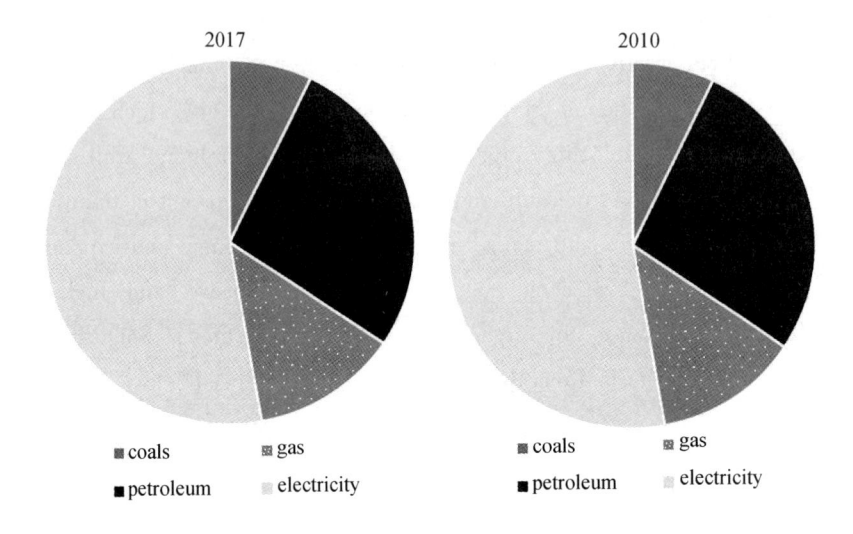

Figure 6 – 2: Diagram of energy structure

transported from inland or imported from abroad. In addition to the huge amount of coal, Shenzhen also has to import huge amounts of fuel oil and liquefied petroleum gas. To solve the energy bottleneck problem of Shenzhen, the city convinced the central government to locate the LNG pilot project first introduced to China at the Dapeng Peninsula in Shenzhen. The project cost over 29 billion yuan. It was approved at the end of 1999, officially commenced at the end of 2003 and phase 1 was put into operation in 2006. Natural gas mined from the seabed in Australia is tanked in LNG cargo ships after pressurization, and sent to Shenzhen's receiving station for unloading, storage and gasification. This project represents a great leap for Shenzhen's energy structure adjustment. After that, Shenzhen has constantly enhanced its utilization of natural gas, nuclear energy, solar energy, biomass energy, wind energy and other clean energies and continues to raise the proportion of clean energies. Shenzhen applied high-efficiency power generation technology and trial applied carbon capture and sequestration methods to lower the carbon emission of the energy industry. Shenzhen also piloted smart grid construction to promote the grid connection of renewable energies.

Greatly increase the proportion of utilization of clean energies

Implement the petroleum replacement strategy by introducing natural gas, expand the supply channels of natural gas resources, seize the strategic opportunity of global energy development and strive to develop and utilize nuclear energy and renewable energies.

- Actively introduce natural gas resources. Greatly promote the planning and construction of natural gas source projects, such as the West-East natural gas transmission line 2 Shenzhen-Hong Kong branch, West-East natural gas transmission line 2, Shenzhen LNG emergency load station and Diefu LNG receiving station to form a multiple source of supply pattern. The natural gas supply capacity will exceed 6.5 billion cubic meters per year and the proportion of natural gas in primary energy structure will increase to around 14 percent.
- Strive to develop nuclear power. Fully utilize the brand and technological advantages of Shenzhen's nuclear power industry, break through the traditional base planning mode and enhance the transformation of concepts from industrial park to the industrial city; and establish an industry cluster with the nuclear power design, R&D, integration and service as the core, and solar energy, wind energy and other new energy and high-end industries as the auxiliaries. Build a national-level new energy (nuclear power) industrial base, and a high-productivity demonstration base of Shenzhen's transformation development, innovation development and low-carbon development, and make it a new window for Shenzhen's external display.
- Promote the utilization of solar energy. All civil buildings with the necessary heat collection conditions must install the solar energy hot water system. Speed up the solar energy-photovoltaic building integration (BIPV) demonstration projects. The area of the solar energy photo-thermal application will exceed 16 million square meters, and the total

installed capacity of solar energy generation will reach 200 MW. Actively carry out the pilot of renewable energy building applications, such as solar energy air conditioning and ground source heat pump. Promote and install new energy products such as solar energy-LED and wind-solar complementary lighting for urban roads and public spaces meeting the necessary conditions.

- Engage in the development and utilization of bio-mass energy. Accelerate the expansion of phase II of the Laohukeng waste incineration plantand the planning and construction of the waste incineration and power generation plant in the eastern part of the city. Enhance the utilization of methane from landfill. Actively engage in the R&D of biodiesel, fuel ethanol and energy plants, and pilot the application of biological liquid fuels at appropriate time. Currently, the four waste incineration and power generation plants operating in Shenzhen can process 5,450 tons of household wastes every day and generate 700 million KWH per year, with emission indexes reaching or exceeding the EU standard. At the same time, Shenzhen is actively promoting three more waste incineration projects: Bao'an Phase III, Nanshan Phase II and the eastern environmental-protection power plant. The Shenzhen Eastern Environmental Protection Power plant under construction will process over 5,000 tons of waste daily. When completed, it will be the largest single garbage power generation plant in the world. When all these projects are completed, Shenzhen will incinerate all household waste for power generation and will become the first city in China to process all household waste in a "harmless, reducing and recycling" manner.

- Actively carry out the demonstration of wind utilization. Combined with wind energy resources and construction conditions, Shenzhen will research and construct the wind power demonstration projects to lead the development of the wind power equipment industry. And Shenzhen will actively carry out a feasibility study of offshore wind power projects according to the offshore wind power project planning of Guangdong

Province.

By 2017, the proportion of non-fossil energy in Shenzhen's primary energy consumption reached 15 percent, while the proportion of clean energy exceeded 90 percent.

Comprehensively lower the carbon emissions of the energy production sector

Encourage the energy production sector to adopt high efficiency power generation technologies, and test the application of carbon capture and sequestration technology (CCS), striving to significantly reduce the carbon emissions of the power industries.

- Accelerate the R&D and application of high efficiency power generation technologies. Encourage power generating enterprises to engage in R&D of high efficiency power generation technology to transform the main equipment of the power generation unit and the important energy-consuming auxiliary system, while focusing on desulfurization and dephosphorization; install pollution control equipment, improve the utilization efficiency of coal and gas for power generation and lower the station's power consumption rate and carbon emissions. Back in 1999, Mawan power station's No. 4 unit completed the construction of the first set of the seawater flue gas desulfurization system, which was a demonstration project of the State Environmental Protection Administration. According to the statistics, Shenzhen invested 1.423 billion yuan in energy-saving and emission reduction technical transformation of the existing coal power plants from 2014 to 2017. As of now, all ten coal power generation units have completed their ultra-low emission transformation; nine of them passed the ultra-low emission acceptance and obtained a preferential electricity price for ultra-low emission.

- Pilot the energy comprehensive integrated supply mode. Pilot the household type or community type small-scale combined supply of cooling, heating and power. Research regional low-carbon energy planning in combination with the new urban functional areas and parks to promote the complementary development of ordinary energies and renewable energies, and establish an integrated energy supply centre. Encourage the pilot of the distributed combined supply of cooling, heating and power of natural gas in buildings meeting necessary conditions. Encourage the construction of energy storage power stations in important venues, and develop ice storage air conditioning and phase-changing materials and other energy storage forms, and increase the efficiency of the energy supply system.

● In order to reduce the air pollution caused by the diesel generators of the coal carriers in the power plant wharf during unloading, Shenzhen Energy Group Co., Ltd. constructed the shore power facility of the Mawan power plant wharf from 2015 and carried out the transformation of the shore power facility of the coal carriers of its subordinate transportation companies at the same time. In September 2016, Shenzhen Energy Group completed the transformation of the shore power facility of all four carriers and passed the handover acceptance in November. It is calculated that the harbour area can reduce exhaust gas emissions by about 4,000 tons per year after the shore power transformation and truly achieve "zero emission" of exhaust gas by ships. It is reported that this project was the very first large-scale bulk cargo terminal shore power construction project in China which successfully utilized low-pressure boarding, which has a positive demonstration effect for the promotion of "terminal shore power" in Shenzhen and even across the country.

Strive to improve the energy utilization efficiency

Take energy-saving and cost-reducing as the important carriers of energy utilization efficiency improvement, and speed up the structural energy-saving, technical energy-saving and management energy-saving. And intensify the energy-saving and cost-reducing measures in fields such as manufacturing, transportation, building and public institutions, reducing the resource and energy consumption and improving the energy utilization efficiency.

- Enhance the energy conservation and emission reduction management of key industries such as electricity, building materials and manufacturing. Actively adopt advanced and suitable energy-saving technologies to reform traditional industries and improve energy efficiency. By 2015, the energy consumption per unit of industrial added value dropped by 20 percent compared to 2010 and reached 0.394 tons of standard coal/ten thousand yuan; Shenzhen strives to bring down the energy consumption per unit of industrial added value by another 10 percent compared to 2015 and reach 0.355 tons of standard coal/ ten thousand yuan.
- Energy-saving of the electric power industry. Shenzhen promote the technical transformation of thermal power generating units and replace them with efficient and clean power generation technologies to bring down the power generating energy consumption and the station service power consumption rate. Accelerate the technical transformation of power transmission, transformation and distribution equipment, as well as the construction of the power grid; gradually eliminate the old equipment with high energy consumption, to lower the power loss during transmission, transformation and distribution. Promote the simplified power grid transformation levels and 20Kv power distribution. Enhance the management of the power-demanding side and carry out energy-saving and power generation scheduling in a comprehensive manner.
- Energy-saving of the building material industry.

Speed up the technical transformation of the glassmaking industry, promote advanced technologies and carry out the technical transformation of the residual heat utilization of the glass kiln. Accelerate the elimination of backward kiln types in the ceramics industry, promote energy-saving and environmental-friendly kiln technologies, optimize the fuel structure and encourage comprehensive resource utilization projects such as recycling of ceramics slag and residual heat.

• Electronic equipment manufacturing industry. Intensify the energy consumption diagnosis and the energy-saving transformation of the electronic equipment manufacturing industry; accelerate the elimination of the backward and high energy consumption electronic equipment such as the motor, draught fan, water pump, injection moulding machine and compressor; guide enterprises to adjust their product structure and divert their focus onto low energy consumption and high added value products; raise the access threshold of the electronic equipment manufacturing industry and strictly monitor the energy consumption of energy-consuming equipment.

• Energy-saving and cost-reducing of key energy-using units. Enhance energy-saving monitoring of key units consuming more than 300 tons of standard coal per year; implement the reporting system regarding energy utilization status; promote energy efficiency benchmarking and encourage the pilot of energy-saving management specialists and energy management system. Increase the capital input to guide enterprises to carry out research on energy-saving technology, organize key energy-using units to engage in energy-saving and cost-reducing services, improve the measuring and detection capability and standards of the energy-using units, as well as calibrate their energy measurement devices and verify their energy measurement data.

Industry transformation and upgrading

As of 2017, the proportion of advanced manufacturing, modern service industries and advantageous traditional industries, respectively in Shenzhen was 0.1 : 41.3 : 58.6, showing a coordinated development pattern of advanced manufacturing, modern service industries and advantageous traditional industries.

The added value of the four mainstay industries: high-tech industry, financial industry, logistics industry and the cultural industry was 1.4 trillion yuan, accounting for 63.4 percent of GDP. The advanced manufacturing industry achieved an added value of 573.387 billion yuan, with a growth rate of 13.1 percent. The proportion of modern service industry in the service industry grew to 70.8 percent, and the added value of the six strategic emerging industries of bio-industry, the Internet, new energy, new-generation information technology, new materials and cultural creativity reached 918.35 billion yuan, accounting for 40.9 percent of GDP. Shenzhen has become one of the cities with the largest scale of strategic emerging industries and the strongest clustering effect in China.

Development of low-carbon emerging industries

Assign great importance to the development of low-carbon emerging industries such as new energy, Internet, biology, new materials, cultural creativity, new-generation information technology, energy-saving services and low-carbon services; seize the commanding height of the development of low-carbon industries and create mainstay industries for low-carbon development.

The new energy industry

Earnestly implement the "Revitalization and Development Plan of the New Energy Industry in Shenzhen (2009 – 2015)" and the Revitalization and Development Policies of the New Energy Industry in Shenzhen, and implement technological innovation, industrial cultivation, development and promotion, application expansion and industry service engineering in aspects of solar, nuclear, wind and biomass energy, energy storage power stations and new energy vehicles to rapidly expand the industrial scales, improve the energy supply proportions and optimize the energy structures. By 2015, the output of the new energy industry reached 250 billion yuan, with an annual replacement of traditional energy of more than 15 million tons of standard coal and a CO_2 emission reduction of more than 20 million tons.

The Internet industry

Accelerate the implementation of the "Revitalization and Development Plan of the Internet Industry in Shenzhen (2009 – 2015)" and the relevant policies, speed up the construction of Internet infrastructures and greatly develop the E-commerce, IT and mobile Internet, strive to promote the integration of the Internet industry and the real economy and bring down energy consumption. By 2015, the output of the Internet industry reached 200 billion yuan.

Bio-industry

Actively implement the "Revitalization and Development Plan of the Bio-industry in Shenzhen (2009 – 2015)" and the relevant policies. Focus on fields such as biological environmental protection, biological energy, biological medicine, biological pharmaceutical and biological manufacturing, and accelerate the R&D of the production of biological environmental protection products and the comprehensive utilization of recycled resources, environmental monitoring, waste disposal, water treatment, exhaust gas treatment technology and set products, biodiesel and fuel ethanol. By 2015, the output of the bio-industry reached 200 billion yuan.

The new material industry

Actively implement the "Revitalization and Development Plan of the New Material Industry in Shenzhen (2009 – 2015)" and the relevant policies. Give full play to the foundation and guiding roles of new materials in low-carbon development. Actively cultivate new material enterprises with promising market potential, intensive technologies, high added values, low resource consumption and environmental friendliness to support the transformation and upgrade of the electronic information industry, the rapid development of low-carbon industries such as the new energy and environmental protection industries, the transformation and upgrade of the advantageous traditional industries and acceleration of the core competitiveness of the low-carbon industry system. By 2015, the output of the new material industry reached 150 billion yuan.

Cultural creativity industry

Actively implement the "Revitalization and Development Plan of the Cultural Creativity Industry in Shenzhen (2009 – 2015)" and the relevant policies. Highlight the high-end, high added value and low-carbon advantages of the cultural creativity industry. Intensify the support given to it, create a good environment and greatly promote the development of industries such as creative design, anime games, digital audio and video, digital publishing, new media, cultural tourism, film and performance, high-end printing, and high-end industrial arts. Develop the emerging industrial mode of the cultural industry of "culture + technology" relying on the high and new-tech, and with the digital contents as the main body and proprietary intellectual property rights as the core to increase added value to cultural products. By 2015, the added value of the cultural creative industry reached 220 billion yuan and the total output of the industry exceeded 580 billion yuan.

New-generation IT industry

Adhere to the principles of "market-oriented, innovation-driven, high-end-guided and advantages highlighted", enhance independent innovation, improve the industry standard, expand the application space, optimize the development environment, promote the interaction and integration of IT innovation, emerging application expansion and new-generation network construction, and promote the rapid and healthy development of the new-generation IT industry. By 2015, the output of the new-generation IT industry reached 1.2 trillion yuan, with an annual growth rate higher than 20 percent; Shenzhen became an important new-generation IT industry base in the world.

Energy-saving service industry

Intensify the support given to the energy-saving service industry and issue supporting policies for the development of the industry; encourage enterprises with a high level of technological and service standard to adopt the energy management contract (EMC) mode and provide "one-stop" energy-saving services of diagnosis, design, financing, reform and operation for the energy-using units. Enhance service innovation, talent cultivation and technological

R&D to make the energy-saving service industry stronger, and improve its comprehensive strength and market competitiveness; and establish a batch of large service enterprises with renowned brands and strong competitiveness to promote the rapid development of the energy-saving service industry, and build a national high ground of the energy-saving service industry.

Low-carbon service industry

Cultivate low-carbon service industries such as carbon emission statistics, carbon standard, carbon labelling, carbon certification, carbon finance and carbon emission permit trading. Encourage enterprises to carry out carbon footprint measurement and product carbon certification and engage in the formulation of carbon standards. Encourage financial and insurance institutions to carry out carbon finance (credit) and insurance businesses to provide funding support for low-carbon development. Explore the trading mechanism of carbon emission permits and carry out the pilot of carbon emission permit trading. Encourage domestic and foreign enterprises with a high level of low-carbon technology research and service to settle in Shenzhen.

Transform and upgrade the high-carbon industry

Find breakthrough via technological innovation of the traditional industries and accelerate the update and transformation. Raise the access threshold of carbon emission on the basis of restricted conditions, such as energy consumption and environment. Adopt clean production and product carbon labelling, and promote the low-carbon transformation and upgrade of traditional industries.

Speed up technical transformation and equipment update

Accelerate the removal of backward technology, process and equipment in accordance with the national industrial restructuring catalogue, as well as the industrial guidance catalogues of Guangdong Province and Shenzhen Municipality. Increase production efficiency and energy utilization efficiency to realize the low-carbon transformation of industry. Enhance the review of backward productivity removal, establish the social announcement system of obsolete productivity and report to the public on a regular basis.

Case 6 – 1: Shenzhen Emission Exchange

Carbon trading is essentially a financial activity, but more closely linked to financial capital and a green technology-based real economy: on the one hand, financial capital invests directly or indirectly in projects and companies that create carbon assets; on the other hand, emission reductions from different projects and companies enter the carbon financial market for trading and are developed into standard financial instruments.

Due to the small emissions in Shenzhen, the National Development and Reform Commission did not initially include Shenzhen when drafting the first batch of cities. Shenzhen is probably included in the national pilot area because of the special nature of Shenzhen's industrial structure. Compared with other cities in the country, Shenzhen does not have large-scale direct emission sources of carbon dioxide such as heavy chemical industry, steel industry and thermal power industry, while carbon emission trading is a market-based means to promote energy saving and emission reduction at a lower cost, and ultimately achieve green and low carbon development. The methods to make the large number of "indirect emission sources" achieve energy saving and emission reduction goals through the establishment of market mechanisms will be the significance of this pilot in Shenzhen.

Shenzhen Municipal Government attached great importance to this project and set up a leading group and office for the pilot of carbon emission trading. Municipal leaders served as the people in charge and set up a working group led by the Municipal Development and Reform Commission, consisting of several governmental organs to carry out extensive and in-depth research, together with expert research teams.

On September 30th, 2010, the Shenzhen Emissions Exchange was established. The Shenzhen carbon emission trading market was officially launched on June 18th, 2013, becoming the first carbon trading pilot in the "Seven Pilots" to open the market, and once again with Shenzhen playing the leading role in innovation and reform.

On June 18th, 2013, the Shenzhen carbon market was launched. It was the first real carbon market in China, and among all developing countries worldwide. Shenzhen is the very first pilot of special carbon trading laws, and it has become the first pilot in China which has relatively comprehensive carbon trading laws consisting of local laws and regulations and local government acts.

As of December 31st, 2017, the cumulative volume of carbon market quotas in Shenzhen was 29.35 million tons, with an accumulated turnover of 904 million yuan. The total volume of CCER (China's Certified Emission Reduction) was 11.05 million tons, with a total turnover of 148 million yuan. The total turnover of the Shenzhen carbon market was 40.40 million tons, and the total turnover was 1.052 billion yuan. Its trading volume and liquidity have been leading the country for a long time.

The Shenzhen carbon market is bold in opening and brave in innovating. In addition to having the first carbon trading law in China, it also has the first organizational-level code and guidance for quantization, reporting and inspection of greenhouse gas in China; it is the first carbon trading system using the benchmarking method for distribution; the first quota game (use concentrated if not game) distribution system; and the first greenhouse gas information management system, registration system andtrading system. The Shenzhen carbon market created several firsts in carbon financial innovations, and found several carbon financial cases which can be reproduced and transferred nationwide: such as carbon asset pledge financing, allowing foreign investors to participate in carbon trading, buy-back financing of domestic and foreign carbon asset, carbon bonds and green structural deposits and so on.

> Shenzhen's carbon market has effectively raised the awareness of emission reductions of enterprises and the public. The construction and operation of this market has enabled more and more Shenzhen enterprises to recognize the issues of climate change and be serious about corporate energy saving and emission reduction, and has encouraged enterprises to incorporate GHG emission reduction into their production management and investment decisions, as well as improve corporate social responsibility. At the same time, with the publicity and promotion of knowledge related to carbon trading, the Shenzhen carbon market not only attracted a number of public welfare members, but also greatly enhanced the public's understanding of low-carbon lifestyles and green travel, and improved energy saving and emission reduction awareness in the whole society.

Control the development of industries with high energy consumption and severe pollution

Implement the management authority linkage mechanism of the newly approved projects and the project approval accountability system. Strictly implement the "Six Necessary Requirements" of projects, i. e. a project must meet the requirements of industry policy and market access standards, project review and approval or filing procedures, pre-review of land usage, environmental impact evaluation and approval, energy-saving evaluation review and credit, as well as safety and urban planning requirements. Fully employ references to energy consumption standard, environmental-protection enforcement, dumping right trading, minimum wage and social security to accelerate the elimination of low-end and backward enterprises, increase the industry access threshold, implement energy-saving access management, strictly control the development of industries with high energy consumption and severe pollution.

Greatly promote clean production

Expand the scale and scope of clean production and bring the concept of clean production into the industry cluster base and the construction process of the industry belt; and carry out the low-carbon reform of enterprises and production bases via the implementation of clean production. Attach great importance to the clean production of traditional industries such as building materials, electroplating, household appliances, jewellery, painting and dyeing, as well as watches. Implement mandatory clean production review of enterprises with pollutant emission exceeding the national, provincial or municipal emission standard or exceeding the rated total control index of pollutant emission, and use the clean production review as one of the constraint conditions for settlement, expansion, relocation and eligibility for preferential policies; control the consumption of resources and energies throughout the full life-cycle of products to lower carbon emission.

Accelerate the spatial agglomeration of traditional industries

Speed up the cluster development of traditional industries, adjust the industrial spatial structure, realize the rational industrial layout, shorten the product transportation distance and bring down energy consumption. Enhance the core competitiveness of industries, increase product quality, lower the unit carbon emission of the product and establish a famous low-carbon brand in Shenzhen via constant innovation.

Develop low-carbon urban agriculture

Based on the low-carbon and ecological restructuring of agriculture, develop modern animal husbandry, aquaculture, planting and fishery with Shenzhen's characteristics. Increase the technological management standard and added value products; increase the utilization efficiencies of land, water resources and energies to the greatest extent possible, and lower carbon emission during agricultural production.

Construct A Green Transportation System

By the end of 2017, a total of 120,000 new energy vehicles were put into use, including 16,359 purely electric buses (all buses in Shenzhen are now purely electric), over 10,000 purely electric taxis (all taxis in Shenzhen will be purely electric by the end of 2018) and over 30,000 purely electric logistics vehicles (Shenzhen has the largest number of new energy logistics vehicles in the world).

Strive to promote the energy-saving and emission reduction of transportation by improving the energy efficiency and emission standards of vehicles. Greatly develop rail transit, public transport and non-motor vehicle road transportation and promote new energy vehicles; establish a low-carbon transportation network, effectively lower the energy consumption of vehicles, control exhaust gas emission and realize the gradual lowering of transportation carbon emission.

Strengthen the energy-saving and emission reduction of transportation. Enhance the control of motor vehicle exhaust pollution, improve the quality of vehicle fuels, increase the carbon emission standard of motor vehicles, enhance the monitoring and control of vehicle exhaust and speed up the elimination and upgrading of high emission vehicles; further increase the proportion of buses using clean energies such as LNG, and gradually establish a monitoring, evaluation and alarm system for motor vehicle pollution. Strictly implement the annual inspection system of vehicles and improve the means of inspection of diesel vehicles, accelerate the elimination of the old high energy consumption vehicles, enhance exhaust gas detection and intensify the punishment of vehicles exceeding the limits in accordance with the applicable laws. Make sure all vehicle fuels reach the national IV standard and pay more attention to the oil-gas recycling of gas stations, oil depots and oil tank trucks; strictly implement the environmental protection classification identification system and the inspection/maintenance system (I/M) of vehicles to reduce the pollutant emission of motor vehicles.

Give priority to the development of public transport. Implement the development strategy of public transport priority and establish a transport development mode dominated by public transport. Optimize and adjust the travel mode of the city and establish an integrated public transport system with rail transit as the framework, conventional transport as the network, taxis as the supplement and the slow-travel system as the extension, building an urban bus system in line with international standards. Enhance the coordination between rail transit and conventional transport; reasonably, orderly and efficiently organize the spatial transfer of the passenger flows of the railway stations; construct a smoothly connected, convenient, efficient and integrated bus system to significantly increase the participation ratio of public transport. By 2015, Shenzhen had built a 229 kilometer rail transit network and established a 400 kilometers (two-way) special bus line; the participation ratio in public transport of motorized travel reached 56 percent, fuel consumption per hundred kilometres dropped by 10 percent; by 2020, the participation ratio in public transport of motorized travel will reach 65 percent and fuel consumption per hundred kilometres will drop by 20 percent.

Increase vehicles' energy efficiency and the emission market's access threshold. Increase the energy efficiency of new vehicles and raise the access threshold of the emission market; accelerate the transformation or elimination of the current low energy efficiency vehicles. Strictly implement the fuel consumption limits of passenger cars and light commercial vehicles; and restrict the growth of vehicles with high oil consumption and high pollution.

Pilot and promote new energy vehicles. Take the construction of the national-level energy-saving and new energy vehicle demonstration and promotion city as an opportunity, speed up the implementation of the Implementation Plan of the Energy-saving and New Energy Vehicles in Shenzhen; pilot and promote new energy buses, taxis, service cars and private cars. Accelerate the formulation of the charging station (or charging pile) construction standard and support policies to speed up the construction of supporting facilities, such as charging stations. Actively establish new energy vehicle demonstration areas in Yantian, Longgang and Guangming to create beneficial conditions for the large-scale promotion and application of new energy vehicles.

By 2015, Shenzhen promoted 50,000 new energy vehicles and realized an annual carbon reduction of 50,000 tons; by 2020, 100 thousand new energy vehicles will be promoted and the annual carbon emission will reach 1 million tons.

> **Case 6 – 2: BR Building**
>
> The project aims to explore the realization mode of green building featuring low cost and soft technologies, and realize maximum savings, efficient utilization of resources, environmental protection and pollution reduction throughout the entire life cycle of the building. BR Building incorporates the research achievements and patented technologies of Shenzhen IBR over the years, and has the dream of practicing green life and green office working methods. It has become a green R&D office building integrating regional characteristics, green technologies and architectural art.
>
> BR Building is located in Futian District of Shenzhen and occupies 3,000 Square meters. It has a plot ratio of 4, a coverage rate of 38.5 percent and a total construction area of 18,170 square meters. The main structure of the building has 12 storeys above ground and 2 storeys underground. BR Building was completed and put into use in March 2009 and has won many domestic and international awards. The building has achieved its original objectives and reached the requirements of Three Stars Level of National Green Building Evaluation Standards and Gold Level of LEED, with a total project cost of 4,000 yuan/square meters. The building

created remarkable social benefits. According to preliminary calculation and analysis, the entire building has a construction area of 18,000Square meters, and can save 1.5 million yuan of operating expenses per year. Compared to conventional buildings, it can save 1.45 million yuan of electricity cost, 54,000 yuan of water cost, 610 tons of standard coal, and reduce 1,600 tons of CO_2 emission. BR Building makes a great contribution to the energy saving and emission reduction enterprise of the whole society.

BR Building made great use of the local natural conditions. Not every green technology costs money. BR Building achieves green and energy saving with "local" and "lean" design principles and suitable design methods and technologies.

As shown by relevant data, BR Building integrated and utilized about 40 green technologies and measures with the idea of "adjusting measures to local conditions", and fully explored the value of natural ecological environment for "green building".

BR Building has become a cosy nest for flowers, birds and fish. In fact, there are many such ingenious designs in BR Building. Every flower and water fountain seems to hide a mystery. Taking the water fountain and the aerial garden on the first floor as an example, it is not only a landscape of the building, but also an "artificial wetland"—the reclaimed water treatment system, which turns the sewage generated by the whole building into "reclaimed water", is used to flush toilets via biological treatment. The fountain system in the regenerating pool also replaces the cooling tower of the air conditioning system; transparent glass is installed at the bottom of the pool to introduce natural light into the basement garden. Every drop of rainwater falling on the BR Building is collected to water the three-dimensional greenery throughout the building.

Green buildings should be alive and living. BR Building is able to generate energy by itself, recycle and use sewage and waste by itself. At the same time, the appearance of the building is not pure glass and concrete; there is a "living coat" on the outside. On the west side of BR Building, the designers designed the shield flower stand, which is filled with various vines and flowers. These vines have covered the entire wall. When spring comes, these plants become beautiful green outfits of the building, which block the heat of the city from entering the building. The flowers and plants on the flower stand often blossom, and attract hummingbirds and butterflies, which even build nests here and treat it as home.

In addition to the three-dimensional green "natural outerwear", BR Building's "artificial outerwear" is also quite distinctive. The outer wall of the low-rise area of the building adopts one-moulding and integrally installed hollow cement fibre extruded board, which is not only environmentally friendly, but also high in strength and light in weight. It can also resist earthquakes and fire as well as insulate sound. This material can serve as interior and exterior decorative surfaces, eliminating the large workload of traditional decoration and making large material savings. Last but not least, it also advocates aesthetics of simple material.

The BR Building saves 1.2 million yuan of operating costs per year. Due to the comprehensive application of low-cost, high-efficiency, localized green building technologies, the comprehensive cost of the BR Building is only 4,300 yuan/square meters. BR Building achieved the three-star green building standard with the construction cost of an ordinary high-rise office building in Shenzhen. By analysing the operational data, compared with the same type of office building in Shenzhen, BR Building's air conditioning energy consumption was reduced by about 63 percent, lighting energy consumption was reduced by about 71 percent, conventional power consumption was reduced by about 66 percent, and total energy consumption was reduced by about 63 percent. According to this calculation, BR Building can save about 10.944 million kWh a year. Since the solar photovoltaic system is installed on the roof, the power generation in the first year of its operation was 75,600 kWh, accounting for 7 percent of the building's annual electricity consumption. With the reduction in electricity charge alone, BR Building can save about 1.17 million yuan a year. In terms of conserving water, the building can save 5,180 tons of water a year because of its reclaimed water and rainwater recycling system. After deducting the operating cost of the reclaimed water system, 15,000 yuan can be saved annually. The utilization rate of non-traditional water is 52 percent, far exceeding the highest standard of 40 percent in the National Green Building Evaluation Standard.

The reason for society's strong recognition of the BR Building is that, it is a green building constructed with localized and low-cost methods. Green buildings, both domestic and foreign, usually strike us as "luxuries". The cost of domestic green building often exceeds 10,000 yuan/square meters, not to mention the more expensive green buildings in developed countries; such a high cost renders green buildings desirable and yet unattainable. The extensive recognition and acceptance of BR Building lie in its moderate cost, 4,300 yuan/square meters. Many visitors said that they would make their buildings green too, when they heard about the cost of BR Building.

Accelerate the construction of pedestrian and bicycle traffic systems. Carry out the planning and construction of slow-traffic infrastructure around railway stations to achieve the extension of the subway and bus services. Promote the construction of slow-traffic passageways and the supporting facilities in combination with Shenzhen's greenway construction and actively create a slow-traffic system atmosphere in the city. Shenzhen built about 200 kilometers of bicycle path network to improve the quality of the citizens' leisure time. Research the system demands, implementation conditions, restrictions and feasibility of public transportation and gradually establish a public bicycle system.

Enhance traffic organization and management. Establish and improve the intelligent traffic management system by improving the construction of the road traffic network and traffic signals and traffic information platforms. Establish the statistics and monitoring system of energy consumption and pollution emission of the traffic industry; formulate effective measures, intensify the control of traffic demands, improve the passing rate of motor vehicles, lower the idling time of vehicles and reduce exhaust emissions.

Promote Green Buildings

Strictly implement laws and regulations such as the Building Energy-saving Rules of Shenzhen Special Economic Zone and Implementation Rules of Public Building Energy-saving Design Standard and make sure 100 percent of the newly built buildings comply with the energy-saving requirements. By 2015, the proportion of green buildings in all newly-built buildings reached 40 percent and will reach 80 percent in 2020.

Establish a green building life cycle management philosophy. The green and low-carbon concept will be integrated into the whole life cycle of building survey, design, construction, operation, property management and demolition. Research and establish a green building standard system of green survey, green design, green construction, green evaluation, green operation and green property with Shenzhen characteristics.

Case 6-3: GEP Evaluation System Created in Yantian District, Shenzhen

In 2015, Yantian District of Shenzhen first introduced Urban GEP in China. GEP is the abbreviation of Gross Ecosystem Production; it refers to the total economic value of the products and services provided by the ecosystem for human well-being. Unlike GDP which is more concerned with the running state of the economic system, GEP, on the other hand, emphasizes the "price tag" put on the ecological environment by the running state of the ecosystem. It provides a quantitative basis for "Beautiful China"; and switches regional development to the mode of "double account, double operation and double improvement" of both GDP and GEP. This system adds the building blocks to the pilot and demonstration area of national ecological civilization, and won the "2015 Chinese Government Innovation Best

Practice" award. Yantian District's Urban GEP Accounting System consists of indicators of three levels: two level 1 indicators: "value of natural ecosystem" and "value of human settlement ecosystem"; eleven level 2 indicators, including ecological products, ecological regulation, ecological culture, maintenance and improvement of atmospheric environment, maintenance and improvement of water environment, maintenance and improvement of soil environment, maintenance and improvement of ecological environment, value of acoustic environment, reasonable disposal of solid wastes, energy saving and emission reduction, and environmental health; and 28 level 3 indicators, including values of food, timber, water resources, etc., which can be directly utilized by human beings, ecological regulation functions such as conservation of water and soil, carbon sequestration and oxygen production, and air purification provided to humans indirectly, cultural and service functions originating from ecological landscapes, and indicators related to water, gas, noise, slag and carbon emission reduction, and pollutant discharge reduction.

A good accounting system must be both general and specific. Hence, the indicators possess universality, and 28 indicators are set for both rural areas and urban areas; but the specific accounting items can be different. For example, in view of the fact that Yantian Port faces a great challenge of environmental pollution treatment, its main accounting item can be set as energy saving and emission reduction.

Promote the energy-saving standards of new buildings. 100 percent of new buildings will implement building energy efficiency standards. Encourage new buildings to implement building energy efficiency labelling systems. Develop green buildings and promote green construction. Taking affordable housing as a breakthrough, we will promote the industrialization and one-time decoration of residential construction, carry out residential performance and parts certification, foster the modernization demonstration bases and projects of the residential industry, and accelerate the construction of modern production components of the residential industry. Efforts will be made to reduce energy consumption in the construction and renovation of new buildings.

Carry out energy-saving transformation of existing buildings. Implement the Energy-saving Transformation Plan of Existing Buildings in Shenzhen and produce energy consumption statistics; carry out energy consumption audits, energy efficiency publicity and energy consumption detection. Mobilize the various departments and units in various districts to establish the existing building energy-saving transformation project database in combination with urban upgrading, large public building transformation, building facade and roof transformation as well as anti-seismic housing enforcement to fully promote the energy-saving transformation of existing buildings and promote the low-carbon transformation of buildings.

Carry out building technology innovation. Encourage the development and use of new building technologies, new materials and new equipment. Encourage the development of high-performance new wall materials and glass curtain wall materials. Vigorously develop high-performance building energy equipment, especially for building air-conditioning energy equipment and power equipment. Encourage enterprises to prepare construction techniques and construction methods.

Promote the application of renewable energies. Implement solar-photovoltaic building integration demonstration projects in public buildings, municipal engineering and high-end residence buildings. Install solar photovoltaic systems and solar-thermal systems on the roofs of the newly-built buildings and existing buildings meeting necessary conditions, such as public buildings, office buildings, industrial areas (parks), hotels, enterprises and residential buildings, and lead the development of solar product application and relevant industries.

Carry out energy-saving transformation of the energy-using equipment in public institutions to eliminate high energy consumption and highly polluting equipment; promote the application of energy-saving equipment and new energy products. Strictly implement energy-saving management, establish energy consumption statistics and a monitoring platform to improve the energy utilization efficiency and reduce the carbon emissions of public institutions.

Promote the energy-saving transformation of public institutions. Attach importance to the energy-saving transformation of air conditioning, lighting and electrical power systems, heating systems, office equipment, elevators, draught fans and pumps and the promotion of clean energies; enhance the daily energy-saving management and carry out energy-saving and emission reduction monitoring, performance evaluation and audit of governmental office buildings and large public buildings; enhance the energy consumption management of service cars, enhance water saving and material saving intensities and improve the construction of the information system for governmental affairs. Promote the paperless office, and strictly implement the air conditioning control standard of 26℃ in summer.

Promote energy-saving lighting products. Gradually eliminate incandescent light bulbs and high pressure mercury lamps in large public buildings, and promote efficient, energy-saving and technically mature LED lamps, T5 lamps and tri-chromatic rare earth fluorescent lamps. By the end of 2015, 70 percent of the main roads in the city have had energy-saving lamps installed or adopted measures such as alternate lighting or intelligent lighting dimming, and realized 30 percent reduction of lighting energy. Promote solar-LED products for urban roads, municipal parks, underground garages, transportation facilities and squares and train stations.

Advocate for A Green and Low-Carbon Lifestyle

Actively carry out low-carbon events such as Land Day, Earth Day, Water Resource Day, Energy Day, Public Transportation Day, Car-free Day, Water-saving Campaign, Plastic Reduction Campaign, and One

Hour Blackout to strengthen the public's low-carbon awareness. For example, in March 2010, Shenzhen launched a series of activities including "Green Action, Green Seed" green travel and "Shenzhen Low Carbon Year" and everyone in the city participated in the "Earth Hour" event. According to the real-time statistics of the Shenzhen Power Supply Bureau, the 33,900 kWh of electricity saved during one hour of Shenzhen's blackout was equivalent to 13.56 tons of standard coal.

The city is the home of its citizens, while relaxation is very important for urban life. The city needs a relatively relaxed and leisurely living atmosphere. Strolling on the streets, the low tempo is like a slow-moving image, allowing people to re-appreciate the neglected landscape and taste the changing flavours of the city's four seasons, so that the city's leisure and elegance can be dissipated, thus reflecting its different tastes and connotations.

The slow traffic system not only makes travelling more convenient, but also tangibly connects the cultural landscapes of the city, becoming an extension of its culture and leisure. The characteristic regional landscapes, regional cultures, business cultures and public culture service networks of the city will be connected and integrated organically through reasonable design to make slow walking more of a leisure choice. This is the essence of urban slow traffic systems. The key to a city's slow traffic system lies in the selection of the route. With that, a fast-moving city can still tolerate light paces and comfortable minds, thus demonstrating the cosy and leisurely side of a city.

We might talk about the slow-traffic life in Yantian District, which only has twisted coastlines, but also 253 kilometers of staggered, greenway slow-traffic network capturing various scenes along the way, making it the best place for Shenzhen's citizens to have a taste of Yantian District's life. At the same time, 6,000 public bicycles distributed in the district allow the public to enjoy the cosiness of the slow life within 300 to 500m from any point in the built-up area, and this is the green welfare brought to the citizens by Yantian District.

Integration of Policy Guidance and Market Mechanism

At the beginning of its development, Shenzhen attracted a large number of "two-high and one-low" enterprises (high energy consumption, high pollution and low benefit). For example, the Longgang River and the Pingshan River basin brought together a lot of heavy pollution enterprises, which generated 13.86 billion yuan of output and 2.12 billion yuan of taxes, accounting for 12.5 percent and 7.8 percent of the entire basin, yet they produced 61.5 percent of the industrial wastewater and 47.7 percent of the industrial chemical oxygen demand of the entire basin. Industry demonstrated a distinct "high-carbon" characteristic and the industrial layout was "scattered, disordered and low-end". There were over 900 industrial parks and areas of all sizes across the city (excluding the high-tech zone and bonded area); the total area of these industrial parks and areas exceeded 150 square kilometers. However, the size of each individual park was rather small; with 74 percent of them having an area of less than 10 hectares and the average plot ratio was only 1.0.

Shenzhen was faced with bottleneck restrictions, with pressures becoming more and more prominent in aspects such as space, resources, population and environment, which the traditional economic development mode could no longer sustain; this called for the elimination and relocation of backward industries and the lowering of emissions of the high-carbon enterprises, making room for traditional industry's transformation and the emerging industry's development.

Shenzhen was able to realize at an early point that the high input and high energy consumption development mode is not sustainable; hence, it stuck fast to the promotion of industrial transformation and upgrading and has always seen energy-saving and emission reduction as an important carrier for low-carbon development. Shenzhen regards industrial structure optimization as the important support of low-carbon development, and built a new Shenzhen path for higher quality growth with lower resource consumption and environmental costs.

It is both a social and economic matter that must be treated carefully for enterprises in the traditional industry to "make room". After all, these enterprises made huge contributions to this city during its early development. The standard for capacity elimination must be defined carefully and scientifically. The standard should neither be too high, hurting a large number of enterprises and employees, and affecting the long-term impetus for economic development, nor too low and failing to generate the effect of lowering carbon-emissions and achieve transformational development.

Case 6 – 4: Comprehensive Demonstration Effect of Shenzhen International Low Carbon City

The green and low-carbon development practices which Shenzhen has adhered to for many years laid a good foundation for the planning and construction of the Low Carbon City, as well as the realization of low-carbon development and upgrading. In 2012, Shenzhen International Low Carbon City was officially launched as a flagship project of China-Europe Sustainable Urbanization Cooperation. International Low Carbon City adheres to the core concept of low carbon and smart cities, and plans to build "Four Areas", i. e. , a Pilot Area of a Climate-friendly City, a Clustering Area of New Low-carbon Industries, a Leading Area of Low-carbon Lifestyle and a Demonstration Area of Low-carbon International Cooperation; it seeks to be a national comprehensive pilot site for low-carbon development. International Low Carbon City has entered the stage of comprehensive construction.

Shenzhen International Low Carbon City is located in a place with a good ecological environment, but relatively backward economic development, where the urban construction was quite coarse and the infrastructure foundation was weak. Shenzhen International Low Carbon City seeks to explore the leap-type low-carbon development mode for the late-developing regions of the city. It promotes the integrated construction of industries and the city with multi-rule coordinating means; it leads industrial upgrade and transformation toward a low-carbon development direction, and employs a mechanism and system in which domestic and international resource innovations are marketized, finding the path and piloting for the new urbanization and low-carbon and green development of the nation.

In the process of construction, Shenzhen International Low Carbon City abandoned the idea of large-scale demolition and construction; instead, it chose to respect the existing conditions and make magic out of it. The Low Carbon City actively carried out local ecological diagnosis, conducted comprehensive carbon verification of existing enterprises, and compiled a low carbon city indicator system to control the carbon indicators of land auction, project access and development in the Low Carbon City. It also established a public platform for carbon emission monitoring to monitor, manage, supervise and evaluate carbon emissions of enterprises; it created a community sharing model and is exploring the sharing mode of public facilities in communities, campuses and parks.

In 2014, Shenzhen International Low Carbon City became one of the top ten examples of new urbanization in the country, and won the "2014 Sustainable Development Planning Project Award" jointly sponsored by China Centre for International Economic Exchange and the American Paulson Institute. It is the only project in China which has won this award. The advantages of its low-carbon development model, as well as its reproducibility and transferability are highly recognized by the planning experts of the low-carbon eco-city (district). In 2015, Shenzhen International Low Carbon City was selected as one of the first batch of national Low Carbon City (town) pilots and ranked first among the eight pilots.

Since the launch of the Shenzhen International Low Carbon City, the total output value of Pingdi Sub-district, where the Low Carbon City is located, increased from 6.545 billion yuan in 2013 to 10.925 billion yuan in 2017, with an average annual growth of 11.3 percent; the total industrial output value increased from 18.237 billion yuan in 2013 to 32.743 billion yuan in 2017, with an average annual growth of 9.4 percent; and the unit GDP carbon emission intensity dropped by 12.67 percent. In fact, since the implementation of the International Low Carbon City, Pingdi Sub-district has not suffered from economic decline due to low carbon city construction and industrial transformation; on the contrary, its economic has achieved steady growth.

The first Low Carbon City Forum was held here from June 17th to 18th, 2013. Up to now, it has been successfully held for 6 years and has generated great repercussions, both at home and abroad. Over 6,000 guests from more than 50 countries and regions attended the forums. The very first carbon market of China was born here; the "Blue Sky Award" for Global Leading Technology in Renewable Energy supervised by United Nations Industrial Development Organization was launched here; and the national low carbon technology fair takes place here. The Low Carbon City Forum has become an important window to showcase the effectiveness of China's efforts to address climate change. It has also become an important platform for exploring the frontier topics in the global low-carbon field, sharing wisdom and developing pragmatic cooperation.

Industrial Policy Guidance

Based on the national industrial restructuring guidance catalogue and local development realities, Shenzhen formulated industrial structure adjustment and optimization and an industrial guidance catalogue, and scientifically defined highly polluting industries and high environmental hazard product standards in terms of energy consumption, emissions, quality and safety. For example, due to its water resource scarcity, Shenzhen established water withdrawal per ten thousand yuan of GDP as a core index of the industrial guidance catalogue; and requested no more than 4 cubic meters of water consumption for every ten thousand yuan of output increase for the communication equipment, computer and other electronic equipment manufacturing industries in their industrial access requirements. Bao'an District has forbidden new projects of high energy consumption, high emission and high pollution, such as chemical engineering, printing and dyeing, electroplating and circuit boards; new enterprises must adopt non-toxic and low-pollution raw materials, and advanced production processes to replace highly toxic materials and backward production processes, thus realizing the efficient utilization and recycling of resources. Since 2008, Shenzhen implemented the management authority linkage mechanism of newly approved projects and the system of project approval accountability, by enhancing the approval and filing of fixed asset investment projects.

Employ the market price leverage

Enterprises with high energy consumption, high pollution and high emissions are normally very sensitive to the cost input due to their low profits. Shenzhen used the price leverage effects of water, electricity, gas and minimum wage to gradually increase the operating cost of low-end enterprises, and drive those low-end enterprises out of the market using the "invisible hand". The city carried out comprehensive investigation and screening for elimination and restricted enterprises in the high energy consumption industries; it published the names of these enterprises; implemented dynamic management and strictly implemented the differentiated water, electricity and gas prices. Shenzhen implemented the non-household plan-exceeding and quota-exceeding cumulative price-raise measures for enterprises with energy consumption exceeding the existing unit product energy consumption (power consumption); intensified the charges to increase the pollutant discharge fees. Shenzhen was the first city to establish a water price mechanism reflecting the scarcity of water resources in the country; it adopted a linked adjustment mode of raw water and tap water prices and constantly optimized the price relationship between raw water, tap water and recycled water. In addition, Shenzhen's minimum wage was increased from 1,000 yuan in 2009 to 2,030 yuan in 2015, achieving "doubling every 7 years"; it continued to maintain the highest level in the entire country. Shenzhen improved the labour cost of labour-intensive enterprises, to force enterprises with low added value to transform. By guiding the low-end manufacturing links to migrate to the outside of the city in an orderly manner, Shenzhen cancelled, revoked and cleaned out over 100,000 low-end enterprises, making precious room for the development of emerging industries and high-end industries.

Employ the incentive role of financial credit

Green Credit is a new credit policy introduced by the Ministry of Environmental Protection, the People's Bank of China and the China Banking Regulatory Commission to curb the blind expansion of high-energy and high-pollution industries. The core is to control credit for enterprises and projects which violate the industrial and environmental policies; the enterprise's environmental protection is taken as one of the necessary conditions for the approval of loans by commercial banks, so the role of finance in promoting environmental protection will be exerted. Through the establishment and improvement of policies and measures of green finance, Shenzhen has strictly controlled the support of bank funds for backward industries, and accelerated the elimination of "two highs and one low" industries.

Shenzhen's environmental protection administration cooperated with the financial system and signed "the Enterprise Environmental Protection Information Provision and Iinformation Search Service Agreement", which incorporated the information of enterprises violating the environmental protection laws into the database of basic enterprise credit information of the financial institutions. Financial institutions will stop providing loans to violating enterprises until rectifications are carried out. According to incomplete statistics, Shenzhen stopped providing 5 billion yuan of loans to over 100 enterprises violating the environmental protection laws, and effectively fought environmental protection violations. According to "the Key Pollution Enterprise Environmental Protection Credit Management Measures of Shenzhen" issued by Shenzhen's government, the city will carry out environmental protection credit evaluation of high pollution enterprises and key, high-volume pollutant discharge enterprises in the electroplating, circuit board and printing and dyeing industries. In 2012, there were 159 green card enterprises among the 760 key pollution enterprises, and the numbers of blue card, yellow card and red card enterprises were 420, 141 and 40, respectively. For red card enterprises, in addition to ordering the enterprise to make rectifications within a limited time, the environmental protection administration may close down the enterprises, refuse to issue subsidies of the special fund for environmental protection or recommend the cooperating banks of Green Credit stop providing loans to such enterprises. The relevant measures of the environmental protection administration significantly incentivized the upstream and downstream enterprises of the industry chain to improve their process and design, which raised their environmental protection standards.

Promote the upgrading and transformation of traditional enterprises via technical transformation

Promoting industrial transformation and upgrading doesn't necessarily mean that traditional industries are to be exterminated; Shenzhen pays equal attention to the green and low-carbon development of traditional industries during its promotion of industrial upgrading and transformation, aiming to raise the scale and benefits of traditional industries to new heights. Taking the fashion consumption industry as an example, Shenzhen adheres to the "three quality" principles of quality brand, quality enterprise and quality product. It has endowed unique cultural values to traditional clothing, gold, jewellery, glass and furniture industries with brand construction as the core and industrial design as the guidance. By doing so, it has enhanced the creativity and design capability of industries, improved the added values of products and constantly promoted the transformation of the traditional advanced industries into fashion consumption industries. After the transformation, more than 70 percent of the enterprises spend over 5 percent of their sales revenues on R&D; and there emerged one world famous brand, 41 famous brands in China and 30 famous brands in Guangdong. Shenzhen's gold and jewellery industry includes 46 percent of the famous national gold and jewellery brands, while its domestic market share of women's fashions has reached 60 percent.

Technical transformation is an investment activity of enterprises using new technologies, new processes, new equipment, new materials and new design to transform and improve the existing facilities and process conditions to realize connotation development; it is an important approach to realize energy-saving and emission reduction. For a long time, Shenzhen's traditional industries such as furniture and watches have adopted a rather coarse development mode; their products lack technical contents and they have a low technical standard, making them quite sensitive to external environmental changes and vulnerable to the ever-fiercer market competition. Shenzhen provides support for more than 100 technical transformation projects of enterprises every year, and accelerates the urban industrial transformation of gold, clothing and watch industries and the digital equipment transformation of mechanical moulds.

According to incomplete statistics, Shenzhen has invested more than 20 billion yuan in upgrading and transformation in 5 years and has attracted over 300 billion yuan of social investment via financial funds or interest subsidies. On the other hand, Shenzhen introduced the concept of clean production into the construction process of the industrial cluster base and industrial belt; it strongly promoted the clustering development of traditional industries such as building materials, electroplating, household appliances, jewellery, printing and dyeing and watchmaking. Shenzhen upgraded and transformed 18 old industrial zones and established 16 characteristic industrial parks, including industrial design and automobile electronics. Shenzhen implemented mandatory clean production review of enterprises with pollutant emissions exceeding the national, provincial or municipal emission standard or exceeding the rated total control index of pollutant emission, and used the clean production review as one of the constraining conditions for settlement, expansion, relocation and eligibility for preferential policies as well as control of the consumption of resources and energies throughout the full life-cycle of products to lower their carbon emissions.

参考文献

World Economic Forum, 2016, "China's Innovation Ecosystem 2016 Creating a city innovation ecosystem through education and technology infrastructure", White Paper.

Beijing Sinocarbon 2014, "Annual Report of China Carbon Market in 2014," Sinocarbon, Innovation and Investment Co., Ltd., Beijing.

Albouy David, Kristian Behrens, Frédéric Robert-Nicoud, Nathan Seegert, 2018.

"The optimal distribution of population across cities", *Journal of Urban Economics*, https://doi.org/10.1016/j.jue.July.2018.

Alonso William, "The Economics of Urban Size", Papers in Regional Science, Vol. 26, No. 1, 1971.

Anagnost Ann, *National Past-Times: Narrative, Representation, and Power in Modern China*, Durham, N. C.: Duke University Press, 1997.

Ashworth Gregory, and Stephen J. Page, "Urban tourism research: Recent progress and current paradoxes," *Tourism Management*, Vol. 32, No. 1, 2011.

Bach Jonathan, "They Come in Peasants and Leave Citizens': Urban Villages and the Making of Shenzhen," *In Learning from Shenzhen: China's Post-Mao Experiment from Special Zone to Model City*, Chicago: University of Chicago Press.

"Shenzhen Faces New Challenges", August 26, 2003, http://www.bjreview.com/special/2010-08/26/content_294280.htm, Retrieved 12th February 2019.

Buckingham, William S., 2014, "Assembling the Chinese City: Production of Place and the Articulation of New Urban Spaces in Wuhan, China", Doctoral Dissertation, University of Washington, Department of Geography.

Buckley Chris, "China's 'Nanny' Overhauls State Enterprises", January 31, 2019, https://www.nytimes.com/2005/06/01/business/worldbusiness/chinas-nanny-overhauls-state-enterprises.html.

Cai Jian, "China City Innovation Ecosystem: Shenzhen's Perspective", White Paper, World Economic Forum, 2016.

Camagni Roberto, "Integrated Spatial Planning: Why and How?", In Seminal Studies in Regional and Urban Economics, Roberta Capello eds. Cham: Springer International Publishing, 2017.

Camagni Roberto, and Roberta Capello, "Beyond Optimal City Size: An Evaluation of Alternative Urban Growth Patterns", *Urban Studies*, Vol. 37, No. 9, 2000.

Campbell Scott, 1996, "Green Cities, Growing Cities, Just Cities? Urban Planning and the Contradictions of Sustainable Development", *Journal of the American Planning Association*, Vol. 62, No. 3, 1996.

Carolye Whitzman, "Suburb, Slum, Urban Village: Cartier, Carolyn", 2011.

Cartier Carolyn, "Urban Growth, Rescaling, and the Spatial Administrative Hierarchy," *Provincial China*, Vol. 3, No. 1. , 2011.

Changjie Zhan, Hans de Bruijn and W. Martin de Jong, "Funding Sustainable Cities: A Comparative Study of Sino-Singapore Tianjin Eco-City and Shenzhen International Low-Carbon City", Article in Sustainability 10 (11): 4256 · November, 2018.

Changjie Zhan, Martin de Jong, "Financing eco-cities and low carbon cities: The case of Shenzhen International Low Carbon City", *Journal of Cleaner Production*, 180: 116 – 125, 2018.

Cheshmehzangi Ali, "China's New-Type Urbanisation Plan (NUP) and the Foreseeing Challenges for Decarbonization of Cities: A Review," *Energy Procedia*, Vol. 104, 2016.

Hong'e, Mo, "China to adopt more flexible policies for hukou registrations in cities." ECNS.cn, March 14, http://www.ecns.cn/cns-wire/2018/03

-14/295700. shtml, 2018.

China Center for Special Economic Zone Research of Shenzhen University, "Introduction of China Center for Special Economic Zone Research, Shenzhen", Website of China Center for Special Economic Zone Research of Shenzhen University, January 31, 2019.

China Center for Special Economic Zone Research of Shenzhen University, "Data Center of China's Special Economic Zones", Website of China Center for Special Economic Zone Research of Shenzhen University, January 31, 2019.

Christine Wong, "Budget Reform in China", *OECD Journal on Budgeting*, Vol. 7 -No. 1.

Cox Wendell, "The Evolving Urban Form: Shenzhen", *New Geography*, May 25, 2012.

"Growth, population and industrialization, and urban land expansion of China", *Journal of Urban Economics*, Vol. 63, No. 1, 96 – 115.

Dou Peng, and Yangbo Chen, "Dynamic monitoring of land-use/land-cover change and urban expansion in Shenzhen using Landsat imagery from 1988 to 2015", *International Journal of Remote Sensing*, Vol. 38, No. 19, 5388 – 5407, 2017.

Fan Gang, "Another 30 Years of Prosperity for Shenzhen in Strategic Choice," *China Opening Journal*, No. 1, 7 – 11, 2011.

Florence Eric, "How to be a Shenzhener: Representations of Migrant Labor in Shenzhen's Second Decade," In Learning from Shenzhen: China's Post-Mao Experiment from Special Zone to Model City, Chicago: University of Chicago Press.

Fong Mei, "Before the Claims of Crispr Babies, There Was China's One-Child Policy", January 31, 2019, https://www.nytimes.com/2018/11/28/opinion/china-crispr-babies.html.

Fujita, Masahisa, *Urban Economic Theory: Land Use and City Size*. Cambridge: Cambridge University Press.

Becker, Gary S., Edward L. Glaeser, and Kevin M. Murphy,

"Population and Economic Growth," *The American Economic Review*, Vol. 82, No. 2, 145 – 149.

Fu, Somerville, Gu and Huang, "Land Use Rights, Government land supply, and the pattern of redevelopment in Shanghai", *International real estate review*, Vol. 2 No 1: pp. 49 – 78, 1999.

Garrick, John, Yan Chang Bennett, China's Socialist Rule of Law Reforms Under Xi Jinping. London: Routledge, 2016.

Geert, Wouter, "Top 100 City Destinations 2018," Euromonitor International, https://go.euromonitor.com/white-paper-travel-2018-100-cities.

George E. Peterson, "Land leasing and land sale as an infrastructure-financing option", World Bank Policy Research Working Paper 4043, November 2000, USA.

Glaeser, Edward L. , The Economics Approach to Cities, National Bureau of Economic Research Working Paper No. 13696, http://www.nber.org/papers/w13696.

Glaeser, Edward L, "Cities, Productivity and Quality of Life," *Science*, Vol. 333, No. 6042, 592 – 594.

G. L. Ou and S. K. Tan, "Study on Sustainable Use of Land Based on Ecological Footprint Model: A Case of Shenzhen", *Applied Mechanics and Materials*, Vols. 295 – 298, pp. 2551 – 2556, 2013.

Granet, Marcel, La Pensée Chinoise. Paris: Éditions Albin Michel,

Hao, Pu, Richard Sliuzas, and Stan Geertman, 2011.

Henderson, J. Vernon, The Effects of Urban Concentration on Economic Growth, National Bureau of Economic Research Working Paper No. 7503, http://www.nber.org/papers/w7503 and Henderson, 2003.

Henderson, J. Vernon, "The Urbanization Process and Economic Growth: The So-What Question," *Journal of Economic Growth*, Vol. 8, 47 – 71.

Heyuan You, "Characterizing the inequalities in urban public green space provision in Shenzhen, China," *Habitat International*, 56: 176 – 180, 2016.

Hirsh, Max, "Simulating Global Mobility at Shenzhen 'International' Airport,"

In Learning from Shenzhen: China's Post-Mao Experiment from Special Zone to Model City, Chicago: University of Chicago Press.

HKTC Research, "Shenzhen Looks to Woo Foreign Investment Through Improved BusinessEnvironment," 22 May 2017.

Howard A. Frank, "Public Financial Management": Taylor and Francis in Public Administration and Public Policy, 2006.

Huang Weiwen, "The Tripartite Origins of Shenzhen: Beijing, Hong Kong and Bao'an," In Learning from Shenzhen: China's Post-Mao Experiment from Special Zone to Model City, Chicago: University of Chicago Press.

Hua, R. and Y. Zhang, "Assessment of water quality improvements using the hydrodynamic simulation approach in regulated cascade reservoirs: A Case Study of drinking water sources of Shenzhen", *China. Water*, 2017. 9 (11): p. 825.

"Jewel in the crown: What China can learn from the Pearl River Delta?" *The Economist*, April 8, 2017.

Jiang, Jing J., Bin Ye, and Xiao Ming Ma, "The construction of Shenzhen's carbon emission trading scheme", *Energy Policy*, Vol. 75, 17 – 21.

Jingru Li, Jian Zuo, Hong Guo, Gaihong He, Han Liu, "Willingness to pay for higher construction waste landfill charge: A comparative study in Shenzhen and Qingdao, China," *Waste Management*, 81: 226 – 233, 2018.

Jiping Zhou et al., Research on the Development of Green Finance in Shenzhen to Boost the Carbon Trading Market. Ser. : Earth Environ. Sci. 81 012073.

Jotzo, F., "Emissions Trading in China: Principles, Design Options and Lessons from International Practice", Centre for Climate Economics and Policy (CCEP), Crawford School of Public Policy, Australian National University, Working Paper No. 1303.

Lafforgue, M. and V. Lenouvel, "Closing the urban water loop: lessons from Singapore and Windhoek," *Environmental Science: Water Research & Technology*, 2015. 1 (5): p. 622 – 631.

Lefebre, Henri, Rhythmanalysis: Space, Time and Everyday Life, New York: A & C Black. "Temporality and Shenzhen Urbanism in the Era of 'China Dreams.'", *Verge: Studies in Global Asias*, Vol. 3, No. 1 (Spring 2017), 189–212.

Lew, Alan A., "Invited commentary: Tourism planning and traditional urban planning theory-the planner as an agent of social change," *Leisure/Loisir*, Vol. 31, No. 2, 383–391, Ashworth and Page, 2011.

Liao Fan, "Quench a Thirst with Poison? Local Government Financing Vehicles' Past, Present and Future", Columbia Law School.

Li Hao, *Shenzhen work anthology*, Central Party Literature Press.

Li, L., "Structure and influencing factors of CO_2 emissions from transport sector in three major metropolitan regions of China: estimation and decomposition. Transportation," https://doi.org/10.1007/s11116-017-9827-6, accessed January 23, 2019.

Liu Lin, Lin Yaoyu, Wang Lina, Cao Junliang, Wang Dan, Xue Puning, Liu Jing, "An integrated local climatic evaluation system for green sustainable eco-city construction: A case study in Shenzhen, China," *Building and Environment*, 114: 82–95, 2017.

Li Tianhong, Li Wenkai, Qian Zhenghan, "Variations in ecosystem service value in response to land use changes in Shenzhen," *Ecological Economics*, 69, 1427–1435, 2010.

Li Wenjiang, Li Linjun, Qiu Guoyu, "Energy consumption and economic cost of typical wastewater treatment systems in Shenzhen, China," *Journal of Cleaner Production*, Volume 163, Supplement, 1 October 2017, pp. S374-S378.

Li Yu, "Low carbon eco-city: New approach for Chinese urbanization," *Habitat International*, 44: 102–110, 2014.

Li Zibin, *Increase the advantages of innovation and move towards modernization: Li Zibin's work collection in Shenzhen*, China Financial & Economic Publishing House.

Ma, Emma Xin, Blackwell, Adrian, "The Political Architecture of the First and Second Lines," In Learning from Shenzhen: China's Post-Mao Experiment from Special Zone to Model City, Chicago: University of Chicago Press.

Mair, Victor, "What Is a Chinese 'Dialect/Topolect?'", Sino-Platonic Papers, 29 (September, 1991).

Mark Mobius, "Shenzhen: A City On The Move", Franklin Templeton Investments.

Martin de Jong, Yu Chang, Chen Xinting, Wang Dong, Margot Weijnen, "Developing robust organizational frameworks for Sino-foreign eco-cities: comparing Sino-Dutch Shenzhen Low Carbon City with other initiatives," *Journal of Cleaner Production*, 57: 209 – 220, 2013.

Mason, Katherine A., "Preparedness and the Shenzhen Model of Public Health," In Learning from *Shenzhen: China's Post-Mao Experiment from Special Zone to Model City. Chicago: University of Chicago Press.*

Mazumdar, Dipak, "Rural-urban migration in developing countries," In Handbook of Regional and Urban Economics, Volume 2, Edwin S. Mills, eds. Amsterdam: Elsevier.

Mead, Margaret, *Culture and Commitment: A Study of the Generation Gap*, New York: Doubleday Press.

Mendola, Daria, and Raffaele Scuderi, "Assessing the beneficial effects of economic growth: The Harmonic Growth Index" In Advanced Statistical Methods for the Analysis of Large Data-Sets, Agostino Di Ciaccio, Mauro Coli, and Jose M. Angulo Ibanez eds., Heidelberg-Berlin: Springer.

Michael Enright, Edith Scott, David Dodwell, *The Hong Kong Advantage*, Oxford University Press. -May 22, 1997.

Ng, Mee K., "City profile: Shenzhen," *Cities*, Vol. 20, No. 6, 429 – 441, 2003.

"The Role of Planning in the Development of Shenzhen, China: Rhetoric and Realities," *Eurasian Geography and Economics*, Vol. 45, No. 3, 190 – 211.

Ng, Mee K., and Wing-Shing Tang, "Theorising Urban Planning in a Transitional Economy: The Case of Shenzhen, People's Republic of

China," *The Town Planning Review*, Vol. 75, No. 2, 173 – 203.

Ng On-cho, "The Epochal Concept of 'Early Modernity' and the Intellectual History of Late Imperial China," *Journal of World History*, Vol. 14, No. 1, 37 – 61.

Nijkamp, Peter, and Adriaan Perrels, *Sustainable Cities in Europe*, London: Earthscan, cited by Camagni et al., 1998, p. 105.

O'Connor, Justin, Lie Liu, "Shenzhen's OCT-LOFT: Creative Space in the City of Design," *City, Culture and Society*, 2014, Vol. 5, 131 – 138.

O'Donnell, Mary Ann, "Dachong Update", Shenzhen Noted (blog of urban change), January 31, 2019, https://shenzhennoted.com/tag/dachong/ Bach, Jonathan (ibid.)

O'Donnell, Mary Ann, 2017, "Heroes of the Special Zone: Modeling Reform and its Limits," In Learning from *Shenzhen: China's Post-Mao Experiment from Special Zone to Model City*, Chicago: University of Chicago Press.

O'Donnell, Mary Ann, 2017, "Laying Siege to the Villages: The Vernacular Geography of Shenzhen," In Learning from *Shenzhen: China's Post-Mao Experiment from Special Zone to Model City*, Chicago: University of Chicago Press.

O'Donnell, Mary Ann, Winnie Wong and Jonathan Bach, "Conclusion: Learning from Shenzhen," In Learning from *Shenzhen: China's Post-Mao Experiment from Special Zone to Model City*, Chicago: University of Chicago Press.

O'Donnell, Mary Ann, Winnie Wong and Jonathan Bach, 2017, "Introduction: Experiments, Exceptions, Extensions," In Learning from *Shenzhen: China's Post-Mao Experiment from Special Zone to Model City*, Chicago: University of Chicago Press.

Ong, B. L., "Green plot ratio: an ecological measure for architecture and urban planning", *Landscape and urban planning*, 2003. 63 (4): p. 197 – 211.

Shi Peijun, Yu Deyong, "Assessing urban environmental resources and services of Shenzhen, China: A landscape-based approach for urban planning and sustainability", *Landscape and Urban Planning*, 125: 290 – 297, 2014.

Rode, P., et al., Towards new urban mobility: the case of London and Berlin, 2015.

Sato, Yasuhiro, and Kazuhiro Yamamoto, "Population concentration, urbanization, and demographic transition," *Journal of Urban Economics*, Vol. 58, No. 1, 45 – 61.

Schneider, Annemarie, and Curtis E. Woodcock, "Compact, Dispersed, Fragmented, Extensive? A Comparison of Urban Growth in Twenty-five Global Cities using Remotely Sensed Data, Pattern Metrics and Census Information," *Urban Studies*, Vol. 45, No. 3, 659 – 692.

Scuderi, Raffaele, "Editorial. Special Focus: Local resources for tourism-from impact to growth," *Tourism Economics*, Vol. 24, No. 3, 294 – 296.

Camagni, Roberto, Roberta Capello, and Peter Nijkamp, "Towards sustainable city policy: an economy-environment technology nexus", *Ecological Economics*, Vol. 24, No. 1, 103 – 118.

Camagni, Roberto, Maria C. Gibelli, and Paolo Rigamonti, "Urban mobility and urban form: the social and environmental costs of different patterns of urban expansion", *Ecological Economics*, Vol. 40, No. 2, 199 – 216.

Shen, Jianfa, and Gordon Kee, "Shenzhen: Innovation and Governments' Roles in Reform and Development," In Development and Planning in Seven Major Coastal Cities in Southern and Eastern China, Cham: Springer International Publishing.

Shen, Jianfa, Kwan-yiu Wong, and Zhiqiang Feng, "State-sponsored and spontaneous urbanization in the Pearl River Delta of South China, 1980 – 1998," *Urban Geography*, Vol. 23, No. 7, 674 – 94.

"Shenzhen Chuangyezhe Pingjun Nianling Zuidi, Bi Quanguo Xiao 5 Sui" [Average age of Shenzhen entrepreneurs is the lowest in the nation, 5 years younger], "calendar. huanqiu. com" 4/23/15; accessed January 31, 2019, http://finance.huanqiu.com/roll/2015-04/6272037.html.

Shenzhen Municipal Bureau of Statistics, "Feedback from Shenzhen

Municipal Bureau of Statistics on the Results of Online Interviews on 'Business Knowledge of Population Data'", Shenzhen Government website, January 31, 2019, http://www.sz.gov.cn/sztjj2015/hdjl/zjhy/201810/t20181019_14302978.htm

Shenzhen Municipal People's Government, "Notice of the Shenzhen Municipal People's Government on Printing and Distributing the Shenzhen Life and Health Industry Development Plan, 2013 – 2020," Shenzhen Municipal People's Government website, January 8, http://www.sz.gov.cn/zfgb/2014/gb865/201401/t20140108_2301119.htm.

SSB (Shenzhen Statistics Bureau and NBS Survey Office in Shenzhen), 2018, *Shenzhen Statistical Yearbook*, Beijing: China Statistics Press.

Stephen Olson, "FDI data, Guangdong, Shenzhen", Accessed: https://www.ceicdata.com/en/china/foreign-direct-investment-capital-utilized-prefecture-level-city/cn-fdi-utilized-guangdong-shenzhen January 28, 2019.

Sun Changxue, "The Structural Reform Exploration of Shenzhen Special Economic Zone and Its Demonstration Value," *Reform*, 2018 No. 5, 18 – 26.

Takasu Masakazu, "Will a Culture Be Born from Shenzhen OCT-loft Area," Website accessed January 31, 2019, https://medium.com/shenzhen-high-tour-by-makers/will-a-culture-be-born-from-shenzhen-oct-loft-area – 21f5e756e94d.

Tang Jie, "New Norms Route of Growth and Support: Case of Shenzhen," *China Opening Journal*, 2014, No. 6, 11 – 18.

Tang Jie, "Promote the Development of Venture Capital Industry from the Source of System Construction," Shenzhen Evening News, July 24, http://wb.sznews.com/html/2016-08/10/content_3591650.htm

Tang Jie, Dai Qun, Li Zhanjie, et al., "Theoretical Research on Shenzhen's Economic Growth," *China Special Economic Zone Research*, 2010, No. 0, 13 – 43.

Tan, P. Y.; Wang, J.; Sia, A., "Perspectives on five decades of the urban greening of Singapore," *Cities* 2013, 32, 24 – 32, doi: 10.1016/

j. cities. 001, February, 2013.

Tong S., "Shanghai: Aspirations and Reality, and Implications for Hong Kong", 2009.

UN Habitat, New York University, and Lincoln Institute of Land Policy, Various years Atlas of Urban Expansion, http://www.atlasofurbanexpansion.org/.

UN (United Nations), World Urbanization Prospects: The 2018 Revision, https://esa.un.org/unpd/wup/Publications/Files/WUP2018-KeyFacts.pdf.

Manz W., Elgendy H., Berger J., Bohringer J., Urban Mobility in China, Institute for Mobility Research, Karlsruhe, Germany, 2017.

Van Ling, Gina Ida, Nationalism with Shenzhen Characteristics: A Case Study of the Shenzhen Museum. Masters' Thesis in Asian Studies, Leiden University Institute for Area Studies, 2015.

Wang Dewei, David, Urban Villages in the New China: Case of Shenzhen, New York: Palgrave Macmillan, 2016.

Wang Jingna, "A Review on China Tourism Destination Competitiveness", *In The Hospitality and Tourism Industry in China: New Growth, Trends, and Developments*, Jinlin Zhao, ed. Waretown, New Jersey: Apple Academic Press, 2019.

Wang, Ya P., Yanglin Wang, Jiansheng Wu, "Urbanization and Informal Development in China: Urban Villages in Shenzhen", *International Journal of Urban and Regional Research*, Vol. 33, No. 4, 957–973.

Wang, Ya P., Wang Yanglin, Wu Jiansheng, 2009. "Urbanization and Informal Development in China: Urban Villages in Shenzhen", *International Journal of Urban and Regional Research*, Vol. 33. No. 4, 957–973.

Hao, Pu, Richard Sliuzas, and Stan Geertman, Wong, Tammy, and Geerhardt Kornatowski, "Domination and Contestation in the Urban Politics of Shenzhen", *disP-The Planning Review*, Vol. 50, No. 4, 6–15.

Webster, Chris, Wu Fulong, and Zhao Yanjing, "China's Modern Walled Cities," In Private Cities: Local and Global Perspectives, G. Glasze, C. J. Webster, and K. Frantz, eds. London: Routledge.

Wheaton, William C., and Hisanobu Shishido, "Urban Concentration,

Agglomeration Economies, and the Level of Economic Development", *Economic Development and Cultural Change*, Vol. 30, No. 1, 17 – 30 and Glaeser, 2011.

Williamson, Jeffrey G., "Regional inequality and the process of national development," *Economic Development and Cultural Change*, Vol. 34, No. 4, 3 – 45, as reported by Davis and Henderson, 2003.

Wong Christine, "Budget Reform in China", *OECD Journal on Budgeting*, Vol. 7 No. 1 ISSN 1608 – 7143.

Wong, Winnie, Van Gogh *on Demand: China and the Readymade*, Chicago: University of Chicago Press.

World Bank, "China: National Development and Sub-National Development", New York, 2002.

WTTC (World Travel and Tourism Council), 2018a. "Travel and Tourism, City Travel & Tourism Impact," https://www.wttc.org/-/media/files/reports/economic-impact-research/ cities – 2018/city-travel-tourism-impact – 2018final.pdf.

WTTC (World Travel and Tourism Council). 2018b. "Travel and Tourism, Economic Impact, 2018, China," https://www.wttc.org/-/media/files/reports/economic-impact-research/countries –2018/china2018.pdf.

Xiao, J., "The Movement of Insurance Companies Headquarters: What are the Attractiveness of Shenzhen?", *The Economic Observer.*

Xue, L. L., Fang, W. L., "Rail Plus Property Development in China: The Pilot Case of Shenzhen", Beijing: World Resource Institute.

Xu Qin, "Breaking the development of 'ceiling' with reform," Shenzhen Special Zone Daily, Mar 12, http://www.huaxia.com/ gdtb/gdyw/ szyw/2014/03/3787620.html.

Ye Wangbei, 2013, "Internal Migration and Citizenship Education in China's Shenzhen City," *Education and Urban Society*, 48 (1), January 2013, 77 – 97.

Ying Huang, LeiLiub, Pan Xiaofeng, "CO_2 emissions structure of local economy: A case of Shenzhen," *Energy Procedia*, 104: 86 – 91, 2016.

Ying Liu, Yanliu Lin, Na Fu, Stan Geertman, Frank van Oort, "Towards inclusive and sustainable transformation in Shenzhen: Urban redevelopment, displacement patterns of migrants and policy implications," *Journal of Cleaner Production*, 173: 24 – 38, 2018.

Yi Yongsheng, "Shenzhen's Independent Innovation and Leading Experience," *Special Zone Economy*, 2012 No. 10, 29 – 31.

Yu Jun, "Shenzhen: Transformation and Upgrading," *China Opening Journal*, 2013 No. 2, 24 – 27.

"Restructuring and repositioning Shenzhen. China's new mega city," *Progress in Planning*, Vol. 73, No. 4, 209 – 249.

Zhan, C.; de Jong, M., "Financing Sino-Singapore Tianjin Eco-City: What Lessons Can Be Drawn for Other Large-scale Sustainable City-projects?", in *Sustainability*, 2017, 9, 201. 30.

Zhan, C.; de Jong, M., "Financing Low Carbon City: The Case of Shenzhen International Low Carbon City," *J. Clean. Prod.*, 2018, 180, 116 – 125.

"For CO2 Emission Trading in China, Can the Market Become a National One, Four Years after Creating Seven Local Markets?" *American Journal of Climate Change*, 7, 218 – 235.

Zhang, Q. and S. Li., "Key Issues of Central and Local Government Finance in the People's Republic of China", ADBI Working Paper, Tokyo: Asian Development Bank Institute.

Zhang, S. and J. Zhao, Assessing Urban Transport Systems through the Lens of Individual Behaviour: Shenzhen and Hong Kong, IEMS Working Papers, 2016. No. 2015 – 34.

Zhao, Simon Xiaobin; Lao, Qionghua; Neo Ying Ming Chan, "The rise of China and the development of financial centres in Hong Kong, Beijing, Shanghai, and Shenzhen," *Journal of Globalization Studies*, Volume 4, Number 1/May 2013.

Zheng, Siqi, Rui Wang, Edward L. Glaeser, and Matthew E. Kahn, "The Greenness of China: Household Carbon Dioxide Emissions and Urban

Development", National Bureau of Economic Research Working Paper, http://www.nber.org/papers/w15621.

Yuan Zhiyuan, Zheng Xinqi, Zhang Lulu and Zhao Guoliang, "Urban Competitiveness Measurement of Chinese Cities Based on a Structural Equation Model", *In Sustainability*, 22 April 2017 MDPI.

后　　记

2018年，深圳市对外文化交流协会与联合国人居署合作开展"深圳故事：经济、社会、环境的转型"项目。联合国人居署采用国际视角、聘请国外学者、借助国际平台，生动阐释深圳改革开放40年来取得的伟大成就，精彩讲述"深圳故事"。该项目英文研究成果已经在"联合国人居署第一届人居大会"和"2019年纽约联合国大会"期间成功发布。

鉴于英文原作研究领域众多、成果数量较大，本书从方便编译出版角度出发，选择与深圳改革发展关联度较高的六个章节，按照其内在逻辑结集成册。对于未能选入的部分内容，我们将通过其他方式研究使用。本书由导言和六个章节组成。其中，导言部分作者为中共深圳市委宣传部常务副部长陈金海；第一章"深圳和珠三角地区的全球价值链"，作者为倪鹏飞（中国社会科学院）、马尔科·卡米亚（联合国人居署）；第二章"城市融资、企业融资和创业融资"，作者为阿洛伊修斯·克莱门斯·莫莎（博茨瓦纳大学）；第三章"现代经济增长、经济特区与工业化"，作者为唐杰［哈尔滨工业大学（深圳）］；第四章"城市增长与城市规划：面对人口增长的挑战"，作者为拉斐尔·斯库德里（意大利恩纳科雷大学）；第五章"基本服务和当地基础设施"，作者为维尔纳·朗、殷实（德国慕尼黑大学）；第六章"环境与生态城市"，作者为王东［哈尔滨工业大学（深圳）］。

为尊重原著，译文未作大的删改，力求和谐流畅，在此基础之上尽可能生动流利，以期向读者全面真实展现原版原貌，从而更好地研究和推广"深圳故事"。

本书凝聚着国内外众多专家学者的智慧，我们要特别感谢联合国副秘书长、人居署执行主任迈穆娜·穆赫德·谢里夫女士对于"深圳故事"项目的大力支持；感谢联合国人居署马尔科·卡米亚、阿南达·维里维塔、张祎项目团队的辛勤付出；感谢戴斯客（南京大学）、孔雯煜（南京大学）、威廉·唐纳德·科尔曼（加拿大滑铁卢大学和麦吉尔大学）等专家们的真知灼见。感谢中国社会科学出版社社长赵剑英先生、副总编辑王茵女士的指导与帮助。同时，在此一并向本书编译团队和文化安全审读团队致谢。

  由于时间紧迫，本书编辑过程比较仓促，不免有疏漏之处，不当和错漏还请读者们批评指正。

编者

2020 年 8 月

版内说明

The designations employed and the presentation of the material in this publication do not imply the expression of any opinion whatsoever on the part of the Secretariat of the United Nations concerning the legal status of any country, territory, city or area or of its authorities, or concerning the delimitation of its frontiers of boundaries.

在本出版物中使用的名称和材料的表示方式并不意味着联合国秘书处就任何国家、地区、城市或其当局的法律地位表达任何意见。包括边界划分。

Views expressed in this publication do not necessarily reflect those of the United Nations Human Settlements Programme, the United Nations, or its Member States.

本出版物中表达的观点不一定反映联合国人居署，联合国或其会员国的观点。

Excerpts may be reproduced without authorization, on condition that the source is indicated.

摘录可在未经授权的情况下进行，但必须注明出处。